# Sustainable Architectures

# Sustainable Architectures

## Cultures and Natures in
## Europe and North America

Edited by Simon Guy and Steven A. Moore

Spon Press
Taylor & Francis Group

NEW YORK AND LONDON

Simon Guy would like to dedicate this book to Joel,
Verity, Guy and Olivia.

Steven Moore would like to dedicate this book to Ian
and Nova, Jenny and Vince.

First published 2005 by Spon Press
270 Madison Ave, New York, NY 10016

Simultaneously published in the UK
by Spon Press
2 Park Square, Milton Park, Abingdon, Oxon OX14 4RN

*Spon Press is an imprint of the Taylor & Francis Group*

© 2005 Taylor & Francis

Typeset in Akzidenz Grotesk by Bookcraft Ltd, Stroud, Gloucestershire
Printed and bound in Great Britain by TJ International, Padstow, Cornwall

*British Library Cataloguing in Publication Data*
A catalogue record for this book is available from the British Library

*Library of Congress Cataloging in Publication data*
Guy, Simon
    Sustainable architectures : cultures and natures in Europe and North America /
Simon Guy and Steven Moore. --1st ed.
        p. cm.
    Includes bibliographical references and index.
    ISBN 0-415-70044-2 (hard cover : alk. paper) -- ISBN 0-415-70045-0 (soft cover :
alk. paper) --ISBN 0-203-41280-X (e-book)
    1. Sustainable architecture.  2. Architecture--Environmental aspects.  3
Architecture--Europe.  4. Architecture--North America   I. Moore, Steven A., 1945-  II.
Title.
NA2542.36.G89 2005
720'.47--dc22

                                        2004008320

ISBN 0-415-70044-2 (hbk)
ISBN 0-415-70045-0 (pbk)

# Contents

List of figures    vii

List of tables    ix

Acknowledgements    x

Contributors    xi

1   Introduction: The paradoxes of sustainable architecture    1
   *Simon Guy and Steven A. Moore*

**Part A Modelling design**    13

2   Hybrid environments
   The spaces of sustainable design    15
   *Graham Farmer and Simon Guy*

3   Theory, practice and proof
   Learning from buildings that teach    31
   *Kathryn Janda and Alexandra von Meier*

4   The social construction of 'green building' codes
   Competing models by industry, government and NGOs    51
   *Steven A. Moore and Nathan Engstrom*

**Part B Responding design**    71

5   The politics of design in cities
   Preconceptions, frameworks and trajectories of sustainable building    73
   *Timothy Moss, Adriaan Slob and Walter Vermeulen*

6   Equal couples in equal houses
   Cultural perspectives on Swedish solar and bio-pellet heating design    89
   *Annette Henning*

Part C  **Competing design**                                                105

  7  Safe houses and green architecture
     Reflections on the lessons of the chemically sensitive           107
     *Jim Wasley*

  8  Revaluing wood                                                   123
     *Ted Cavanagh and Richard Kroeker*

  9  Policing sustainability
     Strategies towards a sustainable architecture in Norway          145
     *Marianne Ryghaug*

Part D  **Alternative design**                                              163

 10  Green buildings in Denmark
     From radical ecology to consumer-oriented market approaches?     165
     *Kirsten Gram-Hanssen and Jesper Ole Jensen*

 11  Leaky walls
     Challenges to sustainable practices in post-disaster communities 185
     *Jamie Horwitz*

 12  Social research on energy-efficient building technologies
     Towards a sociotechnical integration                             201
     *Harald Rohracher*

**Conclusion**                                                             219

 13  Reflection and engagement
     Towards pluralist practices of sustainable architecture          221
     *Simon Guy and Steven A. Moore*

     Bibliography                                                     241
     Index                                                            265

# Figures

2.1    Groundwork Trust's Eco-Centre     17
2.2    Doxford Solar Office     17
2.3    Central Square Offices     18
3.1    The Environmental Technology Center, Sonoma State University, California (© Alexandra von Meier 2002)     32
3.2    The Adam Joseph Lewis Center for Environmental Studies, Oberlin College, Ohio (Robb Williamson 2001 (PIX10855)).     33
3.3    The Adam Joseph Lewis Center with south and east trellis (© Barney Taxel 2001; digital enhancements by William McDonough & Partners)     39
4.1    Commerzbank Frankfurt, Foster & Partners Architects (author's photo)     58
4.2    New Mexico Earthship, Mike Reynolds, Earthship Biotecture (courtesy Earthship Biotecture)     59
4.3    The 'planner's triangle' (derived from Campbell 1996: 468)     59
4.4    A 'five star' rated home in Austin, Texas (Imagiz photograph, courtesy Peter L. Pfieffer, AIA)     62
4.5    A Built Green Colorado home constructed by Village Homes of Colorado, Inc. (courtesy of Village Homes)     64
4.6    The first home rated under the FGBC Green Home Standard (courtesy Steven Spencer, Florida Solar Energy Center)     65
5.1    The sequence of planning processes for building locations (W. Vermeulen)     76
5.2    The Information Centre for Sustainable Living in Utrecht (W. Vermeulen 2003)     78
5.3    Photovoltaic panels integrated in the design of a Berlin office block (W. Vermeulen 2003)     85
6.1    The hallway of a Swedish house (source: Emma Henning)     93
6.2    Pellet burner in a boiler-room (source: Solentek AB)     97
6.3    A pellet-burning stove in living room (source: Solentek AB)     98
6.4    A solar collector on a typical single-family Swedish house (source: Solentek AB)     100
7.1    The porch of the Pitman house (author's photograph)     110
7.2    Pitman house (plan) (author's illustration based on drawings provided by Sue Pitman)     111
7.3    Exterior of Oetzel house (author's photograph)     113
7.4    Barrhaven Community Housing (author's photograph)     114

7.5  Barrhaven roofing being cleaned before installation
     (photograph courtesy of Philip Sharp, Architect, Ltd)                    114
7.6  Exterior of the Nelms house (author's photograph)                        116
7.7  Mechanical ventilation systems in the Nelms house (author's
     illustration, adapted from Drerup et al. 1990)                           117
8.1  A 'raft' of 22,000 timbers (courtesy Special Collections, Dalhousie
     University Libraries)                                                    125
8.2. The range of organisations certifying forestry (redrawn and
     substantially revised from Moffat 1998)                                  129
8.3  Sample grade stamp (photo manipulated (with permission) by
     the author)                                                             130
8.4  The domains of consumption and production for wood products in the
     US (diagram by Ted Cavanagh (author) after concept by Ruth Cowan)       138
8.5  *a, b and c* Buildings and building components for an innovative system
     of building construction (photographs by the author)                    140
9.1  Pilestredet Park (Gardsrom)                                             148
10.1 The zero-energy house of 1975 (Thermal Insulation Laboratory, Institute
     of Building Design, Technical University of Denmark)                     169
10.2 View of the eco-village of Dyssekilde (Gram-Hanssen)                     173
10.3 Andelssamfundet eco-village (Claus Bech-Danielsen)                      174
10.4 The Hedebygade project (Claus Bech-Danielsen)                           177
10.5 Ørestad, a new development area in Copenhagen (Ørestadsselskabet/
     Rambøll 2002)                                                           180
10.6 BO-01 in Malmø (Jesper Ole Jensen)                                      181
11.1 The community plan of the Pattonsburg Design Assistance Team
     (Photoshop modified by the author)                                      189
11.2 A Pattonsburg house being relocated to the new site
     (photograph by the author)                                              192
11.3 Pattonsburg on higher ground, with manufactured and
     relocated houses (photograph by the author)                             193
11.4 *a and b* Two views of the domed school in the new town of
     Pattonsburg (photographs by the author).                               194
11.5 Hollywood makeover of Main Street in the old town of
     Pattonsburg for the film *Ride with the Devil* (photograph
     by the author)                                                          196
11.6 Rachel Whiteread's translucent watertower in New York City
     (photograph by the author)                                              197
12.1 Sociotechnical change as the co-evolution of technology,
     institutions and actor strategies (modified from
     Rohracher 2001b)                                                        210

# Tables

2.1   Summary of design features for the three case study office
      buildings                                                          18
4.1   The competing logics of green building in the United States         61
9.1   Summary of design features of the three case study buildings      147
9.2   Responses in the three case study projects to environmental
      goals and requirements                                            151

# Acknowledgements

This book owes a debt to a number of people. Bernie Williams worked tirelessly to prepare the manuscript, and Mara and David Hincher provided essential design input for the cover. We thank Alexandrine Press and the editors of *Built Environment*, who encouraged the project at the outset, for permission to adapt versions of the papers by Farmer and Guy, Jensen, Moss et al. and Rohracher that first appeared in volume 28, no. 1, in 2002.

The contributors would like to thank the many people who have helped in the development of each chapter. In particular, Simon Guy would like to thank his colleagues in the faculty office for allowing him the freedom to complete this project. He would also like to thank Elizabeth Storey for her constant support and Steven Moore for organising his visit to the University of Texas at the outset of the project. Steven Moore would like to thank his colleagues Michael Benedikt and Andrew Light for their careful reading of portions of the text and for their insightful recommendations for its revision. The Mike Hogg Foundation has supported him for some of the time required to complete this project, and his colleagues in the University of Texas Center for Sustainable Development, particularly Bob Paterson, created additional time by relieving him of other responsibilities. Steven is equally thankful to his graduate students at the University of Texas, who have been more influential in the shaping of ideas than they recognise.

# Contributors

**Ted Cavanagh** is a professor of architecture at Dalhousie University, Nova Scotia. He has a doctorate in the history of technology and is a principal in CoastalPlanners, investigating sustainable community design. He is the author of 'No Here There' in *Architectural Design* (March 2004) and *America Builds: Three Centuries of Wood Construction* (W.W. Norton and the Library of Congress, forthcoming 2004) and co-editor of a theme issue on construction for *The Journal of Architectural Education* (September 2004).

**Nathan Engstrom** is programme director of Green Built Home, one of the leading residential green building programmes in the United States. His work focuses on increasing participation of builders in the programme, fund raising and public outreach and education. His main research interest is in the interrelationships between the built, social and natural worlds. He is a graduate of Northland College in Ashland, Wisconsin, where he earned degrees in sociology and environmental studies, and the University of Texas at Austin, where he earned a master's degree in sustainable design.

**Graham Farmer** is an architect and is the director of the architecture programmes in the School of Architecture, Planning and Landscape at the University of Newcastle, UK. He is a member of the Centre for Tectonic Cultures (CTC) research group, and his recent research interests and publications address the theory and practice of sustainability.

**Kirsten Gram-Hanssen** is a senior researcher at the governmental research institute Danish Building and Urban Research, of the Department of Housing and Urban Renewal. She is educated as a socio-engineer, with a master's degree and a PhD from the Technical University of Denmark. Her main research interest concerns differences in consumption practices related to housing and urban life. She has conducted numerous empirical studies on energy consumption, lifestyle and everyday life.

**Simon Guy** is professor of urban development in the School of Architecture, Planning and Landscape and dean of research in the Faculty of Humanities and Social Sciences at the University of Newcastle. His research interests revolve around the social production and consumption of technology and cities. He has published widely on urban technology and environmental change, including S. Guy and E. Shove, *A Sociology of Energy, Buildings and the Environment: Constructing Knowledge, Designing Practice* (Routledge 2000) and S. Guy, S. Marvin and T. Moss, *Urban Infrastructure in Transition: Networks, Buildings, Plans* (Earthscan 2001). His paper 'Reinterpreting sustainable architecture: the place of technology' (with Graham Farmer) won the *Journal of Architectural Education* best paper of 2001 award.

**Annette Henning** is senior lecturer in social anthropology at Dalarna University. She is a researcher at the Centre for Public Sector Research (CEFOS), University of Göteborg, and at the Solar Energy Research Center (SERC), Dalarna University. Her main research interest is in cultural aspects of energy-related issues. She is the author of *Ambiguous Artefacts: Solar Collectors in Swedish Contexts, On Processes of Cultural Modification*.

**Jamie Horwitz** is associate professor of architecture at Iowa State University, where she has been developing a public health perspective in the interdisciplinary graduate programme in design. She holds a doctorate in environmental psychology and, most recently, her research interests in the diffusion of innovations have resulted in publications about the space of eating, including her co-edited collection, *Eating Architecture* (MIT Press 2004).

**Kathryn Janda** is assistant professor of environmental studies at Oberlin College, Ohio. Her educational training includes degrees in English literature, electrical engineering, and energy and resources. She has held research appointments at Lawrence Berkeley National Laboratory and at the US Environmental Protection Agency. Her research interests include social dimensions of technological change, strategies to increase the understanding and use of climate-responsive building designs, and community-level renewable energy production.

**Jesper Ole Jensen** is assistant professor at the section for planning and management of building processes at the Department of Civil Engineering at DTU (Technical University of Denmark). His interests range from environmental impacts of urban planning and urban renewal to green buildings, lifestyle and everyday consumption.

**Richard Kroeker** is professor of architecture at Dalhousie University in Halifax, Nova Scotia, and Cass Gilbert visiting professor at the University of Minnesota College of Architecture and Landscape Architecture. He has a design practice in Halifax, and has a particular interest in low impact, natural materials and community development strategies.

**Alexandra von Meier** is associate professor in environmental studies and planning at Sonoma State University, where she teaches courses on energy management and design and serves as director of the Environmental Technology Center. Her main research interests involve electric power systems, including technical and cultural dimensions of their operation and the adoption of new technologies.

**Steven A. Moore** is an associate professor of architecture and planning at the University of Texas at Austin, where he is director of the graduate programme in sustainable design and co-director of the university's Center for Sustainable Development. His book *Technology and Place: Sustainable Architecture and the Blueprint Farm* was published by the University of Texas Press in 2001 and received the EDRA/Places award for research in 2002. His research interests are broadly interdisciplinary and focus on the social construction of sustainable technologies, buildings and cities.

**Timothy Moss**, who has a DPhil in urban history, is head of the research department 'Regional institutional change to safeguard public goods' at the Institute for Regional Development and Structural Planning (IRS) in Erkner, near Berlin. At the IRS he has coordinated and conducted a number of national and EU research projects on how institutional change affects the provision and use of environmental resources in cities and regions. This he currently explores with regard to the transformation of technical infrastructure systems (water, energy), the institutionalisation of river basin management (Water Framework Directive) and multi-level strategies for sustainable urban and regional development.

**Harald Rohracher** is director of the Inter-University Research Centre for Technology, Work and Culture (IFZ) in Graz, Austria, and research fellow at the Department of Research on Technology and Science of the Institute for Interdisciplinary Studies of Austrian Universities (IFF). He has studied technical physics and sociology in Graz and science and technology policy at SPRU, University of Sussex, UK. His research interests include the social shaping of technology, diffusion and adoption of environmental technologies, and the role of end users in technological innovation.

**Marianne Ryghaug** is a researcher at the Department of Interdisciplinary Studies of Culture at the Norwegian University of Science and Technology, Trondheim, Norway.

**Adriaan Slob** is senior researcher and member of the management team of TNO Strategy Technology and Policy. He is also initiator of the Pytheas network, which involves cooperation between TNO, Erasmus University Rotterdam, University of Utrecht and the Massachusetts Institute of Technology on new policy processes. His main research interest is in new (interactive) policy processes needed for implementation of innovations to achieve sustainability. His studies concern the role of knowledge and learning in policy processes and the development of new process designs with respect to that role.

**Walter Vermeulen** is a senior researcher and lecturer at the Copernicus Institute for Sustainable Development and Innovation, University of Utrecht, the Netherlands.

**Jim Wasley** is an associate professor in architecture at the University of Wisconsin-Milwaukee. His research concerns the interrelations in practice between the design issues of energy efficiency, resource conservation and human health. He has specific expertise in climate responsive design, daylighting and the creation of 'extreme case' healthy environments. With David Rousseau, he is the co-author of *Healthy by Design: Building and Remodeling Solutions for Creating Healthy Homes*.

# 1

# Introduction

## The paradoxes of sustainable architecture

*Simon Guy and Steven A. Moore*

> Environmental architecture, in other words, is environmental architectures, a plurality
> of approaches with some emphasizing performance over appearance, and some
> appearance over performance.
>
> (Hagan 2001: 4)

This book draws upon a number of contrasting concepts of what sustainable architecture might be – that is, what it might look like, where it might be located, what technologies it might incorporate, what materials it might be constructed from and so on. The
diversity of responses to these choices is quite bewildering and – rather than diminishing over time – appears to be accelerating. Three decades of debate about sustainable architecture and a search for some form of consensus around universal best
environmental practice appear to have failed. This situation often provokes deep
depression amongst environmentalists. For example, James Wines despairs that 'A
major proportion of the architectural profession has remained oblivious to the magnitude of its irresponsible assaults on the land and resources', while contemporary architectural practice tends to 'confuse, rather than reinforce, a progressive image of earth
friendly architecture' (Wines 2000: 11). Of course, some architects disagree. Harry
Gordon argues that sustainable design has now gone mainstream:

> After decades of intense effort by designers, architects, individuals, and organisa-
> tions, a tectonic shift in design thinking has occurred: sustainability is now
> becoming mainstream. Some might even say it has become a societal design norm.
>
> (Gordon 2000: 34)

So the debate rages on between what are often called light green and deep green architects. In this book we want to take a different stance. Rather than argue that we need
revolution or reformation, more or less technology, more pious behaviour, to embrace or
abandon the city, or to develop clearer definitions or standardisation, we want to
explore, even celebrate, the diversity of contemporary debate about sustainable architecture. The book is, then, a collage of differing analyses and intentions, of competing
discourses of cultures and natures.

   In the process of exploring the case studies documented in this collection we will
develop the thesis that the challenge of sustainability is more a matter of local interpretation than of the setting of objective or universal goals. This is not to suggest, as more
radical relativists might, that environmental problems are merely imaginary or that they

are no more important than any other social problem – stray cats included. As Steven Yearley has argued, to 'show that a social problem has been socially constructed is not to undermine or debunk it', and even more importantly, 'The detachment required from social science should not become an excuse for cynical inaction' (Yearley 1991: 186).

As editors we generally follow the 'postmodern' critique of modern science, which is to be highly sceptical of the Enlightenment notion that we can solve the problems of environmental degradation and social injustice simply through the progressive applica- tion of science. In response to a world of 'Kuhnian' paradigm shifts about the ways in which architects conceptualise social and ecological issues, we think it is more produc- tive to explore what architects actually do – to explore the cultural framing of what Bruno Latour (1987) calls 'science in practice'. However, to favour a more contextual, reflec- tive science is not to abandon all hope of tackling environmental challenges. Like Richard Rorty (1998), we will argue that the process of 'achieving' social, political and environmental change is not advanced by developing universal claims about progress (as do many modernists) or by endlessly deconstructing our language and actions (as do many postmodernists). Following John Dewey, Rorty calls on us to abandon 'the attempt to find a (single) theoretical frame of reference within which to evaluate proposals for the human future' (Rorty 1998: 20). How to give up such singular frames at the same time as avoiding the temptation to 'prefer knowledge to hope' (Rorty 1998: 36) is the problem. The effect of this stance, Rorty argues, is to change our under- standing of the meaning of progress. That is, 'Instead of seeing progress as a matter of getting closer to something specifiable in advance, we see it as a matter of solving more problems' (Rorty 1998: 28).

So while we might support and even encourage critical engagement with abstract theory about environmentalism, we are not interested in simply playing language games. Like Macnaughten and Urry we are keen to go beyond the 'rather dull debate between "realists" and "constructivists"' and instead identify 'specific social practices, especially of people's dwellings, which produce, reproduce and transform different natures and different values' (Macnaghten and Urry 1998: 2). Our intention in editing this book is to encourage a deeper engagement with sustainable architecture, one that doesn't shy away from broader sociological or philosophical questions or merely indulge in the narrowly instrumental debates that characterise so much of the green architecture literature. By exploring sustainable architectures in the plural, as competing interpretations of our environmental futures, we can begin to ask new questions and perhaps introduce some fresh thinking about sustainable design. As Fischer and Hajer have argued, this interpretive stance

> opens up the questions: what alternative ways of seeing can we envisage?; how do we analyse environmental problems?; and how do we want to live both in and with nature?
>
> (Fischer and Hajer 1999: vii)

This emphasis on living both 'with' and 'in' nature emphasises that 'neither the natural nor the social can be given paramount status, but that instead a process of "co- construction" needs to be recognised and explored' (Irwin 2001: 16). This is key to our approach and to the chapters in this book. Rather than meet nature as an external pre- given entity to be saved or exploited, the authors represented here appear to under- stand and relate to nature in a number of ways. As Kay Milton reflects, these 'diverse "myths" of nature give rise to different understandings of the risks involved in our use of the environment and the character and the degree of responsibilities towards it' (Milton 1996: 32). She goes on:

> environmentalism is unambiguously part of culture ... it is part of the way in which people understand the world and their place within it. It belongs to the sphere that includes people's feelings, thoughts, interpretations, knowledge, ideology, values, and so on. It is ... a particular way of understanding the world. As such ... environmentalism has implications for, and is expressed in, the things people do.
>
> (Milton 1996: 33)

Note that Milton emphasises that what people 'do' is intimately connected to what they think, feel or claim to know. As an anthropologist she wants to sensitise us to the ways in which 'local knowledge' frames our relationship to nature. As another anthropologist, Clifford Geertz, comments:

> the shapes of knowledge are always ineluctably local, indivisible from their instruments and their encasements. One may veil this fact with ecumenical rhetoric or blur it with strenuous theory, but one cannot really make it go away.
>
> (Geertz 1993: 4)

Geertz argues that to comprehend the complex relationship between knowledge, action and local culture necessitates replacing 'thin descriptions' that focus on the narrowly empirical with 'thick descriptions', explorations and explanations of local contexts which look across a 'multiplicity of complex conceptual stories, many of them superimposed upon or knotted into one another, which are at once strange, irregular, inexplicit' (Geertz 1973: 10). It is the 'strange, irregular, inexplicit' ways in which people both interpret nature and make and inhabit buildings, and how these competing approaches reflect the cultures of people who are involved in this process of architectural making, that are the focus of this book.

Acknowledging the plasticity of culture and nature means that we need to recognise and analyse green buildings as a series of contingent hybrids, an understanding of which is inseparable from the encounter with the people and places that shaped their design and development. Seen this way, each individual design strategy explored in these pages has developed a particular relationship to sustainability, place, technology and the future and has emerged as a response to a situationally specific analysis of the environmental challenge. Rorty usefully describes this analytical approach as 'antirepresentationalist', one that 'does not view knowledge as a matter of getting reality right, but rather as a matter of acquiring habits of action for coping with reality' (Rorty 1991: 1). Our aim, then, is not to provide exemplary cases or particular techniques that might convince people to think differently about nature or adopt some form of 'best practice'. Instead the contributions begin to shed light on a few cultural attitudes which have been more or less successful in creating new forms of architecture and urbanism that point towards more sustainable futures (Brand 2003: 117–69). By collecting together research about sustainable architecture from across Europe and North America, this collection aims to review these alternative ways of seeing and, in doing so, learn about the co-construction of multiple natures and architectures.

## The paradoxes of green architectures

Before we embark on the twists and turns of a set of highly diverse chapters we would like to briefly review how we got to this starting place. Some readers may feel we are overcomplicating matters. For many writers the challenge is rather more straightforward than our theorising would suggest. Stimulated by a growing scarcity in resources, the debate about climate change and the threats of sick building syndrome, more and more architects have taken up the mantle of promoting ecological concerns. They have, in the main, focused on reducing the energy intensity of buildings through the use of insulating materials, low-energy lighting and natural ventilation and have attempted to eschew non-renewable and potentially hazardous toxic materials. Many architects have, then, accepted Deyan Sudjic's challenge to 'address the issue of green urbanism' (Sudjic 1996: 7). Energy economy is a major priority among these practitioners. As Susan Maxman argues, 'it's not like the 1970s, when every house had to be earth-bermed, solar powered, etc etc ... we realise now that it has to make economic sense as well' (quoted in Bilger 1993: 11). This popular view of sustainable architecture renders it roughly synonymous with energy efficiency. If this is the definition of sustainable architecture that is ultimately accepted by a majority it would seem that the theorising offered by the authors of this volume might be productively replaced by radically simplified checklists that itemise 'best practices' or concrete things-to-do. Rorty, has, after all, admonished us to 'put a moratorium on theory' and get on with 'solving the problems of men' (Rorty 1998: 91).

There are, of course, many authors who have approached the challenge of sustainability with just such a 'can do' attitude. In the United Kingdom, for example, Brian Edwards and Paul Hyett have written a *Rough Guide to Sustainability*, published by the Royal Institute of British Architects (RIBA), which confidently links the definition of sustainability to 'a number of important world congresses' through which we have learnt what it means to be sustainable (Edwards and Hyett 2001: 1). Architectural sustainability is linked to the much quoted Brundtland definition through an emphasis on limits to the 'carrying capacity' of the planet, and they point to the UK's Building Services Research and Information Association (BSRIA) definition of sustainable construction as 'the creation and management of healthy buildings based upon resource-efficient and ecological principle' (Edwards and Hyett 2001: 7). Drawing on these sources, Edwards and Hyett argue that a 'large part of designing sustainably is to do with energy conservation', while also recognising that it is also about 'creating spaces that are healthy, economically viable and sensitive to local needs'. However, the rest of their guide has little to say about the wider social and political issues that this volume examines, and it focuses almost exclusively on resource efficiency. Sustainable housing, for instance, is defined as 'housing that creates sustainable communities in a resource-efficient manner' (Edwards and Hyett 2001: 97). Modelling techniques such as the Building Research Establishment Environmental Assessment Method (BREEAM) are emphasised, and a self-assessment sustainability toolkit for architecture students is provided that allots scores for interventions in the areas of energy, materials, resources, access and health. Interestingly, when checklist users total their calculations, all the energy criteria receive a 300 per cent multiplier, whereas issues such as 'contact with nature' attract a 100 per cent multiplier, and criteria to assess the social equity of resource and/or environmental risk distribution are altogether absent.

Our intention here is not to critique this methodology or to argue that the range of environmental innovations that Edwards and Hyett highlight are not valid – socially, commercially or technically – in their own terms. Along with John Hannigan, our analysis aims not to 'discredit environmental claims but rather to understand how they are created, legitimated, and contested' (Hannigan 1995: 3). Following Latour, we wish to open the lid of these 'black boxes' and better understand the values that lie inside their making (Latour 1987: 129–31). The critical point is the apparent self-confidence with which some architects and supporters of the concept view the sustainability challenge. It is precisely such certainty that allows Paul Hyett, who was recently President of the RIBA, to declare:

> Sustainability is at the top of the agenda, firmly and irreversibly, coinciding with a growing public awareness and creating a new mood which should be put to maximum effect. The duty lies collectively with all architects to posit alternative visions of the future that will enable mankind to live in harmony with its host environment.
>
> (Edwards and Hyett 2001: 18)

Edwards and Hyett claim that these alternative visions of how we might best live in harmony with nature can be adequately expressed through an energy-rating model. Harry Gordon concurs from a US perspective when he argues that the 'LEED [Leadership in Energy and Environmental Design] standards, issued in 2000, are creating a common understanding of what it means to build green' (Gordon 2000: 34). Employing similar logic, Paul Hawken, Amory Lovins and Hunter Lovins, in their very influential book *Natural Capitalism*, argue that consumers will automatically embrace radical resource efficiency once they understand that they can reduce consumption 'without diminishing the quantity or quality of services that people want' (Hawken et al. 1999: 176). This level of self-confidence in the compelling transparency of sustainable architecture to produce social and environmental change assumes a purely scientific or quantitative framing of the problem and that there are no barriers, save our awareness, to implementation.

There are, however, others who are less sanguine about our ability to scientifically express our relationship to nature. Eric Schatzberg (2002: 220–1), for example, finds the optimism of Hawken et al. to be a 'flawed' example of 'technological utopianism'. He holds that 'ultimately their faith in technological progress has blinded them to the political dimension of the revolution that they so fervently desire'. The American planner Scott Campbell is similarly concerned with this missing political dimension of moves toward radical efficiency. He would strenuously object to the imbalance implicit in Edwards and Hyett's multipliers and the lack of equal assessment given to issues related to social equity (Campbell 1996: 468). Deyan Sudjic, arguing from another perspective, holds that

> Designing buildings that are truly green is still a far from exact science, and we judge by appearances. We assume that buildings are green if they look hand-made and are built of 'natural materials'.
>
> (Sudjic 1996: 7)

For Sudjic, and the editors of this book, the black box of ecological design is filled with paradoxes rather than certainty. Thus, we now have a situation in which a whole variety of environmental innovations are advanced in the debate about 'sustainable building'. Deyan Sudjic usefully summarises this confusion:

> Despite the dogmatism of many of the specialists about what is and what is not an ecologically sensible approach to architecture there can be no certainty. Like all new religions, there is endless scope for doctrinal dissent. There are many different approaches, from those who believe in low-tech mud walls, to the enthusiasts for hi-tech mechanisms
>
> (Sudjic 1995: 25)

Employing a close textual analysis technique (Multidimensional Scalogram Analysis) Cook and Golton analysed a range of books and articles about sustainable building and found considerable inconsistencies and anomalies between the definitions of environmentalism in each of these groups:

> For example, the London Ecology Centre advocate that 'green' building should use super insulating argon filled windows to increase energy efficiency thereby reducing resource consumption, an acknowledged ecological goal. However these windows require high technology in research and development, and use highly processed or high entropy materials. The windows are not manufactured locally from traditional materials and will require transportation from the point of manufacture to the site.
>
> (Cook and Golton 1994: 680)

However, they found the 'edges' between each competing perspective 'blurred' when considering design priorities, technical choices and architectural principles. This is not surprising. The debate about green building has been characterised by a whole set of awkward analytical questions about the nature of 'true' green design. For instance, Mark Branch points out that 'manufacturers who are looking to minimise their impact on ecology are also concerned about their employees, so they avoid toxins' (Branch 1993: 10). The problem is that 'the kinds of products that tend to be best for people with multiple chemical sensitivities or severe allergies are inert ones such as metals, glass, and concrete – non renewable (though recyclable) materials' (Branch 1993: 10). Similarly, Brenda and Robert Vale ask whether it is 'better to produce a new building that has minimal effect on the environment through only using those resources available to the building from its site', or 'is it better to convert an existing building that will continue to need to use resources and fossil fuels over its lifetime?' (Vale and Vale 1996: 142). The Vales call for more 'hard research to underpin any proposals put forward for a more sustainable urban environment' (Vale and Vale 1996: 142), but as Sudjic points out it isn't that simple:

> A timber structure, for example, doesn't need the energy that goes into smelting aluminium. On the other hand, aluminium structure can easily be recycled, while timber cannot. How do you account for the energy costs of transporting building components to the site? And how about the energy that will be consumed by all the occupants in getting to a building?
>
> (Sudjic 1995: 25)

It would appear that attempting to scientifically define 'green buildings' by privileging specific forms of 'technically proven' environmental innovation is misguided. In fact Cook and Golton, quoting Gaile (1956), suggest definitively that the whole concept of 'green' building is 'ill-conceived', with sustainable architecture embodying an 'essentially contestable concept' (Cook and Golton 1994: 678). Similarly, John Farmer has argued that 'there is no conclusive definition of what "green" means' beyond a range of innovative design approaches which 'either explicitly or subliminally reference themselves in relation to nature' (Farmer 1996: 179).

## Exploring environmental knowledge

> A fundamental feature of the new environmental politics is that there is no one true, or trusted, form of expertise, no single path to the truth
>
> (Jamison 2001: 27)

Turning away now from the search to discover universal definitions of sustainability or standardised forms of best practice design, we must find a different way forward. In order to proceed we must draw upon a wider set of disciplinary sources and begin to connect architectural debate to theory and practice in the humanities and social sciences. As Jamison argues, we 'must wander outside the confines of any one discipline and any one mode of interpretation into the wider worlds of culture and history' (Jamison 2001: 36). Jamison is interested in what he terms the 'making of green knowledge' – that is, the ways that 'different producers of knowledge ... take their point of departure, their problem formulation, from different aspects of reality' (Jamison 2001: 32). By focusing on the process of environmental knowledge making we can avoid setting up bipolar oppositions between different paradigms of thought: the light versus dark green architects or the sociologists versus scientists. Instead we can recognise researchers and practitioners as reflecting differing, often competing, modes of knowledge – that is, as inhabiting different 'epistemic communities' (Haas 1990). Jamison puts it this way:

> There have emerged a number of competing academic, or analytical, responses to the new environmental challenges ... based on different ideals of scientific knowledge, different 'epistemic' criteria, as well as different varieties of scientific practice.
>
> (Jamison 2001: 27–8)

Jamison draws on Jürgen Habermas to suggest that the natural, social and human sciences are all underpinned by differing 'knowledge constituting interests', whether it be, respectively, one of control over nature, the management of nature or a better understanding of nature. To complicate matters more, environmental advocates of every persuasion are adept at creatively drawing upon these different disciplinary traditions to support their respective visions. As Ulrich Beck remarks, 'The observable consequence is that critics (i.e. environmentalism) frequently argue more scientifically than the natural scientists they dispute against' (Beck 1995: 60). Everyone it seems is involved in making what Michel Foucault called 'truth claims', each seeking to frame environmental responses in relation to a particular problem definition. Seen this way, appeals to facts and figures, or aesthetics, or experience, or spirituality, all represent alternative forms of knowledge which should be treated symmetrically. Moreover, given that 'except for the name of "ecology" itself, virtually nothing unites the bioregionalists, Gaians, eco-feminists, eco-Marxists, biocentrecists, eco-anarchists, deep ecologists and social ecologists' (Ross 1994: 5), any attempt to neatly categorise or 'essentialise' forms of environmentalism along a scale of light to dark, or deep to shallow, as some authors have attempted, seems fatally flawed. As David Schlosberg suggests, 'There is no such thing as environmentalism. Any attempt to define the term in a succinct manner necessarily excludes an array of other valid definitions' (Schlosberg 1999: 3).

Departing from an understanding founded on a pre-defined conception of the environmental problem in which appropriate ends (sustainability) and means (technology) are simply assumed, this volume explores the ways in which individuals, groups and institutions embody widely differing perceptions of what environmental innovation is about. As Marteen Hajer argues:

> the present hegemony of the idea of sustainable development in environmental discourse should not be seen as the product of a linear, progressive, and value-free process of convincing actors of the importance of the Green case. It is much more a struggle between various unconventional political coalitions, each made up of such actors as scientists, politicians, activists, or organisations representing such actors, but also having links with specific television channels, journals and newspapers, or even celebrities.
>
> (Hajer 1995: 12–13)

We have only to think of the tensions and interlinkages between the various contributors to the urban environmental debate to spot the opportunity for contestation. In the UK we could think of Prince Charles, the Energy Saving Trust, Friends of the Earth, the British Council of Offices, RIBA, the Alternative Technology Centre, the Building Research Establishment and so on. In the United States we can similarly think of the Sierra Club, Earth First!, the Rocky Mountain Institute, the First Nations of Canada and former vice-president Al Gore as sitting uncomfortably in the same category. Each of these actors and institutions possesses 'a particular way of thinking and talking about environmental politics' reflecting the 'rather different social and cognitive commitments' which become reflected in the 'story-lines' each actor develops about what a green building is or is not (Hajer 1995: 13). So, from this analytical standpoint we cease to view green buildings as merely differently configured technical structures. As Hajer points out, to analyse environmental questions in terms of 'quasi-technical decision-making on well defined physical issues misses the essentially social questions that are implicated in these debates' (Hajer 1995: 18). Analysing discourses of environmentalism 'as a specific ensemble of ideas, concepts, and categorisations that are produced, reproduced, and transformed in a particular set of practices and through which meaning is given to physical and social realities' (Hajer 1995: 44) allows us to view green buildings as social representations of alternative ecological values, or material embodiments of the competing discourses that make up the green buildings debate. Tracing the resonances and dissonances between each of these discourses supports John Dryzek's argument that 'language matters, that the way we construct, interpret, discuss, and analyze environmental problems has all kinds of consequences' (Dryzek 1997: 9). It is these consequences that each of the individual chapters explores in detail and through which we begin to recognise the diversity of stories being told about sustainable architecture today. As Beauregard suggests:

> To contemplate public policy for our cities or to consider acting collectively requires not merely an analysis of the conditions available for success but also a reflective understanding of the language with which we represent those conditions.
>
> (Beauregard 1995: 77)

## Future technologies, environmental futures

Taken as a whole, the contributions to this book present a critique of past research into the environmental impact of buildings and outline the methodological challenges facing a new environmental research agenda. Rejecting any notion of green buildings as merely differently configured technical structures which can be more or less better designed in relation to an external definition of accepted environmental standards, the authors collectively argue for the need to view sustainable buildings as social expressions of competing ecological values. The hope is that by reading across and between the chapters we might begin more clearly to identify the relationship between the competing conceptions of environmental issues and the social and technical processes framing building design. Re-reading green buildings in this way reveals the widely differing motivations and commitments of actors, the diverse range of techniques or technical innovations employed, the variety of contexts and settings in which development occurs and the social and political processes involved in the definition and redefinition of the nature of the environmental problem itself. In this way, we begin to recognise how different discourses of green design are mobilised by different, often competing, actors and are then framed by dynamic social and technical contexts of building development and infrastructure provision. Adopting this way of seeing building design highlights both the competing pathways of innovation and the hybrid nature of the green building.

The approach of the book is, then, to treat technology – like the notion of sustainability itself – as a fundamentally contested concept and to explore the importance of social context for the shaping of environmental innovation. Our use of the term 'technology' here is an expansive one. We mean by it not only the artefacts associated with sustainable architecture – solar collectors, wind generators, biomass boilers and the like – but the knowledge required to construct and use these artefacts, as well as the cultural practices that engage them (MacKenzie and Wajcman 1985: 3–4). This stance echoes that of Andrew Feenberg, who has similarly explored these approaches and emphasised the need to avoid the essentialist fallacy of splitting technology and meaning and to focus instead on the 'struggle between different types of actors differently engaged with technology and meaning' (Feenberg 1999: xiii). For Feenberg, the contexts of technology include such diverse factors as 'relation to vocations, to responsibility, initiative, and authority, to ethics and aesthetics, in sum, to the realm of meaning' (Feenberg 1999: xiii). Wrapped up in each technological artefact, or, in the case of our architectural interests, each building, is an assembly of ideologies, calculations, dreams, political compromises and so on. Seen this way 'technologies are not merely efficient devices or efficiency orientated practices, but include their contexts as these are embodied in design and social insertion' (Feenberg 1999: xiii).

Feenberg usefully gives us an example of a modern Western house which on the one hand has increasingly become an 'elaborate concatenation of devices', the centre of 'electrical, communications, heating, plumbing, and of course, mechanised building technologies' (Feenberg 1999: xi). For builders, houses are often little more than this. On the other hand, houses are much more than 'an efficient device for achieving goals', and as home dwellers we are all skilled at creating a 'domesticated' environment, which has 'little or nothing to do with efficiency' (Feenberg 1999: xi). Feenberg acknowledges that a distinction between the technical (the electric circuit as a technology) and the social (the experience of warmth and light) has a certain validity, for instance in the development of professional technical disciplines. However, to treat each as an essentially distinct category would be to deny that 'from an experiential standpoint these two dimensions – device and meaning, technical and life-world practice – are inextricably intertwined' (Feenberg 1999: xii). Indeed, it is the design intelligence of architects that manages, in the best examples, to pull all of these diverse interests and artefacts together into a coherent whole.

In sum, while we the editors acknowledge how a technical, performative approach to understanding environmental design has brought undoubted benefits in terms of highlighting the issues of energy efficiency in buildings, the aim of this book is to fundamentally revise the focus and scope of the debate about sustainable architecture and to reconnect issues of technological change with the social and cultural contexts within which change occurs. To be clear, this is not a plea to relieve architects of yet more responsibility and render it up to social scientists as another group in the long list of consultants employed to solve problems external to design. It is, rather, a plea for architects to expand the variables of design practice itself. Looking forward to the chapters, the reader can then expect to explore the competing notions of what constitutes 'greenness' in architectural terms; how a building's environmental design is shaped by the strategic priorities of the many actors involved in the planning, design, construction and use of the building; how hybrid designs result as a product of a compromise between several often conflicting interpretations of green design; and how we can identify a range of alternative trajectories of environmental design.

## Incorporation and engagement

### Towards a critical practice of sustainable architecture

Elsewhere we have written of the ways in which interdisciplinary research on sustainable building has been conventionally conceptualised in a linear progression of science into technology into society (Guy and Shove 2000). Seen this way, the role of social science research is to tackle the non-technical barriers to the promotion and implementation of best practice design. In this way social science is 'incorporated' into the techno-economic paradigm as a form of end-of-pipe science, an adjunct to scientific research and engineering solutions to a predefined environmental challenge. Alternatively, we suggested, social science could adopt a different stance, one of 'engagement' with the techno-economic perspective. Drawing upon more critical, interpretive analytical approaches to technological change, this would involve social scientists in both defining the nature of the environmental challenge and exploring a range of context-specific responses. This book follows the spirit of engagement and, while responding to Rorty's admonition to quit 'theorizing' and get on with the work of solving the 'problems of men', emphasises the urgent need for a process of critical reflection through which we may begin to 'figure out' how we might individually and collectively respond to environmental issues. For while both checklists and philosophical specula- tion can be helpful and even necessary to achieve certain objectives, they rarely provoke the wider 'public talk' (Barber 1984) necessary to engage community participation in sustainable design. The authors gathered here are all involved in this collaborative reflection about sustainable architecture; that is, the 'work' of choosing how we want to live – with and in nature – in order to sustain life into the future. This is, we argue, a response to the political debate Rorty is calling for and a contribution to the generation of what he terms 'social hope' about our collective futures.

The collection of essays we have assembled is purposely varied in style, approach, focus and content. Sorting these chapters into a progressive order entailed a number of choices about the key themes and issues that we, as editors, felt were key to each contribution and central to the objectives of the book we have discussed so far. This was not an innocent exercise. As Schlosberg has pointed out, 'Histories are always an exercise in framing, and histories of environmentalism are no exception' (Schlosberg 1999: 21). Our initial reading of the contributions raised an extensive list of cross- cutting issues that included standardisation, politics, liberalisation, health, the role of industry, pedagogy, technological diffusion and so on. Each of the chapters had things to say about a range of these issues and concerns, and we could have told different stories about sustainable architecture by reordering the chapters in different ways. Our final selection of four themed parts with distinct but interlinked concerns was informed as much by our own previous work as by the chapters themselves. In previous books (Guy and Shove 2000; Moore 2001) and in special issues of journals that we have separately edited (Guy 2002; Frampton and Moore 2001), we have both identified problems with the conventional, techno-economic perspective on sustainable architec- ture and begun to explore an alternative, more sociological perspective. This book continues that epistemological journey, and our themed structure allows the reader to review some of the steps along the path we have travelled. Each themed part begins with paragraphs introducing the chapters in that part, highlighting some of their key themes and allowing the reader to follow the progression of the argument.

We begin in Part A, 'Modelling design', by identifying and critiqueing the conven- tional urge to model, quantify and standardise approaches to sustainable architecture. The modern narrative of standardisation is, in this part, challenged by the urge to tell local stories. In Part B, 'Responding design', we explore how the contexts of design and development make a difference to the shape and form of architecture. The postmodern narrative of contextualism is, in this part, challenged by the modern desire to 'defamiliarise' architecture and the patterns of daily life. In Part C, 'Competing design', we examine some of the tensions between different environmental discourses and how these collide, clash and intermingle to produce competing forms of sustainable archi- tecture. In this part we consider the evolutionary versus the revolutionary prospects for sustainable architecture. In Part D, 'Alternative design', we trace through some competing design trajectories. Competing designs are equated with competing visions of the past and corresponding possibilities for the future.

Finally, in the concluding chapter we review what all these stories have told us about sustainable architecture and what challenges remain ahead. In particular, we try to iden- tify connections between our contributors' perspectives. For, as Jamison suggests, although there is an increasingly 'voluminous literature' on environmentalism, there is a critical need for books that explicitly try to make connections across disciplines and social roles, across countries and continents, across the generations, and, perhaps most importantly, across the divisions that have continued to grow between activists and academics, practitioners and theorists, the doers and the thinkers of the emerging ecological culture.

(Jamison 2001: 9)

We hope this book makes a contribution to this broader agenda about sustainability and, more specifically, to a more critical, engaged and interdisciplinary approach to sustainable architecture.

# Part A
# Modelling design

# 2

# Hybrid environments

## The spaces of sustainable design

*Graham Farmer and Simon Guy*

Farmer and Guy argue that despite the apparent consensus around key environmental issues it often seems less clear what factors might define or constitute a green building. They highlight some of the limitations of performance-based and ideological interpretations of sustainable architecture by exploring three recent building developments in the north east of England. Each of the three buildings they examine represents a situated design response to three very particular physical and development contexts. Similarly, each embodies a range of environmental innovations that make distinctive contributions to the development of more sustainable futures. Farmer and Guy suggest, that although these alternative technical strategies can be partially understood to conform to contrasting green values, they do not emerge simply from any preconceived definition of 'greenness'. Instead they are shaped through a merging of distinctive philosophies of green design, embedded in particular social and physical contexts. These diverse design strategies can therefore be understood to represent competing pathways towards sustainability. From this perspective, they argue, we can begin to view individual buildings as complex hybrids – situationally specific responses to the challenges of sustainability shaped by the widely differing motivations and competing social commitments of the actors involved in particular design and development processes.

## Modelling sustainable design

As sustainability enters the mainstream, becoming the accepted goal if not always the practice of governments and architects alike, it seems to be slipping through our fingers. No longer an alternative route out in the cold, green architecture is, as a result, ever more elusive and difficult to define.

(Castle 2001: 5)

Within contemporary architectural discourse and practice there seems to exist a wide consensus on the urgent need to promote environmental innovation in building design. It is rare to find a book about sustainable architecture that does not highlight the contribution of buildings to various forms of environmental degradation. Edwards and Hyett, for example, point out that '50% of all resources consumed across the planet are used in construction, making it the least sustainable industry in the world' (Edwards and Hyett 2001: 1). Deyan Sudjic has suggested that, as a result, 'for any architect not to profess passionate commitment to "green" buildings is professional suicide' (Sudjic 1996: 7). However, beyond an apparent consensus of concern for the environment, it is often less clear what factors might define or constitute a green building. You only have to look through the numerous books on green or sustainable architecture and the myriad of building reviews in architectural periodicals and journals to identify a bewildering array of contrasting types or styles of green building, each emphasising different aspects of the sustainability agenda. For example, in an edition of the *Architectural Review* entitled 'Greening Architecture' we can find articles and building reviews, amongst others, on the environmental relevance of vernacular architecture; a hotel constructed of local building materials; a school based on organic forms; an energy-efficient visitor centre buried underground, and a high-tech skyscraper swathed in plants (Architectural Review 1999). Clearly, if we are to progress towards a more sustainable built environment, policy-makers, researchers and designers have to begin to make sense of the conceptual challenges raised by an apparent variety of pathways towards sustainable design.

One of the most common responses to handling strategic diversity in both environmental policy-making and research has been to try to order it through the development of comparative models that aim to interpret and assess sustainable buildings on the basis of their environmental attributes. Typically, these models tend to fall into two broad categories. First, and most common, are those models that tend to view the existence of a multiplicity of design strategies as somehow distracting to the need to collate, compare and contrast 'real' and measurable data relating to physical issues such as climate change. These consensual models tend to attribute the sustainability of a building to its correlation with a set of predefined performance criteria such as energy efficiency. By contrast, a second group of models highlights the apparent diversity of the debate and the differing approaches to sustainability and associates them with a range of conflicting values, ideologies or philosophical assumptions held by those actors involved in the design of sustainable buildings. We suggest that although both types of model can contribute to an understanding of sustainable design, they also have their limitations when applied to actual buildings, and in this chapter we begin to highlight some of these limitations by examining three recent building developments in the north east of England.

## Designing sustainable futures

The three buildings we have chosen to highlight are the Groundwork Trust Eco-Centre in South Tyneside, the Solar Office at Doxford Business Park in Sunderland and the Central Square office development in Newcastle. Before describing the case studies it is necessary to explain why we selected these particular examples. Firstly, we have chosen the same building type in the same regional context: each is a commercial office building in the north east of England. The buildings do, however, occupy three very different locations. Secondly, each embodies a contrasting and particular building design response to three very different urban locations, and each has been, in its own right, portrayed or promoted as an exemplar of sustainable construction. Table 1 shows a comparative summary of some of the features of each building.

The Groundwork Trust's 'Eco-Centre' in Jarrow, South Tyneside, is conceived both as a demonstration facility and as a working office, providing space for commercial rent. The centre has won several awards for its green credentials. It is located in the Viking Business Park on the south bank of the River Tyne in Hebburn, South Tyneside, an area formerly used by heavy industry but now designated an urban regeneration area.

The Doxford Solar Office is a 4600 $m^2$ speculative office development built by Doxford International, an Akeler Group company, as part of Phase 6 of the 32 hectare

2.1 *Groundwork Trust's Eco-Centre.*

2.2 *Doxford Solar Office.*

*2.3 Central Square Offices.*

Doxford International Business Park development. The site is located by the A19 on the outskirts of Sunderland and in the heart of Sunderland's Enterprise Zone.

The Central Square offices are a 7000 $m^2$ speculative office built by Parabola Estates, a Newcastle-based development company, and the building is located on a

*Table 2.1  Summary of design features for the three case study office buildings*

|  | Groundwork Eco-Centre | Doxford Solar Office | Central Square Offices |
|---|---|---|---|
| Location | Semi-urban business park | Out-of-town business park | City centre |
| Developer | National charitable trust (Groundwork Trust) | International property company (Akeler) | Local developer (Parabola Estates) |
| Cost per $m^2$ (est. gross) | £750 | £950 | £560 |
| Floor area $m^2$ (approx) | 1400 | 4600 | 7000 |
| Funding | Private/public | Private/EU/public | Private |

*Table 2.1 continued*

|  | Groundwork Eco-Centre | Doxford Solar Office | Central Square Offices |
|---|---|---|---|
| Proximity to public transport hubs | Close | Distant | Adjacent |
| Attitude to infrastructure networks | Autonomous | Semi-autonomous | Integrated |
| Renewable energy use | Wind power (electricity) | Solar electric (photovoltaic) | None |
| Key low-energy features | • Passive solar design<br>• Highly insulated<br>• Ground source heat pump for heating and cooling | • Passive solar design<br>• Well-sealed construction | • Use of fabric thermal mass<br>• Use of daylighting |
| Ventilation system | Natural | Natural with flexibility for tenant to install mechanical systems | Mechanical displacement ventilation with comfort cooling |
| Predicted energy consumption (kWh/m$^2$) | 75 | 85 | 180 |
| Attitude to construction materials | Use of recycled and renewable materials sourced locally where possible | Conventional business park specification | Minimised use of virgin materials through re-use of existing building |
| BREEAM* rating | None | Excellent | Excellent |
| Urban vision | City made up of dispersed, independent, autonomous and sovereign buildings | De-centralised city utilising new communication and environmental technologies | Centralised, compact and dense city |

*BREEAM = Building Research Establishment environmental assessment method

Source: Farmer and Guy 2003

city-centre 'brownfield' site in an area bounded by Central Station, Newcastle's main transport hub, and the northern bank of the River Tyne.

Before discussing the three buildings it is important to make two points. First, in highlighting these particular examples we are not suggesting they represent the 'ideal' or the only models of sustainable building. A whole range of possible green design approaches might exist beyond those described. Second, we are not questioning the relative merits of each approach or disputing that each is a commendable example of sustainable design. The question we address is: how well can these buildings be understood by performance or by ideological models of sustainability?

## Building performances

Physical performance has become a central issue in several contemporary models of sustainable architecture. Although these concerns are certainly nothing new in architecture, the interweaving of the concept of 'environmentally friendly' with resource efficiency has tended to be a defining characteristic of the environmental debate since the energy crisis of 1973. Although the concept of sustainable development as it developed through the 1980s and 1990s shifted the environmental debate in architecture beyond a narrow focus on energy efficiency, the 1987 Brundtland Report, the Earth Summit of 1992 and the subsequent Kyoto Protocol of 1997 have tended to be instrumental in framing the environmental 'problem' in the mainly macro-physical terms of greenhouse gas emissions and ozone layer depletion. The main outcome of this global focus for sustainability in terms of building production has been a continuing emphasis on improving physical performance generally and the efficient use of energy in particular. In terms of environmental policies this close link between building performance and sustainability is implicit in the UK government's interpretation of sustainable construction where the key issues relating to buildings are seen as reducing energy consumption through all phases of a building's life coupled with an emphasis on reducing the materials used and waste generated through the construction and demolition of buildings (Raynsford 1999: 421). Within the UK's Climate Change Programme buildings are seen as a key part of the strategy to achieve the domestic goal of reducing carbon dioxide emissions by 20 per cent below the 1990 level by 2010, and one recent outcome of these policies has been an enhancement of Part L of the building regulations, which legislates for energy conservation in buildings.

Within many environmental research programmes this largely physicalist model of buildings has underpinned the production of a series of mainly technical, resource-saving initiatives epitomised by the concept of 'best practice' and that have tended to focus on the efficacy of particular technologies. This image of sustainable building is founded on two core assumptions. The first is the suggestion that the key environmental issues we face are essentially physical in nature and global in scale and that the real environmental issues are those of a 'global physical crisis that threatens survival' (Hajer 1995: 14). The second is that 'rational science can and will provide the understanding of the environment necessary to rectify environmental bads' (Macnaghten and Urry 1998: 1). Following from these assumptions is the belief that the 'greenness' of a building can effectively be predefined or assessed through the use of objective technical analyses such as life-cycle analysis, ecological footprint analysis or environmental assessment methods. Of these methods, environmental assessment methods (EAMs) in particular have come to be viewed as a key way of both modelling and categorising the environmental performance of a building, and during the last decade or so several different environmental rating schemes have been developed throughout the world. In the UK the Building Research Establishment (BRE) developed its own environmental assessment method (BREEAM) in 1990, claimed to be 'the world's most widely used means of reviewing and improving the environmental performance of buildings'.[1] According to Hagan, in the UK BREEAM has been central in both shaping and determining a model of sustainability: 'The arbiter of environmental sustainability in this country is the Building Research Establishment (BRE)' (Hagan 2001: 99–100). BREEAM is designed to cover a range of building types which can be assessed in three ways, depending on timing: at the design stage, during operation or as existing buildings that are not in use. The latest version of BREEAM for offices is extensive, covering 87 separate issues, each of which attracts a certain number of credits. Credits are awarded in each area according to performance. A set of environmental weightings then enables the credits to be added together to produce a single overall score. The building is then rated on an environmental performance scale depending on the minimum number of points awarded of pass, good, very good or excellent.

## Reviewing the buildings

If we review the three case study buildings using physical criteria like those central to BREEAM, it is possible to identify several aspects of each design approach that explicitly address performance-based issues such as energy efficiency. Indeed, in all three buildings resource efficiency has been one of the key aims of the design approach. The Groundwork building has a number of energy-efficient features: it generates its own power from an on-site 80 kW wind turbine; a heat pump provides an efficient source of heating and cooling; and energy use is minimised through high levels of insulation. The building benefits from a passive solar and daylighting strategy and utilises a natural ventilation strategy driven by a central atrium that draws air from occupant-controlled perimeter windows. The building's energy target is set at 75 kWh/m²/yr, compared with 130 kWh/m²/yr for typical non-airconditioned offices (Bunn and Ruyssevelt 1996: 14– 18). Similarly, the Doxford Solar Office generates its own power through the incorporation of 'Europe's largest integrated photovoltaic façade' (Pearson 1998: 14–18). The 532m² photovoltaic panels, imported from Germany, provide between one quarter and one third of the building's electricity demand (Evans 1997: 44–5). Any surplus energy is exported back to the grid. The building incorporates other low-energy measures. Its V-shaped plan has two wings of 15m-wide offices separated by an atrium, allowing daylighting and the use of natural ventilation. The incorporation of exposed thermal mass in the ceilings assists in moderating internal air temperatures and the need for mechanical cooling. The building has been insulated to normal standards but has tightly sealed construction to reduce infiltration heat losses. When these features are taken together, the target energy consumption for the building when occupied by a tenant with conventional power requirements is 85 kWh/m²/yr (Winter 1998: 24–30).

Unlike the other two buildings the Central Square Office development is not a new-build project but a refurbishment of the old Orchard Street Post Office Sorting Centre, built in 1934. The generous floor to ceiling height and the thermal mass of the original construction have been utilised as part of the building's low-energy strategy. The building does not incorporate natural ventilation, except in the atrium space. Instead an efficient mechanical displacement system with comfort cooling has been used, with heating provided by energy-efficient condensing boilers, and underfloor perimeter convectors supply the office perimeter zones. When taken together these measures mean that the building's target energy consumption is set at 180kWh/m$^2$/yr (interview), which compares with good practice for an airconditioned office of 225kWh/m$^2$/yr. Beyond a concern for energy efficiency each of the three buildings can also be understood to make a contribution to reducing the environmental impact of development across a number of best practice indicators ranging from occupants' health to water consumption and through to transport-related issues. Both the Doxford Solar Office and the Central Square building have been assessed by the BREEAM scheme and both achieved an excellent environmental performance rating.

## Deconstructing performance

Having highlighted that physical performance has played an important role in the design of each of the three buildings, the question remains as to the extent to which performance characteristics alone might define their sustainability, or indeed what the role of an analytical framework like BREEAM might be in understanding or categorising the buildings. Certainly a 'bottom-line' performance-based comparison of the three buildings could give a quantitative assessment of their relative energy efficiency, or we could use a tool like BREEAM to provide a performance rating across a number of best practice issues. However, these types of assessment tend to compress the meaning of sustainability to a relatively narrow band of pre-defined issues, and this is fraught with methodological difficulties. One problematic assumption built into EAMs is the possibility of defining a standardised set of targets that can be relevant in any context. As Cole (1998) suggests, referring to EAMs: 'Whereas it is relatively straightforward to simply list environmental criteria, organizing them into useful, related categories, prioritizing them for either design or assessment, is far more problematic' (Cole 1998: 5). One of the key problems confronting EAMs is that they rely on a base or reference condition, a benchmark by which it is possible to compare, usually defined as 'typical' or 'average' performance. As Cole suggests, 'If scrutinized, this choice of benchmark is an extremely difficult one to both define and quantify across all assessment criteria in a consistent manner' (Cole 1998: 7). A simple illustration of this problem is revealed when the Groundwork Trust building is analysed, the one building of the three not to have been assessed by the BREEAM scheme. Project architect Carole Townsend has been quoted as saying 'she is not interested in BREEAM assessments, as she would expect to score far better than "excellent" in every category' (Edwards 1996: 49). This is revealing in the sense that it highlights the way in which standardised targets for performance do not necessarily match the possibilities or indeed the restrictions present within particular development processes. Indeed if we look back at all three buildings they tend to problematise rather than reinforce the notion of both issue and benchmark transferability implicit in BREEAM. The differences in performance targets and the contrasting nature of the technologies employed would tend to suggest that the adoption of energy-saving strategies is anything but standardised or universal, rather that 'technologies and energy-related practices are selectively appropriated within specific social contexts' (Guy and Shove 2000: 10). In understanding the buildings more fully we cannot therefore ignore the way in which 'certain energy-saving strategies and technologies are easily accommodated, positively welcomed and actively promoted within the industry' (Guy and Shove 2000: 10). One example of this maximisation of a particular technology is the photovoltaic façade at Doxford. This element of the design was only made possible by a significant grant from the

European Union, and this part of the building alone exceeded the entire budget for the Groundwork Trust's building.

Abstraction from context is also implicit in the way in which EAMs tend to be based on predicted performance rather than actual performance. In this way performance modelling is simplified by separating it from the embedded functioning of the building (which is far less predictable and will depend on a wide variety of factors). Thus, although each of the buildings might be assessed as potentially energy efficient, this will inevitably depend on how they are utilised across their lifespan. As suggested by Cole this has obvious implications for the presumed sustainability of the buildings: 'There is sufficient evidence to show that a building's performance in use is often markedly different from that anticipated or predicted during design' (Cole 1999: 227). This distinction between the way in which buildings may be used also brings into question the notion of transferable performance targets: 'Beyond external factors such as specific weather conditions during a specific time period, actual performance depends on the behaviour of occupants, tenants and actions of building operators. This brings into play many idiosyncratic operational factors that may not be generally applicable to other buildings' (Cole 1999: 237). For example, in the case of the Doxford offices tenants have the ability to add technologies such as air conditioning should they wish to. The building has been constructed in shell-and-core form only and allows flexibility for tenants to incorporate a mechanical displacement ventilation system or even air conditioning. Although the building has achieved an excellent BREEAM rating, its overall performance will depend heavily on the tenant's choice of building service installation and the way in which they choose to use the building.

In highlighting some of the limitations of performance-based methodologies for interpreting sustainable buildings we are not suggesting that they have no role as a comparative assessment tool. Our concern is that if used in isolation they tend to narrowly frame the environmental debate to a conceptualisation of sustainable buildings as merely differently configured technical structures that can be judged through the exchange and comparison of technical data. In compressing the meaning of green buildings to make them amenable to scientific analysis there is a tendency to focus only on the physical attributes of buildings as static and passive objects in which aspects of desirable 'performance can be defined irrespective of geographical location, patterns of ownership, occupation or operation' (Guy and Shove 2000: 53). These notions also assume that individual building designers or decision-makers will act rationally both in quantifying the benefits of specific building performance and then taking action accordingly. The problematic assumptions here are that knowledge can be transferred seamlessly from one situation to another and that generalised knowledge can be relevant in very different contexts. This linear model of research and development tends to ignore the specific social context of development in which practices are localised in both time and space. As Guy and Shove point out, 'it is one thing to know how to build a low energy office, but another to be in the position to actually do so' (Guy and Shove 2000: 9). Perhaps more importantly, within the broader context of sustainability, in limiting environmental assessment of buildings to those elements of design that are readily quantifiable there is also a tendency to ignore other qualitative factors that may equally account for the sustaining of the built environment and that may only become apparent once a building is nested into a particular social or physical context. As Cole suggests,

Standardization can restrict activity to one methodology which inhibits other potentially viable approaches and prevents creativity in terms of the evolution of new
approaches/processes. More significantly, standardization implies consensus
when environmental issues are not at all consensual and many fail to address the
enormous local, regional and global diversities and may be antithetical to the whole
environmental debate which places greater emphasis on addressing problems
locally and at source.

(Cole 1998: 14)

The emphasis on the local context of development suggested by Cole should be
considered crucial in assessing and understanding the relative environmental benefits
or otherwise of buildings. If we refer back to our three buildings, a quantitative assessment of performance actually reveals very little about what distinguishes three very
different buildings – buildings that quite clearly embody different ambitions and design
strategies and that employ contrasting technologies in distinct locations within the
same regional context. In order to understand the merits of the buildings in environmental terms it is important to reflect on how and why particular issues have been
addressed and on what the relative prioritisation of those issues has been when
compared with other design issues. Further, we would suggest that this type of context-
specific analysis could actually be much more useful to the policy-maker seeking to
encourage sustainable design approaches or to the practitioner facing 'real-life' design
problems than a simple statement of 'bottom-line' performance.

## Ideological buildings

Environmental assessment methods have tended to be portrayed as objective, value-
free tools whose aim is to address those universally agreed and 'real' issues such as
climate change. As a result the role of ideology, values or ethics has tended to be
downplayed in the pursuit of such a consensus. However, it is now becoming more
widely acknowledged that sustainability is a contested concept open to diverse interpretations and, given the apparent diversity of sustainable design strategies, that the
use of value-referred models could play an important role in developing an understanding of sustainable buildings, by emphasising the motivations for addressing particular issues or for utilising particular technologies. Hagan highlights the importance of
values by suggesting two opposing and contradictory tendencies in the sustainable
architecture debate:

At present, environmental architecture is split between an Arcadian minority intent
on returning building to a pre-industrial, ideally pre-urban state, and a rationalist
majority interested in developing the techniques and technologies of contemporary
environmental design, some of which are pre-industrial, most of which are not.

(Hagan 2001: x)

Hagan also suggests that a contemporary emphasis on building performance is not in
itself a value-free approach, and she goes on to suggest that this set of values has
tended to predominate:

It is the rationalist majority who now dominate the field. One has only to look at the proceedings of any conference on environmental architecture in the last twenty years to see the overwhelming emphasis on the scientific and quantitative dimensions of the discipline: thermal conductivity of materials, photovoltaic technology, computer simulations, life cycle analysis, and so on.

(Hagan 2001: x)

Several other authors have developed ideological models or classification systems to account for the differing approaches apparent within the sustainable design debate. Though diverse, these differing models share a similar starting point in that they tend to recognise both the contested nature of the sustainability concept and the need to encompass the differing values of those individuals involved in the design process when understanding buildings. However, within the sustainable architecture literature this focus on ideology has tended to result in a relatively limited dualistic categorisation of values in which the dilemma of environmentalism is often portrayed as an expression of two very different but long-standing traditions, as suggested by Shlosberg: 'The split between more traditional and conservative conservation groups and the more radical parts of the environmental movement today is simply a manifestation of basic differences between the utilitarian and romantic attitudes that began at the turn of the century' (Shlosberg: 1999). This dualism is echoed in numerous works. For example, Sandbach (1980) divides the movement into ecological/scientific and humanist branches. Devall and Sessions (1985) distinguish their brand of deep ecology from more mainstream shallow environmentalism. David Pepper's well-known work on environmentalism identifies a dualistic debate and questions whether 'green strategies' should either follow what is termed an ecocentric or 'radical' approach or follow a technocentric or 'reformist' approach to tackling environmental problems (Pepper 1996: 7). Put simply, technocentrics adhere to a process of 'ecological modernisation' which 'indicates the possibility of overcoming the environmental dilemma without leaving the path of modernisation' (Spaargaren and Mol 1992: 334), whereas ecocentrics believe a radical new way of living is the only way forward if we are to avoid the impending ecological crisis. This technocentric versus ecocentric debate is reflected in debates around green buildings where, for many, 'technology remains the answer to saving the environment', while other sustainable architects 'argue that technology … is the primary cause of destruction of nature, and that expecting it to provide a solution for environmental ills is like using the cause of the disease to cure it' (Steele 1997: 291).

Although Pepper characterises environmental value through attitudes to technology, others have developed categories that are based on the notion of differential environmental performance. Some suggest a distinction between 'green' or 'sustainable' buildings: green buildings are defined as those that achieve incremental improvements in performance relative to typical practice; sustainable buildings on the other hand are those that achieve a more radical 'absolute' performance measured against global 'biosphere health' and 'carrying capacity criteria' (Cole 1999: 232–3). A further distinction is provided by Cole, one highlighting different shades of green:

A deep green building may, for example, refer to one designed from the outset to maximise the use of solar energy, daylighting and natural ventilation, as well as harvest rainwater, treat any wastes on site and use environmentally sound materials in the most efficient way. Light green, by contrast, may refer to buildings that have incorporated one or more green features such as high-efficiency windows, high recycled-content carpets or automatic shut-off systems for lights but are otherwise conventional.

(Cole 1999: 233)

Haughton's similar description of shades of green depends on a building's ability to close the circuits of resource supply and waste. A deep green building would have a circular metabolism, whereas a light green building would have a linear though reduced metabolism (Haughton 1997: 189–95).

## Beyond ideology

A cursory glance back at our case study buildings suggests that it might be possible to categorise them broadly using such value-referred analytical frameworks. The aim of the Groundwork Trust designers to produce a building with a radically reduced ecological footprint in comparison with a conventional office building clearly draws on ecocentric values. During the design process both the client and the architect shared a vision of a totally autonomous office building. The aim was to design and construct a building that could generate all its own electricity, provide all its own water and dispose of all its own waste, an exercise in urban autarky. The building is constructed of a timber frame, clad with second-hand bricks; the roof is made of recycled aluminium, and all timber is from sustainable sources. There is almost no use of toxic paints, glues or varnishes. The external paving slabs are recycled from Gateshead Metrocentre; the car park is made from recycled road surfacing from the streets of Newcastle; and three lengths of defunct rail from the local transport system, Tyne and Wear Metro, form a central column supporting the roof. Referring back to the categories of Pepper and Cole and Haughton, the design would suggest an ecocentric or 'deep green' approach. In contrast, the Central Square offices can perhaps be interpreted as embodying a 'light green' approach to sustainability. Here we have a vision of incremental environmental change, and the design approach places an overriding emphasis on reducing energy consumption and efficient use of resources. This has resulted in a pragmatic attitude to technology, reflected in the sensitive refurbishment and reuse of an existing building and an efficient integration of conventional technologies. The Solar Office at Doxford perhaps represents a model somewhere between the two. Here, we can identify a technocentric, modernist and future-oriented approach, in which the aim has been the incorporation and demonstration of new high-tech techniques, in this case photovoltaics. Here, it is not the overall ecological footprint that has been addressed; and although the building is semi-autonomous in energy terms, the vision is not of a building severed from centralised infrastructure provision but rather of one that can make a positive contribution to the existing supply network.

But how useful are these general categorisations? Although it may be possible to broadly categorise the buildings by referring to a general attitude to technology, a more detailed exploration of the buildings renders the picture far less clear-cut. Each of the buildings actually utilises a mixture of high and low technologies and locally and globally sourced materials, and in each the performance varies across a number of issues. At the level of individual technologies and detailed specification, a simple dualistic categorisation of ecocentric and technocentric, light and dark green, becomes difficult. Seen this way, each of the buildings defies easy definition, and it is difficult to completely capture each through an understanding based on adherence to foundational ideological princi-ples or ethical values. We would suggest that although these ideological models can provide us with some useful analytical tools when interpreting competing design concepts, they also have their limitations when applied to actual buildings. Further, if there is a tendency in ideological models (particularly those based on dualistic categori-sations) to oversimplify the outcomes of sustainable design processes, then the same can be argued for the actual conception (or ignorance) of the processes themselves. In attempting to extract clear and unequivocal values there is a tendency to portray the process of building development as both linear and unproblematic and to view the atti-tudes and intentions of individuals as remaining static throughout the process, thereby informing and shaping the decision-making process in a direct, even deterministic way. This emphasis on the importance of individual agency tends to see the way forward to achieving more sustainable buildings as a problem of convincing key decision-makers and other autonomous individuals involved in the process of the importance of the issues. As Guy and Shove suggest, 'the vocabulary is typically individualized' (Guy and Shove 2000: 63), and the challenge is to change the perceptions, attitudes, opinions and motivations of designers. Furthermore, the 'motivation for tackling a problem comes from our moral obligation and our self-interest in enhancing the resource base and its life' (Trudgill 1990: 105). This emphasis on the role and importance of the individual tends to reinforce a set of attitudes already prevalent in architectural discourse, where there is long tradition of attributing the results of complex development processes typi-cally involving hundreds of people to an individual author (usually a single architect).

## Hybrid buildings

Given the apparent necessity for environmental analysis to engage with a complex combination of materials, components and processes that go together to make up the form and functioning of a contemporary building, we suggest that a more appropriate way to model strategic diversity lies in abandoning a search for a true or incontestable definition of sustainable architecture. Rather than relying on a definition of sustainable design that is based on optimal performance or adherence to a clear set of static values, we prefer to treat the concept in a relational way that is capable of accounting for a much wider spectrum of design possibilities. In our own work we have begun to identify the emergence and coexistence of a variety of environmental logics or competing envi-ronmental discourses, each with the potential to reshape the built environment in a myriad of ways (Guy and Osborn 2001; Guy and Farmer 2000, 2001). In these papers we developed a typology of six competing logics that expanded the relatively narrow set of issues usually associated with sustainable design. In this way we suggested that design strategies may distinctly, or simultaneously, emphasise socially cohesive design; design that promotes health; design that is regionally specific; design that expresses a closer relationship to nature; design that maximises the efficient use of resources; or designs that minimise the environmental footprint of buildings; and so on. Crucially, by treating these competing visions not as foundational values or static blueprints for action but rather as environmental discourses taking their material form in buildings it is possible to recognise both the tensions and the overlaps between differing discourses as they are shaped by particular contexts of development. Utilised in this way, the typology of design logics functions as an interpretive framework, a lens through which it is possible to highlight the social production of sustainable design strategies. Importantly, design logics are not meant to be in any way exclusive, or frozen in time and space. As Benton and Short suggest, 'Discourses are never static and rarely stable' (Benton and Short 1999: 2). That is, through the design process of any particular development, logics may collide, merge, co-inhabit or simply be absent from the debate about issues, form or specification, potentially creating a rich tapestry of competing pathways towards sustainability. From this perspective sustainable buildings are better understood as the product of a number of overlapping discourses and distinct contextual practices rather than simply as physical objects that are the inevitable outcome of a static and unproblematic application of performance targets or environmental values. Indeed we should also recognise that both the notion of performance targets and the promotion of particular environmental values are themselves products of such contextual, social processes.

If we refer back to the three buildings and look beyond the simple list of design features that we have already highlighted it is possible to identify the coexistence of a number of overlapping sustainable design logics. If we examine key aspects of the sustainable design approach in each case we can see that the reality of the completed buildings, the nature of the technologies employed and the way in which they perform have actually been shaped by fluid and dynamic processes in which sustainable design discourses have subsequently been warped by the particularities of context. In each of the three buildings we can identify a range of discourses about ecology, resource efficiency, health and environmental aesthetics, but in each case these have combined with a wide array of economic, commercial, technical, and locational factors to shape the final building design strategy. At Groundwork the initial intention of an ecocentric autonomous building was overtaken by an array of functional and commercial concerns, and as a result the building had to be connected to both the electricity and water mains infrastructure. The eco-technic aim of the Solar Office in demonstrating the potential benefits of new energy-generating technologies was only made possible by an out-of-town location. As a result the building is located within and relies on its extensive car parking. Additionally, the actual energy benefits of the technologies will be affected by future tenants' choice of building servicing system. In the case of Groundwork the economic benefits of locating in a former industrial area made possible the incorporation of renewable energy technologies but have also made the building difficult to access by public transport. Conversely, the location of Central Square next to a public transport hub made the 'healthy' passive servicing strategy used at Groundwork impossible, because of urban noise and pollution.

We could tell similar stories about a whole range of sustainability issues in all three of the buildings, but it is important to note here that we are not simply highlighting the paradoxes of green design or questioning whether or not the buildings are good or bad examples of sustainable design; clearly each has its merits in environmental terms. However, having highlighted the concept of hybrid design it may be appropriate at this point to address why we think the concept might be useful in helping us to understand sustainable architecture generally or these buildings in particular. Firstly, while a process of compromise and negotiation always shapes the design of buildings, much of the current discourse about sustainable design tends to suggest that focusing on these processes is simply a distraction from the urgent need to address 'real' and consensual issues. From this viewpoint the way to achieve sustainable design is through better planning, more effective management or clearer communication and we should all aim to work together to meet agreed performance targets in order to the save the planet. In contrast, we prefer to think of the concept of sustainability as potentially providing a space for meaningful dialogue about the possible appropriate relationships between technology, nature and society. Seen in this way the current interpretation of sustainability prevalent in policy-making is precisely that: the current understanding, which is likely to be outlived by any buildings we construct today. If sustainability is therefore about negotiating a range of choices then we should begin to see hybrid buildings, the material practices of green architecture, as sustainability 'in the making'. As such, rather than viewing the process of developing sustainable buildings as the straightforward implementation of a preconceived plan for action, 'it should be viewed as an on-going transformational process in which different actor interests and struggles are located' (Long and Long 1994: 9). Adopting this way of seeing highlights the fact that 'energy related practices are both socially specific and localized in terms of time and context' (Guy and Shove 2000: 11). Similarly, environmental ethics and values become concepts to be tested, qualified and reconstructed 'through a dynamic process of design innovation' (Guy and Farmer: 2000: 84)

## Conclusions: competing pathways of sustainable architecture

Our aim in this chapter has been to explore the role that universal models might have in helping us to understand the diversity of sustainable architecture practice. We highlighted three completed buildings, not to demonstrate good practice but to show that in reality sustainable buildings are not fully interpreted by utilising static or universal models of sustainability, whether based on technical performance or environmental ideology. Our argument is not to deny that these approaches are important, or even essential, but that we should also recognise that in methodological terms they often fail to capture both the broader social context of development and the way in which the sustainability question gets caught up and reinterpreted in a whole range of debates about the future development of buildings. Despite the fact that each of the three buildings houses a similar function located in the same geographical region, in each case a particular vision of sustainability has developed in response to a particular physical, economic and social context and this has resulted in a contingent set of priorities and practices. We suggest that through their process of development the various design strategies have been shaped by a combination of technical, organisational and commercial considerations to form what might be better classified as complex hybrids. In this sense each of the buildings can be understood to incorporate competing social visions, differing ideas about our relationship to the environment, work, organisations, aesthetics, finance and so on. The three buildings can be interpreted to be the products of a variety of contrasting green logics that collide, clash and mesh to produce hybrid designs, situationally specific responses to the challenge of sustainability. Central to this understanding is that design and development actors do not simply pick up on and implement a pre-defined notion of environmentalism, whether performance or value based. Instead, the notion of the 'environment' tends to broken up and re-interpreted by construction actors as they pursue new building strategies. Thinking about environmental innovation in this way, we must become sensitive to the way in which environmental visions are shaped, encouraged, curtailed or warped by the very particular context of development, a process that inevitably results in a range of possible logics of innovation.

When viewed as sociotechnical constructs, the three case studies can serve as illuminating examples of the paradoxes that inevitably face policy and research strategies aimed at promoting 'sustainable' buildings and cities. We are concerned that the current tendency for policy-making to rely on abstracted models of sustainable building may actually be counterproductive in that standardised solutions may only have a limited application in certain contexts, or worse still they might actually act to marginalise other opportunities for environmental innovation which may have difficulty in building a social context for themselves. We suggest that if we seriously want to promote green buildings we need to gain a fuller understanding of the complex social and technical processes that underpin the development of these different approaches to environmental design. In doing so we have to account for a complex combination of differing development actors and funding regimes together with particular locational constraints and possibilities. If we seriously want to locate opportunities for environmental innovation then we have to begin to identify more closely the ways in which particular logics of environmental innovation take root in changing development practices. This inevitably means rejecting any notion of buildings as simply technical structures that can be more or less better designed related to an external model of accepted environmental standards. Instead we must accept that both are 'part of the conflicting and contradictory struggle of differing forces, interest groups and movements' (Borden and Dunster 1995: 4) and therefore contingent on the particular strategic objectives of those design and development actors with the power to implement their chosen design strategy. By demonstrating the interpretive flexibility and plasticity of environmental design strategies, our emphasis on understanding differing logics of environmental innovation raises significant questions about the framing of sustainable architectural practice in terms of technical or ethical models alone. By suggesting that the interplay of competing urban visions and alternative design logics shapes the techno-environmental profiles of green building development, we have highlighted the contested nature of environmental innovation. Seen this way, alternative technological strategies are the result not of technical superiority, but of distinct approaches to green design embedded in particular design and development processes. That is, the concept of sustainable building is fundamentally a social construct. In order to more fully understand green buildings we therefore have to account for the social structuring of both the identification of environmental problems and their resulting embodiment in built forms through multiple technical development pathways. In understanding green buildings we therefore have to be sensitive not only to the widely differing motivations and commitments of actors, but also to the range of techniques or technical innovations employed, the variety of contexts and settings in which development occurs, and the social processes involved in the definition and redefinition of the nature of the environmental problem itself. In this way, we may begin to understand how different logics of green design are mobilised by designers, developers and planners with distinct environmental strategies, and are then framed by dynamic social and technical contexts of urban development. Adopting this way of seeing building design we might better recognise both the hybrid nature of green building and the competing pathways towards sustainable buildings.

## Note

1   See www.bre.co.uk/services/BREEAM_and_EcoHomes.html

# 3

# Theory, practice and proof

## Learning from buildings that teach

*Kathryn Janda and Alexandra von Meier*

Janda and von Meier investigate two 'green' academic buildings: the Environmental Technology Center at Sonoma State University and the Adam Joseph Lewis Center at Oberlin College. Both are designed for use as teaching tools and both demonstrate sustainable architecture. Both employ a variety of passive and active systems to achieve their goals. Both have 'epic' stories to tell about the evaluation of their performance. As self-proclaimed exemplars of sustainable architecture these buildings were set apart from standard construction practice by a heightened degree of 'inspection, assessment and expectation'. But did the measures adopted by engineers and critics reflect the intentions of the builders or did they quantify something different? What was it that the buildings were designed to teach? The authors argue that the quantitative data collected 'may raise more questions about building performance than they resolve'. Noting that 'numbers rarely change our notions of what we already believe to be true', Janda and von Meier thus bring into question the use of quantitative data taken at a particular moment in time as the sole criterion for the 'goodness' of buildings.

## Introduction

Buildings present a significant challenge for the natural environment. Roodman and Lenssen (1995: 5) claim, for instance, that buildings account for 16 per cent of the world's water use, 20 per cent of its wood harvest and 40 per cent of its material and energy flows. Although new buildings can be constructed in a more sustainable fashion, quite often they are not. What can we learn from those constructed to be sustainable? Technical lessons are often sought from such exemplars. Did the argon-filled, double-paned windows in this building save energy? Did using paint low in volatile organic compounds in that building reduce off-gassing? While such questions are important stepping stones to 'better' designs, each green building example contains a set of social lessons as well. David Orr (1993) has coined the phrase 'architecture as pedagogy' to describe the concept that we learn *from* buildings, not just in them. Similarly, W. J. Rohwedder (2003) extends this idea to describe 'pedagogy of place'.

To explore the lessons learned from specific architectures in particular places, we investigate two 'green' academic buildings: the Environmental Technology Center (ETC) at Sonoma State University, California, and the Adam Joseph Lewis Center (AJLC) at Oberlin College, Ohio. Both are designed to be used as teaching tools and both demonstrate sustainable architecture. Both employ passive and active systems to achieve these goals. Both also have 'epic' stories to tell about the social structures and institutional values that resulted in the adoption of some architectural strategies and the rejection of others. Finally, each author has first-hand knowledge of and daily experience with one of these buildings. Our own participation with these structures and our observation of other uses and users helps to frame our understanding of the differences and similarities between them. Through our comparative analysis, we hope to raise new questions concerning the social and institutional context in which sustainable buildings are constructed, used and evaluated.

These buildings were designed to be far better than average, but by what measure are they better? Are there ways in which they are worse? Despite much public critical acclaim, people involved with both buildings are frequently called on to prove that the pedagogical, architectural and environmental theories behind them are working in practice. Among many dimensions, we focus on the presence, absence and use of 'data', looking at several factors with respect to data gathering, use and evaluation. First, we examine how the presence or absence of quantitative data enhances or obscures stories of building performance. Second, we describe how institutional requirements shape the desire for and impact of 'hard numbers'. Finally, we discuss who learns what from 'buildings that teach': students, faculty and the academic institutions themselves.

## Background

Although both the ETC and the AJLC have ample amounts of glass on the south side and use thermal mass for passive heating and cooling, these buildings do not shout 'sustainability' to passers-by. Neither structure relies visually on elements that the general public would likely identify as 'green': a biomorphic shape, obvious photovoltaic arrays or windmills, or a garden on the roof.[1] Instead, both building designs share a

*3.1  The Environmental Technology Center at Sonoma State University, California.*

modern aesthetic and a geometric vocabulary typical of today's commercial and institutional structures (Figs 3.1 and 3.2).

The Environmental Technology Center at Sonoma State University (SSU) is a 2,200 square foot (204 square metre) building with one large seminar room that functions as an auditorium, classroom and laboratory. It is situated on a site internal to the SSU campus, which is located about an hour north of San Francisco. Funded in part by grants from the National Science Foundation and the California Energy Commission and completed in 2001, the ETC was conceived as a 'building that teaches' (Rohwedder 1998), offering an immediate hands-on experience of high-efficiency technology and green building to general audiences as well as an abundance of real-time data for building science buffs.

Use of the ETC comprises university classes – including technical courses on energy, environmental studies courses and selected courses from other departments – and classes and events involving outside agencies and the general public. These include, for example, meetings by the local chapter of the Green Building Council, training workshops for energy auditors, work meetings for Sonoma County's Climate Protection Campaign and public events such as the Green Building Expo, with lectures and vendor exhibits. The ETC has also become a favourite classroom for two other departments: the Psychology of Yoga class appreciates the warm floor in addition to the light and spacious feel, and the *a cappella* Chamber Singers enjoy the acoustics.

*3.2 The Adam Joseph Lewis Center (AJLC) for Environmental Studies at Oberlin College in Ohio.*

The ETC was the subject of Congressional testimony before the House Energy Subcommittee by its director (von Meier 2001), at the invitation of Congresswoman Lynn Woolsey (Democrat), who had supported the ETC since its inception. Representative Woolsey subsequently arranged for an Energy Subcommittee field hearing to take place at the ETC, chaired by Congresswoman Judy Biggert (Republican, Illinois). Nationally recognised energy experts testified at the field hearing (US House of Representatives 2002), with the space of the ETC serving as a concrete example of the concepts of energy efficiency and renewable resource use they advocated.

Like the ETC, the Adam Joseph Lewis Center for Environmental Studies serves many purposes. The AJLC is a two-storey, 13,600 square foot (1,260 square metre) building with three classrooms, a library, an auditorium, six offices, a conference room and a kitchen. It also houses a 'Living Machine' that treats and internally recycles wastewater from within the building, which is sited on the edge of the Oberlin College campus, near Richardsonian Romanesque academic buildings and down the street from Victorian-era homes. Like the ETC, it was designed as a building that teaches. In the words of David Orr, the chair of Oberlin's Environmental Studies Program, the project team wanted a building that would 'help redefine the relationship between humankind and the environment – one that would expand our sense of ecological possibilities' (Reis 2000).

The AJLC has enjoyed considerable critical acclaim. It has received architectural awards from the American Institute of Architects, construction awards from national and state contractors' organisations and an Ohio governor's award for energy efficiency and has been named one of the thirty 'Milestone Buildings for the Twentieth Century' by the US Department of Energy. An early model of the building is included in an architectural textbook on the interactive effects of buildings and the environment (Fitch and Bobenhausen 1999: 336), a diagram appears in a popular environmental science textbook (Miller 2001b: 537), and it has been the subject of numerous articles in the press. Part of its notoriety has to do with its star architectural team, William McDonough and Partners, which is famous for several sustainable buildings as well as a book on the topic of sustainability (McDonough and Braungart 2002). Part also has to do with the dedication and eloquence of its on-campus champion, David Orr, who is a prolific writer and a dynamic speaker and has published several articles about the AJLC's design process (Orr 2002, 2003a, 2003b). Orr also plans to use the AJLC as the basis of a book on the subject of design and organisational learning.

Equally the AJLC has been the subject of much controversy. At the centre of this debate is a contested statement that one of the goals of the AJLC was to be a 'net energy exporter'. An Oberlin faculty member outside the Environmental Studies Program has argued that the building consumes far more energy than the photovoltaic (PV) array delivers (Scofield 2002a, 2002b, 2002c). Proponents of the building do not deny that it currently uses more energy than it generates; early documentation indicates that the goal of net energy exportation was a long-term one, intended to be reached only as PV efficiencies improved beyond the 15 per cent that is common today.

We believe that the stories surrounding these two buildings – including the range of perspectives on how 'efficient' or 'consumptive' they are, as well as how their performance is accounted for and by whom – have much to say about how expectations for sustainable architecture are shaped. Although framed in technical terms (such as air changes per hour or Btu per square foot) these goals have social implications as well as technical bases.

## Comparing theory with practice

On completion, both the ETC and the AJLC had departed from their initial designs in numerous dimensions of varying significance (depending not least on who is judging). In this section, we compare expectations with reality in the realms of the construction process and design intent.

### Process and construction

The sustainable design literature is full of phrases – 'tunneling through the cost barrier' (Hawken et al. 1999) and a 'free lunch we're paid to eat' (Gilman 1986) – that suggest sustainable design is both cheaper and easier than standard construction. Strong theoretical arguments can be made that in the long run this should be true. Construction experience with both buildings, however, provides little direct support for this hypothesis. Instead, the evidence suggests that, compared with conventional buildings, realising sustainable goals within present economic frameworks requires more time, money and effort up-front. Although some individual measures may have negative costs, construction industry standards tend to inflict penalties on designs or materials that diverge from the norm in any dimension, including sustainability. Moreover, how and when these initial costs pay off through savings down the road depends in part on what is being counted and who is doing the accounting.

### ETC

The ETC was initiated by faculty and students in the Energy Management and Design (EMD) Program at SSU. They sought to replace a recently demolished solar energy laboratory with a new teaching facility. The university administration's position in the 1980s was that the project could proceed if the programme could raise sufficient external funds. Fundraising efforts by the faculty, supported by local politicians and Congresswoman Woolsey, finally met with success in 1998 through a $370,000 National Science Foundation grant and $215,000 from the Department of Energy's Petroleum Violation Escrow Account, administered by the California Energy Commission. An earlier $5,000 grant from Pacific Gas & Electric Co funded initial design collaboration with local architect George Beeler, SSU faculty and students and other energy professionals, including researchers from the National Laboratories.

The project went out to bid in 1999, and construction began in the spring of 2000. A combination of circumstances, including weather, a local construction boom, and communication and coordination issues between campus facilities personnel, contractors and the design team, soon put the project behind schedule and over budget. Initially estimated to cost $700,000, SSU President Armiñana authorised university funding to meet the final tab, which, by the time furniture and a rooftop PV system were included, came close to $1 million. This represented a substantial buy-in on the part of the university administration. In summary, it would be fair to say that people on the Sonoma State campus were enthusiastic about the idea of the ETC but found themselves in various degrees of distress about the level of effort and sacrifice the project required in a time of limited resources.

*AJLC*

Like the ETC, the idea for the AJLC emerged from student and faculty collaboration. In 1992–3, David Orr organised an experimental class with students and architects that established a set of goals for an Environmental Studies Center at Oberlin (Orr 1997). The class considered renovation projects but ultimately decided that only a new building could reach all the goals envisioned. These goals included the following charges: that the building would discharge no wastewater, be integrated with the landscape, use no known carcinogens, use energy efficiently and generate more electricity than it used. The initial planning stages involved 13 design charrettes with approximately 250 students, faculty and community members. In addition to the architecture firm of William McDonough and Partners, the AJLC's full design team included experts from the Rocky Mountain Institute, NASA scientists and leading ecological engineers and landscape architects.

Construction began in 1998 and was completed in 2000. Like the ETC, it was supported by funds garnered from sources outside the usual academic channels. In fact, the terms of the Environmental Studies Program's agreement with the college required that Orr obtain funding from 'sources not otherwise likely to give to the college'. The construction costs were initially estimated to be $2.5 million, but the final price for the full project was $7.1 million, including a building endowment, design fees and the costs of research and construction (Orr 2003a). As with the ETC, relations with the college administration were strained over construction costs and process.

## Apples and oranges

Both the ETC and AJLC illustrate the inherent problems in making meaningful cost comparisons among structures as complex and different as conventional and sustainable buildings. The single most frequently asked question by building professionals visiting the ETC is, 'What did it cost per square foot?' Depending on which cost components are included, the answer is approximately $400 per square foot ($4,320 per square metre), which sounds discouragingly high when compared with typical first-cost construction of school or office buildings. At the same time, this figure compares reasonably with university laboratory costs. To enable a better comparison, then, we might like to dissect the construction costs and isolate those associated with laboratory or teaching capabilities. However, the major costs associated with making the ETC a building that not only performs but teaches do not appear as line items; rather, they pervade the budget in the form of many labour hours on contractors' bills with no obvious way to disentangle them.

The total project cost of the AJLC was $7.1 million. Divided by the size of the building, this works out to about $500 per square foot ($5,400 per square metre) – even higher than the ETC. David Orr (2003a) argues that a better basis for comparing the AJLC's cost with other buildings is to subtract the research, endowment and design fees, leaving a construction cost of $4.8 million. Using construction costs instead of total costs drops the initial cost of the AJLC to $350 per square foot ($3,780 per square metre). Further, since most buildings do not include a sewage treatment facility or a power plant, Orr asserts that an 'apples to apples' comparison would subtract an additional $1.2 million for unconventional construction costs, such as those associated with constructing the Living Machine and purchasing the 4,700 square foot (435 square metre) photovoltaic array.

This brings the initial cost of the AJLC to $250 per square foot ($2,700 per square metre), which is comparable with office and school averages at a similar scale and in the 1998 bid environment. The key problem might be paraphrased in general terms, in that conventional buildings do not account for the infrastructure that enables their environmental comfort, whereas sustainable buildings to some extent do.

Simply put, then, conventional rules of thumb for first costs do not compare favourably with our cases, nor are such rules apt to characterise these cases' important features. Performing a complete lifecycle cost analysis, and relating costs to benefits, is beyond the scope of this chapter, but it would level the playing field between sustainable and conventional buildings. As more sustainable buildings are constructed, another way to 'normalise' them is to compare them with each other rather than with conventional practice: apples to apples rather than apples to oranges. Identifying and describing the full initial costs of existing sustainable projects may serve to lay a foundation that others can build on. Otherwise, each new project with sustainable goals must reinvent its own wheel of justification and proof.

## Design intent versus as-built specifications

Having emerged from a construction process that could be described as 'epic', both buildings depart from their initial design plans in numerous dimensions of varying significance. We must remind the reader that differences between design intent and actuality are fairly common in standard building practice. We would also expect such differences to become more pronounced in experimental projects such as these, where less reference to convention means fewer shared assumptions. The translation from a set of two-dimensional plans and quarter-inch-to-the-foot scale models to full-scale, three-dimensional reality is fraught with issues, including variations in quality of materials, quality of craftsmanship and real versus imagined occupancy schedules. Call it Murphy's Law or the Second Law of Thermodynamics, but when moving from design to demonstration there are simply more ways for things to go wrong than for things accidentally to go better than planned.

### ETC

A key problem area for the ETC has been building control, including the custom software, sensors and hardware on operable devices (such as windows and blinds). These technical challenges in conjunction with funding constraints have considerably compromised the ETC's laboratory function. A combination of factors during the construction and commissioning phases resulted in an only partially functional building management system (BMS) with a restricted range of controls that to date makes available only a fraction of the anticipated plethora of scientific data. First, the challenges and complexity of the programming task, in which Alerton control software was adapted to the needs of this building, were underestimated by everyone, including the hopeful design team and the subcontractor who furnished an optimistic initial bid. Subsequent 'value engineering' required a reduction in the number of sensor points installed in different parts of the building. The budget constraints also left no room for hiring the programmers (who had already spent many *pro bono* hours on the project) to do what it would take to create the flexibility of data processing and control that were initially envisioned. An additional part of the design intent was to make ETC building data available in real-time on the Internet, but the first stage of these efforts had to be abandoned because of network security considerations. Finally, once the BMS was up and running, a hard-drive crash wreaked havoc that proved surprisingly difficult to repair. While new programming work was being performed in 2003 to enable systematic data analysis and control of all the existing hardware (and thus finally turn the ETC into the laboratory it was conceived to be), at the time of writing the BMS was recording only essential variables like indoor and outdoor temperature and performing rudimentary functions such as opening and closing windows.

*AJLC*

There are several ways in which the AJLC departed physically from its initial vision. We describe three examples of varying significance here. From an energy standpoint, perhaps the largest problem with the as-built AJLC was the installation of an electric boiler rather than a heat pump to heat the atrium. The engineers made this substitution on the construction documents, and the architects did not catch the change at this stage. The boiler served as the primary heat source for the atrium for almost two years, causing substantial increases in energy use.

In addition to the substitution of the electric boiler, other differences are evident in two very different images of the AJLC available on the internet. One, available at the Environmental Studies Program's website, shows the AJLC's southeast corner on a summer morning (see Fig. 3.2). The second, displayed in the William McDonough and Partners photo gallery, shows the same corner on a summer evening (Fig. 3.3). In the architect's photo the entire building is illuminated, and the vine-covered trellis is reflected in the pond below.

The problem with the evening image from the architect's photo gallery is that this view of the building does not reflect reality. Despite its photorealistic qualities, the vine-covered trellis on the east and south sides of the building does not exist. As the trellis was part of the design package accepted by the college, the architect has a legitimate right to claim credit for its intended addition. But the image itself is oddly disconcerting to someone familiar with the current building – a little like seeing a normally clean-shaven man wearing a moustache. Plans for adding the trellis on the east side of the building have recently been made, but as of June 2003 the college has yet to build it. In lieu of the trellis on the south, oak trees were planted on Arbor Day 2003. Reasons for this substitution will be discussed in the next section.

A third alteration between design and completion has to do with the occupancy sensors in the office spaces. Occupancy sensors are a favourite strategy in the energy-efficiency community, because they ostensibly solve the intractable problem of people leaving lights on when they leave a room.[2] Often combined with daylighting sensors, these gizmos are thought by many to be the foolproof way to provide light only when it is needed: when daylight alone is insufficient and when there are people present to perform the tasks at hand. In the building occupancy community, however, such sensors are one of the least liked energy-efficiency strategies. If one is sitting diligently at one's desk, the sensor may not sense the occupant and turns the lights off. This may also happen in conference rooms, when the speaker is moving and the listeners are not. Getting the sensor to turn the lights back on requires a certain level of arm waving. Ordinarily, these sensors can be 'tuned' to increase their sensitivity and direction, which decreases the amount of movement needed to trigger them.

*3.3 The Adam Joseph Lewis Center with south and east trellis.*

When one of the authors began working in her office at the AJLC, she discovered that the occupancy sensor was extraordinarily insensitive to her presence. At night, the lights would dim and go off within the first 15 minutes of computer work. She could get the lights to return to full power only by standing in the centre of the room and waving vigorously. Knowing that the sensor was designed to save energy not waste time, this author first attempted to adjust the sensor herself to preclude the latter problem. On removal of the sensor's faceplate, the internal circuitry showed none of the adjustment screws typical of this device. Conceding defeat and vowing to be held personally responsible for her lighting use, the author called in an electrician and asked to have the sensor disabled and exchanged for a basic on/off switch. In troubleshooting her problem, the electrician learned that the sensor had been installed upside down. As a result the sensor looked out into the room and up towards the ceiling, rather than out into the room and down toward the floor, where someone seated at a desk might be sensed. The electrician inverted the author's sensor and, for good measure, checked the sensors in the five other offices. He discovered that two of the other sensors had also been installed incorrectly, and he rectified this mistake.

According to the product literature, the sensors used in the AJLC offices have a two-tiered, multi-cell viewing Fresnel lens with a 180 degree field of view. They are not, however, labelled 'This end up' on the units themselves; nor is this problem indicated on the installation instructions under 'Troubleshooting'. Although this is a small example of the difference between design intent and reality, it illustrates the very real gap between the world as imagined by technology designers and the conventional practice of users

and installers. For instance, a standard US single light switch is usually installed verti-
cally rather than horizontally. Moreover, the light is usually 'on' when the switch is up and
'off' when it is down. But the switch itself is invertible: it performs equally well if installed
right side up or upside down. It would be cheap and easy for the manufacturer of the
occupancy sensor to add 'top' and 'bottom' stickers to the sensors to signify that these
deviate from the norm: they are *not* invertible. Perhaps in the world of occupancy sensor
designers, it goes without saying that the Fresnel lens goes beneath the switch instead
of above it. In the material world, however, this convention does not yet exist.

## Measures of success

Although the ETC and the AJLC are subject to the same laws of gravity and thermodynamics as other buildings, what sets them apart from standard practice is the higher
degree of inspection, assessment and expectation associated with them. Here we
begin to see how the standards of success tend to be measured against the initial
claims of the buildings' proponents (some of which they do not meet), instead of using
an average level of performance of other buildings (most of which they exceed).

### Public performance

To most people, understanding building performance is more difficult than, say, understanding automobile performance. Benchmarks for automobile performance are widely
publicised and fairly well understood. For instance, everyone of driving age in the United
States knows that '15 miles per gallon' is not a 'good' number. Even here, however,
standards of performance have cultural underpinnings. If this relationship was
expressed as 16.7 litres per 100 km the understanding of 'goodness' would vanish for
most of our US audience and materialise for our European readers. Moreover,
standardisation of a performance indicator that is based solely on distance travelled per
volume of fuel may obscure other significant sustainability criteria (say, emissions). But
what about average building performance? What rubrics do people use to understand
thermal comfort and visual sensation? Although both the AJLC and the ETC are
designed to use quantitative data to assist occupants and visitors in their understanding
of building performance, we find that, in both, qualitative sensory experience seems to
matter more than figures and graphs.

### ETC

The ETC is widely experienced as a success, especially with regard to its outstanding
thermal performance. Here the simplest of passive solar design strategies – daylighting
and incorporation of ample thermal mass – turned out to be the big winners, both in terms
of energy savings and, perhaps even more importantly, occupants' comfort. Perhaps the
most remarkable success is that the ETC maintains pleasant indoor temperatures during
summer heatwaves without any active cooling whatsoever. Combined with interesting
materials, angles and aesthetics, the experience of comfort seems to leave occupants
and visitors with an overwhelmingly positive impression and inspiration.

Because of difficulties with the BMS, information that occupants and visitors actually
receive from the building about its performance is essentially limited to their immediate
experience through the senses, rather than figures or graphs from the computer.

Thermal comfort, air quality and lighting are obviously key factors; what also get noticed are the seminar room's problematic acoustics on the one hand and the pleasant absence of operating noises on the other. Aside from the building's net electric meter, which dramatically illustrates the effect of solar generation by spinning backwards, energy generation and consumption data are not yet readily accessible to the visiting public in visually compelling trend logs or real-time displays. Nevertheless, the ETC's visitors are generally content with qualitative information through their own impressions (combined with the director's vigorous oral assertions on the subject).

## AJLC

In contrast to the ETC, the AJLC has had a chequered experience with thermal comfort. Despite complicated building schedules designed to minimise energy use, matching thermal comfort with building occupancy has proved a challenge during much of the heating and cooling seasons. During the unusually cold winter of 2002–3, the AJLC's heat pumps did not deliver adequate heat. Because of the high thermal mass of the building, classrooms take a long time to heat up, and a longer time when the heat pumps deliver lower temperatures than as designed. Discomfort in the building was so pronounced that at least one class scheduled to be held in the AJLC relocated to another building. Although the AJLC did not provide adequate temperatures, it does provide more than adequate access to daylight. A professor of Caribbean literature told one of the authors that she wished to keep her class in the AJLC, even if it was cold. She said, 'You can't teach my subject without sunlight'.

In the summer, high thermal mass and small swings in diurnal temperature make it difficult to keep the AJLC's atrium cool. Additionally, the south and east façades of the atrium allow a large amount of solar gain into the building. These gains would have been mitigated by the external vine-covered trellises, had they been built. But energy simulations conducted using the computer program DOE–2 could not prove that the trellises were cost-effective. Because the construction cost of the south trellis was higher than the energy savings it would deliver, the college chose a lower-cost alternative: planting trees.

### Qualitative versus quantitative data

Interestingly, qualitative impressions rather than quantitative 'hard' data seem to be what most people want to get from the ETC, anyway. One obvious reason is that the great majority of visitors are lay people with regard to building energy analysis. With the exception of a number of building professionals and a handful of scientists who frequent the ETC, most builders and members of the general public alike have little mental framework with which to integrate quantitative building performance data. The number of air changes or the Btu consumption for heating can actually be less meaningful than the qualitative impression that 'the air smells fresh but it doesn't feel drafty' or 'it's nice and cool in here on a hot summer day'. The situation is somewhat different for the students majoring in energy management and design, who are working on establishing just such a quantitative framework and for whose benefit it is ultimately crucial to upgrade the BMS capabilities.

A second reason why the paucity of quantitative data at the ETC may not be seen as tragic even by building professionals is that the qualitative information tends to be more generalisable. Most visitors care less about the performance of the ETC per se than about the possibilities for applying certain of the ETC design concepts elsewhere, whether in their own home or their professional construction work or even in the building codes they recommend and implement as public officials. While numerical data certainly serve to support qualitative statements such as 'the Trombe wall supplies heat to the office space after sunset' or 'the clerestory dramatically reduces the need for active lighting', the quantitative measures themselves would not be transferable to any other building, where all the parameters from floor plan to incident sunshine will, of course, be different. For example, no reasonable person would extrapolate that a clerestory will save their building $x$ number of kilowatt-hours per year just because it does so in the ETC. The key information being communicated, rather, consists of the ideas for employing certain design elements, examples of their execution in a particular setting and their perceptible function in terms of sensory impressions (heat, light, sound, smell, touch, sense of space) and aesthetics. Thus, what a typical visitor would want to take home with them is not a measurement of how many Btu per hour are coming through the ETC's Trombe wall, but a thought like 'I'll see about including a Trombe wall in my new house, because the one at the ETC felt very nice'. This finding is consistent with the phenomenological understanding of intentionality in design: we intend material experiences, not abstract expressions such as Btu per square foot per year.

## Performance by numbers

If qualitative impressions of building performance seem subjective and unscientific as evaluation tools, a case can be made that quantitative measurements may, too, be just that. Guy and Shove (2000) argue that 'epistemic regimes' tend to bracket knowledge in ways that prop up their own authority. One way of doing that is simply to discount different forms of knowledge as legitimate. At issue here are not likes and dislikes, but divergent definitions of what quantitative measures constitute desirable performance and how these data are to be obtained.

### ETC

One paradigmatic example of divergent definitions of performance in the ETC was the issue of air infiltration rates. The architect had specified the building to allow 0.2 air changes per hour (ach), which to him and the design team represented an ambitious but plausible goal for a state-of-the-art, airtight commercial building. The builders, on the other hand, considered this figure to be idealistic and unattainable in practice. Achieving such low infiltration rates would have required an uncommon level of attention during the early construction phase, scrutinising every crack and crevice in walls, floor and ceiling for possible air leakage. From the architect's perspective, it seemed realistic to expect the contractor to exercise such care, as the building envelope represents an integral component of the building's final energy performance. From the contractor's perspective, 'airtightness' was not a familiar performance criterion for structural elements, which were understood to count for mechanical strength and thermal resistance (R-value) on a macro rather than a micro scale. It is easy to imagine how, to the workers on the construction site, the architect's concern about air coming through nail holes (let alone all the fuss over the multiple, ultra-tight window latches) would have seemed rather silly if not downright obsessive.

When it came time for the blower door test, the design team was disappointed by the results, which initially were above 1 ach. But the fascinating thing is what happened next. In an effort to reconcile data with expectations, the contractor undertook a special preparation of the building for a second blower door test. Workers spent an entire day covering all visible orifices, from door handle joints to electrical outlets, in blue masking tape. The new and improved ETC measured 0.5 ach – still not meeting the original specifications, but a number that would be considered decent for a commercial building and ultimately represent an acceptable compromise.

During this process, with all parties anxious to finally complete a behind-schedule, over-budget project in reasonably collegial spirits, nobody (including one of the authors) dared call attention to the obvious disconnect between the data measured (the infiltration rate of the taped-up building) and the building's actual performance when occupied (which certainly does not involve masking tape). The measured air change figure became a legal entity rather than a physical datum. It was the number of record that could be pointed to in judging success or failure, crediting diligence or assigning blame, yet it had very little to do with the finished building's air circulation, its energy consumption or the comfort experienced by its occupants.

It turns out that, owing to the other insulating and thermal storage techniques, the building seems hardly affected by the greater-than-specified air infiltration. During its first two heating seasons, the hydronic floor active heating system has only been operated sparingly on the few days when passive solar gains were insufficient for occupant comfort – totalling less than a dozen or so days per year. Thus, while infiltration rates certainly affect the efficiency of space heating, the ultimate impact on annual energy use is small, owing to the small amount of heating energy used to begin with. Of course, heat loss from infiltration also affects the building temperature on passive heating days and might conceivably result in active heating being used on some days when, without the excess infiltration, it could be avoided. This scenario has not been modelled quantitatively. However, the actual number of active heating days suggests an upper bound for the total heating energy impact. If one assumed generously that 10 per cent of heat losses were attributable to excess infiltration, this would imply no more than about one day's worth of heating energy consumed per year as a result. (Note that, on passive heating days with sufficient solar gains, the heat flows resulting from unplanned infiltration are not countable as 'losses', because given that occupants are comfortable with the temperature as it is they would presumably begin to open windows if the building were any warmer.)

Since there is no active cooling, warm air infiltration in the summer has no impact on energy consumption. Even though greater airtightness would undoubtedly allow the building to stay even cooler during hot days, this hypothetical comparison is not one that presents itself to occupants. Rather, the operative standard would be other campus buildings, and here the ETC compares rather favourably. When other classrooms are cooled to 68°F (20°C), the temperatures around 70°F (21°C) in the ETC on hot summer days appear quite similar – especially subjectively, after walking through sweltering heat to reach the building. Indeed, after the California electricity crisis in the summer of 2001, when the chancellor ordered thermostats in all California State University buildings to be reset to 78°F (26°C), the ETC became literally the coolest building on campus (prompting President Armiñana to quip that it was no doubt in violation of the chancellor's directive).

*AJLC*

In contrast to the lack of quantitative data for the ETC, the AJLC is overflowing with it. Funded in part by a grant from the Andrew W. Mellon Foundation and installed in collaboration with the National Renewable Energy Laboratory, the AJLC has 148 data points that collect data on the flow of energy and matter through the building and its landscape (Petersen 2002). These sensors collect data on a minute-to-minute basis, and their real-time reflection of the relationship between the building and the environment is posted on the web and displayed in the atrium lobby (see www.oberlin.edu/ajlc/). These data and the graphs they create provide a quantitative frame through which to view the AJLC's contribution to environmental problem-solving.

What is interesting about these data is that they seem to create more controversy than they resolve. In addition to the data points monitored by the Environmental Studies Program faculty, there are additional data available through a separate energy monitoring system and tabulated by a faculty member in physics. The raw data collected by the sensors are not disputed. However, there has been some disagreement regarding the interpretation. Depending on the time period chosen and the context selected for analysis, the AJLC uses either more or less energy than its peers. In terms of its site energy, Petersen (2002) shows that the AJLC's gross energy consumption between April 2001 and April 2002 was 30,000 Btu per square foot (95 kWh/m²). Compared with a national average reported for educational buildings, this is roughly 62 per cent better than normal. Compared with nine other buildings on Oberlin's campus, the AJLC's energy performance is 64 per cent better. When the production of energy produced by the AJLC's extensive PV array is included, its net energy consumption is just 14,000 Btu per square foot (44 kWh/m²). This figure suggests that the AJLC imports only 17 per cent of the average energy consumed by Oberlin's other buildings.

While these numbers seem definitive, Scofield (2002a, 2002b, 2002c) uses the same data sources to paint a different picture. Instead of focusing on the amount of power generated by the PV array, for instance, it is possible to look at the differences between actual generation and projected energy output. From this perspective, Scofield shows that total energy production from the AJLC's PV array for 2001 was 15 per cent below projections.

This kind of deficit is typical for PV arrays, yet it affects the AJLC's ability to meet its annual load without assistance from the grid. In terms of energy consumption, Scofield uses data from January 2000 to December 2001 to show that the building used 48,000 Btu per square foot (152 kWh/m²). Using this number as a basis of comparison, the AJLC's gross energy use is only about 37 per cent better than the average educational building in Ohio's climate. Moreover, Scofield argues that a better basis for comparison should be source energy consumption, not site energy consumption. Because the AJLC is all-electric, any electricity not produced with its own PV array is most likely generated by burning coal in a local power plant. This process is only about 33 per cent efficient, which means it takes three units of coal to produce one unit of electricity. Because the AJLC does not meet its entire annual energy budget with its own PV array, Scofield suggests that the as-built AJLC may have been 'greener' if it wasn't all-electric.

If the AJLC 'succeeds' according to one quantitative analysis and 'fails' according to another, what are readers of either or both analyses to make of these interpretations? To some degree, the difference between these assessments stems from *koan*-like questions about whether it is better to see the glass as half full or half empty. Both Petersen and Scofield assess the AJLC's performance over time, but their analyses use different time periods. Scofield uses data from the building's initial operation; Petersen uses data from a later period. If buildings have a learning curve, the part of the curve selected for analysis inevitably influences the construction of the assessment itself. Imagine, for instance, using only a year or two of data to evaluate the whole of a human life. How would this evaluation differ if the person was viewed in infancy, adolescence or old age? Quantitative data are often expected to provide 'proof' that somehow exceeds qualitative impressions, but in our view they may raise more questions about building performance than they resolve. Such questions should be considered as opportunities rather than challenges, particularly in an academic environment where the exploration of objective and normative truths should be fair game. These examples demonstrate how quantitative data have been used to influence socially constructed concepts (such as what constitutes 'success') while maintaining an aura of objectivity.

## Teaching functions

Despite their relative youth, both buildings have already performed their teaching functions on more levels than could have been imagined at the outset. Many of these lessons could be treated from a technical perspective – what does and does not work in an educational green building. They have been the subject of much study. Relative to other buildings, both the ETC and AJLC have an explicit charge to serve as teaching tools. Toward this end both have their own websites (www.sonoma.edu/ensp/etc and www.oberlin.edu/ajlc/). But what are they teaching, and to whom? In this section, we consider the ways in which the ETC and AJLC are serving as models for students and the community around them.

### Teaching the students

For buildings that teach, a key measure of their success should be the learning opportunities that they provide their students.

### ETC

At the ETC, the anticipated plethora of physical measurements has not yet materialised, owing mainly to the difficulties in getting the BMS to work. While students have measured light levels and radiant temperatures with handheld instruments, they have yet to download and analyse batches of trend logs from the building's own brain. Instead, the ETC's main role for the classroom has been to provide an example of specific design elements as well as the integrated concept of a 'healthy' building.

Demonstrating specific techniques is obviously important in such courses as Passive Solar Design, where energy management majors learn about key design elements and can immediately recognise them implemented in their classroom. For example, seasonal shading is illustrated by overhangs, deciduous vines, an awning, exterior venetian blinds and light shelves. On the subject of thermal mass, there are the concrete floor slab, masonry units and a rammed earth wall. This variety of materials and techniques entailed high construction cost with its diseconomy of the many different small things (not to mention the many different subcontractors), but its value lies in the depth and richness it offers. Quantitatively, we hope to be able eventually to compare the functioning of various alternatives – say, to measure heat transfer through concrete masonry blocks versus rammed earth. But even more fundamentally, the diversity of techniques used in the ETC shows qualitatively that there is more than one solution to a given design problem.

This message of diversity of design solutions may also come across to some extent to students from majors other than energy management, who constitute the majority with regularly scheduled classes in the ETC. We don't know how many of them actually read the coloured posters explaining the various features of the building or how much of their professor's introductory speech they might retain. Yet it seems reasonable to claim that students and faculty who use the ETC take away a qualitative sense of this building being 'special'. The empirical evidence for this claim is simple and twofold. First, people increasingly request the ETC as a classroom space. Second, after two years of occupancy no graffiti are to be found on the ETC furniture. Though it may seem trivial, the absence of graffiti stands in remarkable contrast with other university classrooms and, to this author, indicates a subtle but important attitudinal shift.

*AJLC*

The building and its landscape have proved a popular location for studying the principles of ecological design across disciplines, from biology to dance and from economics to computer science and maths. Students created the initial design of the website for the building as part of a seminar. Next fall, there will be a practicum that focuses entirely on the AJLC as a medium to study ecological design. The building has become the topic of private readings, summer fellowships and winter-term and work-study projects. Students are developing a new technique for monitoring whole ecosystem metabolism in the Living Machine and for testing hypotheses regarding the effect of plant growth on patterns of water flow in its marsh.

**Teaching the community**

Creating sustainability on college campuses does not lie in individual buildings, but in the 'greening the campus' movement as a whole. The ETC and the AJLC are a small but significant part of this effort. Despite their different levels of support and success, the pedagogy behind these buildings is diffusing to other buildings nearby.

*ETC*

The SSU campus was established in 1961. The present decade marks a period of intense construction activity, including the remodelling of several first-generation buildings and several new construction projects completed, in progress and planned – on a scale that rather dwarfs the ETC in terms of both dollars and square feet.

Interestingly, both of the major construction projects initiated since the ETC incorporate substantial and remarkable elements of 'green building'. The first is a complete remodel of the 115,000 square foot (10,650 square metre) Salazar Building, formerly a library that now houses office space and classrooms. The Salazar Building has a combined indirect/direct evaporative cooling (I/DEC) system which, in California's dry climate, should provide dramatic energy savings compared with conventional air conditioning, and a 96 kilowatt PV system on its roof. The project's viability hinged on two rebates, about $106,000 from Pacific Gas & Electric's Savings by Design Program for energy efficiency and a $340,000 state subsidy for the PV system. A performance study by Lawrence Berkeley National Laboratory researchers is under way, as the Salazar Building promises to set new records in both conceptual innovation and energy efficiency. The second major project is a new, student-funded centre for recreational sports. Construction was just beginning as of early 2003, but plans also call for I/DEC as well as passive and active solar components.

Unlike the ETC, whose 'green' features were specifically conceived for teaching purposes, the design of both the Salazar Building and the recreation centre was driven strictly by economic considerations. While the positive publicity about the Salazar Building has certainly been welcome, the building is not set up as a demonstration for students or the general public, and its benefits to the campus are quantified solely in terms of financial savings.

The question presents itself as to what extent the ETC's presence influenced the university administration's decision to proceed with these major new commitments to green building. Personal initiative on the part of the campus design engineer was a key factor in both the Salazar remodel and the recreation centre, as was the timing with respect to Californian energy politics. One interpretation of events is that the tangible experience with the ETC made it possible to take the 'green' plans seriously and bolstered administrators' confidence that the unconventional features proposed by the design engineer would actually work and pay for themselves.

For example, although the ETC's PV system measures only a modest 3 kW, the university had to go through the complete contractual process involved with its installation, including grid interconnection and the California state rebate that pays up to half the capital cost. Initially, counting the ETC's $12,000 PV rebate funds as a 'credit' pending completion of the project elicited a certain scepticism on the part of the university's accounting staff. The second time around – despite much higher stakes – trust in the rebate process had clearly been established, as it was essential for authorisation of the project.

Similarly, the campus had become familiar with the notion of unconventional cooling systems. The ETC design had called for an I/DEC system, but this was omitted during construction because of funding constraints, in the hope that the building could sustain acceptable comfort levels with thermal mass and night-time ventilation alone. This wager turned out to be a resounding success: steady indoor temperatures of around 70°F (21°C) even during a heat wave in the ETC's first summer season (with outside temperatures near 100°F (38°C) for days on end) validated the idea that air conditioning is avoidable by careful design without loss of comfort.

## AJLC

In addition to providing learning opportunities for students, the AJLC has catalysed the creation of several regional groups, including the Cleveland Green Building Coalition, the Ecological Design Innovation Center and the Oberlin Design Initiative. Over 8,000 visitors toured the centre in its first two years of operation, and it also hosted workshops organised by the National Science Foundation, Second Nature and the Institute for Ecological Economics (Petersen 2002).

On the Oberlin College campus, only one new major building has been completed since the AJLC: the Science Center. This building was, by all accounts, quite conventional in its design. It contains some obvious design flaws: a series of uplights that face skylights (instead of light-coloured ceilings) and that remain on at both day and night. Ironically, since neither the college nor the design team set its sights on a higher plane for this building, they are not being held accountable for its failings. Were these design flaws made in the AJLC, they would have been the subject of intense debate and discussion.

Two new building projects are, however, on the drawing boards for the Oberlin campus, and both of these are being designed with sustainability in mind. The first is a small environmental studies laboratory that will be constructed adjacent to the AJLC. The lab will adaptively reuse an existing Victorian Italianate house on the property, and it is being designed as a Leadership in Energy and Environmental Design (LEED) project. Although the college agreed to support LEED ideals, the Environmental Studies Program is responsible for bearing the certification costs of this process.

The second project is for new student housing. Many of the students who have learned from the AJLC have asked the college to incorporate sustainable principles in its design practices. The college hired the same design team for the student housing project that the environmental studies faculty selected for its new lab. One of the architects on this team is active in the US Green Building Council and the American Institute of Architects' National Committee on the Environment. The college's choice of this team represents some willingness on the administration's part to explore green building opportunities outside the context of the Environmental Studies Program. Although SSU's decision to install green features in its new buildings was driven in part by economic opportunities available from the state and its local utility, Oberlin College cannot avail itself of these benefits. Ohio has few state or utility subsidies available for green or sustainable features. Oberlin College does, however, heed the interest of its students and is cautiously recognising the learning opportunities for students created through ecological design.

## Future directions

The work done to date on the pedagogy of buildings and place has implications for generalisable results. What architectural lessons can be translated from one place and time to another? If two buildings in different climates have the same goals, could (or should) they achieve them the same way? Whereas the ETC validated the premise of passive cooling and heating to the SSU community, the AJLC has not provided a similar learning experience to Oberlin College. This comparison is technically askew, because the design challenge of providing adequate levels of thermal comfort in sunny, dry northern California is not as difficult as providing them in snowy, humid northeast Ohio. In other words, it would be unfair to expect an Ohio building to embody the message that 'it's easy to do without air conditioning or heat'. Nevertheless, since neither the general public nor university administrators are trained to think in terms of degree days and wet bulb temperatures, the level of thermal comfort actually experienced in each building remains a key empirical standard by which performance is judged.

Buildings cannot behave as exemplars for all things at the same time. It is very unlikely, for instance, that a single structure will simultaneously be the easiest to measure, be the simplest to manage, achieve the highest benefits, incur the lowest costs, teach everything to everyone, and be as sustainable as possible. The AJLC and the ETC are both successful buildings, but in very different ways. The ETC, despite lacks in its monitoring system, is empirically satisfying and thermally comfortable. Its proof is in the pudding, as they say. The AJLC, in its conception as a holistic entity, integrated with the landscape and the Living Machine, has been a source of debate, discussion and inspiration.

Relative to other buildings, what role does the presence or absence of quantitative data play? The data certainly form an epistemological lens for formal debate and discussion, as described above. But how does this lens interact with the phenomenological one used for most buildings? That is, does 'performance by numbers' override performance through experience? On an instantaneous basis, we would have to say 'no'. As is common in expert debates, numbers rarely change our notions of what we already believe to be true. For instance, visitors to the AJLC can observe a computer display that shows graphically and in real time whether the building is producing more energy than it is consuming. As most tours are given during the day, the PV array often produces enough energy to show that the AJLC is a net energy exporter at that moment. If the tours were given at night, however, the 'take away' image would be different. These data confirm what our senses would expect. If the graph said otherwise, visitors would expect something was wrong with the sensors. On a cumulative basis, however, the quantitative data provide information that our senses cannot effectively collect and analyse. Another graph in the AJLC atrium integrates building consumption and energy production information over time, showing the annual pattern of energy exports and imports. This graph displays information that the viewer could not intuit just by standing in the atrium.

In his novel *Slaughterhouse-Five*, Kurt Vonnegut explored the notion of being 'unstuck in time'. We suggest that the notion of time should be incorporated more explicitly into explorations of building evaluation and sustainability. In particular, what is the right period of time to use for a quantitative assessment? If understanding climatic responsiveness is a goal, at least one cycle of four seasons is required. But a building that is expected to change its performance over time complicates the selection of the 'best' date to begin a time-series assessment. When, for instance, does the AJLC begin its 'real' performance? Is it after the drywall is hung, but before the electric boiler has been replaced? Or must its true potential lie patiently in wait, firstly for the building of its trellis, then the growth of its vines and finally for its saplings to turn into mighty oaks?[3]

More generally, the very notion of being 'sustainable' implies a projection in time: an assessment of what would happen if practices and processes in question were continued indefinitely into the future or at least for a time period much longer than conventional planning horizons. Any economic evaluation of sustainable building measures also relies on time as a key variable, since present costs are almost always compared with some form of future savings. Standard discounting techniques from finance, while suited to a narrow and literalist interpretation of cost–benefit analysis, offer little guidance in the way of estimating the overall value or benefit to society of undertaking sustainable building: who decides on the correct discount rate; and how, in the long run, does one weigh the interests of different generations who bear the costs and reap the benefits of today's decisions?

Given the inherent limitations of quantitative standards and performance measures, meaningful inclusion of a time dimension should prove a challenging and worthwhile endeavour. By contrast, in the area of phenomenological satisfaction, we require no conceptual innovation but patience. How will these buildings hold up, and how will people feel about them as they age? Only time will tell.

## Acknowledgements

The authors would like to thank the editors and their colleagues for their insights and suggestions. At Oberlin College, John Petersen, David Orr, John Scofield and Andrew Shanken informed this telling of the AJLC's tale. Special thanks to Barney Taxel and Kyle Copas for illustrating it. At SSU, W. J. 'Rocky' Rohwedder, who led the ETC's design team, has been a steady source of initiative and perspective.

## Notes

1   It may be argued that biomorphism is more an indicator of natural building (see for example Kennedy et al. 2002) than green design. We believe the general public would be unlikely to make this distinction, and our point here is simply that neither of these buildings looks like Earthships (www.earthship.org).
2   For a recent review of lighting controls and strategies see Wilson (2003).
3   For those actively engaged in measuring building performance, this question may be as scientifically and socially contentious as determining the precise moment of conception. For many building users, however, the simple notion that building performance is variable instead of constant is hard enough to grasp.

# 4

# The social construction of 'green building' codes

## Competing models by industry, government and NGOs

### Steven A. Moore and Nathan Engstrom

In 1992 the city of Austin, Texas, was the first in the country to create a residential green building programme and by the end of the century about 26 similar ones emerged in 16 different states. Moore and Engstrom argue two related points. The first is that 'green building' reflects the latent fusion of two powerful late-nineteenth-century ideas, preservation of the natural environment and protection of the public health. These two concepts were so ideologically opposed at the turn of the twentieth century that it took a full century of changing conditions to reconcile the opposing assumptions that motivated their respective supporters. Second, the authors hold that, once reconciled under the broad umbrella of 'sustainable development', green building programmes foreshadow North American building codes of the twenty-first century. Some US green building 'programmes' are departments within municipal governments, others are the products of homebuilder associations, and at least two are non-profit non-governmental organisations. Taken collectively, these 'programmes' reflect a changing cultural horizon with regard to public health and the built environment. Taken individually, however, they reflect contradictory social values that vie to redefine how a private house embodies a public 'good'. The authors' project is not to predict how these conflicting social values will become resolved, but to better understand the social construction of green building programmes as antecedents of twenty-first-century cultural values that will ultimately become realised as standardised building codes.

## Green building as good building

Building codes in the United States derive principally from English precedents. Their adoption can be understood as acceptance by mid-nineteenth-century Americans of those utilitarian values which made it possible to restrict some individual freedoms, like shoddy building practices, in favour of general health, safety and welfare. The political will to pass such legislation was, no doubt, strongly influenced by a series of devastating fires that damaged or destroyed eleven nineteenth-century American cities and the chronic outbreaks of typhus, yellow fever and smallpox that plagued many other cities (AIA 1990: 9). These crises were inevitably followed by legislation and the founding of institutions intent on eliminating those building practices that would most obviously contribute to repeat fires and epidemics. Historians generally refer to this phenomenon as the era of 'sanitary reform' or the 'public health movement'.

If we accept this dialectical relation of crisis and reform it is tempting to interpret the appearance of 'green building programmes' in the US, not as a new phenomenon, but as a continuation of two nineteenth-century social movements: the public health movement and the environmental movement. The environmental crises experienced by contemporary city dwellers are, after all, not different in kind from those experienced by nineteenth-century urban dwellers. Poor air quality, fouled water and general environmental degradation are the unintended consequences of industrial development that are shared by both periods. It does not really matter if the sources of pollution have shifted from smokestacks to tailpipes – the threat is the same. What is different in our current situation is that the dramatic fires and epidemics of the nineteenth century have been replaced by more subtle and pervasive effects that derive from long-term industrial development. Energy scarcity, water scarcity, climate change and chemical sensitivity are environmental conditions that even the economically comfortable can no longer avoid by moving further out of town. It is now solidly middle-class citizens, not only the industrial proletariat, who experience the crisis of environmental degradation and seek environmental security from government, industry or third-party experts. The risks associated with environmental degradation have, then, been somewhat democratised. And with the democratisation of risk has come economic and political controversy (Beck 1992: 191–9).

The production of environmental programmes and building codes is, of course, not entirely a matter of science. Rather, it is a highly social and contentious process in which some interests are suppressed and others are reinforced. The presence of competing interests is reflected in the confusing array of codes and green building standards that have emerged in response to contemporary environmental conditions. Commercial construction certification schemes like LEED (Leadership in Energy and Environmental Design), BEES (Building for Economic and Environmental Sustainability) and BREEAM (Building Research Establishment Environmental Assessment Method) are just a few examples. Such conflicting standards tend to frame problems and propose solutions in ways that define opposing 'goods'. All manufacturing standards are, in this view, socially constructed agreements that favour a particular set of actors because they contain the interests of the standard-makers (Latour 1987: 201).[1]

Beginning with the sociologist Max Weber (1864–1920), many have argued that the history of modernisation has been synonymous with standardisation (Weber 1958: 181–2; Feenberg 1995: 4). Weber understood that the institutions of modern commerce are better able to optimise exchange value by imposing a single structure on diverse populations and spaces. This logic suggests that those outside an emergent technological network run the risk of being excluded from certain exchanges. If your locomotive is of the wrong gauge, your motor of the wrong voltage or your software of the wrong operating system, you are excluded. The mechanisms of commerce, then, favour dominance by a single technological standard. It does not really matter what that standard is – DOS versus MAC, for example – so long as it is commensurable with the endless array of local conditions. If we apply the logic of modernisation to the home-building industry, it suggests that the emergence of multiple green building programmes and model environmental codes are competing attempts to standardise the many variables of 'good' building to include 'green' building practices.

On this basis, we hypothesise that standards designed by industry, government, and non-governmental organisation (NGO) environmentalists will differ. This hypothesis is based on the assumptions that these organisational types generally represent opposing political interests and that with authorship of a building code comes the power to regulate the social and technical constitution of the artefact. We also assume that, in practice, standardised codes represent, to one degree or another, the negotiated interests of industry, government and environmentalists. Building codes can, then, be understood as the temporary resolution of social conflicts that are, in turn, materialised as buildings. The establishment of codes, by any means, pushes the building industry down a particular technological path. Green building codes will, for example, push us away from paints that rely on volatile organic compounds to those that do not and from harvesting old-growth timber towards substitute technologies such as engineered wood products. In these and other similar cases some technological networks will benefit and others will necessarily suffer.

Green building programmes intend to challenge existing building codes and seek to redefine the agreements that shaped them on the grounds of the general welfare. According to this utilitarian logic, private dwellings contribute to or detract from several kinds of public resources or public goods. With regard to the construction of private houses, two types of damage to public resources can be assessed by environmental accountants. The first are those negative environmental impacts that derive from gathering building materials and energy from distant locales. Water pollution caused by timber 'clear-cutting' or strip mining is an example of this type, where costs are borne by downstream citizens reliant on access to clean water. The second is the public cost to maintain the health and welfare of those citizens who build badly, either out of ignorance or malice. An example of this type is personal injury and property damage derived from building on a flood plain, where costs are borne by taxpayers. In the eyes of utilitarians, the loss of either type of public good trumps private property rights because such ruinous acts increase the public cost to maintain the 'civic economy'. If we agree, then, that the general welfare is promoted by green building we have also agreed in principle that green building is a necessary if insufficient condition for good building.

The balance of this chapter is in four sections. The first section establishes the early linkage between building codes and the public health movement and the delayed linkage of building codes to the environmental movement. The second section examines how changing technological standards both reflect and attempt to resolve cultural conflict. To make these arguments concrete, we will, in the third section, empirically examine three cases that demonstrate how government, industry and environmentalists infuse technological standards with opposing values. Finally, our conclusion will argue that through a process of crisis, reform, codification and standardisation today's green building programmes foreshadow the social construction of twenty-first-century building codes.

## Building codes, public health, environmental preservation

In this section we argue that the long-term development of building codes related to human health is rooted in nineteenth-century utilitarian thought and becomes fused with the environmental preservation movement at the beginning of the twenty-first century.

The codification of building standards, as all architecture students learn early in their careers, begins with Article 229 of the Code of King Hammurabi (Mesopotamia 1780 BCE) (Sanderson 1969: 5). The Greeks and Romans certainly contributed to the establishment of construction standards, but it wasn't until 1189 in England that a building act representing municipal legislative power was developed. Five hundred years later, in 1676, a document resembling a modern building code was created through an Act of Parliament to regulate the rebuilding of London after the devastating fire of 1666 (AIA 1990: 8). These pre-modern codes were, in emphasis, fire-prevention ordinances. The emergence of the industrial revolution and rapid urbanisation in the nineteenth century, however, created new conditions that catalysed the codification of building standards.

The idea that there is a collective or 'public' health, and that it is linked to environmental conditions, emerged in mid-nineteenth-century England as 'the sanitary idea'. Most historians attribute the first or most prominent articulation of this idea to Edwin Chadwick, son of James. The elder Chadwick was a devotee of the revolutionary Tom Paine and had sufficient status among radical thinkers of his day to gain his son a position as the personal secretary to Jeremy Bentham, a progenitor of utilitarianism. It was Bentham who argued for the 'greatest happiness principle', that 'the end of life, ethically speaking is "the greatest good for the greatest number"' (Reese 1980: 53). Although the younger Chadwick was profoundly influenced by the utilitarians in philosophical matters, he is remembered, not as a thinker, but as a civil servant and man of action. At the behest of Parliament, he published in 1842 his *Report on the Sanitary Condition of the Labouring Population of Great Britain*, which proved to be as historically influential as it was then controversial. Chadwick's report was considered radical because, first, it relied on rigorously gathered empirical data rather than deductive logic, and second, it employed such methods to reject the commonly held idea that disease was the fatalistic imposition of God's will. With equal temerity, Chadwick challenged the received wisdom that held poverty to be the main cause of ill health. Chadwick argued the reverse, that 'the attack of fever precedes the destitution, not the destitution the disease' (Chadwick 1965: 210). For Chadwick and his fellow 'sanitarians', disease was not an outward sign of moral depravity, but the misfortune of those subjected to degraded environments. In the eyes of historian William Luckin, Chadwick was a 'proto-environmentalist' because he identified an environmental cause of disease before there was any scientific understanding of pathogenic organisms (Melosi 2000: 46). It was not until some 20 years after the publication of Chadwick's report that 'germ theory', based on the work of Pasteur and others, would begin to supplant the then dominant 'miasma' theory of disease.

Chadwick's medical logic might have remained simply prescient were it not for the political implications of the sanitary idea. Beginning with the utilitarian formula of 'the greatest good for the greatest number', he reasoned that true 'civic economy' required 'preventative measures in raising the standard of health and the chances of life' (Chadwick 1965: 246). It was a short mental step from advocating the economic value of public health to advocating the creation of a general building code backed up by a strong central government capable of enforcing such standards (Chadwick 1965: 339–47). The utilitarians were, then, precursors of the modern welfare state.

In recent years utilitarianism has been much criticised for its easy disregard for the civil rights of minorities. Bentham, Chadwick and their followers constructed an attitude towards social order that we now regard as highly authoritarian and technocratic. They were not predisposed to trust in the ability of common citizens to make sensible choices concerning much of anything. Rather, their idea of 'civic economy' relied on an educated elite to manage efficiently the interests of society, which they conceived to be essentially economic in nature.

Such an efficiently managed or sanitised society was the nightmare of Michel Foucault (1975). In Foucault's view, the institutions of public health constructed by nineteenth-century utilitarians were little more than the illegitimate mechanisms of the modern bureaucratic state through which social deviancy might be eradicated. The ethical dilemma posed by the doctrines of public health, then, is characterised by a confrontation between two seemingly rational desires. First is the desire of those who, like Chadwick, wish to minimise the waste of resources associated with environmental degradation. Second are those who, like Foucault, see the management of private, existential risks by the state as a totalitarian scheme intent upon the production of a monoculture constituted of happy and productive workers.[2] For the purposes of this discussion it will suffice to say that the social construction of 'the sanitary idea' was not without repressive tendencies (Moore: unpublished manuscript 2004).

We should take care, however, to understand Chadwick's proposals as a response, at least in part, to the social and economic chaos fostered by the industrial revolution and to the extreme laissez-faire political climate of the time. In this historical context the proposals by Bentham, Mill and Chadwick to limit the rights of landlords and industrialists on behalf of working citizens seem only reasonable, because we have benefited so much from them. The British Public Health Act of 1848 was the culmination of Chadwick's activism and is considered so significant because it marked a conceptual shift in how we understand the role of government. The sanitary idea that informed this legislation required, for the first time in history, that government act proactively to protect the health of the citizenry. And, like the industrial revolution that preceded it, the sanitary idea crossed the Atlantic about 1880 (Melosi 2000: 48).

The utilitarian rationale to guard public health fell into very different political circumstances in North America. Here, citizens found no reason to organise strong municipal governments until they were faced with the capital-intensive need to construct the infrastructure demanded by rapid industrialisation and by the demonstrated need for fire protection (Melosi 2000: 35). 'In the United States, New York ... was the first to enact laws governing the erection and alteration of buildings' (Fryer 1891: 69). The New York Building Law was developed collaboratively in 1860 by the New York City Fire Department, the American Institute of Architects (AIA) and the Mechanics and Tradesmen's Society. But, as in England, such chaotic conditions stimulated the emergence of a new class of visionary technocrats pressed from the same utilitarian mould as Chadwick. Colonel George Waring, who at one time was manager of Frederick Law Olmstead's Staten Island Farm, became a major, if not the first, proponent of public health legislation and public works. First in Memphis, and later as Street Cleaning Commissioner of New York City in 1895, Waring articulated a progressive, if paternalistic doctrine that guided the American public health movement for nearly a century (Melosi 2000: 157). We can characterise the movement as a hybrid of medical science and engineering pragmatism focused on the economic benefits of human health. By the turn of the twentieth century some observers argued that, through the leadership of Waring and others, the codification of health-related building standards in the United States had already exceeded English precedents (Cubitt 1906: 180).

New York, of course, was not an isolated case. Other major cities, including Chicago, Seattle and Boston, developed health-related building codes that sought to protect citizens, particularly in public buildings. However, as early as 1891, observers understood that a 'building law can advance no faster than the prejudices of interested persons will allow' (Fryer 1891: 82). When considering the large number of persons economically interested in how design and construction are regulated, it should come as no surprise that demands to standardise building codes rose simultaneously with the adoption of health-related building codes by American cities.

By 1908, not only were building codes deemed essential for large cities, but efforts were organised to implement standardised building codes for smaller villages and towns, too (Fitzpatrick 1908: 54). As building codes spread out in space there was increasing recognition that older codes, like those of New York City, needed to be modernised. In 1921 D. K. Boyd argued that 'these codes fail to take into consideration the advances made in the scientific and efficient use of structural materials' and did not adequately address issues of quality, safety and public health (Boyd 1921: 77). By the mid-twentieth century the often confusing jurisdiction of health-related building codes had become a complex network of competing interests in which what was permitted was as significant as what was not. The lack of standardisation made it increasingly difficult to apply the same products and design solutions in different locales.

In the eyes of contemporary environmental activists, however, the American public health movement was slow to relate its own agenda to that of nature preservation. In North America the concept of environmental preservation is almost as long-standing as that of the public health. It was actively promoted by the administration of Teddy Roosevelt (1901–9) and was famously, if differently, advocated by John Muir (1838–1914) and Gifford Pinchot (1865–1946). Michael McCally, a professor at Oregon Health Sciences University, holds that nearly 100 years after the Roosevelt administration, at the time of the United Nations Conference on Environment and Development (UNCED) at Rio de Janeiro (1992), 'the [human] health dimensions of environmental degradation had been neglected' (McCally 2002: 3). Public health officials, like most other Americans, have historically understood environmentalism as limited to nature preservation – an ecocentric doctrine, not directly related to the anthropocentric origins of the human public health movement. It took events like the 1962 publication of Rachel Carson's *Silent Spring*, the 1969 burning of the Cuyahoga River in Cleveland or the 1977 Love Canal industrial pollution disaster near Niagara Falls to challenge that perception. It is important to recall that the very term 'sustainable development', which explicitly relates human well-being to environmental preservation, was not coined until 1980.[3] In this context, the historical distance between American institutions focused on human health and those focused on environmental health is less surprising.

A purely political lens might also serve to explain how, in spite of utilitarian doctrines, the public health and environmental movements remained estranged for so long. Put simply, their ideological roots were allergic to one another. Where the concept of public health emerged from the left wing, the concept of nature preservation emerged on the right. Those utilitarians and socialists who advocated the sanitary idea simply could not imagine common cause with those social elites who advocated nature preservation, and vice versa (Brulle 2000: 133–72). From this dialectical perspective, fusion between these social movements would remain impossible until their ideological allergy was overcome by middle-class concerns that linked the health of humans to general environmental degradation.

Robert Rubin's book *Critical Condition: America's Health in Jeopardy* (1988) can be credited with renewing the conceptual link between environmental and public health conceptualised by Chadwick 146 years before. Although environmental philosophers, Murray Bookchin in particular, made this association much earlier (1962), followed by Barry Commoner (1971), the point here is that the connection between public health and environmental preservation had to be re-established by those within the public health movement, not by philosophers of environmental ethics. By the date of Michael McCally's book *Life Support*, published 14 years after Rubin's – on the eve of the UNCED-sponsored Johannesburg Summit in 2002 – McCally was able to document the existence of 'an international environmental health movement' (McCally 2002: viii).[4] On the basis of work by McCally and others we can argue that, although rigidly ecocentric environmentalists may reject human health as a dimension of 'sustainability', the public health movement and the environmental movement have belatedly, but irrevocably, become fused (Frumkin 2002: 201–17).[5]

In sum, we can construct two related arguments that derive from the same utilitarian logic that informed Chadwick and contemporary public health advocates nearly 150 years apart. First is the proposition that health-related building codes initially appeared in response to local crises related to rapid industrialisation and urbanisation. This phenomenon occurred simultaneously in scattered locations affected by similar structural conditions of political economy. However, such local reactions were problematic for those whose interests extended across municipal boundaries. Second is the proposition that standardisation tends to follow codification. Not only do competing codes tend to reduce the exchange value of local goods and services, but cities that wish to be proactive in protecting the public or environmental health tend to appropriate and adapt the situated codes of others. Standardisation is the process by which exchange value is seemingly optimised and threats to public health are seemingly minimised. Utilitarian logic, then, tends toward the standardisation of codes intent upon securing the health of a majority of humans and non-humans alike. It was, however, just this kind of standardisation that so concerned Max Weber in 1905.

## Conflicting constructions of 'the good'

By arguing that the concept of sustainable development can be understood as the fusion of the public health and environmental preservation movements, we do not mean to suggest that there is a single logic or set of ideas associated with the concept. Rather, we will argue two points in this section. First, that 'sustainability' has become an umbrella for a number of competing social values, and second, that contrary to an idealised model of sustainability in which competing values become balanced, it is far more likely that one set of values, or standards, will come to dominate the field.

In their exhaustive review of the literature concerning contemporary sustainable architecture, Simon Guy and Graham Farmer found not one but six coherent systems of social value (Guy and Farmer 2001). Employing the research methods and assumptions of social constructivists, Guy and Farmer were able to reconstruct the social values, or 'logics', employed in the production of works of architecture. The reconstructed values found in their study are exemplified by projects as diverse as Foster and Partners' technologically driven Commerzbank project in Frankfurt (Fig. 4.1) and Mike Reynolds' off-the-grid, romantic fantasies in rural New Mexico (Fig 4.2). Each of these projects makes explicit claim to being 'sustainable', yet few projects could be culturally, visually or technologically so dissimilar. Guy and Farmer did not challenge the validity of any claim to being an exemplar of sustainable architecture, but simply concluded 'that implicit within alternative technological strategies are distinct philosophies of environmental place making' (ibid.: 146).

Guy and Farmer's findings suggest that technological choices are prefigured by differing conceptions of economic, political and cultural realities. From these differing perspectives, both the problem of unsustainability and the transformation of those conditions are imagined, with sometimes conflicting values. Those values refer, in turn, to different power and authority structures. For example, the Commerzbank tower embodies the anthropocentric values of energy and corporate efficiency achieved through high technology. In contrast, the house by Reynolds embodies the ecocentric values of minimal environmental impact achieved through low technology. Our selection

*4.1 Commerzbank Frankfurt, Foster & Partners Architects. This highly urban and technologically sophisticated project is commonly associated with the concept of sustainable architecture.*

of a particular technological vocabulary, then, acts to legitimate and lend authority to all that comes with it. As Langdon Winner argues, 'we do not use technologies so much as live them' (Winner 1977: 202). As these two cases suggest, the big umbrella of sustainability can shelter very different ways of living.

*4.2 New Mexico Earthship, Mike Reynolds, Earthship Biotecture. This rural and very low-tech project is also commonly associated with the concept of sustainable architecture.*

The planner Scott Campbell has developed a particularly elegant model of sustainable development, illustrated in somewhat modified form in Figure 4.3. This model conceptualises sustainability as constituted of three competing variables: economic development, environmental protection and social equity. Equally important in Campbell's construction is the presence of three social conflicts (Campbell 1996: 468). The heart of Campbell's proposal is that these conflicts, seemingly inevitable in a society as diverse as our own, might be mediated or balanced through democratic discourse managed by a skilled planner. The responsibility of planners, in Campbell's view, is to mediate technological choices that come to rest at the triangle's geometric centre. In this sense Campbell's model is an idealised one because the resolution of conflicting social values requires the presence of what Sandra Harding has called a 'valuable

*4.3 The 'planner's triangle', derived from Campbell (1996: 468).*

stranger' (Harding 1991: 124). Unfortunately, when valuable strangers are in short supply, the resolution of social conflict tends to drift to the corner of the triangle inhabited by the most powerful players. In Weber's terms, then, creative public conflict and alternative technological choices tend to be suppressed by the process of standardisation promoted by market forces and the state, which consistently favour the interest of economic development over those of environmental protection or social equity.

Another critique of Campbell's triangulated model is that it represents sustainability as a static or balanced condition existing only at the centre of the triangle. The advocates of complexity theory argue, in opposition, that systems capable of sustaining themselves are always in motion – no system ever comes to rest except at the moment before death. In their view, a state of equilibrium is a moment of exhaustion, not a moment of ideal community life (McDaniel 2001: 22). If complex adaptive systems are ever-emergent we should consider the standards and codes that govern technological networks to be temporary agreements about how we will live together, not immutable laws. Donna Haraway has famously argued that all knowledge claims are 'power moves, not moves toward truth' (Haraway 1995: 176). Arguing that one knows how to build better or more healthfully is, then, only a way to redistribute power relations within the triangle of competing interests constructed by Campbell. Selecting a particular building logic is akin to selecting a particular conceptualisation of the world.

## Industry, municipal and NGO perspectives

In this section we examine empirical evidence, in which competing conceptualisations of the world are inscribed. Specifically, we examined the publications of fourteen US residential 'green building programmes'. Where necessary, this textual data has been supplemented by interviews with representatives of those organisations. Our method has been, first, to categorise the implicit values contained in the various green building programme criteria, and second, to select one of the programmes in each category for further study. Third, we have attempted to articulate the values that inform each logic in simplified tabular form. The table that summarises our findings helps us, in the conclusion of this chapter, to test the hypothesis stated at the outset.

Each of the fourteen green building programmes we examined is operationalised by a rating tool, or checklist, in which the technical characteristics of the houses in question are quantitatively measured against established energy and environmental standards. This is a seemingly objective process. It is, however, our contention that although these rating tools are perceived as scientific definitions of 'green building', they represent highly selective and contextual values. By proposing definitions of 'green', these programmes act to condition our understanding of the public good embodied in private homes. It is important, then, to reconstruct the values that inform various green building standards if we are to critically evaluate them while they are still in a formative state.

One way of slicing the data is by recognising the organisational type of the fourteen sponsoring institutions. We found three: government, industry and NGOs. In the opening section of this chapter, we hypothesised that these three perspectives exemplify the competing viewpoints of stakeholders interested in the green building debate as well as the public health and environmental movements in general. To test this hypothesis we selected one case of each organisational type for further investigation: Austin, Texas, as a specific case of green building defined by government; the Built Green Colorado programme as a case defined by industry; and the Florida Green Home

Standard as a case defined by an NGO. The Austin, Colorado and Florida programmes were chosen for the high quality of available data and to provide for geographic and cultural diversity. The selected cases also represent the oldest (Austin) and one of the newest (Florida) of US green building programmes. The table provides an overview of these three green building programmes as well as eleven others that employ rating tools to assess new single-family homes.

Table 4.1   *The competing logics of green building in the United States*

| | Type of logic | | | |
| --- | --- | --- | --- | --- |
| | *Restrictive* | *Strategic* | *Adaptive* | *Expansive* |
| *Modes of qualification* | Membership, education, documentation | Inspection, submission, scoring | Regulation, review, rating | Verification, assessment, confirmation |
| *Modes of certification* | Review, testing | Checklist | Checklist | Checklist, programme inspection |
| *Definition of 'green' building* | Efficient use of resources | The rational trade-off of economic for ecological goods | The dynamic balancing of economic, ecological and social e7quity interests | The technological redescription of civilisational values |
| *Implicit world-view* | Positivist or post-positivist | | Constructivist | Emancipatory |
| *Type and location of individual programmes:* | | | | |
| *Government organisations* | • Frisco, Texas<br>• Boulder | | • Portland | • Austin*<br>• Scottsdale |
| *Industry organisations* | • Albuquerque<br>• Kansas City | • Atlanta<br>• Denver*<br>• Kitsap County | • Hawaii<br>• King and Snohomish | |
| *Non-governmental organisations* | | • Madison | • Florida* | |

* Selected case studies.

## *Austin, Texas – green building defined by government*

### Austin Energy Green Building Program

Austin has always listened to a different drummer. We have a style all our own, part Texas individualism, idealism from the 60s, a willingness to embrace high-tech, yet a love of things simple and common sense. Located in the heart of the state, we rest at a historical cultural crossroads. Around us are rolling hills, azure lakes and rivers, and below us is one of the country's most pristine aquifers. It was in this environment that some very forward thinking individuals created the Green Building Program, the first comprehensive program to encourage using sustainable building techniques in residential, multifamily, commercial and municipal construction.

(From the Austin Energy Green Building Program website)

Austin's market-driven, voluntary green building programme, housed in the city's municipal electric utility company, Austin Energy, is well known for being the nation's first residential green building programme and is a much copied national model. Before being known for green building, however, the city of Austin implemented a variety of municipal energy conservation programmes in the mid- to late 1980s. Over 6,000 homes were rated by one such, the Austin Energy Star Program. By the early 1990s, however, there was a growing local awareness of the negative environmental impacts of construction. In Austin, energy conservation activist Laurence Doxsey, along with Pliny Fisk III and Gail Vittori, co-directors of the Center for Maximum Potential Building Systems, developed the original concept for Austin's green building programme. The city of Austin embraced these ideas as a natural evolution of its Energy Star Program. Since its inception in 1992, this green building programme has certified well over 3,100 homes as 'green' (Fig. 4.4)

*4.4 A 'five star' rated home in Austin, Texas.*

The single-family residential rating tool of Austin Energy's Green Building Program is a comprehensive, weighted checklist of items used to rate new homes on a scale from one to five stars. To receive a green building rating, the home must be built in the Austin Energy service area. The builder or architect must also be a member of the programme and have attended the requisite half-day training session. A self-certification rating application must be submitted for all homes, and additional energy tests administered by a third party are required for four and five star rated homes. The checklist is divided into six categories: energy, testing, materials, water, health and safety, and community. Under each is a series of building features, each in turn with a corresponding point value. Builders and home owners select a set of features whose cumulative point value is sufficient for the rating they desire. A one star home is required to earn a minimum of 40 points, a two star home 60 points, a three star home 90 points, a four star home 130 points and a five star home 180 points, out of a maximum 274. In addition, there are 14 requirements as well as additional required checklist items for four and five star rated homes.

### Denver, Colorado – green building defined by industry

#### Built Green Colorado

We're the second-oldest program in the country, and we're familiar with the pioneering Austin program. A group of progressively-minded builders, local govern-ment, and general LOHAS-types [Lifestyles of Health and Sustainability] began to launch the idea of a program, and the Denver HBA [Home Builder's Association] took on the job, in 1995, of hosting a program in one of the country's fastest-growing markets, along the Front Range of the Colorado Rockies ... [W]e're the only program funded by industry-types ('industry leaders') and are as such subject to the particular challenges working with for-profit parties in that capacity. Our main objective is to affect a shift toward sustainable building practices in as large a segment of the Colorado home-building industry as possible. We have done and continue to do this by building a marketable brand that adds value for participating builders, and by educating homebuyers of the value of an environmentally sensitive home.

(K. Slattery, Built Green Colorado, e-mail message to author, February 2003)

The Built Green Colorado programme was introduced in 1995 as a creation of the Home Builder's Association of metropolitan Denver, the Governor's Office of Energy Management and Conservation, Excel Energy and E-Star Colorado.[6] It is currently the nation's largest green building programme, with over 100 builder members, 45 sponsor members and 10 members of the Built Green Industry Leaders group throughout Colo-rado. In 2002 alone, Built Green Colorado certified approximately 4,000 homes as green, more than double the number of homes rated by the second most prolific programme in the nation (Fig. 4.5). Since its inception in 1995 more than 14,000 homes have been built green. Unlike some of the 13 similar programmes, Built Green Colorado derives its operating budget not only from the dues and fees of builder and sponsor members, but also from the substantial financial contributions of members of the industry leaders' group such as Excel Energy, Colorado Rockies Brick Council, James Hardie Building Products, Rheem Company, Boise Cascade, Trex Decking, Whirlpool Corporation, Kurowski Development Co., McStain Enterprises and US Home.

*4.5 A Built Green Colorado home constructed by Village Homes of Colorado, Inc.*

The Built Green Colorado rating tool is a comprehensive weighted checklist that rates new homes as 'Built Green'. Unlike the Austin rating tool, the Colorado programme does not currently issue tiered or graduated ratings (such as stars), although a change to a tiered system is planned in the near future to allow builders to further differentiate themselves in the marketplace. To receive a Built Green rating, builders must enrol, submit a home registration form and accumulate the required points. It is not required to select points from each category. Five per cent of all residential homes are inspected on a random basis by third party services, and many checklist items require documentation at the time of the random testing. The checklist is divided into four primary categories: energy efficiency, materials, health and safety, and resource conservation. Each primary category consists of several related sub-categories of increased specificity, such as 'envelope' in the energy efficiency category. Builders are required to choose one of three methods of meeting the energy efficiency minimum requirement and then reach a cumulative point total of 70 from anywhere in the checklist.

### Florida – green building defined by an NGO

#### Florida Green Home Standard
The Florida Green Building Coalition (FGBC) was conceived and founded in the belief that green building programs will be most successful if there are clear and meaningful principles on which 'green' qualification and marketing are based.

FGBC is devoting considerable effort to developing technical standards for a variety of green practices. The standards are developed to provide independent third-party verification, via FGBC, for a project's green planning and actions. As such, FGBC hopes that consumers and government agencies can rely on the FGBC symbol to assure there is no 'greenwashing'. Each of these standards requires appropriate environmental stewardship for certain activities. In this sense, green building is conceived as a process, not simply a noun.

(From the Florida Green Building Program website)

The Florida Green Building Coalition is a non-profit corporation in Florida whose expressed mission is to provide a statewide green building programme with environmental and economic benefits. Its primary means of achieving this goal is the development and implementation of certification for green building practices, the Florida Green Home Standard rating tool. Incorporated in 2001, the FGBC is a membership-based organisation governed by an eight member board of directors, elected by vote of the general membership. Membership is open to all interested individuals, non-profit organisations, government agencies and businesses willing and able to pay fees that range from $25 for full-time students to $475 for large businesses with 50 or more employees. The FGBC has five standing committees – education, nomination, research and technical, programme and promotion, and standards – established by the board of directors and charged with specific tasks outlined in the coalition's by-laws.

*4.6 The first home rated under the Florida Green Building Coalition's Green Home Standard.*

The Florida Green Home Standard features a comprehensive, weighted checklist with minimum point requirements for each category as well as maximum allowable points per category. The sum of the minimums is 190 points and an additional 10 points must be accumulated from anywhere on the list. If any category minimums cannot be achieved, point deficiencies may be made up by adding the deficiency to the total minimum score. Similar to the Colorado rating tool, the FGBC's does not feature a tiered or graduated rating system. To receive certification builders must complete the Florida Green Home Standard checklist, a certifying agent must verify specified measures and the FGBC must receive the required submittals for other selected measures. The FGBC standard is also geographically specific, with requirements for pools and spas as well as waterfront considerations. Similarly, it also contains a disaster mitigation category that contains required and optional items related to hurricanes, floods, wild fires and termites. Other categories include energy, water, site, health, materials and general. In 2002, only three homes were certified under the Florida Green Home Standard (Fig. 4.6).

### Analysis of the three case studies

Each case has been examined with regard to the modes of qualification employed, the modes of certification utilised, the definitions of green implicitly and explicitly articulated and the implicit worldview that guides each logic. By modes of qualification we refer to the processes by which builders or architects comply with the specific technical standards. Similarly, modes of certification address the concrete mechanisms used to rate a particular project. Definition of 'green' refers to the stated and implicit values contained within the modes of certification and qualification. In the final category of analysis, implicit worldview, we refer to the four dominant paradigms of inquiry, or metaphysical traditions of science, that are generally accepted by social scientists. In this framework, positivists and post-positivists inquire so as to 'predict and control' nature; constructivists inquire so as to 'understand' or 'reconstruct' reality; and finally, critical theorists inquire so as to 'emancipate' or 'transform' history (Denzin and Lincoln 1994: 112).

Using these four lenses, we then categorised each programme as consistent with one of four logics: restrictive, strategic, adaptive or expansive. Each of these logics prefigures a specific range of technological choices and seeks to associate such choices with the general public welfare on the grounds of protection to environmental and public health. The four logics are best understood as 'nested' or progressive values and can be summarised as follows (Table 4.1).

The organisations that employ restrictive logic tend to value efficiency for its own sake. This logic suggests that an unsustainable condition is a product only of inefficient industrial processes, thus a green solution will optimise both human and non-human resources and, at the same time, maximise economic growth through the use of advanced technology. This worldview relies on positivistic or post-positivistic assumptions in that it tends to characterise concerns related to social equity and environmental ethics as lying outside the realm of quantifiable knowledge. Where positivists see nature as knowable, post-positivists see it as describable within acceptable limits. In our view this logic conceptualises nature and human health through the reductive neo-classical economic models that have been thoroughly criticised elsewhere (Daly 1996). Many observers will identify this logic with 'greenwashing'.

The organisations that employ strategic logic also value efficiency, but as a means to protect the interests of both home owners and industry. The environmental problem is defined by these organisations not only in terms of inefficiency but also, more importantly, in terms of conflict between economic growth and environmental protection. This is what Andrew Feenberg refers to as the 'trade-off problem' – the perceived need to give up some economic good so as to afford either environmental protection or public health (Feenberg 2002: 18, 187). A green solution for these organisations must balance the competing interests of environmental protection and economic growth through the same kind of positivistic or post-positivistic procedures as those who employ restrictive logic. Concern for social equity as a dimension of sustainable development is not emphasised. This is a more sociocultural approach that requires collaboration among stakeholders to reduce utility bills, increase comfort, lessen impact on the environment and pre-empt government regulation. The changes advocated by this logic are dependent on educating industry, government, environmentalists and the public of their common interests, which can be realised only through a politically strategic way of thinking.

The organisations that employ adaptive logic certainly value efficiency and strategic political thinking, but they are also proactive – as were nineteenth-century utilitarians – in seeking long-term solutions to social and environmental quality problems. Advocates of this logic perceive environmental problems as related not only to utility costs and human comfort, but also explicitly to public health concerns such as the off-gassing of highly processed construction materials. Adaptive logic seeks solutions that not only balance a variety of competing interests in the present, as in the strategic logic, but also continuously redefine relationships among industry, government, the public and the environment in the future. The implicit worldview of these organisations is constructivist – meaning that reality is a socially constructed agreement between individuals and groups associated with competing interests.

Finally, the organisations that employ expansive logic tend to value efficiency, strategic political thinking, adaptability and public health, but not for their own sake. For these organisations the environmental problem is understood not as a natural site in need of a technological fix, but as a social problem requiring reform. This logic requires a whole-systems approach to protecting the health and well-being of citizens and the natural environment alike. Such a project is what Feenberg refers to as 'civilizational change' – a discursive process through which society explicitly modifies its values through the revision of 'technical codes'. Citizens who employ this logic give up the trade-off model in which economic goods are sacrificed on the account of environmental protection or social equity. Rather than looking for trade-offs, or rebalancing competing interests, these organisations seek two related goals. First, they seek what Feenberg refers to as 'concretization' – a (design) process through which buildings are integrated into the natural energy-flows of a place, as with passive ventilation, rather than attempting to overcome environmental problems by adding on appliances external to the building concept. Such add-ons are typically those that depend on fossil fuels, like air conditioning, but also might be those that depend on renewable energy, like photovoltaic solar collectors that are only stuck onto the envelope. In the latter case, the more expensive solar technologies are easily deleted during times of economic constraint (Feenberg 1999: 220). Secondly, these organisations seek to fundamentally redefine the limits within which economic choices can be made. Green buildings defined expansively would not restrict otherwise desirable economic activity but would redefine the cultural values within which economic activity takes place (Feenberg 2003). This worldview is clearly emancipatory in that the purpose of creating better building science is not to predict and control nature (as is the case for positivists and post-positivists), nor only to better understand and thus balance competing reality claims (as is the case for constructivists), but to liberate humans and non-humans alike from unsustainable conditions.

From our analysis of these cases, it is apparent that competing definitions of green are being advanced by various organisations. However, as the table indicates, the logics of green building we have reconstructed do not correlate strongly to the organisational types of government, industry or NGOs as we had originally hypothesised. The industry-driven programme in Hawaii employs, for example, an adaptive logic, while the municipally driven one in Frisco, Texas, employs a restrictive logic. This finding is somewhat surprising. Like many observers, we hypothesised, on the basis of perceived self-interests, that industry-based organisations would consistently construct the most restrictive of green programmes, that environmental NGOs would consistently construct the most expansive ones, and that government would fall somewhere between.

The data contradict such an a priori bias and suggest three propositions. First, the values underlying each logic are strongly influenced by local political discourses. Second, local codes are freely appropriated by green building programmes in distant communities with differing organisational structures. And third, programmes implemented by one type of organisation – home builders in the case of Colorado – are negotiated in their formative stages with other organisational types – government – in order to gain credibility.

With such a limited sample and inconclusive data it is difficult to generalise about the social values of organisational types. Instead, a programme's position within the table reflects the hybrid nature of green building logics in practice rather than the purity of ideological principles. This finding only enhances our ability to raise questions concerning the future of green building programmes and their influence on general building codes.

## Conclusions

In their current state of development, North American residential green building programmes should be understood as local attempts to resolve social conflicts, across organisational types, that have emerged in the residential construction industry. Were our analysis to end here, however, it would leave the reader pondering four separate and distinct definitions of green building. But, as we argued above, it is not likely that these four definitions will remain distinct for long. Rather, there are powerful incentives to standardise the definition of green building as a new social 'good' that is commensurable across political jurisdictions. The social construction of this definition will be highly contentious and will ultimately depend on enlisting those middle-class citizens who increasingly characterise their own health and environment as in a state of crisis and who seek security from any source that seems credible. Cities that wish to be proactive rather than reactive in satisfying public anxieties tend to adapt the codes of others towards their own unique goals and objectives. Standardisation is, for better or worse, the process by which local conflicts are commonly resolved. Interpreting this phenomenon positively would be to argue that the standardisation of green building practices reflects a changing cultural horizon and anticipates new technical codes intent upon altering the definition of 'good building'. To interpret this phenomenon sceptically would be to argue that standardisation tends to suppress those local discourses that constitute what Kenneth Frampton has called 'tectonic culture' (Frampton 1995). The question remains: who decides? The answer, in many ways, seems to be whoever acts first.

The US Green Building Council's LEED programme is a prime example of early-market capture in the commercial construction industry – a position that foreshadows the residential construction industry. Initially organised in 1995, the Green Building Council has rapidly promoted the LEED standard to become the de facto rating tool for commercial buildings worldwide. They have achieved this through a commanding market presence, the creation of a value-added saleable product and impeccable timing that beat similar efforts out of the gate. LEED has succeeded so widely in the commercial sector because its authors have standardised the less comprehensive and sometimes less relevant codes constructed by local discourses in places like Austin, Colorado and Florida, among others, and made their LEED Green Building Rating System™ valuable to stakeholders. The degree to which LEED will be able to redefine 'good building' for the twenty-first century depends, of course, on the flexibility of its code and its ability to recruit the interests of environmentalists, public health advocates, government and the building industry.

The standardisation of green building practices will surely occur in the routine context of modernisation foreseen by Weber. However, too many interests are at stake to anticipate which logic – restrictive, strategic, adaptive or expansive – will be reinforced and which will be suppressed. The very proliferation of green building programmes, however, is a strong indicator that we are rapidly approaching the moment in history when green building will no longer be considered an add-on to basic values like durability, economy and style that are already demanded by citizens. Rather, protecting public health, as an indivisible element of ecosystem health, will be understood as a basic condition of civilisation from which retreat will seem no more possible than a return to slavery, child labour or unregulated construction. What remains unclear is whether the process of defining green building will be directed by market forces, special interest groups or local democratic discourse.

## Notes

1 This phenomenon is what Bruno Latour refers to as a 'technological network'. He means by this term, not only networks of human interests, but the non-human resources tied to those human relations.

2 The same dilemma continues to be articulated between contemporary authors such as Ulrich Beck (1992) and Peter Marsh (2000). Beck argues that it is unjust that those who control the means of production generally escape the health risks associated with environmental pollution while those of modest means suffer such risks disproportionately. In contrast, Marsh, who describes himself as a left-wing libertarian, objects to 'the level of concern (some might say "obsession") with dietary, health and lifestyle correctness that characterises contemporary Western societies, and the UK and the United States in particular. This pursuit of novel, narrow concepts of so-called "health" and "fitness" has led us to create new outcasts – those who fail to conform to the increasing catalogue of prescriptions for what is "best for us" – those who, contrary to the advice of self-appointed arbiters of modern rectitude, persist with "bad habits".'

3 The term 'sustainability' was first used in its current environmental, economic and social context in *World Conservation Strategy*, a 1980 publication by the International Union for the Conservation of Nature and Natural Resources (IUCN 1980). That document defined 'sustainable development' as 'those paths of social, economic, and political progress that meet the needs of the present without compromising the ability of future generations to meet

their own needs'. In the first decades of the twentieth century Gifford Pinchot used the term in the context of sustained-yield forestry. However, he did not yet anticipate the concerns of social equity that the term now incorporates.

4　The University of Texas School of Nursing and Student Community Center (2003) is a concrete example of how public health educators and officials had, by the turn of the twenty-first century, become advocates and patrons of sustainable architecture.

5　Further support for this logic was found in a routine keyword search at the Environmental Policy Index database, EBSCO (http://search.epnet.com/), which reported 551 links to articles related to 'public health' and 'sustainable development'. A web search of *Rachel's News* (www.rachel.org/bulletin/index.cfm?St=4) provided a link to 764 articles that relate 'environmental protection' to 'human health'.

6　E-Star is a Colorado non-profit making organisation working to advance energy efficiency in housing.

# Part B

# Responding design

# 5

# The politics of design in cities

## Preconceptions, frameworks and trajectories of sustainable building[1]

*Timothy Moss, Adriaan Slob and Walter Vermeulen*

Moss, Slob and Vermeulen address the limited impact of local policy and planning initiatives in promoting the introduction of sustainable energy technologies in the design of new housing. They begin with a critique of the policy response of removing individual 'barriers' to technology take-up, commonly identified as inadequate regulations, funding and information. They then argue the need for a broader understanding of how local policy contexts shape decision-making processes in this field and how recent shifts in these contexts – relating, in particular, to market competition, new constellations of actors and technological diversity – are creating new windows of opportunity for green housing. In this way the authors question the view that the diffusion of proven environmentally beneficial technologies and construction techniques is simply a technical challenge. Instead they suggest that in order to assess the changing opportunities for actors in design and development to put their already existing knowledge into practice, we must deepen our understanding of the competing social and technical logics governing development processes.

## Introduction

The process of designing, planning and creating sustainable buildings is tied up in a complex web of problem perceptions, actors' interests, decision-making procedures and policy frameworks. Experiences in practical application suggest that these factors are not peripheral or trivial. They shape the process of implementation significantly and can have a substantive influence over the design and features of the building or development. There is a growing recognition in the literature on sustainable architecture that some of the dominant assumptions on how sustainable and energy-efficient building can best be promoted are fundamentally flawed (Guy and Shove 2000). Broadly speaking the critique is, firstly, that policy-makers and planners pursue a rational choice logic that is often at odds with everyday experiences of human behaviour. Secondly, the role of key individuals in decision-making processes is often overemphasised at the expense of consideration of the real and potential contribution of other affected parties. Thirdly, the notion of implementation following a linear path from original design to ultimate construction, overcoming 'barriers' encountered on the way, overlooks the inherent complexity, unpredictability and reversibility of the implementation process. Several chapters in this book take up this critique and investigate different dimensions to the broader picture of promoting sustainable buildings.

The purpose of this chapter is to explore one of these dimensions – sustainable building policy in urban contexts – as a way to contribute to this debate and raise our understanding of the contextual forces that frame opportunities for energy efficiency.

The focus is not on the choice of technology or the design of buildings but rather on the ways these issues are framed and shaped by policy priorities, actor engagement and urban development forces. Drawing on experiences in European countries with strong traditions of municipal influence over local energy and housing policy – in particular the Netherlands – we investigate urban contexts that contribute to, or otherwise affect, efforts to create more sustainable locations and designs for new housing.

We characterise our perspective on the debate as 'the politics of design in cities'. The terminology is deliberately chosen to capture a number of different 'worlds' that interact in efforts to promote sustainable building in urban contexts: the world of politics, where power is exercised and interests negotiated (Fearon 1998), the world of policy-making, with its beliefs in planning and control and its institutional structures, the world of design, which strives to combine aesthetics with functionality (von Meiss 1998), and the world of the urban environment, with its multiple physical dimensions and social interpretations. Each of these worlds engages a particular constellation of actor groups – local politicians, planners, architects, developers and so on – who pursue their interests and responsibilities according to their own perceptions of problems and logics of action. Increasing sensitivity towards the relevance of these different worldviews and interests is one objective of this chapter.

A second objective is to raise awareness of the dependence of sustainable building on a wide range of policy issues. Even in the context of a single locality, efforts to promote sustainable building get caught up in debates and issues not readily associated with the immediate task at hand. Sustainable building can be significantly affected, for instance, by local transportation policy, the structure of technical infrastructure networks or the activities of technology consultants. How these contextual factors can shape initiatives in sustainable building has not been well documented to date. In particular, little is known about how shifting contexts of action can create new openings for promoting sustainable building or undermine the premises on which current building policy is based. The liberalisation of energy markets, for example, can substantially alter the interest of the local energy utility in contributing to a sustainable building programme. Finally, we need to know more about the combined effect of these diverse factors in specific urban contexts. Identifying contributory factors alone is not enough; understanding ways in which they interact is important to identifying the emergence of windows of opportunity for policy action. It is contested here that the 'mainstreaming' of sustainable building practices cannot be achieved without a good understanding of the politics of design.

The chapter begins by exploring the gap in policy implementation that exists in promoting sustainable building, setting the ambitious policy objectives against the relatively modest results. In the subsequent section we identify some common explanations given by local authorities for the low rate of dissemination of sustainable building practices – including inadequate regulations, lack of funding and information deficiencies – and criticise how these problem perceptions often lead to selective solutions. On the basis of this problem analysis we then set out our own conceptual understanding of the politics of (sustainable) design in urban contexts. This broadens the perspective to encompass the multiple factors which influence the decisions of investors, developers, housing associations and owners to adopt or reject sustainable technologies when building, refurbishing or managing housing. The paper then indicates how some of these frameworks of action are currently shifting, creating new openings for sustainable technologies and practices and requiring novel approaches to planning sustainable housing in the future. The following section then gives examples of more context-sensitive approaches to pursuing sustainable building objectives and exploiting the new windows of opportunity being created. We conclude by summarising the implications of the findings for future ways of promoting sustainable building in urban contexts and for the role local authorities can play to this end. Examples drawn from empirical research from the Netherlands, in particular, serve to illustrate the central arguments of each section.

## The policy implementation gap

Many European countries have strong traditions of municipal influence over local housing and energy issues. Local authorities possess various powers, ranging from planning regulations and ownership of housing to responsibility for relevant policy fields to promote sustainable building. They are also well placed to create pilot projects of sustainable housing, encouraging the take-up of innovative technologies such as high-efficiency condensing boilers, solar domestic hot-water systems, heat pumps and combined heat and power. The Agenda 21 document of the Rio Conference on Environment and Development recognises the pioneering role of local authorities in promoting sustainable development. In recent years considerable steps have been made by local authorities in advancing energy efficiency in buildings. In the Netherlands, the central government has successfully introduced energy performance standards, financial incentives and voluntary agreements with the building and construction industries (Haarman et al. 2000). Extensive checklists of possible techniques and designs are available, such as the national packages for sustainable building (Anink et al. 1996). These policies have been supported and often elaborated by local energy-efficiency policies. As a result, by 1998, 32 per cent of all new building permits met a specified minimum standard for sustainable building, the so-called 'yardstick' (Novem 1999). Although this appears to be quite an achievement, a comparison across Europe shows the Netherlands to be somewhere in the mid-field in terms of environmental innovations (van Hal and Dulski 1999).

Despite a number of success stories and growing recognition of the multiple benefits of energy-efficient housing, it cannot be denied that many local policies to promote sustainable building fail to live up to expectations. Criticism is levelled in particular at the relatively low rates of technology dissemination (van der Waals 2001). Even if individual pilot projects of sustainable housing prove successful in their own right they seldom stimulate significant take-up of the innovative technologies on a broader scale. Without the favourable financial backing, involvement of actors and exemption from regulations that pilot projects have available, the technologies they advance often prove unattractive and unviable. There exists a substantial gap in policy implementation. Compared with the ambitious policy objectives, the outcomes have been modest.

This generally acknowledged observation has been substantiated by empirical research in the Netherlands on the role of sustainable building in planning processes for urban development and urban renewal. Studying the early generation of government-endorsed demonstration projects of the early 1990s Silvester concluded that the focus of these projects had been merely on 'getting the demonstration done' (Silvester 1996). It took almost ten years for a target-group oriented communication strategy to be developed for disseminating the acquired knowledge. Similar findings for other European countries have been made by van Hal (2000).

A more recent study examined the degree to which major urban development projects of the late 1990s in the Netherlands met national policy targets on energy and transport (van der Waals et al. 1999). The survey covered 26 locations, each including at least 4000 new dwellings and together covering 36 per cent of the planned new dwellings in all large urban expansion plans in the country, for the period 1995 to 2005. It was found that, although sustainable building was generally given a high priority at the strategic planning level, many of the more ambitious objectives were not carried over to the following implementation phases or taken up by the respective sets of actors (van der Waals et al. 1999: 21–33; van der Waals and Vermeulen 2000. See Figure 5.1). This applied to many urban design and technological options generally considered highly important to sustainable building, such as the location and orientation of the buildings, access to public transport and ways to minimise car use.

A further study on the implementation of $CO_2$ reduction targets in urban reconstruction plans reveals an even larger implementation gap (van der Waals et al. 2003). In projects of this kind many opportunities for $CO_2$ reduction are being overlooked. The few technical options introduced, such as insulation, condensing boilers and high-performance glass, were often applied to only some of the houses or part of the house shell. The take-up of technologies would appear to depend to a substantial degree on the market viability and maturity of each technology, as perceived by developers and property owners.

These studies show some 'successes' but also various dimensions of an implementation gap. Discussions on levels of success are always strongly coloured by the perceptions of what 'sustainable building' actually is. In the Dutch case, 'preferable packages' have been formulated in consultation with authorities, businesses and experts, creating one practical definition of sustainable building. The government's claim to success rests on the level of implementation of these 'preferable packages', which offer considerable

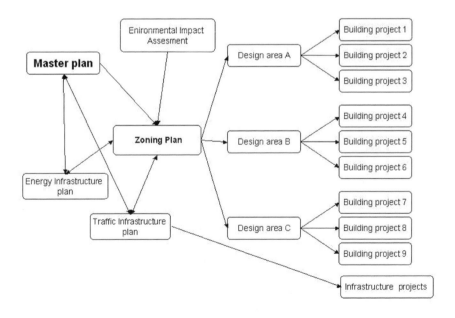

*5.1 The sequence of planning processes for building locations.*

freedom of choice over individual measures while limiting additional costs for new housing to between 2 per cent and 3 per cent. However, seen from the perspective of specific design options, as in the studies discussed, levels of success clearly vary according to the option. Here, the degree of maturity and market viability of the technologies is important. Given the growing attention being paid to sustainable building, the pace of technological development in this field is rapid and accelerating. Technologies which only recently were experimental are breaking through into the mainstream, creating a challenge for businesses and authorities to keep up with developments.

## Perceived problems and selective solutions

Local policy-makers are well aware of this implementation gap between policy objectives and operational achievements. Those engaged in promoting sustainable building are frustrated that years of demonstration projects backed by considerable resources have generally not succeeded in mainstreaming energy-efficient technologies and practices that exceed the regulatory requirements. They attribute limited dissemination to specific obstacles encountered during the process of implementation. These barriers, it is widely held, relate essentially to a lack of information among key actors about the technological options, inadequate financial incentives for actors to adopt sustainable technologies and market forces that favour short-term cost-saving for the developer over long-term benefits for the user of a building. These three barriers are similar to the 'barriers' cited in Guy and Shove (2000: 60–1): lack of knowledge and information, capital priority and market distortions.

It follows from this definition of the problem that the solutions, in the eyes of many protagonists, are to be found in improving knowledge transfer, providing additional subsidies and tightening the regulatory net to favour energy-efficiency measures (Ministerie van VROM 1995). These three strategies are examined in more detail here.

### *The conventional toolbox*

#### *Tightening the regulatory net*

One general explanation for the limited dissemination of innovative energy technologies is that building regulations are not strict enough (Umweltbundesamt 1998). This line of argument is based on the understanding that architects, developers and builders tend, for commercial reasons, to follow the minimum legal requirements when designing and building housing. Disseminating environmentally sustainable technologies not (yet) commercially viable will, it is argued, require adequate regulatory incentives and sanctions. Following this logic, regulations in many European countries have been made more stringent in order to raise levels of insulation, promote the use of double glazing and increase the efficiency of heating equipment. Experiences in Denmark and the Netherlands have shown that raising standards for insulation may indeed contribute to a decrease in the energy used for heating buildings (Ministry of Foreign Affairs 1996; RIVM 2000).

At the local level municipalities may be able to add their own regulations. The city of Eindhoven, for instance, required developers on the Meerhoven site (owned by the city) to sign a letter of intent binding them to meet high environmental standards and requiring the construction companies to contribute to the cost of installing a combined heat and power system (van der Waals et al. 1999: 66). In Nieuwland, the new district

*5.2  The Information Centre for Sustainable Living in Utrecht, the Netherlands. It was built as a 'zero-energy house' with 50 m² of photovoltaic panels integrated in the roof and high isolation levels (roof and façades 6 m².K/W; floor 5 m².K/W; triple windows 0.7 W/m².K). It is intended to have a modern, non-alternative look. (For more information see Duurzaam Huis 2004.)*

of Amersfoort, building companies that wanted to be engaged had to agree with a list of requirements drawn up by the municipality and the developer.

### Covering additional costs

A second explanation frequently given for the limited dissemination of sustainable energy technologies is lack of funding. The argument here is that new energy technologies are relatively expensive, being at an early stage of development, and require initial subsidies to help them become commercially viable and more widely established. Early subsidies may in time even reduce production costs by increasing production numbers.

Here, again, local authorities can provide financial incentives of their own. The city of Rotterdam, when building the Kop van Zuid, introduced a checklist of environmental measures with a point-scoring system for implementation. Developers scoring 70 points or more receive a subsidy of €455. In this way, the municipality knows what measures are taken and has some degree of control over developers. The city also grants subsidies, funded from the sale of the development site, for meeting the strict energy performance coefficient of the Rotterdam Energy Plan and for introducing solar domestic hot-water systems. A special fund is used to promote options of a more exper-imental nature, such as photovoltaic systems, heat pumps or combined heat and power (van der Waals et al.1999: 62).

*Removing information deficiencies*

A third common explanation for poor dissemination levels is lack of information and inade-quate information transfer. The underlying assumption is that the relevant actors, provided with proper information, will act rationally in ways framed by their knowledge base. They follow, it is held, largely predictable patterns based on maximising benefits for the organi-sations they belong to and for themselves individually. The logical solution has been to seek ways of improving data collection, information transfer and communication (Nijkamp and Perrels 1994; Selman 1996; Umweltbundesamt 1998). In several countries available knowledge has been collected in sizeable technical handbooks, such as those developed by the Danish and Dutch governments (Miljørigtig projektering 1998; Stichting Bouwresearch 1999). Other forms of information transfer are encouraged through the help of information centres, training programmes for professionals, information campaigns or energy advisory services for housing associations and households.

Some local authorities have developed sophisticated forms of knowledge transfer. For example, the city of Amersfoort introduced an environmental supervisor for the new urban district of Nieuwland whose job it was to check plans at various stages of the implementation process and to inform developers of options for environmental improve-ment. In addition, project teams were formed to manage building projects, each team comprising an 'environmental architect' alongside a 'design architect' and 'housing expert'. Workshops were held to raise awareness of environmental options, and media coverage helped to create a positive public image of the project and those involved (van der Waals et al. 1999: 64–5).

## Limitations of the conventional toolbox

Solutions of this kind have undoubtedly contributed to overcoming some of the difficul-ties encountered in promoting sustainable technologies and building practices. Experi-ences indicate, however, that each has its own structural deficits that have limited their overall impact. Some of these are briefly outlined here.

*Limitations to tightening the regulatory net*

With regard to the process of rule making, regulations on sustainable building have to be integrated into a complex web of existing building regulations addressing a variety of situa-tions. Exceptions are often necessary, as uniform rules tend to lack context sensitivity. Efforts to make the rules more contextually sensitive are often strongly opposed. An addi-tional problem lies in keeping pace with the rapidly changing technologies for sustainable building. Considerable time can elapse between the introduction of a technology on the market and its prescription by regulations. A time lag of 10 to 15 years is not exceptional. During the process of rule enforcement, regulations designed to promote sustainable energy technologies can have negative side effects. Thorough enforcement often demands a major commitment of resources, particularly on the part of local authorities. Furthermore, unpopular regulations tend to generate creative ways of avoiding their stipulations.

*Limitations to covering additional costs*

Here, too, a time lag can be observed between the emergence of new technologies and their inclusion in funding schemes. Another limitation revealed by research is that the use of subsidies is subject to what is termed the 'Matthews effect'. This refers to the frequent cases where those who receive subsidies would have introduced the technologies anyway without additional funding. Limited effectiveness may also be explained in part by the complexity of funding programmes. Developers and investors are often outfaced by the bureaucracy involved in applying for, and meeting the requirements of, funding schemes. These limitations seriously question the assumption that subsidised pilot projects will lead to widespread future dissemination.

*Limitations to removing information deficiencies*

In practice, there is often a discrepancy between the information that is needed and what is available. Information can be aimed at specific target groups only, missing actors deemed peripheral to the central decision-making process. It may be presented in a way that overlooks the fact that most of those being addressed act not simply according to rational choice models but under multiple constraints. Supply of information, often part of a 'technology push' strategy, may also be heavily technical; contextual information, by contrast, is often missing (Almlund et al. 2001). A study by van Hal (2000) of demonstration projects for environmental innovations in housing across Europe shows that information transfer is often poorly organised. Attention is often directed at the innovation itself and how to implement the demonstration project rather than at attracting wider interest.

More significantly, efforts of this kind have, collectively, not succeeded in enabling the mainstreaming of more sustainable building practices. Besides their inherent limitations it would appear that the challenge of promoting sustainable building involves more than overcoming the barriers of lack of funds, regulations and information commonly identified. It raises the question of what other factors need to be addressed when promoting sustainable building and, more fundamentally, whether the notion of overcoming readily identifiable 'barriers' is a helpful way of understanding the problem. This leads us to consider the politics of design in urban contexts.

## Conceptualising the politics of design

In their pioneering book on the sociology of energy and building Guy and Shove (2000) challenged a number of assumptions underpinning the conventional discourse on sustainable building and set out an alternative way of conceptualising the processes involved. Their critique is essentially three-fold. Firstly, they challenge the common notion of 'removing' non-technical 'barriers' to progress and the confidence placed in using improved knowledge dissemination to this end. Without denying the relevance of problems that confront efforts to promote sustainable building, they claim that these problems can rarely be readily isolated from all other factors and 'removed' by means of providing better information or applying incentives or sanctions. Processes of creating sustainable building, they argue, are much more complex. From this follows, secondly, their criticism of the linear narrative surrounding the development of sustainable technologies: from invention, design and demonstration to application and dissemination. The reality of technology diffusion, they argue, is frequently at odds with this model path. More consideration is needed of the delays, setbacks and reversals that generally accompany processes of technological innovation. Thirdly, they challenge the focus, in promoting sustainable building, on creating incentives for individuals assumed to be acting according to rational motives alone and on targeting select groups of decision-makers in particular. This narrow focus runs the risk, they argue, of overlooking the contextual factors preventing individuals from acting rationally and the potential importance of actor groups beyond the immediate decision-makers.

On the basis of this critique Guy and Shove develop an alternative way of conceptualising processes of urban design. They emphasise the existence of multiple potential 'design routes' (Guy and Shove 2000: 67) for a sustainable building, rather than a single linear model. These varied options and trajectories available to the actors are influenced substantially by the local context of action, not merely by the inner rationale of a specific policy. Time and place take on particular importance in framing the opportunities available (Guy and Shove 2000: 69, 110). When planning and implementing sustainable building projects it is important to consider how some contextual factors can be used to advantage and how others may pose difficulties to implementation. Broadening the perspective in this way means also considering the role of actor groups other than those immediately responsible for a sustainable building project. Introducing environmental technologies, altering the local infrastructure or creating new development locations can affect the interests of a wide range of organisations and individuals (Guy and Shove 2000: 68). Identifying this web of interests and enrolling particular actors to support a project poses a major challenge to those responsible. In essence, it means shifting the emphasis of policy away from influencing the decision-making process in isolation towards structuring choice in such a way as to draw benefit from potential windows of opportunity as they present themselves or are created (Guy and Shove 2000: 95).

We build on this line of argument, focusing on two aspects in particular: the policy domain and urban contexts of sustainable building. Critical to the policy domain of sustainable building is the extent and degree of access to the decision-making process. The various stages of design, planning and construction are generally characterised by a high level of exclusivity, with clear roles for a set number of expert groups: architects, engineering consultants, urban planners, property owners and developers. Open planning processes that engage, for instance, residents, local businesses or utilities are rare (van der Waals et al. 2000). Yet actors like these have important and relevant interests in urban development processes of this kind that can potentially have a determining influence on the degree of success of a sustainable building project. Commonly, these peripheral actor groups are – initially at least – not strongly motivated by the project. Their interest in sustainable building is shaped by the extent to which it ties in with their other concerns. It follows that enrolling such actors can be significant in creating greater sensitivity to local contextual factors and identifying potentially beneficial ways in which these can be taken into consideration when implementing a particular project. Such a process is inherently political. It entails extending access to decision-making to those not directly responsible and creating procedures for negotiation between actors with diverse interests and power bases. It is about acknowledging and managing the politics of design in a broader context.

## Contexts of design in transition

Exploiting the opportunities offered by local contextual factors requires not only identification of those most pertinent to sustainable building but an understanding of how they may be changing. External pressures, such as globalisation and liberalisation, and internal pressures, such as budget deficits and socio-economic restructuring, combine to alter the operational framework of development projects of this kind. Such shifts can have a determining influence on the effectiveness of policy instruments and the success of project implementation. In this section we select three areas of change of direct relevance to the pursuit of sustainable building in cities: changing markets, new actor networks and technology dynamics.

### Changing markets

The influence of housing or energy markets on the diffusion of sustainable building and sustainable technologies in buildings has received little attention in the past. If considered at all it is largely as constants representing the economic framework for action rather than as drivers of change themselves. Yet markets for energy as well as for housing are changing quite dramatically across Europe – albeit in very differing degrees – creating new openings for energy technologies.

The liberalisation of energy services is the more obvious case in point. As territorial monopolies of supply for electricity and gas are eroded and competition between utilities increases, new market dynamics are emerging, encouraging new types of entrepreneurs to access this market (Guy et al. 1997; Guy and Marvin 1996; Guy et al. 2001, Agterbosch et al. 2004). In their efforts to cut costs and retain or attract customers, energy utilities are gradually distancing themselves from the costly 'build and supply' logic that so characterised infrastructure management in the past (Guy et al. 1997). Instead, they are reorienting their business strategies towards raising cost efficiency and providing a wider range of energy services. This new approach to energy management is creating a number of opportunities for sustainable energy use. Housing associations and developers, being key determinants of energy consumption in residential buildings, represent important customers for electricity or gas utilities. In a competitive energy market they can often be beneficiaries of energy services, such as free energy audits or tailor-made packages for a whole housing estate that might comprise the installation and management of low-energy heating appliances. In the Netherlands, for instance, social housing corporations have negotiated collectively with energy companies for low-price electricity for their tenants. Whereas some supply just partially green electricity, other corporations (such as DUWO in The Hague region) supply their tenants with cheaper green electricity, benefiting from major supply contracts.

Changes in the housing market can also create new opportunities for energy-efficient technologies. In the past the status of a local housing or building market was rarely considered a factor influencing the diffusion of environmental technologies; yet recent localised shifts in the supply and demand of housing suggest this can be crucial to technology up-take. In a buyers' market environmental technologies can give the edge over the competition. Conversely, the omission of energy-saving measures can, in certain hotly contested markets, leave houses unsold (van der Waals et al. 2000). We can observe how, in several European countries, green technologies have acquired an important image-building function under certain market conditions (Roedekro Kommune 2000).

It is worth noting that, parallel to the housing sector, the market in environmental technologies has its own dynamics that influence green building. The emergence of a large number of companies specialising in the manufacture, installation and mainten-ance of energy-efficient technologies has in recent years created a substantial driving force for technology diffusion in new and refurbished housing (van der Waals 2001). These emerging market dynamics offer considerable potential for energy-saving tech-nologies. Those involved in promoting green housing could benefit from ensuring that their strategies build on, rather than ignore or run counter to, these dynamics.

## New actors, new roles, new relationships

These shifts in market structures are encouraging the emergence of new actors, altering the roles of those involved and giving rise to new relationships among actors. Following the liberalisation of utility services, the traditional relationship between energy provider and user – limited essentially to one-directional contact via the annual bill – is giving way to more complex forms of interaction involving a wider range of actors. New services such as energy audits, price deals and appliance management are creating a more intensive relationship between energy utility and consumer, as well as engaging third parties – such as independent energy consultants or contractors – operating between utility and the end user (Guy et al. 1997; Guy and Marvin 1996). In the housing sector these emergent actor constellations are particularly apparent where substantial contractual commitments exist, as with larger housing associations or developers.

Contributing to this emergence of new actor groups and forms of interaction is the growing diffusion of small-scale energy technologies that engage a wider range of actors than under centralised systems of energy generation and distribution. The decision to install a solar collector or photovoltaic units is made by the house owner, not the utility; its opera-tion is similarly a matter for the owner, if necessary with professional assistance. What we can observe, therefore, is not only the emergence of new actors in the energy management of housing but also the redistribution of roles and responsibilities among a larger number of actor groups, a process often requiring the renegotiation of established positions. To take one example: in Berlin the local gas utility offers owners of apartments the installation and maintenance of block-type combined heat and power plants, relieving the owner of mainte-nance tasks, providing a more cost-efficient source of heating and electricity for tenants and developing a market niche for itself in an increasingly competitive local energy market.

The changing social organisation of energy provision and consumption requires a rethinking of the role of the state in promoting sustainable energy use. Local authorities need to consider, when designing their energy policies, what different options might mean in terms of the actor groups involved, their interests and lifestyles, their scope for action and their relations to other relevant groups.

## Technology dynamics

The emergence of small-scale environmental technologies that are economically viable has created multiple openings for energy-efficient housing. The traditional dominance of large-scale, centralised power generation and distribution systems is being gradually eroded – or, at least, complemented – by decentralised systems. Dunn (2000) argues that many OECD countries are today on the threshold of a new era of micro-power. This transition, he predicts, will necessarily be accompanied by the adaptation of the original market rules developed to protect the centralised monopoly structures of the past. Both in the United States and Europe new tariff and regulatory systems are being designed to accommodate small-scale, sustainable energy technologies, enabling market access for new entrepreneurs (Dunn 2000: 50–4). This is creating new opportunities for green housing projects to place greater emphasis on promoting innovative decentralised technologies at the micro-level of a building.

The problem with addressing only the end point of the energy distribution chain, however, is that technological diffusion of this type tends to create 'islands of sustainability' that relate little or not at all to the surrounding technical networks of power lines and gas pipes. Proponents of green housing rarely show any interest in the compatibility between their new technologies and existing technical systems. This may be accidental, but it often reflects a deliberate attempt to escape the influence of large-scale, centralised technical systems. Recent research suggests that incompatibility between small-scale technologies and existing infrastructure networks – whether of a physical, social or economic nature – limits the effectiveness of the small-scale technologies (Jensen 2001). The more successful cases of technology diffusion in buildings are those that respect the wider technological environment of infrastructure networks. If this entails some adaptation of original designs to meet local circumstances, it need not mean following the dominant logic of the existing system. Rather, it requires understanding this logic and identifying opportunities for integrating specific technologies within this context. Failure to respect the socio-economic as well as the technical rationales underpinning large-scale supply systems – as in the familiar conflict between district heating and solar heating in Denmark and elsewhere (Elle 2001) – can seriously limit the dissemination of new technologies. To summarise, we can observe how the contextual factor 'existing physical infrastructure' acts primarily as a limiting factor for technology diffusion but is itself undergoing transformation as the old mono-structural, centralised networks are complemented by new, smaller-scale technologies.

Interestingly, local authorities often regard these recent changes to the contexts of sustainable building as a threat to their traditional avenues of power. They point rightly to their loss of influence over municipal utilities following the liberalisation and privatisation of energy services. The emergence of new actors and actor constellations in the dissemination of sustainable energy technologies has, furthermore, made local energy policy and planning more complex. As a result, local authorities find it harder to implement their energy policies and to control processes of technology dissemination. The command and control logic of the past (including control over utilities) is being undermined.

On the other hand, changes in energy, housing and technology markets are creating new openings for local government involvement. To a greater or lesser extent the new market opportunities require increasingly detailed knowledge of a locality: its economic development, physical infrastructure, consumption patterns and spatial development plans. Energy utilities keen to maximise use of their existing technical networks for commercial reasons are showing a growing interest in the performance of individual sub-networks, differentiating between areas of high and low demand (Moss 2003). The introduction of small-scale power or heat generation plants within larger energy supply networks also requires a more spatially sensitive approach to infrastructure planning than in the past. Such examples illustrate the need for new forms of cooperation between energy service providers and local agencies responsible for spatial planning and economic development, through which local authorities could influence decisions relevant to energy in housing and other sectors.

*5.3 Photovoltaic panels integrated in the design of a Berlin office block.*

## Building on shifting urban concepts

What are the implications of these findings for those engaged in promoting sustainable buildings in urban environments? More specifically, how can windows of opportunity emerging in specific urban contexts be exploited to promote sustainable building and housing? The answer, we argue, lies in appreciating the (urban) politics of design and devising projects and programmes to reflect a broad range of institutional and non-institutional factors that could contribute to their success. Mainstreaming sustainable building requires building on, rather than merely operating within, a local political context.

What do proponents of sustainable building need to consider in order to draw maximum benefit from a particular urban setting? As a preliminary step, they need to identify what contextual factors have the potential to contribute to – or to work against – the overall objectives. Here it is important to appreciate that solutions may well lie in policy fields not readily associated with sustainable building. The aim should be to pinpoint drivers for change and areas of uncertainty where shifting contexts and their impacts are hard to predict. Secondly, on the basis of this broader perspective the relevant actor groups can be identified and their (potential) interest in sustainable building assessed. This requires looking beyond the immediate circle of 'experts' and prime movers to others less directly implicated but whose involvement may nevertheless be crucial. At the same time the strength of vested interests and the persistence of established rules and procedures need to be taken into consideration. It should then be possible, thirdly, to assess the range of possible options for embedding the strategic approach and instruments for promoting sustainable building in the local policy context. Here it is important to consider the process not as one of implementing a preconceived plan but of structuring choice and framing the decisions so as to derive maximum benefit from the identified contextual factors and actor interests. It should then be possible, fourthly, to map the possible trajectories, or pathways, for pursuing the policy objectives. The purpose of this step is not to limit the number of trajectories, prematurely excluding potentially useful options, but to think through the progress along each pathway, bearing in mind potential setbacks, critical junctures and inherent weaknesses. Finally, ways need to be developed for enrolling the relevant actors in the process, creating openings for greater access to decision-making. This requires special consideration of the wide range of actors involved and the different degrees of interest in a project.

To illustrate one possible point of entry to a process of this kind we draw on one example of a policy experiment in open, collaborative design in the Netherlands. In the city of Hoorn a workshop-based procedure was introduced in 1999–2000 to highlight opportunities for reducing $CO_2$ emissions at a planned urban development scheme at Bangert Oosterpolder (van der Waals and Vermeulen 2002; van Hoorn et al. 2001). An unusually wide range of local actors was involved in the workshop, ranging from the local authority, housing association and developer to representatives from the local building industry, the energy utility, the public transport company, non-governmental organisations and future residents. The intensive, open exchange resulted in a number of agreed targets and proposed measures for reducing $CO_2$ emissions that were considerably more ambitious than those identified by the group at the start of the workshop. These included building 'low-energy houses' with an energy performance coefficient of 0.75, capable of reducing $CO_2$ emissions by between 40 per cent and 60 per cent of the 1987 figures, and ensuring that 20 per cent of the energy used in the houses and buildings would come from renewable sources.

Subsequent to the workshop the level of commitment of the participants to the joint declaration of intent was evaluated on two separate occasions. After three months the majority remained committed to implementing the agreed actions. However, it subsequently transpired that many of the recommendations were not adequately pursued during the construction of the new locations. The workshop was not effectively bound into the formal planning procedure. In retrospect it would have been advantageous to have followed up the workshop with further activities, such as elaborating on the actions agreed, in a continuous consultation process, guaranteeing the continued involvement of all participants, discussing necessary adjustments in response to changing contexts of operation and monitoring progress, providing feedback to those involved.

## Conclusions

The purpose of this chapter has been to illustrate how a broader, contextually sensitive approach to promoting sustainable building – considering what we term the politics of design – can contribute to a better understanding of the range of contributory factors and how they might be harnessed to better effect. Our point of departure was the policy implementation gap over sustainable building, widely acknowledged by the principal proponents. Despite considerable advances in establishing sustainable building on the political agenda, the achievements have generally failed to live up to expectations.

Practical applications in many instances fall well behind policy objectives. Even in relatively favourable urban contexts with influential local authorities, as in the Netherlands, energy efficiency and sustainability principles have not become mainstreamed in the design and construction of buildings beyond the legal requirements.

Our analysis of policy implementation processes suggests that part of the problem lies in the way decision-makers perceive barriers to implementation and how this perception gives rise to particularly selective solutions. We have identified three common problem perceptions – inadequate regulations, funding and information – deemed to be restricting the take-up of sustainable technologies and practices in the building sector. In order to remove or, at least, lower these 'barriers' to more effective implementation, policy-makers seek to tighten the regulatory net, offset additional costs with targeted subsidies and improve knowledge dissemination of best practices and technological options. This strategy is pursued not only by national governments but also, as we have demonstrated in the case of the Netherlands, by local authorities keen to promote sustainable building practices.

The limited overall impact of this strategy of overcoming barriers indicates that other factors beyond the immediate incentives may play a significant role in framing the opportunities for sustainable building. We have argued here for the need to appreciate how efforts to promote sustainable building get caught up in a wide range of policy agendas and actor interests that may not, at first sight, seem directly relevant. A policy initiative to improve energy efficiency in a new housing settlement touches, for example, on urban transportation policy, local power and gas infrastructure systems and the state of the housing market. Behind each of these relevant issues lie actor interests that may, or may not, be sympathetic to a particular aspect of sustainable building. It is important to identify these forces and understand how they work in a specific urban context. This arena we have termed the (urban) politics of design in order to focus attention on the political nature of the process of enrolling actors and negotiating positions.

It is important to appreciate, in addition, that urban contexts are dynamic. The wide range of institutional and non-institutional factors relevant to sustainable building can change – sometimes radically – in response to external or internal pressures. We selected three examples to demonstrate how recent shifts in energy, housing and technology markets are creating new openings for energy-efficient technologies. To a greater or lesser extent the new market opportunities require increasingly detailed knowledge of a locality: its economic development, physical infrastructure, consumption patterns and spatial development plans. Energy utilities keen to maximise use of their existing technical networks for commercial reasons are showing a growing interest in the spatial distribution of demand. The introduction of small-scale power or heat generation plants within larger energy supply networks also requires a more spatially sensitive approach to infrastructure planning than in the past. Both examples illustrate the need for new forms of cooperation between energy service providers and local agencies responsible for spatial planning and economic development through which local authorities could influence energy-relevant decisions in housing and construction.

This leads us to a final observation on the future role of local authorities in stimulating greater actor interest and involvement in sustainable building. If local authorities were to initiate and coordinate a collaborative process of this kind they could gain some influence over local energy planning and management, compensating at least to some extent for that lost in recent years. The kind of influence exerted would, however, differ from the past practices, which were reliant on restrictive planning powers, distribution of subsidies and ownership of local utilities. Rather than intervening in decision-making processes to rectify a perceived problem with the help of more regulations, money or information, local authorities would be acting as facilitators of a mutual exchange of ideas between a wide range of actors relevant to the policy process. They would be framing the debate, seeking windows of opportunity, structuring the options and managing the process of selecting the ones most suitable to their particular urban context.

## Note

1  This chapter is based on a shorter paper published in *Built Environment* entitled 'Rethinking Local Housing and Energy Planning: The Importance of Contextual Dynamics' (Elle et al. 2002). We are grateful to the publisher for permission to publish brief excerpts of this paper here.

# 6

# Equal couples in equal houses
## Cultural perspectives on Swedish solar and bio-pellet heating design

*Annette Henning*

Knowing how to design a heating system that will work mechanically is quite different from knowing how to design a system that users perceive as responsive to their domestic practices and values. In this chapter, social anthropologist Henning argues that the challenge for designers involved in the development or marketing of green buildings with heating systems that are based on renewable sources of energy is to see things from the perspective of those who are supposed to live in these buildings. The chapter focuses on three culture-specific aspects of Swedish households and single-family houses: perceptions of house and home, of private and public space, and of male and female space. Through these three angles, some clues are given as to how design, performance and location of solar and bio-pellet heating systems could be made to resonate with predominant experiences, habits and ways of thinking among both men and women.

## Introduction

Scandinavia is inhabited by 'kitchen-people' (Gullestad 1984). They are a people who dwell in well-built, well-insulated houses with pitched roofs; a people who love spending time with family and friends in the kitchen, and who put a lot of effort into making their homes warm and cosy. They are a people who tend to emphasise similarity as a sign of equality and who, consequently, tend to de-emphasise the gender division of household responsibilities (Gullestad 1992).

Professionals engaged in the development and construction of sustainable buildings and renewable energy systems could contribute more actively to the reduction of $CO_2$ emissions, were they to take a wider interest in culture-specific ways of living. In a recent design handbook for solar combi-systems, Bergmann et al. (2003) focus to a large extent on the aesthetic taste of architects and argue for a better collaboration between engineers, architects and planners. My argument here, however, is that it is important not only for the implementation of solar heating that the design and planning of buildings are coordinated with research and development of solar collector components; even more important is to put the presumptive users considerably more into focus than is the case today. This means that cultural variation has to be taken into consideration and that it is not enough to consider climatic conditions or the traditional form of the house to understand how and why solar heating has been put into use at different times and in different parts of the world (Butti and Perlin 1980; Henning 2000). Questions also have to be asked concerning the priorities and everyday lives of specific groups of people.

This chapter provides an illustration taken from Swedish single-family houses and the households that inhabit them. I have chosen to focus on three culture-specific aspects:

perceptions of house and home, of private and public space, and of male and female space. From these three angles, I give some clues as to how the design, performance and location of solar and bio-pellet heating systems could be made resonant with predominant experiences, habits and ways of thinking among both men and women. The chapter also gives clues as to how the marketing, design and possible locations of such heating systems may have an impact on household installation decisions.

Part of the background to this chapter is the Swedish government's aim to reduce the amount of oil and electricity consumed for heating. Another part is the fact that a substantial number of single-family houses in Sweden have been constructed without a basement, boiler room or other space suitable for a house-based heating system. Wider use of solar and pellet heating systems is one way of reducing the amount of fossil fuels used for heating purposes, and the chapter deals with the question of how such systems could be fitted into single-family houses that do not have a basement or boiler room. (Pellets are small pieces of compressed bio-fuel, often sawdust, a byproduct of the forestry industry. The use of this fuel is increasing rapidly in Sweden. It is easy to transport and handle, and because of its effective combustion, emissions that are dangerous to health are reduced.)

## Methods and theoretical approach

I have drawn upon material from two research projects. In the first, I studied attempts to implement solar heating systems in various Swedish contexts. Conclusions and examples used here were collected during an extensive field study conducted over a period of four years (Henning 2000). In the second, a multi-disciplinary project, I focused on the conversion of Swedish single-family houses from electric resistance heating to heating systems that combine solar heating with the burning of bio-pellets (Henning 2001, 2003a, 2003b, 2004). My conclusions from this project are based on literature studies and supported by results from series of interviews with both husband and wife in ten households.

Social anthropologists have tended to focus either on the house as a local idiom for lineage-like groupings or on households and economy (Hugh-Jones 1996: 248). However, Carsten and Hugh-Jones (1996) have asked not only for a greater anthropological interest in how houses are built and used by ordinary people in their day-to-day affairs, but for a sharper focus on the building itself. The anthropological approach chosen here takes as one of its starting points culture-specific ways of using and perceiving various spaces of the dwelling. However, I also attempt to combine the cultural meaning of the Swedish house and home with culture-specific ways of perceiving solar collectors and pellet-fuelled stoves and boilers.

There can, of course, never be an objective opinion about the appearance of a heating system or part of such a system, for example a solar collector. When material, form and size are taken into account in anthropological research, this is always done with an awareness of there being no simple connections between, for example, the size of an artefact and its role as a cultural representation. It is even seen as one of the major tasks of social anthropology to convey to a broader public the crucial importance of cultural context for understanding the meaning of artefacts and habits. When Appadurai (1990) proclaimed his interest in the artefacts per se, his primary intention was to point out that a commodity is not in the first place a special kind of artefact, but an artefact in a certain situation. We find a similar approach to material objects in Thomas's book *Entangled Objects* (1991). With the possible exceptions of archaeological anthropology and anthropology of art, I believe Miller (1992) to be one of the few social anthropologists who, in recent years, has explicitly argued that the physical forms of artefacts definitely can have a complicated, albeit fully analysable, connection to the cultural context. Both these approaches are considered in this chapter.

## Background

Partly because of the long, cold winters, the buildings and housing sector is the single largest consumer of energy in Sweden. The heating of buildings has gone through much change since the beginning of the twentieth century. In the late 1940s, there was a great breakthrough in waterborne central heating, which was installed in the majority of new houses. District heating was introduced at the beginning of the 1950s, and heating delivered through waterborne district heating increased rapidly between 1965 and 1980 (SOU 1995: 140–2, para. 10f). The next big change began in the mid-1970s and accelerated in the early 1980s. This was the conversion to electric resistance heating, largely a result of a dramatic rise in oil prices, while at the same time the price for electricity and electric equipment was low. The change was also due to extensive construction of nuclear power plants in Sweden from 1970 onwards, leading to the largest nuclear power programme in the world, per capita (Summerton 1994).

In 1997, the Swedish government agreed on a strategy for adjusting the national energy systems (Energimyndigheten 2003b). This energy programme comprised two parts, one aimed at reducing $CO_2$ emissions, the other at replacing electricity produced by nuclear power. The use of oil-only boilers has been steadily decreasing for some time in single-family houses. Also district heating is increasingly using bio-fuel rather than oil.

At present, interest is increasing among house owners in replacing or combining electric heating or oil with bio-fuel, and at least 460,000 of the 1.5 million single-family houses in Sweden now have some kind of combined solution for heating (Energimyndigheten 2003a; Overland and Sandberg 2003). Yet, many single-family houses have little space in which a home-based heating system can easily be installed, as around 40 per cent of the houses are electrically heated, and more than 10 per cent are connected to the district heating system (Overland and Sandberg 2003; SCB 2002). Many of these houses were constructed for electric resistance radiators or a heat exchanger alone. They do not have a basement, boiler room or any other space in which a new heating system could easily be fitted.

## The 'equal' house

Most commonly, the Swedish single-family house displays an ethos of equality rather than one of individuality and hierarchy, and it does so in a double sense of the word. Very similar single-family houses may be seen throughout Sweden, from the very north down through 1650 kilometres to the south. Orders from building contractors to a few large firms making prefabricated houses, and the number of regulations concerning how one is allowed to build a house, are two explanations for this similarity. Another reason is the cold climate, which makes solid, well-insulated houses a necessity. The sometimes heavy snowfalls are also one reason why most single-family houses have pitched roofs, clad in roofing tiles, to allow the snow to slide off the roof and thus not weigh too heavily on it.

However, there is also in Sweden an ideology of equality that contributes to this similarity. All over the world houses are usually treated just as a commonplace setting for living (Henning 2000). They should not draw attention to themselves by appearing in some way wrong or inappropriate (Henning 2000; Miller 1992). This is true whether houses display wealth and power, as they tend to in south east Asia (Waterson 1996), or similarity and equality, as in Sweden (Henning 2000). Nevertheless, because of this ideology of equality, house owners in Sweden generally try to make sure that the appearance of their houses does not differ too much from neighbouring houses.

As the exterior of the house can be observed by every neighbour or person that passes by, it is the most public part of the home. The identity that it lends the household may get widely spread. Furthermore, the possibilities of controlling the ways in which others perceive the house and (thereby) its inhabitants, is primarily restricted by economic resources when choosing a house or by the ability to work upon the façade (Carsten and Hugh-Jones 1996; Waterson 1996). Therefore, the fact that a solar collector installed on top of the roof singles out a house from its neighbours has a bearing on interest in solar heating systems, as described below.

### Public and private space

Unlike, for instance, the Mediterranean region (Booth 1999; James and Kalisperis 1999; Lawrence 1987), in Scandinavia there is often a sharp boundary between outdoor and indoor activities. This is particularly obvious during the cold months of the year, when people do not leave their houses so much and when most activities are carried out indoors. People also meet more often at home, at work or through recreational courses (the popular 'study circles') than in restaurants, pubs or cafés (Blid 1989; Gullestad 1992; Sjögren 1993).

Much more than the outside of the house, the interior conveys detailed information about the house owner's age, gender, family history, taste, lifestyle and feeling for order (Blanton 1994). Primarily, the inside of the house is a meeting place for relatives and close friends (Birdwell-Pheasant and Lawrence-Zúniga 1999; Sjögren 1993). The front door marks a social boundary, and one that allows control over how the boundary operates. However, as Miller (2001a) and Clarke (2001) have also pointed out and demonstrated, there is no clear dichotomy between private indoor and public outdoor space. Gardens surrounding Swedish single-family houses are, for instance, considered very private, despite their often invisible boundaries (Björklund 1983; Sjögren 1993). And inside the house, certain zones are more public than others. It is in these more public indoor spaces that members of the household socialise with friends and relatives who do not belong to the household (Birdwell-Pheasant and Lawrence-Zúniga 1999; Gullestad 1992; Junkala 1998).

The hallway of the house works like a floodgate or checkpoint, where people may either be turned away or invited into the house (Gullestad 1992; Junkala 1998). It is therefore one of the most public zones of the interior and the first space you enter when coming through the front door. One of the women in the study by Lövgren and Ramberg (1997) commented that her apartment must have been planned by a man, since 'no woman would put the entrance directly into the living-room without a hallway in between'.

### The social multi-functional kitchen

Booth's description of how entire housing areas were reconstructed after a big earthquake in Sicily in 1968 clearly illustrates the importance of cultural awareness in

*6.1 The hallway of a Swedish house – a boundary between public and private space.*

architecture and the importance of architects and planners not taking too much for granted, even when building for people in the same country (Booth 1999). When reconstructing these housing areas in Sicily, planners from northern Italy made well-equipped but fairly small kitchens located at the back of the houses. They took for granted a desire for privacy as well as a general desire for 'modern' kitchens for people working mainly outside the home. However, a majority of the Sicilian women saw the new kitchens as both inconvenient and limiting, and many of them used a substantial part of the household income for changing their new home. The solution was to transform the garage into a traditional kitchen. Here, the women could again both work and socialise with neighbours and friends.

Similarly, studies from Sweden, Finland and Norway show how displeased people get when they are stuck with a small kitchen. A Scandinavian kitchen should be cosy, warm and pleasant, and it should be big enough to fit at least all the members of the household around the kitchen table (Gullestad 1992; Junkala 1998; Lövgren and Ramberg 1997). The kitchen is the primary dining area and the space in which household members have most of their meals (Lindqvist et al. 1980; Londos 1993; Lövgren and Ramberg 1997).

But the kitchen is also a public space of the house used by male and female household members of all ages, not merely when socialising with one another, but when socialising with friends and relatives as well. The kitchen and living room could be described as complementary social rooms that are used in a flexible way. If one couple comes to see another couple, for example, the women may go into the kitchen to be able to chat more intimately with each other, while the two men go into the living room. Furthermore, the complementary function of these rooms makes it possible to manipulate a situation and to choose how it should be defined. Thus, showing a guest into the living room could either be a way of honouring him or her or be a way of creating a distance (Gullestad 1992). These are some of the reasons why many people do not want an open-plan solution with no door and wall between living room and kitchen.

Kitchens may have several other functions besides cooking and socialising. A study from Finland shows that important papers such as household bills are kept in this space (Junkala 1998). And a Norwegian study shows that women even keep cosmetics, hair brushes and combs in the kitchen and describes how they sit there when putting on their make-up and arranging their hair (Gullestad 1992). A parallel could be drawn here between the modern Scandinavian kitchen and the many functions that used to take place around the open fire in houses in the countryside up to the end of the nineteenth century (Junkala 1998; Palmqvist 1999).

The Scandinavian kitchen, a social space with many functions, differs completely from the idea of the kitchen in other countries, for example the Indian kitchen. Unlike in Sweden, in many parts of India the kitchen is considered a private zone by many middle-class families. Guests are seldom invited into the kitchen, and in some cases even the entry of children or other members of the household may be restricted during cooking.

### The tidy, decorated living room

The living room has a greater importance than other parts of the house. It is often kept very clean and tidy, so that a visitor may understand that those who live in this house are orderly people. This space usually contains the best furniture, lamps and paintings. Cloths and ornaments decorate tables and other furniture, and flowers and patterned curtains decorate the windows. The room is almost never used for work, and children are seldom allowed to play in here. In this room you will find wedding photos and family portraits, along with other artefacts giving evidence of the lives and social positions of the household members (Gullestad 1992; Londos 1993). At night, household members gather in the living room to relax. Usually this means drinking coffee and watching TV or listening to music. Someone might read or possibly sew or knit.

As ever before, people in Scandinavia take an interest in making their houses into homes. Although most people no longer spend time on making clothes or jam, they spend more and more time, money and energy on decorating their homes. They do not just renovate their homes or rearrange their furniture when they move or when things get worn out; they do it for the sake of renewal in itself (Garvey 2001; Gullestad 1992; Wallensteen-Jaeger 1975). Or rather, they do it in order to express values, lifestyle, identity and social standing (Daun 1974; Junkala 1998; Miller 1992). And they do it to prove to themselves, their friends and their relatives that they are a 'real' family (Gullestad 1992).

## The equal couple

Scandinavian couples tend to see themselves as teams that share household tasks and responsibilities. They do, however, also tend to believe they follow that principle more than they actually do. The culture-specific and predominant ideals of sharing and equality defined as sameness imply that traditional gender roles can no longer be fully taken for granted. Household tasks are often negotiated, even though some tasks more than others have accumulated and retained symbolic value as belonging to one gender or the other (Gullestad 1992). People more or less consciously tend to perceive, side by side with the 'do it together' ideology, certain tasks as more male and others as more female (Gullestad 1984; Kugelberg 1999; Nordenmark 1997).

Home decoration and reconstruction projects are popular joint husband-and-wife tasks. In these projects, as in other parts of everyday life, men are expected to be handy and good at construction work and repairs, while women are seen as aesthetic and emotional specialists, having the main responsibility for the creation of a cosy and tasteful home. At the same time, home improvement projects are perfect ways of creating and maintaining the ideals of togetherness and equality, and for many women they provide a tangible symbol of the man's interest in the home and thus in her and the rest of the family (Gullestad 1984, 1992; Rosengren 1991).

### Male and female space

Certain zones of residential buildings are treated as more male or female than others (Ardener 1997). Even if men and women in Sweden normally do not themselves think of the home as anything but gender neutral, the woman is usually responsible not only for coordinating activities of the household members (Mårtensson et al. 1993) but for the overall planning of the interior of the house (Almqvist 1993; Friberg 1990; Gunnemark 1998; Jakobsen and Karlsson 1993). This responsibility does not merely mean taking the initiative as to when the vacuum cleaner should be used; it also means that she, at least to a certain degree, controls where objects and people should be located. Certain areas, however, are treated as male spaces in which few women would take an interest. The boiler room and the garage are examples of such male zones of the interior (Gullestad 1984, 1992; Gunnemark 1998).

A study by Rosengren (1991) describes how young Swedish couples build a house of their own. Here, the gender division of tasks is clearly associated with the inside and the outside of the house. Rosengren describes how both spouses were committed to a house building project in the initial stage and how they discussed it and made decisions together. Nevertheless, as the construction work continued, their different decision responsibilities became more and more detailed and separated. Craftsmanship was more his responsibility; aesthetic thinking more hers. The main dividing line was drawn between the outside of the house, which was his area, and the inside of the house, which was considered her sphere of interest and competence. Sometimes one spouse would have opinions on matters considered more the responsibility of the other, although in such cases he or she easily gave way to the other person if they did not agree. One of the most interesting findings of this study, I believe, is that the only time a husband and wife really argued was on issues where the outside and the inside met, such as the colour of the window frames or whether the area in front of the main entrance should have asphalt or stone. The meeting point of outside and inside was, thus, also the meeting point of the male and female spheres of interest, competence and decision.

### A male heater in a male space – the pellet burner success

To begin this section, here are some definitions. A stove is an enclosed space for combustion, designed for use in the living quarters; it may or may not have a water jacket connected to the hot water system of the house. A boiler is similar to a stove, typically larger and designed to be placed in a separate room; it usually contains a small hot water storage tank for domestic hot water and is always connected to the house's heating system (in Sweden generally a waterborne system). A burner combusts a fuel and is part of, or connected to, the boiler. A heat store is a hot water storage tank, typically 500 litres.

Despite the fact that the pellet stove was introduced in Sweden prior to the pellet burner, the burner has been a far greater success so far. Only a sixth of the pellet heating systems sold have been stoves. It seems clear that the introduction of the burner has been more successful in several respects. Firstly, single-family houses where pellet burners are installed normally have a basement and a boiler room. This means there are few problems with fitting the heating system into the house. Secondly, the boiler room is a male space, as handling a boiler with its burner and hot water store is primarily considered a male task. Women in Scandinavian households would rarely question the opinions of the men in such clearly traditionally male areas (Gullestad 1984; Londos 1993; Mårtensson and Pettersson 1998; Mårtensson et al. 1993). Thus, in several respects, the decision to purchase a pellet burner is a straightforward one and could be taken by the man alone.

Thirdly, no radical change to the previous heating system is needed. About half of the pellet burners have been installed in boilers previously run on oil, the other half in boilers previously run on logs of wood or heated by electricity (Energimagasinet 2003; Fiedler 2004). Also, there are few other special requirements for the design of the burner and boiler, as the boiler room is constructed solely for the purpose of housing the boiler. The burner, boiler and heat store do not have to be neat, small, clean and presentable to guests. The challenge lies rather in fitting boilers and hot water stores into single-family houses that lack basements and boiler rooms. A short discussion on technical requirements for smaller systems can be found in Kovacs and Weiss (2003).

### A male heater in a female space – conflicting interests

For single-family houses with no basement or boiler room, the laundry might be used for a boiler or hot water store connected to a solar heating system or waterborne pellet system. We might, however, expect to find conflicts of opinion within the household concerning the coexistence of boiler and washing machine in this location. Certain household tasks (such as laundry), and tasks perceived as technical (like handling a boiler), are more than many others marked as female and male, respectively (Nordenmark 1997; Londos 1993; Mårtensson and Pettersson 1998).

*6.2 Pellet burner in a boiler-room.*

In such cases the equipment would have to be substantially smaller, cleaner and neater in appearance than is standard in Sweden. Integrated pellet boilers with automatic cleaning, similar to products in the Austrian and German markets, would have to be used (Fiedler 2004). Even so, whether or not boilers and washing machines can share space depends not only on the design of the boiler but also on the ability of husband and wife to come to an agreement concerning their respective interests and responsibilities.

### A heater in a public space – cosy, tidy and aesthetically appealing

The hallway, the kitchen or the living room may all be possible locations for a pellet stove. Since the hallway is the first room a guest enters, the style and cleanliness of a stove or boiler in this space is of utmost importance for its acceptance. Most probably, the stove

*6.3 A pellet-burning stove in living room.*

would also have to be quite small to fit into this room. From a technical point of view, the hallway would make a perfect spot for a pellet stove, since it would then be located in a central position in the house with close connection to several rooms. Also, the hallway could be kept at a higher temperature than other rooms, as household members do not usually spend any length of time there. This way, the heat would be used and distributed in the most effective way (Persson and Nordlander 2003). Bedrooms, often located on the top floor, would be cooler, which is well in line with the wishes of most Swedish house owners (Gaunt 1985; Henning 2003b). These reasons for locating a heating system in the hallway do not apply, however, to a boiler or water-jacketed stove.

In the projects on which this chapter is based only a few interviews have so far been made with members of households with a stove, boiler or open fire in the kitchen, but these interviews show very pleased reactions to the location (Henning 2003b). Taking into account the multifunctionality of the kitchen and the desire for warmth and cosiness when people are gathered there, it should be possible to make pellet stoves or boilers attractive enough to be fitted in this space. The popularity of spending time and money on the reconstruction of kitchens and of interior design magazines featuring pictures of kitchens with an open fire should also contribute to this location being accepted for this location. Most probably it would be women who would mainly be interested in this location, even though gender responsibility for the kitchen varies with age and social class (Gullestad 1992; Junkala 1998), and female responsibility in the kitchen does not predominate in northern Europe to the extent that it does in many other parts of the world.

However, the living room might be the most obvious space in which to place a pellet stove, as this is where members of the household would prefer to gather around an open fire – if they had room and could afford one, that is. A pellet stove in the living room needs to be silent so that it can operate at the same time as a television or CD player. One of the women in my interview study (Henning 2003b) complained about the pecu-liarity of a small, green, attractive stove that 'sounds as if it belongs in a boiler room in the basement'. In their household they had to shut down the stove when they wished to watch television.

If pellet stoves are to be more widely accepted, the fact that many people try to keep their living rooms clean and tidy has to be taken into account. To decorate, furnish and arrange a home in the right style is a lot about placing the right objects in the right spots. Representations of dirt and cleanliness are very much about this sense of order: about keeping everything in the right place in a way that is culturally understood (Douglas and Isherwood 1988). This means that a sooty boiler would not be a problem in a boiler room, which is meant to accommodate exactly such an artefact. Such a boiler or stove in the kitchen, bathroom, laundry, hallway or living room, however, would be quite another thing.

The aesthetic consideration is even more important when a stove, or even a boiler, is located in the living room. Although one of the impediments in the introduction to the market of solar heating systems has been an extremely strong focus on installation costs (Henning 2000), I am sure that such concerns will not be the case with pellet stoves. One reason for my making such an assertive prediction is Swedish people's willingness to spend money on furniture and other artefacts that may improve the feeling of cosiness and a homelike atmosphere.

The design of a pellet stove has to achieve a balance between several requirements (Henning 2003b). Stoves need to be easy to handle and should not prevent their owners from keeping the living-rooms tidy. However, when contemplating ways in which to increase the popularity of pellet stoves, one should also consider the fact that a Swedish home is seen as attractive, comfortable and 'cosy' (*hemtrevligt, mysigt*) when it is perceived as 'warm' in both a literal and figurative sense. Ornaments, curtains, flowers and other decorations enhance the perception of the home as warm and welcoming, as do candles and the warmth from a stove or open fire. A decorative pellet stove could contribute to this perception of a 'warm' home. Most probably, it could also be made to resemble an open fire, which not only engages the senses but evokes positive memories of togetherness, childhood experiences and culture-specific dreams of a 'red cottage by a lake'.

## The insecure solar collector

I also begin this section with some definitions. A solar thermal system for the single-family house in Sweden consists of a solar collector, a heat store in the form of an insulated tank filled with water, and connecting pipes, a pump and a heat exchanger. In Sweden, small systems produce domestic hot water from May through to September. More common, however, are the larger combi-systems, which also provide hot water to the house heating system from early spring to late autumn. An auxiliary heat source is needed for periods of little or no sunshine.

In Greece and the United States, solar collectors are often mounted on stands and placed on top of flat roofs. In Sweden, they have instead become more and more integrated into the roofs, thus becoming more fully part of the buildings. One of the most characteristic features of Swedish solar heating systems for individual homes is the extreme visibility of the collectors. This visibility is partly due to the importance put on the look of the building, as described earlier, but also to the unfamiliarity of solar collector-covered roofs.

To many people it is not clear how the solar collector should be classed (Henning 2000). It is obviously a part of the house and most often a part of the roof, but it is more noticeable than the chimney, for example, in spite of its less prominent form. The chimney just sits there like it always has; house owners do not need to wonder about what it might look like. With the solar collector, things are different. People seem to

*6.4 A solar collector on a typical single-family Swedish house.*

wonder how this artefact really appears: if it is all right to have it on their house, and what their friends and neighbours will say. The glass of the collector makes it shiny like a window. It is, however, much bigger than a skylight or a dormer window, and it does not have a little roof above it as the dormer window usually does. Neither, with its flat shiny surface, does it look like roofing tiles.

However, to a large extent the visibility of the solar collector is a result of the ambiguous way in which it has been perceived and discussed in Sweden since it was first introduced in the 1970s (Henning 2000). On the one hand, the solar collector in Sweden is a strong positive symbol for an environmentally benign future. On the other hand, there is a lingering insecurity concerning its present feasibility. One of the reasons for this ambiguous position is the role solar energy technologies played in the discourse surrounding the nuclear power referendum in 1980. This was a time when heated debates and conflicts concerning national energy policy tended to split families and friends all over Sweden.

Today, solar heating systems are increasingly treated in less ambivalent ways, as issues of climate change and $CO_2$ emissions gain legitimacy, and as roof-integrated solar collectors gradually become a more common sight. Still, implicit conflicts in opinions and differences in how these artefacts are culturally understood tend to leave potential owners of solar collectors uncertain as to how they will be looked on by others were they to decide to install one (Henning 2000). There is also an insufficient social structure of producers, installers and promoters with enough economic resources to change this situation and fully carry through the process of introduction and implementation (Edquist and Edqvist 1980; Henning 2000; Shove 2003).

Not just solar collectors but their users as well are perceived differently in different cultural contexts, and cultural variation does not stop at the national border but extends down to the habits, experiences and modes of thought that individuals share to a larger or smaller extent with certain others (Henning 2000). In some places and situations, people can feel pretty certain of what their closest neighbours and friends will think of them, while in other places people may show a great concern and uncertainty about how others will react. In a place such as Orust (the third largest Swedish island), which has become an area dense in solar collectors, people no longer stand out as different or signal anything special if they put collectors on their roofs. But in a village with only one installation, people might start talking: 'He has always been a little odd. He has all that stuff in his barn, so whenever someone in the village needs a special screw or something they go to him. So when he put that solar collector on his roof, that was so typical!' (Henning 2000).

## Solar design, marketing and cultural values

As with all artefacts, the ways in which solar collectors are perceived differ across the world. They may lend prestige, as in Poland or Central America. They may be seen as ugly, as in southern Italy. Or they may just be seen as functional, as in Greece. In Sweden, the combination of conflicts surrounding the initial introduction of solar heating, the extremely public location on the roof and the importance put on house and home and on having an 'equal house', in the double sense of the word, has produced an uncertainty about solar collectors.

So, which design strategy would be best suited to the purpose of marketing solar collectors in the Swedish situation of uncertainty and insecurity? Perhaps it would be best to pay attention to concerns about what other people might think about how collectors look and to strive to make this a less salient factor? Or perhaps a better strategy would be to try to subvert the insecurity by making solar collectors very conspicuous? Or maybe the strategy should be based on the fact that solar collectors are very differently perceived in different neighbourhoods and among different groups of people? Such a strategy would, I presume, lead to a much greater variety in solar collector designs than we see in Sweden today.

My personal favourite, however, is the idea of making better use of the fact that solar collectors, through innovative design thinking, can be made into really good advertisements for combined pellet and solar heating systems. The promotion of such combined heating systems would also be a perfect way of avoiding a difficult pedagogic problem in the marketing of solar heating systems in Sweden, a problem actually caused by the experience people have of their climate. To produce hot water, solar collectors primarily need a clear sky, not a warm outdoor temperature. This is the reason why they are able to produce heat in the autumn and the spring, when there is a great need for heating Swedish houses. However, men and women who grew up in Sweden link sunshine with warm summers. It is hard for them to understand that indoor heat can be produced by sunshine when, outside, cold northerly winds sweep over their houses (Henning 2000).

## Motives, responsibilities and decision-making

Male or female motives, responsibilities and interests connected with different heating systems vary with (among other things) the space in which the system is placed. The location of the heating system also influences household negotiations in deciding on a change of heating system.

We have seen that in couples in Swedish households the woman would rarely question the opinions of the man in such clearly traditionally male areas as the boiler room and the task of handling a boiler with its burner and hot water store. Any man interested in installing a pellet stove in a hallway, kitchen or living room, on the other hand, would most probably have to come to an agreement with his wife about his wishes, as the general understanding is that it is the woman who has the main interest and responsibility for creating a pleasant home in the right style.

However, while in the case of the stove the man would have to come to an agreement with his wife, the gender situation is reversed in the case of solar heating systems. Women who wish to have a system installed in their home tend to act indirectly through their husbands (Henning 2000). One explanation of why they do not themselves act in a more direct way can be found in the dominant and, of course, culture-specific gender role division of household responsibilities and interests. Despite the fact that many women value solar heating systems highly, not merely for the hot water they provide but for their ability to reduce $CO_2$ emissions, for the most part they do not have the main responsibility for construction work or for the outside of the house. These are the husbands' responsibilities. A household decision on a solar heating installation depends either on the wishes of the man or on the woman's ability to persuade her husband (Henning 2000).

## Conclusions

Important in the background of writing this chapter was the Swedish government's aim to reduce $CO_2$ emissions produced through the heating of residential buildings. One way of realising these aims would be to cut down on the burning of fossil fuels (which increases the production of $CO_2$ overall) through wider use of efficient stoves and boilers for bio-fuel combustion (which adds no more $CO_2$ emissions to the atmosphere than if the plants or trees had just decomposed) (Fryk 1999). Another way of realising the aim would be to cut down on the use of any fuel through increasing the proportion of direct use of solar energy, a solution that seems increasingly necessary for a sustainable global energy future (Weiss 2003).

Culture is not inherent nor given once and for all. Even so, the primary task for social scientists engaged in energy research should not be to persuade individuals to change their habits in order to accept renewable energies and sustainable architecture (as has often been the case) but rather should be to help making such artefacts resonant with the habits and interests of both men and women (Carlsson-Kanyama and Lindén 2002; Henning 2003b; Nordell 2003; Shove 2003; Wilhite 2000).

For planners, architects, building contractors, engineers, designers or salesmen, the challenge is to see things from the perspective of those household members who use the buildings or heating systems. Knowing how to design a heating system that will work is quite different from knowing how to design or market a system that users can perceive as responding to their domestic practices and values.

The importance of socialising in a large and cosy kitchen and the importance of decorating the home so that it is experienced as warm and welcoming are only two examples of how various spaces of a dwelling are culturally perceived and used in this part of the world. When combining culture-specific ways of using and thinking of various spaces of the building with the ways in which certain heating systems are handled and looked on, we may get some clues as to what should be expected of the appearance, performance and marketing of such technologies. Thus, a 'male' boiler located in a 'female' laundry, a dusty but 'cosy' (*mysig*) stove located in a tidy, decorated living room and an 'insecure' solar collector located on the publicly visible roof tell us something about the kind of interest or lack of interest men and women in Swedish households have in these heating systems.

One of my arguments has been that cultural variation in people's perception of heating systems that are based on renewable energies could inspire design thinking. Cultural analysis is, I argue, an important way for architects, engineers, designers and others involved in the development of sustainable buildings and heating systems based on renewable energies to be actively involved in setting the course towards a sustainable energy future.

# Part C
# Competing design

# 7

# Safe houses and green architecture

## Reflections on the lessons of the chemically sensitive[1]

*Jim Wasley*

Multiple chemical sensitivity (MCS) is a controversial condition involving heightened sensitivities by individuals to chemicals and allergens. According to those who suffer from this condition, retreating to 'safe' environments is the best available therapy. 'Safe' environments for victims of MCS have been offered by other observers as exemplars of 'green architecture'. They have, however, also been parodied to ridicule environmental concern as the romantic dream of anti-urbanites who imagine themselves to be contaminated by modern industrial life and cured by the house-as-healer. Reflecting on his study of dwellings built by people with MCS in the United States and Canada, Wasley seeks to clarify the relationship of these unique constructions to ecologically minded architecture as a whole. He argues that 'safe' houses are not necessarily 'green', and conversely that 'green' houses are not necessarily 'safe'. In this study of competing discourses Wasley argues that the dialogue between 'safe' and 'green' points not towards the eventual domination of one, but towards their synthesis.

## Introduction

Multiple chemical sensitivity (MCS) is a controversial medical syndrome involving a heightened sensitivity to chemicals now commonly found in the built environment, as well as to allergens such as natural terpenes, pollens and moulds. Although MCS is experienced as a range of debilitating physical ailments, there is no clearly established medical explanation of the body's reactions to what are commonly considered harmless doses of environmental toxins. There is also no single treatment that can restore a victim's health, leaving isolation from potential irritants as the best available therapy. The resulting 'safe' dwellings offer compelling studies in the design of contaminant-free, healthful environments.

'Green architecture' has come to represent the holistic concern for a broad array of environmental topics in architecture, from energy efficiency and indoor air quality to resource conservation and land use planning, and from an accounting for the environmental impacts of raw materials acquisition through to the life of a building and beyond. Broadly stated, 'green architecture' seeks to design for the health of both the individual and the planet. This rubric suggests the close identification of 'safe' and 'green' agendas.

As depicted with painful ambiguity in the film *Safe*, MCS has also become a lightning rod eliciting strong emotions on both sides of the environmental debate. For those convinced of the dangers of our industrial culture, MCS is proof of its insidious effects. For those ridiculing environmental concern, belief in MCS is proof of the irrationality of such fears.

This highly charged situation is reflected in public discussion of MSC dwellings and the general lessons that they might offer. Ecologically oriented design books have often used 'safe haven' environments as exemplars of 'green' architecture, blending their description into general discussions of health and aesthetic concerns. Such narratives tend to play down the specificity of MCS dwellings and even conflate them with environments unacceptable to chemically sensitive individuals.[2] Mass media characterisations of MCS dwellings, such as the idiosyncratic geodesic dome on the television sitcom *Northern Exposure* or stock depictions of trailer homes lined with tin foil, dwell only on their novelty. This sensationalism generally obscures the similarities between designs responding to MCS and the broader front of 'green' design.

Seeking to clarify the relationship between the extreme case solutions of the chemically sensitive and the 'green' movement in general, in the summer of 1994 the author documented eleven MCS dwellings scattered across the United States and Canada. Reflecting on these structures through the eyes of those who built and inhabit them leads to a more informed discussion of their potential as exemplars of 'green' or 'sustainable' design. In holding a mirror up to both 'safe' and 'green' philosophies, the case studies point out limitations and contradictions in the design programmes of both camps. Finally, they offer strategies to overcome such conflicts and inconsistencies. All of this suggests that 'safe' and 'green' concerns should not be confused but can and should be reconciled.[3]

## Background

As a medical disorder, multiple chemical sensitivity (also known as 'environmental hypersensitivity', 'environmental illness' or EI and other names specific to different medical theories) is a poorly understood condition in which low-level exposures to a wide variety of chemical compounds cause extraordinary symptoms throughout the body, such as headaches, nausea, disorientation, lack of muscle control, mood disorders and so on. Often, but not always, these health problems can be traced to specific exposure events. Rather than diminishing over time, however, symptoms advance and recede unpredictably, and reactions tend to spread to everyday exposures such as foods, caffeine and alcoholic beverages, items that may at one time have been quite well tolerated by the affected individual. In the extreme, MCS can be physically debilitating.

The emergence of MCS is circumstantially linked to the explosive rise in the use of chemicals and synthetic materials in the environment since the Second World War. Among respondents to one 1989 survey of 6,800 self-described 'chemically sensitive' individuals, roughly half specifically cited exposure to pesticides as the initiating cause of their illness. Other recognisable groups of people with MCS include industrial workers, residents of chemically contaminated communities and, more recently, Gulf War veterans and women with medical complaints caused by silicone breast implants (Miller and Ashford 2001).

MCS is also strongly associated with the widespread construction of tightly sealed and poorly ventilated houses and office buildings after the 1973 energy crisis. These environments had the effect of amplifying the health impacts of the synthetic products with which they were constructed, as well as creating the potential for severe mould exposure problems. In this way, MCS is associated with sick building syndrome (SBS). SBS differs from MSC, however, in being a clearly understood range of conditions in which cause and effect are closely related, and where symptoms ease when the source of exposure is removed (Ashford and Miller 1998).

Though the National Academy of Sciences has estimated that 15 per cent of the population may experience some sort of 'increased allergic sensitivity' to chemicals, the wide range of potential causes and expressions of the illness has made the diagnosis of MCS itself exceedingly controversial (Ashford and Miller 1998: 26). The mainstream medical establishment in the United States does not recognise MCS as a valid diag-nosis, and medical models for how the brain and body could be affected in so many different ways by such low levels of exposure are only recently beginning to be seriously considered.[4] Research that has been difficult to fund in the past is now being driven by the needs of those suffering from Gulf War syndrome and by the United States govern-ment's interest in understanding chemical exposures generated by the war on terrorism. Reflecting a host of differences both cultural and institutional, the medical communities of Canada, Great Britain and several European countries do recognise MCS, and the Japanese government has recently funded the construction of several clinical research facilities aimed at understanding and treating MCS (Kanke 2003).

In the absence of medical consensus on the issue, the premise of this case study research mirrors the logic often articulated by design professionals working with chemically sensitive clients. The potentials for adverse health effects from toxins such as formaldehyde, pesticides and mould are well documented in both the medical and architectural literature, and many indoor air quality consultants have in fact trained their sense of smell to detect these contaminants. It is thus reasonable to grant that a heightened sensitisation to these irritants is possible, or at minimum that a heightened awareness of them is possible. Once we grant a heightened awareness, it is reasonable to respect the commitment with which these people pursue the task of creating toxin-free environments for themselves. The research shows that MCS dwellings do, in fact, both build on and surpass widely accepted 'best practice' standards for avoiding indoor air quality problems.

The research has involved documenting the physical details of various exemplary dwellings and interviewing their occupants, builders and architects. Nine houses and two apartment buildings have been catalogued, representing several different climates and types of client. The results are subjective in so far as they are based on the experi-ences of those involved. In most cases these dwellings have given their occupants distinct relief from their symptoms, and many occupants have over time recovered a measure of health. All spoke of the sanctuaries they had constructed as allowing them to rebuild their lives, even if their sensitivities remained. Given a living space that was not constantly making them feel sick, they were free to test their reactions to other potential triggers and to retreat from situations that they found problematic.

## An overview of 'safe' design

As with 'green' design, 'safe' design demands a rethinking of architecture from the ground up. This critique bears on everything from site selection and site response to space adjacencies, materials selection, envelope design, mechanical, electrical and plumbing systems design and the supervision of the construction process. Many of these topics are highly climate dependent and so present a range of strategies, depending on location.

The elimination of suspected irritants is the clear priority of all of the documented structures, making the selection of building materials a central issue. Potential irritants can be direct attributes of a material such as the formaldehyde-based glue found in manufactured wood products, secondary attributes such as the biocidal additives that extend the shelf life of latex paints or even unintended attributes such as the residue of

7.1 *The porch of the Pitman house, looking towards the combined kitchen and living cabin.*

machine oil on metal. As mentioned previously, pesticides are seen as posing the greatest possible threat, and materials that contain pesticides or biocides are avoided, both inside the dwelling and in the landscape. Likewise, materials that might support biological activity are avoided, one of several reasons that carpeting was completely absent from the dwellings documented. Materials are also chosen on the basis of maintenance, so that the dwelling can be maintained without the use of toxic household products. Finally, the adhesives, sealants, solvents and lubricants that typically facilitate the process of construction are often problematic, and supervision to ensure that such things are not unthinkingly introduced is of primary importance.

Where potentially toxic materials cannot be eliminated, strategies of isolation and encapsulation come to the fore. The desire to avoid contamination of the job site also often leads to an emphasis on prefabrication, either of components or entire structures.

An acute awareness of air quality and air movement, both within spaces and in construction assemblies, makes ventilation the complementary strategy to source control. Responses vary greatly, depending on the climate, but access to unpolluted air and the ability to thoroughly flush the interior are constants. The dwellings also offer examples of novel and intelligent space planning related to ventilation, tending towards the extremes of either compartmentalisation or openness.

Four case studies presented here offer specific examples of these design issues. The Pitman house presents an architecturally compelling vision of 'safe' space planning. The Oetzel house exemplifies 'safe' materials selection. Barrhaven Community Housing for the Environmentally Hypersensitive highlights 'safe' construction practices, while the Nelms house makes the case for 'safe' mechanical ventilation. The Pitman and Oetzel houses reflect a hot and humid setting, while Barrhaven and the Nelms house reflect the demands of a cold climate.[5]

The Pitman residence is a country home expressive of its site and climate in a way that reflects as much on the sensibilities of its owners as it does on the requirements for

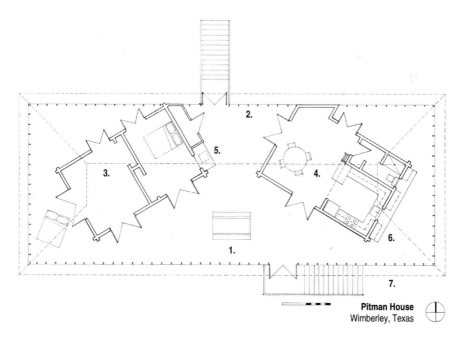

Pitman House
Wimberley, Texas

*7.2 Pitman house (plan): 1. screened porch; 2. northern screen wall between cabins fitted with storm windows in winter to deflect northern winds; 3. sleeping cabin; 4. living and kitchen cabin; 5. coat closet with dehumidifier, television cabinet; 6. household storage, including storage of potentially irritating hobby supplies; 7. path to garage.*

creating a clean air environment. It is notable for the simplicity of its palette of materials and for its calculated elimination of pesticides. Above all, its design offers a dramatic example of how spatial relationships can be manipulated to enhance indoor air quality.

The Pitman family's biography of health, illness and gradual recovery can stand for the experiences of most of the people interviewed. Sue Pitman and her two children first began to have health problems in 1977, the winter after they moved into a new and tightly sealed suburban house in the Lake Bluff area of Chicago. A second house in the same area proved better, but the neighbourhood's heavy use of lawn pesticides also began to appear connected to the family's health problems. In 1984 Sue's husband's work shifted to Austin, Texas, and the family built the first of two 'healthy' homes in Wimberley (Figs 7.1 and 7.2). Both Sue's health and the health of her children had improved dramatically by the time that we met in 1994.

The plan of this second, larger home is a contemporary interpretation of the 'dog-trot' log cabin that is vernacular to this part of Texas. Two log cabins each of two levels sit within a 28 foot by 84 foot screened porch enclosure. One cabin houses only the sleeping rooms. The other contains the living, dining and study areas, as well as the kitchen and bathroom. The entire structure is raised eight feet above the ground, exposing the posts and footings for easy termite inspection. The special treatment of the bedroom as an isolated space appears repeatedly in MCS houses; in the case of the Pitman house the plan was described more specifically in terms of isolating the kitchen and bathroom to control potential mould sources.

The house is oriented east–west, with the primary entry and porch facing the south, serving both to catch the sun in the winter and, more importantly, to face the prevailing southern breeze in the summer. The effect of the breeze is amplified by the inflection of the two cabins, which together create a venturi that funnels the breeze through the centre of the house. Corners of the cabins touch the northern wall, creating a smaller opening to the north that can be effectively closed off in the winter with storm windows. Northern winter winds are in this way directed around the house rather than through it, making the porch habitable year round.

The life of the house happens on the porch, where most of the storage space is also found. In one isolated and breezy corner is a cabinet with the teenage son's model airplane supplies, along with cleaning supplies. At the other end of the house, the master bed rolls out of the bedroom and onto the porch when the weather permits. Shaker pegs decorate much of the remaining wall space, allowing clothes and other items to be aired out before entering the cabins.

The final key to the spare lifestyle that the house promotes is a detached garage and laundry with a large storage room above, isolated from the offgassing of the automobiles through its construction and venting. The detached storage room was especially important to Sue, because it allowed her to remove herself from most of her belongings without throwing them away, making the process of seeking a safe haven less emotionally draining. As the family's health has improved, personal items have one by one been brought out of storage and into the primary living space.

The Oetzel house (Fig. 7.3) is a single-storey wood-frame structure, located on a large and isolated lot outside Wimberley. It is characterised by its siting, landscaping to minimise insect habitats, energy-efficient design and, most importantly, by its rigorous materials palette.

Mary Oetzel is an architectural consultant on issues of indoor air quality and designing for chemical sensitivities. Oetzel's approach in both her own house and in her

*7.3 Exterior of Oetzel house.*

consulting is to adapt conventional plans through substitution of materials and attention to the construction process, rather than through novel design. Her own house is made visually distinctive by its unfinished cement plaster walls, but otherwise its special features are invisible to the casual observer. Where the Pitmans enjoy the uniqueness of their house, Mary's house strives to create a place of refuge without calling attention to a condition that is by its nature socially isolating.[6]

The ceramic tile floors in this slab-on-grade house are set in the traditional manner in additive-free Portland cement and sand. Beneath the stone-clad walls, the exterior sheathing is a formaldehyde-free compressed fibreglass sheathing board. Fibreglass batts are isolated from the interior by carefully taping their foil facing to create a vapour barrier. All interior walls and ceilings are finished with traditional cement plaster containing no chemical additives. Most of the walls are otherwise unfinished. As a test, Oetzel painted her office with oil-based enamel, which is free of the biocides of latex paint. Ultimately she found this to be an acceptable finish, though complete curing took over a year and consequently she no longer recommends it. In contrast, the utility and bathrooms are painted with a custom-manufactured preservative-free latex paint. Kitchen countertops are of tiles, wet cured in a deep grout bed as opposed to a latex-based thinset. The cabinetry is solid oak, built without back panels rather than the typical particleboard.

Mary Oetzel's considerable experience as a consultant provides many illustrations of how difficult choosing materials can be. One of the products that she counsels against using is exterior latex caulk, since the latex contains mildewcides. At the same time, certain clients have had such allergic reactions to mildew that she has found the exterior use of mildewcides at times advisable. The compromise that she has adopted is to recommend their use as the situation demands it, but only for areas remote from close contact and never on a porch or patio. This degree of nuance is typical of MCS materials palettes.

7.4 *Barrhaven Community Housing for the Environmentally Hypersensitive. Exterior view across the 'pesticide free' municipal park.*

7.5 *Barrhaven roofing being cleaned before installation.*

The Barrhaven Community Housing project (Figs 7.4 and 7.5) is by far the most innovative structure documented here – a reflection on the problem-solving orientation of its architect, Philip Sharp. A part of a larger social housing project sponsored by the Barrhaven United Church, the seven-unit structure is characterised by simplification to offset the cost of higher standards of materials, by the elimination of all possible construction cavities in order to design away potential habitat for mould and by a design that allows complete access behind all major appliances and easy demountability of the duct system for periodic cleaning. The approach is in large measure a response to the dilemma of designing for future residents whose specific sensitivities are unknown.

The degree of caution exercised in the design was also reflected in the construction process. Drerup Armstrong Ltd was brought in to act as the contractor for this specific structure, on the strength of Oliver Drerup's successful history with Ottawa's chemically sensitive community. Drerup employed a small crew that was fully aware of the health-related objectives of the project and enjoyed the enforced standards of care and craftsmanship required. Letters of commitment to these standards were also secured from each subcontractor.

The primary structure of the building is exposed to the interior, necessitating high levels of workmanship and special procedures of fabrication and installation. Concrete floors were polished with a terrazzo grinder to produce an elegant, low-cost finish. Exposed concrete masonry unit walls with cores grouted full serve as both structure and interior finish material. All other interior partitions are plank walls of solid basswood. With no hidden cavities anywhere in the construction, the plumbing, ductwork and electrical wiring are fully exposed.

Both the precast planks and concrete blocks required special additive-free concrete mixes, and in the case of the planks the substitution of health soaps for diesel fuel as a form-release agent. The use of plant-based soap was embraced by the precast workers, who enjoyed working without the permeating odour of diesel fuel, but it did allow the steel forms to rust and stain the floor planks. This in turn meant that the planks had to be painted in the field, counter to the intention of eliminating all such applied surface treatments.

The site was kept exceedingly clean throughout construction and every effort was made to prevent inadvertent contamination of the interior. No cleaning fluids, lubricants or gasoline containers were allowed in the structure. All rest breaks were taken off site. Smoking was not allowed on site. Exhaust fumes from delivery trucks and from the terrazzo grinder were ducted away from the structure. Vehicles were not allowed to idle near the site. Storage was handled carefully, with all potentially problematic substances being stored off site. A large container of soap was always on hand, and people washed oil off their hands and tools constantly. Metal roofing was washed before installation. Standard galvanised ductwork was washed with a dilute solution of muriatic acid, with the pleasant consequence of giving the metal a dull patina. Even the finish screws were washed in bulk to remove residual machine oil.

Even with such standards of care, the construction process is fraught with potential for unintended contamination. A hydraulic hose on the precast plank hoist burst as the second floor was being erected. Fortunately, the thick red fluid sprayed away from the structure, but the previously polished first floor slab was reground rather than simply cleaned and a fluid-soaked pallet of concrete blocks and several yards of topsoil had to be disposed of. From that time on tarpaulins were hung between all large machinery and the structure.

The Nelms house is an elegant single-family house on a remote wooded lot approximately an hour from Ottawa, Ontario (Fig. 7.6). It is characterised by its siting, passive solar design, super-insulated construction, elegant materials palette and its highly developed mechanical ventilation. The Nelms house offers a counterpoint to Barrhaven in the same way that the Oetzel house offers a counterpoint to the Pitman house. High standards of indoor air quality are achieved without altering the home's traditional aesthetics. Though the house has facilitated Catherine Nelms' recovery from a state of extreme ill health, it was designed so that it would retain its resale value in a conventional market.

The Nelms credited the energy-conserving mechanical system with making the house a successful healing environment. The ability to continually flush the house with fresh air, even in the middle of winter, seemed to them to be central to Catherine's recovery.

Built in 1983, the house's ventilation system (Fig. 7.7) is an early experiment in the types of ducted fresh air systems with heat recovery ventilators seen in all of the colder climate houses documented. It owes this experimental quality to Oliver Drerup, the contractor for this house as well as for Barrhaven. Drerup is a nationally known spokesperson for the Canadian government's 'R–2000 program', which seeks to educate the general population about energy-efficient construction practices. This house was Drerup's first for an environmentally hypersensitive client, coming ten years before Barrhaven.

The fresh air system is separate from the heating system, an arrangement that eliminates the potential for 'fried dust' generation, or the recirculation of combustion products from particles in the return air stream. Space heating is provided by an electric boiler and fin tube radiation. Ventilation air is provided independently and was designed to provide high volumes of fresh air with no recirculation. The incoming air is brought into the house through a dormer on the roof, away from any potential local

*7.6 Exterior of the Nelms house.*

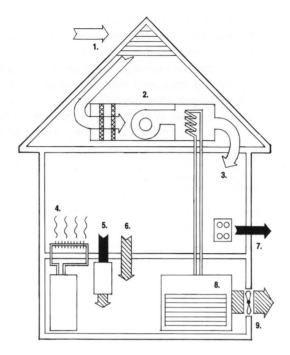

*7.7 Mechanical ventilation systems in the Nelms house: 1. ducted fresh air intake; 2. dual flow (balanced) ventilation system, including two passive electrostatic filters, blower motor mounted outside of air stream, glycol loop heat transfer coil; 3. tempered air supply to all rooms; 4. space heat provided by electric boiler and hydronic fin-tube radiation; 5. central vacuum system vented to mechanical room; 6. house exhaust ducted from bathrooms, kitchen, laundry and closets; 7. downdraft cooker top independently exhausted to exterior; 8. customised heat pump with integrated glycol loop heat recovery; 9. continual exhaust through heat recovery unit maintains negative pressure of the mechanical room, and centrally located fan for all ducted exhaust minimises fan noise. (Adapted from Drerup et al. 1990.)*

contamination. It passes by two electrostatic filters and over a fan coil unit, where it is heated by a glycol loop drawing heat via a heat pump from the house exhaust. The fan driving this supply is mounted outside of the air stream, isolating the incoming air from odours generated by the fan's electric motor.

Tempered fresh air is distributed to every room in the house, and stale air is collected from the baths, clothes closets and laundry and from behind the refrigerator and oven. This stale air is ducted into the mechanical room, where it is exhausted by a single fan pulling all exhaust air through the glycol heat recovery loop. The mechanical room serves as the exhaust plenum for the central vacuum system as well. This allows for some heat recovery from the vacuum exhaust while solving the pressure-balancing problems associated with appliances that extract air from the house, leaving only the range hood independently exhausted. The mechanical room is kept at a constant negative pressure regardless of the amount of air being dumped into it, keeping contaminants from being drawn back into the house. The single large fan at the exit point works to keep the house as quiet as possible and ensures that fan-generated contaminants leave the building.

The heat recovery system has been tinkered with several times over the years as both Catherine's health and the available technology have improved. Most recently, the levels of fresh air supplied have been scaled back, the glycol loop has been disconnected and a commercially available air-to-air heat exchanger installed. In each subsequent design, the underlying logic of providing dedicated exhaust, separating the airstream from potential in-line contaminants and economically providing fresh air, has been upheld. At the same time, the only feature of the current heat exchanger that sets it apart as distinctively 'safe' is the upgrade to a stainless steel core, eliminating the potential for offgassing from the less expensive plastic variety.

## Characterising the architecture of MCS

As seen in these examples, 'safe' houses are excellent case studies of the technical issues of creating healthful environments, offering broadly applicable lessons on a variety of topics. Grounded by such strict limitations, they also often achieve a compelling poetic presence that makes them appealing as exemplars and teaching tools.

At the same time, there are strong reasons to differentiate this housing from the bulk of 'green' design and to carefully consider its use in promoting 'green' architecture. A holistic concern for the environment is simply not the driving issue behind MCS design, even if people with MCS often identify themselves as environmentalists. MCS environments respond first and foremost to immediate health concerns rather than ecological concerns.[7]

Conversely, while one can argue that the lessons of dealing with MCS are broadly applicable, the case studies illustrate that the problems of designing for MCS can be specific and demanding. Being a 'green' architect may be a good starting point for understanding the needs of a chemically sensitive client, but it does not guarantee a positive outcome. 'Safe' is not necessarily 'green', and 'green' is not necessarily 'safe'.

### *'Safe' is not necessarily 'green'*

Two aspects of the case study dwellings raise significant environmental questions if they are to be identified with 'green' design, especially as they play into desires that the 'green' movement is itself divided by. The first is the question of site selection. For the most part, the houses give clear expression to the decision to seek uncontaminated air away from human activity. Wimberley, for example, has become a centre of the MCS community for several reasons. It is a resort community, taking advantage of the relative cool and definite beauty of the Texas hill country. Outdoor living is possible almost year round. The land itself is not fertile enough to support agriculture, guaranteeing freedom from agricultural pesticides. Wimberley is also within an hour's drive of Austin, to which both Mary Oetzel and the Pitman family commute. The same could be said for the siting of many MCS houses, including the Nelms' house outside Ottawa. They are colonising the countryside by means of the automobile.

The case studies do offer qualifications familiar to anyone who has wrestled with the ecological implications of exurban development. Mary Oetzel and John Nelms each have independent businesses with home offices. The Pitmans have a specially renovated apartment in town that at times serves as their primary residence.

Still, if these MCS houses are taken to represent 'green' architecture, they trade on conflicted imagery. Is the notion of a car-dependent retreat into the rural landscape itself ecologically desirable? In holding up such examples, is the 'green' movement using the health concerns of the MCS community as a means of rationalising pastoral cultural preferences? The question of whether the good life is best lived in the city or the country is as old as the Greek poets mourning the loss of the Golden Age and debating the relative merits of nature and art. This debate in contemporary culture is shaped both by the Romantic reaction to the ills of the nineteenth-century industrial city and by the uniquely twentieth-century experience of the automobile's destructive and liberatory power. In public presentations of this research I have become keenly aware of the seductive power of these rural homes to win the sympathies of the audience. I have also faced visceral condemnations, claiming that I am promoting sprawl simply by discussing them.

A second place where the strict requirements of these MCS houses come into conflict with other environmental objectives is in the choice of materials. Should the use of manufactured wood products, for example, be ruled out unconditionally because of their reliance on formaldehyde-based glues? Can the world's forests support the technological simplicity of the Pitman house, where stud construction is eliminated in favour of solid logs or where the need for toxic preservatives is eliminated by the use of redwood decking? Many MCS dwellings are strident in their use of only 'natural' materials. This gives them a strong aesthetic appeal that is again problematic, potentially undermining that aspect of the 'green' movement that seeks to promote resource conservation. If these dwellings are exemplars of 'green' design, how can we argue that old-growth timber is more beautiful left standing than incorporated into 'natural' dwellings?

The research again offers qualifications to this extreme formulation. MCS dwellings are often bitter critiques of post-war construction, but even so, only those in the warmest climates can afford to simply turn back the clock. In Ontario, both Barrhaven and the Nelms house offer examples where highly insulated, resource-conserving building envelopes are made 'safe'. Perhaps a full accounting of environmental costs would even vindicate log construction in Texas, owing to the minimal processing that it requires. The real dilemma here for the 'green' movement is that because of the nature of MCS as an illness each case remains unique. Materials solutions that advance both health and other objectives can be struck in individual cases, but they cannot be endorsed as a rule in 'safe' design.

### 'Green' is not necessarily 'safe'

Because each MCS case is unique, a general commitment to sustainable design does not guarantee that the results will be acceptable to a person with MCS. A classic conflict between 'green' and 'safe' on a symbolic as well as a physical level is seen in the issue of house plants. Rooms filled with living plants are the very symbol of harmony for many environmentally minded people. And yet, plants other than cacti are totally absent from the houses documented. Most people with any sort of severe chemical sensitivities are also strongly affected by moulds and pollens and hence avoid having plants in their living spaces. Greenery is literally unsafe.

Are the needs of people with MCS distinct from any other intuition of what constitutes healthy design? The answer again is, 'Yes, but ... '. This answer is qualified because experts see the condition as constituting a spectrum from health to extreme disability. For the many who may suffer from minor sensitivities without even realising it, the insights of building for health can be stated in universal terms. This level of health-conscious design is precisely what 'green' architecture seeks to accomplish. The architectural needs of the extremely sensitive minority, however, are distinct. These distinct needs are also individual, even idiosyncratic. Especially at the extremes of ill health, individual sensitivities vary greatly within the general categories of known irritants. Sue Pitman can tolerate softwoods and used them extensively, for example, while others in Wimberley cannot tolerate visiting her log house.

An architect or builder simply cannot offer a blanket solution to an extremely sensitised person. What is called for instead is a methodology for untangling individual reactions and making specific choices. Where this is impossible, as with the apartment buildings documented, a huge risk is that after everything is said and done the environment will still prove unacceptable to specific individuals. California's Ecology House, for example, which was funded by the US Housing and Urban Development Department, experienced wrenching problems in its first months of occupancy. Only after two additional years of working through specific complaints could Ecology House claim success.

### Towards the synthesis of 'safe' and 'green'

One way to think of the relation of 'safe' and 'green' architecture is to see these MCS houses as uncompromising voices on the health side of a debate between the values of personal health and environmental sustainability. To a great degree, contemporary concern for both objectives is an outgrowth of the limitations of the environmental architecture of the 1970s. This architecture put great emphasis on improving the energy efficiency of buildings, but often unintentionally produced dangerously unhealthy environments. Likewise, the focus on energy efficiency eventually came to seem too narrow to account for the true environmental cost of building, promoting the introduction of insulation materials that later turned out to be destructive of the ozone layer, for example. If 'green' architecture represents the current horizon of environmentally concerned architecture, then the purpose of the debate should be not just to articulate differences but to find simultaneous solutions to the problems of design faced by all sides.

Signs of such a synthesis can be seen in the combination of MCS concerns and super-insulation practices in many of the dwellings documented. The Nelms house offers one such example of 'safe and green' envelope construction. The exterior wall is built with 2 foot by 6 foot studs, strapped on both sides and braced with let-in diagonal bracing rather than sheet sheathing. The exterior strapping provides a large and thermally broken cavity for the recycled cellulose insulation. The elimination of sheathing excludes a potential source of formaldehyde from the building while conserving resources. The interior strapping creates a chase for the electrical wiring on the warm side of the vapour barrier, eliminating penetrations. These details create an energy-efficient and resource-efficient shell that also effectively isolates the materials of the envelope from the dwelling space.

Barrhaven provides two more examples of 'safe and green' synthesis. The first offers a solution to the dilemma posed by the notion of MCS dwellings as country retreats, primarily because the parishioners did not have the luxury of relocating to virgin land. As the architect tells the story, concern over the use of pesticides at the adjacent municipal park led to a request that the city not spray in the area during construction. Outreach was also conducted to ask the same of the adjacent property owners. As the neighbourhood was brought into the process, the idea gradually gained acceptance. This eventually led the neighbourhood to extend the pesticides ban in the park indefinitely, with many neighbours eliminating the use of pesticides and gas-powered mowers on their own property as well.

In the second instance, the crew of the precast plant where the floor planks were made reportedly found it such an improvement to abandon diesel fuel as a release agent that they continued the practice of using organic soap even after the order was filled. Whether this apocryphal story is true or not, since Barrhaven was built several lines of non-toxic release agents have entered the market, catering to this confluence of health and environmental concerns.

In the Nelms house, the synthesis of 'safe' and 'green' is a model of technical mastery. Problems are solved without compromise through the skill and the care of the builder, who devised hybrid solutions relying on both traditional and contemporary building practices. Barrhaven presents an alternative strategy that is both more ambitious and more earth bound. Conflict is overcome by changing the context of the problem through social action. Both strategies are alternatives on a conceptual level to the withdrawal from the world that these dwellings for the chemically sensitive can easily be interpreted as promoting. Both show the way for this extreme-case architecture of safe havens to engage and enrich mainstream 'green' design.

## Notes

1   The rough outlines of the argument in this chapter were presented at a conference (Wasley 1996a) and a previous version published (Wasley 2000).

2   See for example David Pearson, *The Natural House Book: Creating a Healthy, Harmonious, and Ecologically-Sound Home Environment* (Pearson 1989). On page 241 Pearson discusses the concept of a sanctuary for an environmentally sensitive person. Page 242 features a shag-carpeted sitting area surrounded by dense foliage that would be an anathema to the MCS sufferers documented in this essay, as will be discussed in the main body of the text. To be fair, this blurring of distinctions is also found to an extent in *Healthy by Design* (Rousseau and Wasley 1999), in as much as the book is aimed at a larger audience than those with severe chemical sensitivities.

3   This essay frames the issue of the contribution of the chemically sensitive community to the project of green architecture as a study of the specific in relation to the general. For a slightly different frame of reference consistent with the structure of this collection of essays, see Guy and Farmer's 'Re-interpreting Sustainable Architecture: The Place of Technology' (2001), in which they parse the discourse on sustainable design into six competing 'logics' grounded respectively in technical, ethical, aesthetic, cultural, medical and social perspectives.

In this formulation, 'safe' architecture falls within the 'eco-medical' camp, as one voice in what this author would characterise as the 'healthy house movement', which is itself only one of several communities of interest forwarding health-oriented perspectives on the built environment. To appreciate the diversity of these voices, consider the irony that the tobacco industry has been a major funding source for reseach into indoor air quality, embodying a seventh, 'eco-libertarian' logic perhaps?

While the argument is understated in deference to the 'part to whole' analysis indicated by this chapter's title, a central difference that this chapter seeks to articulate is between the physical needs of the MCS community and the broader social and aesthetic values Guy and Farmer ascribe to eco-medically oriented designers. This is the same conflation of medical and aesthetic concerns illustrated by the reference to Pearson's *The Natural House Book*. In the terminology of Guy and Farmer, Pearson is guided by the image of 'a natural and tactile environment which insures health, well-being, and quality of life for individuals' (Guy and Farmer 2001: 141). Another early and well-known example of this conflation might be *Healing Environments: Your Guide to Indoor Well Being*, by Carol Venolia (1988). Where Pearson's book incorporates aesthetic topics and sensuous imagery within a broad discussion of 'green' issues in residential design, Venolia's book is specifically about this experiential dimension. As the back cover notes claim, '*Healing Environments* goes way beyond the concept of "safe" – and often sterile – nontoxic housing'.

My point here is not to deny the impulse to tie an uplifting aesthetic to the more pragmatic concerns of ensuring a physical environment free of potential irritants, or to deny that beauty has a role to play in creating a sense of well-being, but to simply point out that, for reasons explored in the main body of the text, the individuals whose dwellings are documented here didn't express these concerns. By implication, several of the subjects interviewed would in fact feel marginalised to have their needs discussed as such. If their houses had any agency in healing them, it was consistently represented as a 'matter of fact' result of creating a physical sanctuary.

It should be of no surprise that at least this one of the six 'eco-logics' is itself full of conflicting positions, as they are all at best useful abstractions overlaid onto what Guy and Farmer powerfully characterise as 'contested terrain'. 'Green architecture' is, by its nature, an evolving consensus, and, as 'Re-interpreting Sustainable Architecture' is at pains to point out, the different discourses that define it are neither exclusive nor fixed.

4  Personal conversations with Dr Claudia Miller, University of Texas Health Science Center at San Antonio. Dr Miller discusses her own hypothesis of 'toxicant-induced loss of tolerance' in 'Are We on the Threshold of a New Theory of Disease? Toxicant-Induced Loss of Tolerance and its Relationship to Addiction and Abdiction' (Miller 1999). This theory is also covered in Ashford and Miller (1998) and Miller and Ashford (2000).

5  Each of these topics is explored in greater detail in other publications: Wasley 1995a (building materials selection), Wasley 1996b (space planning) and Wasley 1997 (ventilation). Case studies of the Pitman house, the Oetzel house and the Barrhaven Community Housing project are presented in Rousseau and Wasley (1999).

6  This point bears directly on the issue of distinguishing these dwellings from a more general, and more aesthetically identified, interest in health and well-being. For many of those interviewed, MSC is socially isolating both in the physical isolation that it imposes and in the sense of social rejection implicit in having, or in fearing, a negative physical reaction to other people and everyday settings. This social stigma is a strong theme of most accounts of MCS, as for example in the film *Safe*. As a result, the desire to 'blend in' is a powerful force in most of the dwellings documented.

The desire to blend in also typifies most people and most housing the world over. As an academic committed to the project of creating a sustainable society, I have found that one of the most interesting aspects of these case studies is this tension between the extreme nature of their circumstances and the range of expressions that they have taken on. To highlight a second point glossed over in the text, two of the four examples discussed are unhesitatingly bold in their problem-solving expression and two are deliberately understated. This opens up another possible set of 'logics' through which to interpret sustainable architecture: the impulse towards either radicalism or reform. This dimension of the case studies is hinted at in 'Multiple Chemical Sensitivity Syndrome and "Traditional Concepts of Architecture"' (Wasley 1995b). Much more could be done.

7  And though the dwellings documented do share strongly aesthetic qualities, these are most suggestive of other cultural expressions of an extreme concern for hygiene, such as embodied in Shaker and Scandinavian design, rather than the sensuous and spiritualistic aesthetic represented here by Pearson and Venolia.

# 8

# Revaluing wood

*Ted Cavanagh and Richard Kroeker*

Although the standardisation of contemporary wood products and practices is the apparent subject of their investigation, Cavanagh and Kroeker argue that beneath the surface lies a conflict between two much older discourses: the universal versus the local, or modern industrialism versus sustainable sylviculture – a discourse at least as old as the seventeenth-century English natural philosopher John Evelyn. Like Anthony Ashley Cooper, the 3rd Earl of Shaftesbury (1671–1713), the Whig advocate of the English picturesque, the authors envision a landscape of particularity that is resistant to universalising forces, be they aesthetic (classicism) or economic (global capital). Wood has distinct advantages and disadvantages that will influence emerging technologies and consumer standards. The authors' purpose is to explore the interests concealed in those universalising standards by documenting local alternatives to the now dominant practice of industrial forestry. Firstly, they consider the apparent linkages between consumption and land use by comparing new 'forest certification programmes' and current grading conventions. Secondly, they focus on three cases of wood production in Atlantic Canada: an exemplary woodlot operation, the contemporary export of North American wood technologies to Europe, and the development of a new building technique based on local culture and ecology. The authors argue that these local cases provide alternative futures based on 'multiple sovereign practices' rather than 'a new orthodoxy of sustainability'.

> The environment will always balance itself, with or without humans. Essentially, sustainability is a human rights issue.
>
> (Albert Marshall, private interview, 8 December 2002)

## Land use and consumption

Since there is nothing which seems more fatally to threaten a weakening, if not a dissolution of the strength of this famous and flourishing nation, than the sensible and notorious decay of her wooden walls ... For it has not been the late increase in shipping alone, the multiplication of Glass-Works, Iron-Furnaces, and the like, from whence this impolitick diminution of our Timber has proceeded; but from the disproportionate spreading of Tillage, ... tempted, not only to fell and cut down, but utterly extirpate, demolish, and raze, as it were, all those many goodly Woods, and Forests, which our more prudent Ancestors left standing ... this devastation is now become Epidemical, that unless some favourable expedient offer it self, and a way be seriously, and speedily resolv'd upon, for a future store, one of the most glorious, and considerable Bulwarks of this Nation, will, within a short time, be totally wanting to it. ... Truly, the waste, and destruction of our Woods, has been universal.

(Evelyn 2001: 1–2)

For the last four hundred years, demand for heat and building material has led to the intensifying commodification of forests and the repeated prediction of their imminent depletion. During this time, the excesses of the wood industry have caused substantial harm. Human impact, from inconsiderate land use to overconsumption, has been detrimental to the environment. Nevertheless, wood does have many natural advantages over other building materials and, in many simple ways, it creates buildings that are efficient, ecological and sustainable. Wood is genuinely renewable, particularly when based in sustainable land practices, local procurement and manufacturing, and recycling. It is rooted in the local, in the cycles of nature and in the diversity of wildlife habitat – and deep in the human psyche. Its low embodied energy is recognised in the Kyoto Accord, a global agreement that values energy-efficient modes of production and gives explicit value to forests as oxygen producers and carbon fixers. As a result, and sometimes by default, the wood industry continues to play a leading role in defining the very standards of sustainability.

Sustainable architecture requires consideration of how building materials, among other variables, affect land use. This chapter focuses on some of the optimistic and/or likely outcomes for the reconfiguration of wood production from the point of view of Atlantic Canada and North America. It argues for the support of alternative technologies, varied management strategies and innovation, and it argues against standardisation either as prescriptive practice or through a drift to global normative practice. It considers aspects of the culture, technology and history of wood use to support the case for diversity of response leading to resilient places. It simplifies the history of wood as a building material by exemplifying Europeans as proponents of systems of consumption and North Americans as developers of massive systems of production.

Writing in 1662, John Evelyn presented one of the first arguments for sylviculture and sustainable wood production. He asked for the king's support in reforesting Britain to help supply industry and the British navy. It would, he believed, return Britain to the 'prudent' practices lost after the breakdown of land traditions and 'the disproportionate spreading of Tillage' during the time of Oliver Cromwell. He identified wood as a renewable material with a direct relationship to land use. These persuasive arguments established wood as the framework and a simple indicator of sustainability across a wide range of human practices, well before the introduction of iron and other industrial materials into building. Of course, the parameters used to compare materials, such as measurement and standards, are contested as well (Manzini 1986: 37). Since the definition of sustainability has emerged from a consideration of wood use, one would expect its continuing advantage in competition with other materials.

Nova Scotia is situated between Europe and the United States both geographically and historically. It is a small area, 22,308 square miles or 57,778 square kilometres, part island and part peninsula attached to the eastern edge of North America. Its forests are transitional, both boreal and northern hardwood. It was a wilderness forest unlike those in Europe; as Longfellow wrote of Nova Scotia: 'This is the forest primeval' (Longfellow 1847). It flew the flag of France for 100 years, Britain for 150 years and Canada for 150 years. It was the first area of North America to export timber to Europe, one thousand years ago when European traders came to harvest wood for their buildings in Greenland. In 1612, it was the site of the first North American sawmill, constructed to export barrel-staves and planks back to France. The legislature introduced standards of wood production in the early days of the colony: 'Boards shall be one-inch thick, shingles 18 inches long, at least four inches broad and one-half inch thick at the thick end, clapboards shall be five inches broad and one-half inch thick at the back and four foot four inches long' (Nova Scotia Legislature 1774). Atlantic Canada has a long history of wood production influenced by EU requirements.

As Evelyn had warned, Britain was soon dependent on imported timber, and in 1774 the surveyor general recommended that the whole island of Cape Breton in Nova Scotia (10,311 square kilometres) 'should be reserved for the purposes of preserving for His Majesty's use Timber for Shipbuilding and other uses – this Island being the nearest tract of land to England' (Johnson 1986: 42), and so it was. In the eighteenth century, the main role of royal land surveys was to identify tracts of forest and to emblazon 'broad arrow' marks on pines of 24 inches in diameter suitable as masts for the British navy. As a result, lone pines were often left standing in agricultural fields reserved for navy use (the flag of Maine depicts its independence from this British policy). After US independence from Britain, the law creating the Cape Breton reserve was repealed to provide land for the resettlement of Loyalists. Nova Scotia now found itself placed between the United States and Europe. Britain's appetite for pine was legendary, 'but subsequent American demand was even greater' (Riley 1999: 14) (Fig. 8.1). In the 1860s, Nova Scotia had the third largest merchant marine in the world after Britain and France. Some

THE GREAT TIMBER RAFT FROM JOGGINS, NOVA SCOTIA.

*8.1 A 'raft' of 22,000 timbers averaging 40 feet long, equivalent to the cargo of 44 vessels, was towed from Joggins to New York City in 1888, near the end of the wooden boat building era.*

3,000 vessels were built annually, making Nova Scotia the largest shipbuilding country in the world. The local history of wood use is substantial, if not sustainable.

Today, European and North American practices of consumption of wood are distinct. In 1986, François Diagenet used a particularly resonant metaphor for a 2 foot by 4 foot wood stud as an extravagant 'fillet' – a meaty, prime cut of wood (Manzini 1986: 14). We North Americans find this European description remarkable and strange, as we have constructed a fundamentally different attitude to building in wood. For us, wood is a local material; it is plentiful and part of the ordinary construction and renovation of houses. Whereas North Americans produce what they consume, since the earliest times colonists have exported wood products back to their European countries of origin. European values of consumption continue to affect North American production; as recently as the 1980s this emphasis led Europeans to initiate '[rain]forest certification programmes'. At the same time, on the production side, North Americans are becoming very successful at exporting their methods of building wood-frame houses to Europe. While differences in attitude will continue to cause discrepancies in international standards of wood production, the conjunction of these two forces, increased certification and the spread of wood-frame house production will direct the new parameters of sustainable architecture towards global standardisation rather than to local and diverse practices.

### Linking the principled use of land with consumption

Native North Americans understand sustainability through principles rooted in their cultural and technological traditions and see Europeans as relative newcomers to this way of thinking. Algonquian First Nations groups are codifying an approach to resources that they see as part of their own history. Culture and environment are inseparable in the indigenous North American tradition. This influences treaty interpretations and 'resource claims'.[1] Eighteenth- and nineteenth-century treaties had forfeited their formal land title to the British Crown, but control of the resources, and by extension the environment from which they came, was maintained to sustain their culture.

In 1978, perhaps for the first time, this native North American ethic of sustainability rooted in the land was allied with a contemporary European ethic based in the principled practice of consumption. At that time, a multinational forestry company with headquarters in Stockholm, Sweden, was quite intensively spraying forests in Cape Breton with the biocide 2,4,5-T (Agent Orange). The purpose of the spraying programme was to increase forest production by removing 'nuisance species'. Basing their conclusions on medical information, Albert and Murdena Marshall believed 2,4,5-T to be the possible and probable trigger that ultimately resulted in their son's tragic death from aplastic anaemia, a relatively rare disease usually caused by a chemical trigger (A. and M. Marshall, interview, 8 December 2002). Albert Marshall sold his construction company and flew to Europe to embark on an education campaign, with the support of the Sami and Swedish environmentalist Eva Bealone. From Sweden, he toured extensively through Germany, Austria and Holland. Over a period of three months, he spoke at universities, churches and town halls and conducted media interviews, with the logistical support of a well-organised network of European environmentalists.

By this time, Sweden and Europe had banned spraying with the chemical agents being used in Atlantic Canada. When offered assistance by sympathetic audiences, Marshall told them he was not targeting the multinational forestry company. The company was, after all, complying with Canadian law and was acting in its interests to maximise economic returns. Instead, he asked his supporters to write and telephone Canadian government embassies concerning the inappropriate use of chemicals in Canada, to raise awareness about the growing imbalance in the forests under government jurisdiction and advise them on how to protect forest environments. As part of the strategy for seeking an end to a destructive practice, Marshall appealed to existing power structures and their claims to authority. He questioned the increasingly seamless relationship between government and large-scale commercial interests and reinforced the established principle that governmental power is politically and morally rooted in the environment, which includes people.[2] The principles were clear. The United States banned the immediate suspect chemical in 1979 and Canada allowed it to continue in use until further action by the US Environmental Protection Agency prohibited the manufacturer from exporting old stock to Canada. The battle against airborne chemical spraying is ongoing on a case-by-case basis (Sierra Club 2000), accentuating once again the alliance between the European consumer and North American land use.

### Voluntary standards: the case of local FSC certification

By the 1980s, European attention to environmental issues had begun to focus on wood production in the countries of origin. Wood held an historical advantage in discussions of sustainability, and perhaps for that very reason the environmental movement singled out the wood sector for its unsustainable practices. No longer were governments relied on to set appropriate standards of sustainable practice in their own countries. Non-governmental organisations began to organise information campaigns and consumer boycotts. For boycotts to be effective, third-party certification programmes had to be in place that defined acceptable sustainable practices (Hansen 1997: 17). The first boycotts and certification programmes targeted rainforest depletion but soon included the North American forest products industry as well. By virtue of their ability to create a consumer boycott or a credible threat of one, non-governmental organisations took a leading role in defining sustainable practice.

The Forest Stewardship Council (FSC) was founded in 1993 as a non-governmental organisation to develop a set of certification standards for sustainable wood products throughout the world. Its certification programme is one of the leading international standards; it has ten principles and fifty-six criteria with provisions for extension and localisation in each region. The FSC does not actually check forests for compliance; instead it accredits those who do. The FSC is organised in three chambers (economic, ecological and social) each for two hemispheres (north and south).[3] Memberships are granted to either individuals or organisations. It operates on the basis of consensus and tries to be democratic and representative in its structure, balancing regional interests. This form of organisation is both its strength and weakness. Organised so that no one interest group has power, it is seen by some as being very cumbersome. Nevertheless, this method of organisation produces one of the world's most credible forestry certification programmes.

In January 1996, the FSC formed an organisation for Canada, and the Canadian board of directors set up working groups to develop standards for each region compatible with FSC international principles and criteria. The first of these North American regional standards was for Atlantic Canada and included representatives from large-scale industry, owners of small-scale woodlots and sawmills, and First Nations groups, as well as observers from government (J. Drescher, Atlantic Regional Committee of the Canadian Forest Stewardship Council, interview, 2003; FSCCanada 2002). The Atlantic regional committee met over a four year period and, in November 2000, briefly came to a tentative agreement. Its criteria included extending certification to those who eliminated three forestry practices: the use of biocides, replanting to exotic species and conversion of forests to plantations. This event demonstrates the tuning of FSC certification to local values.

Consensus in the regional committee broke down, however, as first one and then a second representative from large-scale industry withdrew support. In addition, a tension between global and local standards emerged. In the absence of regional standards, international standards form the basis of evaluation. One industry member of the regional committee had simultaneously hired an accredited evaluator to pursue FSC certification based on the more lenient international standards. This was granted in 1998.[4] Clearly, certification was beginning to have economic value.[5] Since regional standards, once in place, demand compliance within one year, it might not be in the interest of those already certified internationally to cooperate in the development of more stringent regional standards.

An agreement was reached in the summer of 2002, with the three contentious standards rewritten. Even though these were compromised, Jim Drescher, who chaired the process, believes it important to have some standards in place, rather than no agreement at all. Since that regional agreement was reached, the 'conversion of natural forest to plantations' standard has been tightened at the international level. This shows the influence of the regional organisations within the FSC and highlights a major difference: North America is in the process of developing extensive plantation forestry while Europe, author of the earlier, less stringent standard, has fewer 'natural forests' to worry about.[6]

As in the example of lumber grading explained below, the impetus to simple global certification standards may be irresistible; however, even its proponents do not anticipate influencing the majority of forests worldwide. The certifications do not have the force of law and are themselves not subject to regulation or coordination (Fig. 8.2). Possibly, some are established by industry to mask unsustainable practices. The evaluating organisation, who apply certification criteria, and the applicants, who manage the forest, are in the continuing business relationship. This is mitigated by requirements for transparent process and, in the case of the FSC, for peer review of the findings (Upton and Bass 1996: 78). The status of the evaluating organisations and their relationship to industry is unclear, and it is here that the fundamental negotiations between criteria and application occur, on the basis of everything from bottom-line economics to ecology. Closer ties between the forest and the consumer are privileged in the FSC process and standards; industry has to segregate supply streams to maintain the integrity of the product from the forest through every step of production (Groves et al. 1996: 77). The patchwork of standards is not well understood by consumers.[7] For the moment at least, the certification organisations create a kind of layered democracy and act in a quasi-legislative capacity, but are not subject to the same sort of scrutiny we give to our publicly elected legislators. They can also become the reason for civic inaction, by creating the misleading impression that issues related to sustainable use, sustainable development and sustainable production can be conflated and are effectively regulated by the private sector or the NGO sector, rendering government regulation unnecessary (von Mirbach 1997: 8).

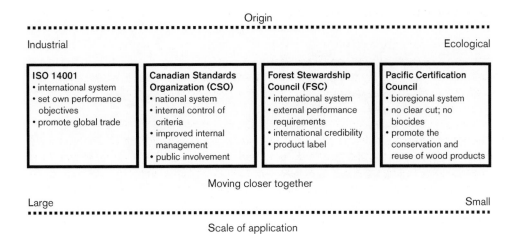

Origin

Industrial            Ecological

| ISO 14001 | Canadian Standards | Forest Stewardship | Pacific Certification |
|---|---|---|---|
| • international system | Organization (CSO) | Council (FSC) | Council |
| • set own performance | • national system | • international system | • bioregional system |
| objectives | • internal control of | • external performance | • no clear cut; no |
| • promote global trade | criteria | requirements | biocides |
| | • improved internal | • international credibility | • promote the |
| | management | • product label | conservation and |
| | • public involvement | | reuse of wood products |

Moving closer together

Large            Small

Scale of application

*8.2. The range of organisations certifying forestry, from those sponsored by industry, on the left, to those sponsored by environmentalists, on the right. Despite the difficulty, many forestry operations are considering dual certification.*

On the other hand, unless certification takes local ecological and cultural diversity into account, uniform certification standards will reinforce and extend the massive current system of wood production. There are difficulties with local standards, however. Within the FSC, the issue of the level of standard is interpreted by nations and regions differently; Sweden, for instance, is committed to finding widespread support for the standard rather than certifying a smaller set of exemplary suppliers (Swedish FSC Working Group 1997). The FSC is well on its way to reinforcing diversity and local values. The process of regional elaboration of international standards seems to be working well. Small operators can achieve certification for very little cost by associating with an umbrella organisation that manages the certification, and biological diversity is one of the FSC international standards. The extent to which the forestry sector will adopt certification depends on its use in the buying decisions of architects, builders and home buyers. Consumer-oriented information such as certification is much better today than it was ten years ago, but after all, the FSC standard was established in 1993, a very short time compared with the lifespan of a tree.

### Voluntary standards: NLGA/ASLS grading and global trade

There is a history of standards applied to wood production. By 1750, urban producers and builders had arrived at conventions for lumber dimensions and approximate grades of quality in the US Northeast. With the introduction of these standards, rural sawmillers and urban lumber merchants were able to conduct business effectively over great distances (Rilling 2001: 99). Eventually, lumber-manufacturer associations established standards for members, and in 1924 the US Department of Commerce standardised lumber grades throughout the United States (Cutter 1993). There remain, however, distinctly regional aspects to this system, reflecting the variations of climate and tree species throughout North America. For softwoods, it is a coarse structural classification system with many species lumped together, and downgraded to the weakest of the

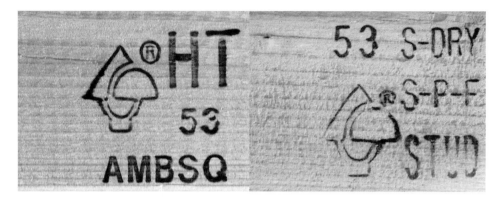

*8.3 Sample grade stamp. The grade assigned to an individual piece of dimension lumber is stamped on each piece. This stamp contains the following information: the grading agency that wrote the rules and issued the grade stamp, the species of lumber, the grade itself, the mill identification, and the moisture content of the wood at the mill when the stamp is applied.*

species in the group (Fig. 8.3). Initially intended to facilitate trade and communication, like any standard operating over time it has become a key determinant of production and forest management.

Today, as the primary production standard, grading has a huge influence on sylviculture and the type of trees grown in Nova Scotia forests. Regionally, there are two basic grades: SPF, which is approved for framing and includes spruce, jack pine and balsam fir, and the lower-priced 'North Species' grade, which is not approved for residential structures and includes eastern hemlock, white pine, red pine, tamarack (juniper) and cedar. For many plantation foresters, hemlock is considered a weed. Eastern hemlock and tamarack have never been tested and remain classed as 'North Species'. Jack pine, which grows well in plantations, is graded SPF. An attempt to upgrade a species to the SPF category or to create a new grade, costs about C$200,000. The price of these time-consuming tests is paid by industry and requires samples from every region where the species grows. Effectively, a 'threshold of entry' has been created by grading. The way that it simple-mindedly privileges one species over another runs counter to efforts to promote biodiversity.

Eastern hemlock and tamarack will continue to be graded as structurally inferior species until private industry funds the tests required to upgrade their rating. In the long term, this leads to the disappearance of certain species; for example, cedar is fast disappearing from Nova Scotia and tamarack may follow. Hemlock, which needs some shade in its early growth stage, doesn't grow well in second-growth clear cuts. In contrast, Norway spruce, an introduced species that does well in plantation and clear cuts, is currently being funded for tests to raise its status to SPF. Clearly, grading influences the make up of our forests, and large-scale industry influences grading.

Places with weak or nonexistent wood-grading requirements have different difficulties; wood tends to have a poor record in both the uptake and the quality of its application (UNIDO 1969: 13; Dudley et al. 1995: 141). Again, local biodiversity loses. Poor forestry practices are promoted by the lack of grading standards or by grading only a few select species.

Grading has an important influence on trade, and grading standards are often exported. Russian logs, graded using Scandinavian criteria, have replaced most Canadian lumber exports to the European Union (M. Albright, Wood Science and Technology Centre, Fredericton, New Brunswick, interview 11 March 2003). Recently, Japan has rewritten its building codes to reduce the moisture content of wood to prevent rot in timber joints, because many houses built with 'green' western hemlock failed during the 1995 Kobe earthquake. This has a significant impact on North American exporters, as western hemlock is not easy to kiln dry. In addition, the Japanese have developed their own JAS grade, which is more stringent with respect to appearance defects such as splits, wane, white speck and knot size. Accordingly, to produce any quantity of JAS-grade construction lumber, a Canadian mill must substantially change its production process, sacrificing recovery or rate of production, or both. More often, exporting companies purchase graded and kiln-dried lumber and then regrade and/or remanufacture it to JAS-grading standards (Neil 1998).[8] New national building code requirements in Japan have stalled efforts to increase exports of Canadian-graded lumber, demonstrating the links between trade and building standards. This push to export often occurs in conjunction with a campaign to introduce or expand the practice of North American light-wood frame construction techniques in places such as Japan, Britain, Germany, Korea and China.

In Nova Scotia, grading promotes the introduction of new species and large-scale sylviculture. Until now, Nova Scotia has not been a particularly good example of sustainable land use or forestry practices. We have borrowed against the future by placing a huge debt load against our forested land. Official report after official report during the twentieth century pointed out that the total annual cut exceeded the annual growth of wood (Fernow 1912; Canadian Society of Forest Engineers 1944; Dawson 1944; Hawboldt and Bulmer 1958).[9] The choices are to repay the debt by replenishing our natural level of resource or squeeze yet one more cut out of the existing forests.

Currently, the pressures of trade are exacerbating an already poor record. Of great impact on forests in Atlantic Canada has been a decade-long trade dispute over the import of Canadian softwood lumber into the United States. Atlantic Canada accounted for a small percentage of Canada's lumber production until five years ago, when production in Nova Scotia and New Brunswick soared '62 per cent to more than 1.2 billion board feet' (CBC News 2001). It was the one region exempt from US countervailing duties on Canadian lumber, and in 'New Brunswick alone, 90 per cent of its softwood lumber exports go to the United States' (ibid.). The reason for the exemption is that lumber harvested in Atlantic Canada is mostly from private land, like that in the United States. In this dispute Nova Scotia is once again in the middle, this time between the United States and Canada.

Except in the Atlantic region, Canadian land use for wood production is regulated and forested land is publicly owned. Large corporations have long-term rights to harvest public forests and pay fees at regionally negotiated rates, whereas in the United States the price of harvest is determined by market auction of cutting rights. Nevertheless, the two regimes have had similar results (Sierra Club 2002; Banuri and Apffel Marglin 1990: 45). Despite the extensive public ownership of forested land in Canada, both countries have failed to promote small business or a diversity of response designed for local circumstances and preferences. This diversity of response includes the possibility of small, profitable, carefully stewarded forests like Windhorse Farm, described in the next section.

### Alternative technology: a local forest operation

Forestry in the Atlantic region maintains some resilience: it has an incredible diversity of ownership and the natural advantages of the Acadian forest mix with few catastrophes such as hurricane or fire. This diversity, and the small scale of most of the forestry operations, suggests the possibility of viable small forestry businesses and, even more optimistically, operations based in diverse response, local employment and sustainable practices.

Jim Drescher continues a seven-generation tradition of forest management that creates a sustainable woodlot by maximising biodiversity. Windhorse Farm in New Germany, Nova Scotia, is a woodlot operation with sawmill, planers and kilns, as well as a forestry school. As part of a strategy of maximising the biological envelope, the tallest trees are left standing. Windhorse Farm considers the habitat it provides to indigenous flora and fauna. For instance, deadwood is left standing in place to provide habitat for forest insect life, which in turn supports other levels up the forest food chain. The proportion left in place is based on observation of existing old-growth forests in the area.

The rough sawing of the wood is done with mobile sawmills brought to sawing locations in the forest by draught horses. This ensures that biomass from sawdust and slabs remains part of the nutrient balance of the forest.[10] Slabs and sawdust are used to construct forestry roads, so that the subsurface life of the forest and the water network are continuous across roads and aren't disrupted by packed soil or drainage ditches. Each year's harvest is based on the amount of biomass added to the forest in that year. Trees are selected on the basis of optimising the habitat left behind and on the tree's stage of life. The best trees are left to become seed stock for subsequent generations, and the tallest are left to maximise the growth zone.

The practices employed at Windhorse Farm exceed the standards presently defined by FSC certification (Drescher chaired the group developing the Maritime Standard). Its relatively small forest operation is certified by FSC and by a more stringent ecological standard. Its method of management requires an intimate familiarity with the forest and a constant monitoring process. The production strategy adds maximum value to the wood product before shipping. It values the wood in terms of man-hours of high-quality employment, provided as close to the forest source as possible. The integrity of their market depends on customer awareness of the environmental and social ethic underlying their operation. Clearly, this is a small operation based in a local community.

Drescher has ideas that make his a model operation, as evident in his contribution to certification, his commitment to schooling others and, particularly, his arguments for full-cost accounting, restoration and 'slow-grading'. He is critical of current business practices that promote the 'increase in profits by getting others to pay the costs … Commonly externalized costs include loss of biodiversity, environmental degradation, health problems, unemployment, community disintegration, and resource depletion' (Windhorse Farm 2003). Full-cost accounting keeps the whole score; easy to say, difficult to measure (Heaton and Donovan 1996: 6). Restoration uses comparison old-growth forests as a model and techniques such as retaining and enhancing dead wood, large snags and coarse woody debris. 'Slow-grading' has been the method of harvest for 150 years; they cut the slowest-growing trees regardless of size but never the tallest trees, even if they have stopped growing. Like any operation, Windhorse Farm elaborates on these concepts for its particular context and integrates them into a viable set of practices.

At the moment, Windhorse Farm can compete economically with other operations that are not based on the same principles of sustainability. Certification supports its position. In general, the certification of established well-managed forests might be a contributing factor to the early ascription to FSC certification; possibly, a new 'threshold of entry' is being created between the already certified and the uncertifiable. The Menominee forest in Minnesota, 88,320 hectares (321 square miles) managed carefully since 1854, was certified easily (Burgess 1996: 268). Neither example indicates a way to repay the debt and replenish our natural level of forest resource. Perhaps, an imaginative use of certification standards containing a principle of improvement (such as a net increase in the forest resource) will help.

It is beyond the scope of this chapter to suggest future policy for local forestry, but it is probably worthwhile to mention some concerns about the continued depletion of wood resources and current trends in production. One concern is the instrumental bias of 'scientific forestry', whether as an ideal, as practised or as usurped by bureaucratic and commercial interests – for example, the label 'scientific' is used to justify short-horizon commercial practices, not long-term social and environmental health.

> One can interpret scientific forestry as saying that individual control was likely to be undesirable, given the short time horizon of individual actors, and that therefore some form of organised control was necessary for good management. Our alternative view would emphasise a third possibility, the role of communities, whose long time horizons are inscribed into their rituals, beliefs, and world-views – in other words into their systems of knowledge. The neglect of this possibility has limited the debate to only two alternatives, both of which are instrumental, and neither of which we find desirable. The actual practice, however, differs from the intellectual debate in that the third possibility is always present; indeed, in our view, this third possibility is what determines whether the outcome will be good or bad.
>
> (Banuri and Apffel Marglin 1990: 43)

In Maine, although clearcutting and herbiciding have declined recently, there is a trend for logging contractors to invest in expensive equipment and for large-scale wood producers to practice 'whole-tree' forestry, where they raze the forest and then market every part of the tree (Vail 1990: 167; St Pierre and Vail 2001). This shows the increasing demand for wood, wood chips and biomass. It involves heavy capitalisation in big equipment and reduced labour cost. As Drescher points out, this practice leads to unemployment and community disintegration. The lack of 'waste' left after whole-tree clearcutting is even more detrimental than clearcutting alone, and shows the extent to which the industry can deplete a landscape in a way that precludes any easy recovery (Dahlgren and Driscoll 1994; Duffy and Meier 1992; Schneidereit 2002). Typically, sylviculture leads to a loss of biodiversity, and whole-tree forestry leads to environmental degradation and resource depletion. There is no economic disadvantage to these forestry practices, despite their negative long-term economic and environmental outcomes, nor is there any competitive advantage for those, like Drescher, who promote a balance between environment and production.

At a larger scale, Nova Scotia must find a balance between environment and production. It has virtually no old-growth, pre-colonial forest. It does have reserves and lands held in trust, but biological diversity cannot be protected solely in reserves. The challenge is to design and effectively manage 'semi-natural' lands as multipurpose landscapes (Harris 1984; Hunter 1990; Gamborg and Larsen 2003). The recent recommendations of a Canadian Senate subcommittee suggest a strategy:

In order to accommodate all of the competing demands on the boreal forest, the Subcommittee recommends that serious consideration be given to a natural landscape-based forest use regime that apportions the boreal forest into three distinct categories. One category, comprising up to 20 per cent of the forest land base, would be managed intensively for timber production. A second category, which would comprise the majority of the boreal forest, would be managed less intensively for a variety of values, but with preservation of biodiversity as the primary objective. The third category, comprising up to 20 per cent of the forest land base, would be set aside as protected areas to preserve ecologically and culturally significant areas.

(Canada Senate 1999)

Other recommendations include reforms to the tax system to support woodlot owners, showing consideration of the unique aspect of longevity as regards tree crops and plantation practices. The subcommittee estimates an eightfold increase in productivity through the application of intensive forest management practices (category one above). As a result, the province of Ontario is recommending the increase of the annual cut to be offset by this predicted increased production capability. This is unethical, according to some, and repeats a 1970s scenario where management described as intensive was applied extensively rather than in the targeted way apparently intended (Oliver 1999; Whan 2000). The political debate is beginning to engage the real choices to be made; it remains to be seen whether industry and government can lead effectively.

## The system of wood production

Traditionally, a material was thought of as an elementary system whose task was to 'give structure' to a more complex system.

(Manzini 1986: 39)

Writing in 1989 about the future, Thomas Hughes identified the increased momentum of large systems of production. They 'mature, grow large and rigid, then resist further social construction' and often repackage existing practices for competitive advantage rather than radically retooling to address fundamental shortcomings (Hughes 1989: 470). In his view, everything from industrial organisations to reforestation should be considered 'the technology of wood'. Contemporary wood production organises the harvesting, processing, construction and reuse of wood into a complex distribution of technologies: a 'massive technological system'.

Today, building houses is understood as an industry. Most building construction combines factory and on-site fabrication – unusual in the historical literature about industrialisation (Rilling 2001; Burley, Horsefall, and Brandon 1992; Nash 1987; Laurie 1989; Cordulack 1975). Construction is an industry with complex aspects of production and consumption. The house has been converted into a series of components and processes that reflect patterns of geography and consumption. Although this is not simple industrialisation, arguably, the very dispersal of building production is more influential, levelling building practices in different localities through the introduction of standardised industrial building materials and components.

Wood is a material with a unique economic geography. Lumber is politically and economically a nineteenth-century commodity. Its production combines aspects of agricultural harvesting and mining – basic extractive industries that depend on the 'boundless' resources of the land, privilege monocultural production and define numerous by-products as waste. It is based in a formal and linear process that produces dimension lumber, sash and moulding – building components that are defined by dimension, profile and assembly-line sequence. It is made to conform to the mechanical exigencies of production (Giedion 1948). Lumber was essentially a new and experimental product for house structure in the 1800s. Dimension lumber reacts differently than timber or even planks, so selecting lumber, seasoning and storing it, and assembling it into a building would have required allowances quite different from timber construction.

In general, the twentieth century developed wood products based on engineering principles – plywood, glue-laminated beams and parallel-strand materials. Plywood is a typical material of the twentieth century: engineered, laminated and effectively isotropic, with structural properties quite distinct from timber or lumber (Marrey 1994: 195). Plywood is more rigid, more difficult to form and transform, and requires a different set of tools and processes, because of its decreased workability. Its isotropic nature suited old engineering theories demanding predictability and uniformity. Plywood is a good example of a modern industrial product; value is added to the basic material in the production process. In comparison to lumber, its processing is more complex, demanding more dexterity, care and judgment before and during its production. The basic expenditures of capital, material, energy and pollution are quite different. Plywood changes our understanding of wood's properties, and there is a reduced potential for ordinary interaction with wood in this form. It is perceived as stronger than wood: an ideal, stable, planar substrate in shear walls, high-traffic floors and counter-tops. Although both lumber and plywood are industrial products, plywood is more obviously manufactured and, as a result, is open to ambivalent interpretation: sometimes as material, sometimes as product.

> The capital threshold of entry rose several fold in the antebellum years. Capital demands precipitated mainly by technological innovations squeezed out or barred most small entrepreneurs. Standardization of quality and dimensions worked in concert with the rise of commission traders and wholesalers ... [this furthered the] integration of production and distribution in the trade.
>
> (Rilling 2001: 99–103)

In North America, change to diverse local and ethnic building traditions occurred in the interstices between the traditions, accelerated and overtaken by technological, economic, environmental and demographic events of the mid-nineteenth century. In rural United States, itinerant tradesmen and peddlers established networks of commercial relations that combined production and sales (Jaffee 1991; Benes and Benes 1984). Speculative land practices tied the capitalisation of wood production to surplus farming. Housewrights integrated networks of knowledge and skill with networks of exchange in land and new wood products. Machines first took over the monotonous and quickly learned tasks of joinery. In this context of diversity and change, however, the introduction of industrial products and new technical routines were not immediately reductive.

By the mid-nineteenth century, most repetitive tasks were replaced by mouldings, lumber, sash and other extruded products of lineal factory processes (Peters 1996: 245). Items such as windows, doors and blinds were stocked year round. 'Wages for employees of sash and door firms compared favorably to carpenters in nonmechanical settings. In fact, employment around the seasons probably raised the standard of living for those workers above their artisan contemporaries' (Rilling 2001: 132). In general, change in building practice accelerated when local trading relations were established, based on exchange value. These were gradually and sporadically appropriated by larger and larger networks of trade organised from ever more distant industrial centres. Typically, at the scale of the individual, land was the first item that was bought on the basis of exchange value. This was extended into surplus farming, building materials and construction skills. The reason for the initial development of the balloon frame in the region of the Midwest was the strength and popularity of market exchange, amplified by the short duration of its introduction during initial settlement (Cavanagh 2002). It was change, introduced in this concentrated way, that stimulated its introduction in the Midwest rather than any other region of North America. The change affected material and practice in a way that continually extended the influence of the system of wood production.

### Exporting North American conventions

Today, John Greenough, a Nova Scotian builder, exports North American light-wood framing techniques and materials to Europe. He speaks of the difference between German and North American construction practices in very straightforward terms: 'Why should we pay carpenters in Germany C$150 an hour while we teach them how to build light-wood frame houses, when our carpenters know how to build it, do it well, and will do it for less?' (J. Greenough, interview, 10 March 2003). In North America, we have created a pervasive way of constructing houses; the light-wood frame construction system has been a stable practice for nearly two hundred years (Cavanagh 1997). It has organised and conditioned residential building practice and house form. Today, in a time of increased international trade, the light-wood frame continues its diffusion across the globe. Many countries now import North American softwood lumber, and as a by-product import the techniques of light-wood frame construction (DOTC 1965; OHC 196–; CMHC 1997; Larden Muniak and Youn 1998). It commands an increasing proportion of wood construction practices throughout the world, displacing local diversity and cultural traditions.[11]

Greenough is not alone in citing compelling reasons for this shift to North American practices. These arguments of economic advantage are similar to those used in nineteenth-century North America and contemporary Japan: it 'has many benefits over the traditional post-and-beam home-building system, still widely used in Japan. It takes less time to build and lends itself readily to the use of prefab components. It is also better able to withstand earthquake shocks' (Neil 1998). In Greenough's case, he built light-wood frame houses near Hanover for an average cost of C$285,000, compared with C$550,000 for conventional German house building.

A number of Canadian companies are building houses in Europe, and others are exporting precut houses for construction by European workers. Greenough was willing to spend time organising a 'turn-key' product because of a number of distinct advantages, some particular to the German situation. He was able to work with local desires for affordable housing and to work around stringent labour laws. The Canadian workers who built the houses were considered part of a skilled crew assembling a product beyond German capabilities. Only one German engineer was willing to certify the structural integrity of the construction, and only after the Canadian government guaranteed the compliance of the structure with the National Building Code of Canada. The wood was milled and kiln dried in Canada with an additional high-temperature treatment to certify that it was insect free. At the time, Germany had an oversupply of Bavarian fir, but it was not even of sufficient quality to meet German standards for oriented-strand board. For light-wood frame applications, this local wood requires at least 50 per cent more cross-sectional area for studs and joists. Perhaps, this is the reason that the engineers were reluctant to verify the structural integrity of light-wood frame and that a German architect predicted that it would 'rot out' in a few years. A recent drop in the German economy and a high demand in Nova Scotia mean that Greenough has put further projects on hold, but he will be doing it again. Meanwhile he has left the information with agencies of the Canadian government to pass on to others, for, as he says, 'The more that frame construction happens in Germany, the more accepted it will become, and the easier it will be to educate them on the values of [light-wood] frame'.

## Massive displacement and the system of consumption

The historian Daniel Boorstin writes of 'consumption communities'. They existed on at least two levels, household and market, and contained two equally important elements, goods and social relations. Building practices that used local materials in construction reinforced the local nature of construction. The kinds of goods being used and their point of origin mattered: 'these goods were used to forge new social relations, social relations that existed within the community (and were fostered by the household mode of production) and beyond the community (and were fostered by the capitalist mode of production)' (Orser 1991: 14). Wood became competitive in its various forms – as trees, as logs and as lumber. As the cost of wooded land increased, it became seen as a commodity to exchange. Not that trees couldn't be used from the actual site of the building, just that the house building trade fractured into different strategies according to exchange value.

Early on, felling and hewing timber might take place on the same piece of land as the house.[12] Carpenters would assess the quality of the material supply as part of their trade. The carpenter's tradition of evaluating live trees, felling, curing and laying out the cutting of the timber was first displaced by lumber supplied by local sawmills fed from forests upstream. As local material became scarce, importation became the norm and construction changed. Within this general drift to imported industrial products, there were cyclical variations in availability that induced economic competition between local and imported materials and among building components produced on site, in local shops and in distant factories. 'Jean-Christophe Agnew has argued that in the first stages of capitalism the market became dislodged from an actual sense of place and became an amorphous entity, a free-floating concept' (Jaffee 1991: 527). In other words, a local 'marketplace' becomes the placeless 'market'. This shift away from local trade in materials was momentous. The massive importation of construction material and practices into the US Midwest contributed to the establishment of communities strongly influenced by imported production. Like other developments, this happened in stages and unevenly.[13]

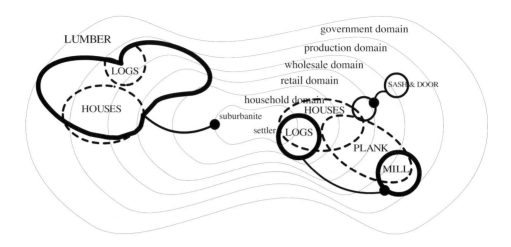

*8.4  Two diagrams show the domains of consumption and production for wood prod-
ucts in the US; the earliest period (right side) until c.1810 in the Midwest and c. 1840
in the East, and the later period (left side) after c. 1820 in the Midwest and after c.
1850 in the East. It is possible to contrast an earlier time, when the sources of supply
were logs from the building site and plank from local mill, with a later time when the
lumber industry was organised nationwide.*

The organisation of wood supply for houses is shown graphically in a diagram of the
'consumption junction' that looks at the sources of supply from the consumer's point of
view (Fig. 8.4). The contours in the diagram move outward from the consumer, whether
settler or suburbanite, through various domains – household, retail, wholesale, production and government. The diagram represents some interesting changes interpreted by
one of this chapter's authors from general evidence. The house itself has migrated
outward from the consumer to lie nearly exclusively in the retail domain. Consumers in
the later period are almost exclusively involved in maintenance and small renovations,
and the logs, the raw material of wood construction, are no longer obtained locally. In
the earlier period, the production domain included the sawmills and the sash-and-door
manufacturers that have existed since colonial times. The caption to the diagram
suggests that the Midwest moved to the wider organisation of wood supply earlier than
the Atlantic Coast.

Many historians have commented on the balloon frame as a strategy for building on
the treeless prairie, but they have failed to remark on the larger implications of this
occurrence. From 1830 to 1850, nine trans-Appalachian states had a combined
population increase of more than 4.5 million, and the area was by far the most rapidly
growing in the country. 'Based on an average household size of 5.55 persons in 1850,
a minimum of 827,000 residential structures would have had to have been
constructed in these regions to accommodate the increased population' (Loveday
1983: 47). The Midwest received this incredible number of settlers at a time when the
improvement of the transportation network allowed vast quantities of materials to be

transported to the Midwest. For probably the first time in history, the method of constructing houses for an entire region no longer depended on, nor indeed drew its quality from, local materials. This intrinsic rejection of local materials was by implication a rejection of one of the inherent properties of regional building that was based in a vernacular tradition.

The volume of lumber used to build houses in the new Midwest and prairie settlements created possibly the first instance of a commercially determined, materially driven vernacular architecture. These houses depended on a cheap transportation system as well as an abundant supply of forest – firstly that replaced by the agrarian landscape of the Piedmont and Trans-Appalachia, then the forests surrounding Lakes Huron, Michigan and Superior. The displacement of materials from Ohio, western New York, western Pennsylvania and the region around the Great Lakes was one of the largest in history. Building with wood on the prairies was the first instance of a major displacement of building materials, a displacement so vast that it rivals major material displacements of the twentieth century (Cavanagh 2002).

### *Alternative technology: construction, culture and environment*

Wood still provides the best point of comparison for material efficiency. Instead of the massive displacement of wood products outlined in the previous section, local procurement reinforces the advantages of wood as a sustainable building material. In Eskasoni, Nova Scotia, building practices created by one of the authors takes advantage of the self-optimisation principle in nature and of wood as a product of nature (Kroeker 1998). This work exemplifies locally defined sustainable technology.

It draws on traditional cultural building practices of the Algonquian First Nations people, practices based on natural efficiency. Wood, as it comes directly from the forest, is already optimally configured in concentric tubes of cellulose fibre, continuous from end to end. While it is green and uncut, wood has built-in flexibility. Utilising these basic properties, local structures in the Mi'kmaq tradition were not sawn, and were often bent while green into buildings to gain structural advantage from curvature.

In Kroeker's work, forms derived from a study of traditional wood use have generated a system of binding and shear connections that give these bent structural members their stability and predictable tolerances (Figs 8.5a, b and c). These new building practices seek to follow traditional principles to minimise the embodied energy of the material and maximise their structural advantage. Small-diameter red and black spruce tree thinnings are harvested from the local forest, then bent into structures while still green, using bending jigs and a system of connections. Once the erected structure dries in place, there is checking of the round wood components but very little movement, as the cellulose fibres remain continuous, even around knots. This technique creates buildings to modern specifications using locally available materials, with very little additional embodied energy. In this case, the material is a free by-product of forest optimisation (thinning).

Apart from its material efficiencies, this method of building is giving cultural continuity to the built environment of the Mi'kmaq people, who have lived in this region for many thousands of years. The intent of the research has been to seek efficiencies, to resist the importation of wood technologies based in European or US practices, and as a result, reinforce the connection between a culture and its environment.

8.5a, b and c  Buildings and building components for an innovative system of building construction. Environmental, building material and cultural factors combine to create prototypes for new ways of building with wood.

## Conclusions

The adjustments necessary to convert current building practices to sustainable ones are of the magnitude of those that occurred during the first industrial revolution, when changes in the processes of production led to new patterns of consumption. As we have seen, the scale and unity of the forces of consumption are now exerting their influence on wood production processes. In the current context, consumer values and perceptions are increasingly important and have the potential to reinforce locality, diversity and social justice as important indicators of sustainability.

Wood has strong claims to a sustainable architecture based in locality, diversity and the links between culture and environment. These claims are rooted in history, but times of transition are times of jeopardy. Clearly, leaders of the wood industry are worried. The American Forest and Paper Association, representing 80 per cent of wood producers in the United States, is campaigning to 'halt the development of new ISO standards on sustainable building construction which have the potential to limit market access of wood globally and favor non-wood products in building systems in general' (AF&PA 2002). In addition, the association has concerns about the US Green Building Council's 'Leadership in Energy and Environmental Design' (LEED) Building Rating System and the potential impact of these new voluntary standards on contemporary wood production. LEED ratings encourage construction techniques that reduce the quantity of wood in conventional wood frame by up to 30 per cent. Further, proposed LEED standards require wood that is FSC certified, is locally manufactured and contains recycled content. Definitions of sustainable practice will introduce new standards, and the danger is that these will lead to a more pervasive and proscriptive technological system of wood production. Because wood continues to play the role of lead indicator in discussions about sustainability, the manner and quality of this adjustment will influence the entire building industry and any of its claims of sustainability in the future.

A new orthodoxy of sustainability might have a radically reductive impact on local and even national practices. In the view of the authors, however, reductive tendencies can be countered by an ongoing critique that values diversity, redundancy and adaptability within a long-term economic and cultural context. This creates room for the construction of multiple sovereign practices within the strong values of sustainability. This is a basic strategy for resilience.

In this chapter, we have elaborated on cases that place wood at the forefront of these important questions of sustainable architecture. To capitalise on its historical and ecological advantages, the wood industry must extend its influence far beyond the sites of its harvest and fabrication, despite the complexities raised by extending this influence into political, social and ethical realms.[14] By the same token, the discussion around other materials and processes of architecture must extend beyond the site of their consumption to look also at the long-term environmental, ethical and political issues around their mining, harvesting and processing.

Sustainability, technology and culture are inextricably linked. Currently a wide and diverse set of wood construction practices is being made more heterogeneous by the introduction of new criteria of sustainable practice. The heterogeneity of wood technologies suggests the possibility of new creative combinations built on the values of sustainability. In summing up historical Mi'kmaq definitions of sustainability, Albert Marshall refers to two fundamental principles that make these concepts universally accessible: firstly, actions should be examined in the context of their individual and collective effects for seven generations; and secondly, there is a consciousness of spirit in all living things that connects them. These principles are a reminder that current considerations of sustainability are part of a long and significant history – values indigenous to Nova Scotia and North America.

## Notes

1 An important ruling by the Supreme Court of Canada supported this principle. On 17 September 1999 the court overruled the Provincial Court of Nova Scotia and the Nova Scotia Appeal Court and supported the argument of Donald Marshall, a Mi'kmaq. Treaties from the 1760s between the Crown and the Mi'kmaq people gave him the right, as a Mi'kmaq, to catch fish for sale and excused him from current government fisheries regulations. This supported a Mi'kmaq view that control of resources within their traditional territories remained with them and was embedded in their treaties.

2 The Innu of Labrador were in Europe protesting the environmental impact of low-level training flights by NATO over their territory when Albert Marshall was on his campaign. Objibway and Cree groups came later to campaign against clear-cut forestry practices in northern Ontario and Quebec. In the 1980s, the Oglala Sioux promoted cultural preservation, which they linked to the environment. John Sark travelled to the Vatican to press for recognition of an historic treaty between the Vatican and the Mi'kmaq nation (A. Marshall, private interview, 8 December 2002).

3 The economic chamber is restricted to 25 per cent of the membership; this has led to a lack of industry support in Canada (Dudley et al. 1995: 147; Moffat 1998: 47). The Canadian organisation created a fourth chamber to represent the interests of First Nations.

4 The legitimacy of this 1998 certification was challenged by environmentalists at the time (Sierra Club 2001). Their challenge was based, in particular, on the continuing use of biocides in their forests.

5 Currently the demand for FSC-certified products by far exceeds the supply.

6 In most cases the trees that are used in plantations are exotic species, which are often very invasive and seriously harm surrounding natural indigenous ecosystems. Government support for plantation forestry and its island ecology makes New Zealand a focus of current debate and study.

7 For example, the International Organization for Standardization (ISO) deals with the efficacy of environmental management processes, in other words the effectiveness of managing for production to whatever forestry standard has been established (ISO 1998; von Zharen 1996: 40). ISO and the compatible but more specific Canadian Standards Association standard is moving from conformance to performance, with increased emphasis on improvement and customer satisfaction and/or public participation (ISO 9001-2000, CSA Z-808-96 and Z-809-96). Generally both government and industry have schemes of their own: SFI (USA and Canada), CSA (Canada) and various national governments of Europe led by Finland (Moffat 1998; Canada Senate 1999; Finnish Forest Certification Committee 1997).

8 Remilling is complex. After moisture content has been checked, there are four basic sorts. 'The primary sort is for pieces that meet the JAS grade standard … The other sorts are for acceptable JAS after trimming, remanufacturing or rejects for resale in the local market … Through reprocessing, remanufacturing and fabrication, about 85 percent is recovered' (Neil 1998).

9 Although there is general agreement that current practices are unsustainable and data unreliable, one estimate for New Brunswick puts production level at 150 per cent of the 'annual allowable cut' – a coarse measure of volume of wood that, in the government's estimate, is economically sustainable.

10 Slabs are the four thin, half-round, bark-covered slices created by the initial squaring of the log.

11 See, for instance, the statistical increase in various countries outside North America, such as Japan: 80,000 units in 1997 for 13 per cent of wood-frame construction, up from 9 per cent in 1994 (USDA 2002). Canadians train Chinese builders as an export strategy (COFI 2002). A proponent of light-wood frame construction was Walter Segal, a UK architect who built a reputation that was partly based on its introduction and refinement.

12 One defining characteristic of vernacular building is materials with low transport costs. For Cumbria, UK, the limit of twenty miles for timber in the seventeenth and eighteenth centuries has been suggested (Tyson 1998: 77).
13 Everything develops unevenly. Small craft production persists alongside the factory production of building materials. The scale of the manufacturing operation was influenced by situation rather than following any model of continuous development. In other words, development depends on spatial attributes rather than just temporal and causal ones (Safley and Rosenband 1993).
14 For example, the wood industry has to address the genetic manipulation of trees as well as a range of new wood production processes, cyber-organic and genetically engineered products that break down the dichotomy of nature and culture to create hybrids that generate previously unknown materials (Manzini 1986: 14–15). Writing about a future generation of materials created using nanotechnology, scientist Ralph Merkle says of this new family of material, 'It gives the ultimate in flexibility consistent with physical law. And ultimately it will be low cost, less than $1.00 per kilogram, roughly the price of wood' (Fouke 2000: 47).

# 9

# Policing sustainability

## Strategies towards a sustainable architecture in Norway

*Marianne Ryghaug*

Norwegian architects have not been much occupied with sustainable design, according to Ryghaug. Her chapter analyses three examples of building projects in Norway that have tried to incorporate sustainability in their design and planning. The chapter's main goal is to identify the potential existence of underlying conditions in these processes that are favourable to the promotion of sustainable buildings. Her analysis explores the process of 'policing sustainability' in order to promote sustainable buildings. The analysis suggests that achievement of sustainability depends on key actors championing the process of green design. She suggests at least two ways in which this may happen. Either the sustainability concerns may be safeguarded by means of duty, such as through an environmental management programme, or there must be someone, preferably a building owner, who sees it as his or her responsibility to pursue such concerns. As such processes are embedded, a form of 'social learning' can develop that may ultimately accelerate the up-take of sustainable technologies.

## The challenge of promoting sustainable buildings

Norwegian architects have not been much occupied with sustainable design. Most of them do not seem to regard sustainability as an aspect to which they have to relate, and even less as something that they should integrate into their practice. Thus, sustainable design is 'domesticated' only by a minor part of the profession (Silverstone et al. 1989; Sørensen 1996). One reason for this is probably that most Norwegian architects struggle with defining sustainability as a core part of their profession. The dominant architectural discourse is experimenting with form, function and shape (Ryghaug 2002). Moreover, sustainable architecture has traditionally been associated with out-groups and a particular image of buildings that breaks with the modernism preferred by most architects. This alternative building image is often coupled with two opposing traditions: low-tech and high-tech ecological architecture. The low-tech movement is associated with the use of wooden materials, turf roofs and a style similar to traditional mountain cabins, the high-tech energy-efficient buildings with double glass façades or complicated ventilation systems and buildings where technology is thought to be more important than the shape or design. Similar approaches to sustainable buildings are identified by Guy and Farmer (2001) and by Sudjic (1995), quoted in Guy (2002). This debate is also referred to as a technocentric versus ecocentric debate (Farmer and Guy 2002).

Furthermore, few policy instruments or institutional frameworks have been set up with the intent of promoting sustainable buildings in Norway, and the measures that exist seem both uncoordinated and occasional. Viewed against this background, it is obvious that realising sustainable buildings is not an easy task. Thus, it is important to identify what strategies and measures may be needed to cope with the present challenges.

This chapter analyses three recent Norwegian projects that have aimed at sustainable design, in order to assess their success and to study how problems are addressed in practice. Given that most architects do not seem very interested in sustainable architecture, how is it possible to imagine the realisation of sustainable buildings? In what way is it possible to set up processes of building design and planning that promote sustainable architecture? It is also interesting to consider how these building projects dealt with the problem of aesthetics.

One goal of this chapter is to identify any general underlying conditions in these processes that seem favourable to the promotion of sustainable buildings. It is obvious that, in order to encourage green buildings, we need to improve our understanding of the social and technological processes that underpin the development of environmentally sound designs. The answers to these questions might give some clues as to what could make the realisation of sustainable architecture more successful in the future.

The analysis is based on qualitative interviews with key actors in each building project who have had an influence on the design of the building (building owners, developers, architects, engineers, consultants and researchers) and on relevant written material (e.g. environmental management programmes, reports, brochures and journals) and websites. The first section gives a general presentation of the three buildings and a description of the design process. The second discusses the different features of each building with regard to environmental goals and aspects of sustainability. The third summarises the features that seem to be helpful to the realisation of sustainable buildings, and the concluding section gives an actor-differentiated summary.

## The process of designing sustainable buildings

The three different building projects chosen as case study objects are Pilestredet Park, a large residential project in Oslo; Kvernhuset, an ecological school project; and Telenor Fornebu, the largest office building in Norway. Each project made pronounced efforts to incorporate sustainability into its design and planning. The cases fulfil different functions and differ in size and location, the Kvernhuset project being significantly smaller than the other two and situated outside the Oslo region. The Kvernhuset project also differs from the other two as it is a public project, while the others are private sector initiatives. Table 9.1 summarises the features of each building. The buildings also differ with respect to the design process, involvement of research activities and environmental goals.

The municipality of Fredrikstad owns Kvernhuset Junior High School. Apart from constructing Norway's most environmentally friendly school, Fredrikstad municipality had two main goals: first, to develop a school that minimised the consumption of energy, materials and economic resources during the lifetime of the building and used renewable resources as much as possible, and second, to create a school where the building itself was a learning tool for achieving sustainability. Construction started in May 2000.

Kvernhuset is part of the municipality's programme for Local Agenda 21. It was already decided in the planning phase that the school was to be based on the principle of sustainable development, in line with 'the environmentally friendly city of Fredrikstad' project. Fredrikstad was one of five cities in Norway given official status as an environmentally friendly city. The school was to be located in woods, but still at the centre of the

*Table 9.1 Summary of design features of the three case study buildings*

|  | Kvernhuset | Pilestredet Park | Telenor Fornebu |
|---|---|---|---|
| Function | School building | Residences | Office building |
| Location | Semi-urban | City centre | Out-of-town business park |
| Developer | Local: Fredrikstad municipality | Local: property company (PPB) | Local developer (Telenor) |
| Floor area (m²) | 8,500 | 28,570* | 140,000 |
| Funding | Public | Private | Private |
| Architect competition | Open | Closed | Open |
| Research involvement | Yes | Yes | No |

*Total area that the architects' firm GASA was responsible for

intake area for the school. The planning process took place with the cooperation and involvement of pupils, parents, teachers, the health service and so on, to produce a solid programme that formed the basis for the competition for an architect. In addition, a major consultation exercise within Fredrikstad municipality was organised, with the participation of the different municipal departments and local bureaucrats.

Initially, the planning committee travelled to Sweden and Denmark to look for a holistic model project but could only find fragmentary solutions. They also sought help from the National Association of Norwegian Architects (NAL) in finding a reference project in Scandinavia, but without any luck. In the absence of any examples, they allowed themselves to spend some time fantasising before deciding what to choose. NAL put the planning committee in touch with the association Norwegian Architects for Sustainable Architecture (NABU), which assisted the municipality in planning a three-day workshop. The goal of the workshop was to establish a platform of ideas to inform the plan for the school. The workshop also functioned as a pre-qualification exercise for the architect competition and gave the prospective architects a chance to hear directly from the users what they desired.

The first day of the workshop involved a visit to the site. A climate analysis was conducted, the biological diversity of the site was mapped out, and a historical profile of the area was presented. On the second day users presented their wishes, followed by teamwork sessions on the topic. The results from these two days were presented on day three, together with different environmental and energy-efficient solutions. The school was programmed on the basis of the work of the planning committee and the workshops.

With all the preconditions in place the architect competition was announced and six of the best propositions were selected. These architects were invited to a seminar in Fredrikstad, where they were presented with the new learning plan and some of the ongoing environmental work of the municipality, and were given the opportunity to ask questions. The municipality stressed that the environmental challenges were to be taken seriously, as earlier experiences showed this was not always the case.

The joint project of Pir II, an architecture firm in Trondheim, and Duncan Lewis Architects, of Paris, was announced the winner. According to the jury leader, this was the best project because of its exciting solutions and careful planning. The jury's assessment was that 'the architect tries to use the significant qualities of the site – the mountain, the forest, the light – within the concept of sustainable development' (Pir II Arkitektkontor 1998). The project focused on making the building and the surroundings grow together, and it had unconventional plans for co-use of some areas in the building.

Financial support for the project came from EcoBuild, a national action-oriented programme meant to improve eco-efficiency in the building industry by introducing profitable solutions, regulations and support. The purpose of the support was to cover additional expenses in the planning process, allowing the time and resources needed to explore natural and hybrid ventilation solutions and to achieve an environmentally friendly building. The EcoBuild programme also financed two other research institutes to monitor and report the experiences of the project.

Pilestredet Park, the second case study project, has been marketed as a 'green oasis in the centre of Oslo', situated as it is in the capital's most attractive residential area (Fig.

*9.1 Pilestredet Park.*

9.1). The Directorate of Public Construction and Property (Statsbygg) and the municipality of Oslo collaborated in steering the development through. The area was to be rebuilt for housing, a college, industry and public utilities, including a national medical museum. Of the 110,000 square metres of existing buildings, 50,000 square metres were to be demolished in an environmentally friendly way to allow 75,000 square metres of new houses and apartments. Construction of the first building started in August 2001.

Pilestredet Park is envisioned as a project that unites the best environmental solutions, forming a totality that promotes and stands out as a leading example of sustainable urban development efforts. According to Statsbygg, the project is a way of seriously shaping the future in the building industry.

In 1999, Selmer Bolig and OBOS Utviking AS, two large property development firms, bought three of the areas within Pilestredet Park from Statsbygg, with the aim of building 400 residences. Together they formed a new firm, Pilestredet Park Boligutbygging ANS, which managed the project development. One of the points in the sales contract referred to a 'Miljøoppfølgingsprogram' for Pilestredet Park: an environmental management programme (EMP) for sustainable, environmental and energy-efficient buildings to which companies buying into the park committed themselves.

Thus, the project's development was based on a goal-oriented commitment to environment and health. The architect competition was a pre-qualification exercise requiring competence, capacity and prices. An architects' firm famous for its experience in sustainable design, GASA, was given the assignment, together with Lund and Slaatto Architects AS. The project was supported by €480,000 from an integrated project of an EU research programme. This funding enabled consideration of various different solutions, the systematic collation and cross-disciplinary analysis of various actors' experiences of sustainable solutions, and the installation of solutions that would not have been chosen but for the environmental demands.

The third case study, Telenor's new headquarters at Fornebu, on the outskirts of Oslo, is the largest single-company office complex in northern Europe. The plan was to relocate 7,000 Telenor employees to Fornebu from more than 35 offices located throughout the greater Oslo area. In September 1999, approximately one year after the start of the project, construction of 40,000 square metres of buildings and 40,000 to 50,000 square metres of parking began.

At Fornebu, Telenor aimed to create 'the foremost innovative and prosperous working environment in all of the Nordic countries' (www.telenor.co). The company's new headquarters was intended to enhance Telenor's profile and to proclaim its identity, ambitions and self-understanding to its employees, while at the same time being a centralised location for the company. The project was thought to have a functional, aesthetic and environmental profile that would reflect Telenor's ambitious technological development but also take people and nature into consideration (Paulsen 2003). The ambition was to create an architectural milestone at the start of a new millennium.

The process of creating Telenor's new headquarters started in 1997 when Telenor issued an international invitation to interested architectural teams to enter a pre-qualifying competition. The remit was for an extensive building programme that included the overall visions of the project. Three juries evaluated the project proposals (on economical aspects, functionality and the building as a workplace). Of the seven sketches submitted three were considered interesting, and these contenders were invited to participate in the second round.

A consortium of three architectural firms – two Norwegian firms, HUS Architects and Per Knudsen Architect Office AS (PKA), and NBBJ from Seattle – won the competition. Their project was judged as more architecturally exciting and better profiled than the others. Their building was seen as having a strong functional character with a clear structure, and the analysis of the programme intentions was perceived as perfect. At first the jury found the concept difficult to understand and felt that it was not feasible for economic reasons, as it used far too much glass (50 per cent to 60 per cent of the façade). However, it later came to the conclusion that the project did in fact fit the brief – it took up less area than was envisioned in the original remit and was structured more like 'a suite in the park' than a typical urban structure. An updated building programme and an environmental management programme were later produced and formed the basis for the project work.

## Features linked to sustainability

The three case study buildings differ with respect to environmental and sustainability features. The buildings embody quite contrasting and particular building design responses to the different environmental goals and requirements faced in each case. Not only do they represent different technical and physical solutions or pathways to the problem of sustainable design, they also have very different approaches to how one should produce sustainable designs, in terms of the design process. This may be partly linked to the way the energy and environmental goals in these different projects have been formulated and the degree to which the building owner or developer played the role of initiator of the environmental aspects in the projects. Table 9.2 summarises the features relating to the sustainability goals, processes and solutions in the three buildings.

The Kvernhuset project surpasses the building codes, which are often perceived as being too loose and out of touch with the latest technology. Its environmental goals cover everything from demanding a 'clean building' process to quite particular considerations with regard to transportation, handling the building site, data on materials, etc. The energy efficiency and energy conservation strategies were the use of:

- daylight to reduce the consumption of electricity for artificial lighting;
- separately operating zones for artificial lighting and control by daylight sensors;
- natural forces such as air pressure and wind for ventilation, to minimise power used for fans;
- control of airflow, heat recovery and low-emitting building materials;
- geothermal heat;
- alternative building materials, e.g. transparent, environmentally friendly insulation in façades.

(www.sintef.no/units/civil/ark/ark/Norsk/Prosjekter/Kvernhuset)

The different buildings in the school were given different colours to reflect the main theme of each, the yellow buildings focusing on energy, green on growth and reuse of materials and blue on circulation of water. The buildings are composed of simple rectangular volumes, ensuring rational constructions. Technical solutions integrated into the design contribute to energy saving and a better indoor climate. The school has a thermal ventilation system based on underground culverts that minimise the need for air

*Table 9.2* *Responses in the three case study projects to environmental goals and requirements*

|  | Kvernhuset | Pilestredet Park | Telenor |
|---|---|---|---|
| *Type of goals* | Qualitative | Quantitative | Qualitive and quantitative |
| *Infrastructure networks* | Semi-autonomous | Integrated | Semi-autonomous |
| *Key low-energy features* | • Passive solar design<br>• Transparent façades<br>• Use of daylight<br>• Ground source heat pump<br>• Thermal ventilation system<br>• Low-emitting materials | • Well-sealed construction<br>• Building shape and orientation<br>• Improved insulation<br>• Energy efficient ventilation<br>• Energy efficient equipment | • Seawater heat pump<br>• District heating– local renewable energy source<br>• Better windows<br>• Low-emitting materials<br>• Effective use of floor space<br>• Zoned control of heating and lighting |
| *Technical strategies* | Innovative, pedagogical | Semi-conventional, remunerative | Conventional minimal requirements |
| *Developer/owner the initiator of sustainability?* | Yes | No | No |
| *Design process/ strategy* | Integrated | Semi-integrated | Traditional |
| *Contractual goals* | No | Yes (EMP) | Yes (EMP) |
| *Political initiators* | Local Agenda 21 Environmental community | Statsbygg | Statsbygg |

EMP = environmental management programme

filters, heating and cooling. A heat pump provides as much as possible of the energy for cooling and heating. Daylight enters the building through ceiling lights and transparent façades to increase the energy efficiency and give better working conditions. A treatment plant for discharge water takes care of the sewerage. The interior is filled with plants to purify the indoor air and regulate the moisture level (Kvernhuset Ungdomskole 2000). The most important energy solution is the heat pump, which helps the project in many ways as it allows the use of much more glass than would otherwise be considered acceptable from an energy efficiency point of view.

The Kvernhuset project won EcoBuild's environment prize in 2000 and has attracted extensive attention. It was one of the main attractions at the World Exposition of Architecture in Venice in 2001. The project was also nominated for the prestigious Mies van der Rohe Award 2003 and has gained a lot of publicity in Norwegian and international professional journals (Lewis 1999, 2000).

The EMP for Pilestredet Park and Oslo's ecological programme are the two pillars that are meant to ensure sustainable and ecological urban development in the whole Pilestredet Park area. They are framed as a number of goals and intentions with regard to environmental aspects. The construction of the building according to environmentally sound principles was to be based on:

- creating a good indoor climate;
- protecting against traffic noise;
- a focus on health and safety during the construction;
- 'clean building' processes and protection from damp during the construction phase;
- building techniques and materials that minimise environmental strain and energy consumption;
- documenting the properties of the materials used throughout the whole life cycle of the project.

The goal was to reduce energy consumption by designing the building in an energy-conscious way, in terms of architecture and building techniques as well as exploiting the local sunshine and climate conditions. Electricity was not be used for heating purposes, and district heating was to be employed in combination with solar energy and recycled energy, water-saving fittings and low-energy lamps in fixed installations. Both Statsbygg and the municipality of Oslo envisioned these guidelines and goals for the whole area (Statsbygg 2000). As they were part of the sales contract, they also applied to the residential project of Selmer Bolig and OBOS Utviking AS, studied here.

The EMP demands that the project has an overall responsibility to introduce environmental goals in building plans and architect competitions and when inviting tenders and entering into contracts. In the pre-project phase this responsibility went to GASA, which had been assigned the role of environmental coordinator for the project. GASA also had the responsibility for developing a control plan. It has been a deliberate policy to integrate the environmental aspects as a core part of the project so that the environmental demands are not treated separately. The project's management has been involved with all the groups of actors, such as the environmental group, and there has been a focus on quality assurance and fostering motivation in all stages of the process, right down to the person nailing bolts.

The overall energy goal of the project was that annual energy consumption for the gross floor area that is heated should not exceed 100 kWh/m$^2$. Other goals arising from the final contracts are a demand for flexibility in energy sources for heating systems through connection to the district heating network, more effective energy use through the use of IT systems, and alternative heating sources. In addition, there are demands for the zoned division of apartments to ensure good heating efficiency and high thermal mass construction.[1] Apart from the specific energy requirement not to exceed 100 kWh/m$^2$, there were few restrictions on the choice of solution.

The heat, ventilation and air conditioning (HVAC) consultant planned a series of energy saving measures together with the architect, prioritising those measures that have major effects. These included the use of windows with a better thermal heat transfer coefficient (U-value) than normal, thicker insulation in walls and roofs, 'green' plantation roofs on a third of the roof area, stopping up details by windows and in the wall–floor and wall–roof transitions, energy-efficient ventilation aggregates and energy-saving lighting. Together, these measures have been calculated to give an energy consumption of 99 kWh/m$^2$ a year.[2]

The buildings have straight walls without a lot of fancy detail, and the apartments are quite small. Energy efficiency considerations are the basis for the choice of room plan. For example, there is as little façade as possible per apartment, and the bedrooms are placed on the shady side of the building. The bay window solution that the architect demanded for aesthetic reasons, with lots of glass and woodwork, is probably the least energy-efficient feature of the building.

According to the project manager, a cost-efficient way to save energy was used in this project. Stricter controls on energy consumption would have demanded more 'drastic' measures, as many measures, such as insulation, have a limited effect (efficiency does not increase in proportion to the amount used). One of the solutions the architects wanted was solar collectors on the roof, but this solution was rejected in the project as the building owners considered it too expensive. The property developer did not want experimentation in such a large project, so acceptable conventional solutions were mainly chosen. Thus, it will be interesting to compare the Pilestredet Park project with more high-tech sustainable buildings that achieve about the same estimated total energy savings, because if the project reaches its energy goals without the need for unconventional technological measures, this will be an important signal that the energy demands in Norwegian building codes can be tightened without implying extra costs.

In the Telenor project a special EMP was prepared that has the declared aim of 'ensuring that an understanding of its impact on nature, resources, the environment and society are systematically incorporated into each stage of planning, projecting, and development at Fornebu'. This programme is based on a document called the general environmental programme (GEP) for Fornebu, produced by the City of Oslo and Statsbygg. In the area of energy supply and consumption it has three goals: to adopt an energy supply and usage patterns that are sustainable, to create a flexible system that allows transformation to use of future energy sources and to prioritise the use of renewable energy sources. As a challenge to today's energy technology, a contest was organised to find an energy solution for the Fornebu area. The chosen solution was based on the winning entry, a combination of sea-water heat pumps and district heating.

The local planning authorities included the GEP in the final master plan for the Fornebu area to ensure that the environmental objectives and measures were incorporated at an early stage of the project. Special environmental plans for infrastructure, waste handling and renovation and repairs were also established. The landowners inform new owners about the environmental programme, and the new owners are responsible for the programme through the sale contracts. Thus all developers in the area, such as Telenor, are required to integrate the environmental programme into their planning and construction, including building plans, architectural design competitions, calls for tenders and contracts. This means that they are obliged to develop their own environmental plans, including a set of objectives and measures that is supposed to contribute to the achievement of an environmentally sustainable Fornebu (Folkestad 2000). The goals of Telenor's environmental management programme, based on the GEP, were that:

- environmental considerations shall underpin the choice of materials;
- land use shall be reduced by 40 per cent of the current figure;
- more than 50 per cent of energy consumption shall be derived from local renewable energy resources through the use of sea water;
- in the construction phase 70 per cent of the waste shall be sorted on site, and 90 per cent in the operational stage;
- in the construction phase the total amount of building waste shall not exceed 65 pounds per square yard;
- all managers in the construction companies working for Telenor Eiendom Fornebu are required to take a course in health, environment and safety and external environment issues.

(Strom 1988)

Concerning the amount of energy used, the plan emphasises the importance of choosing technical solutions that make the running of the building consume as little energy as possible, for example through the use of low-energy products and energy efficiency measures. The relevant measures include:

- establishing a system for energy planning and control;
- the heating systems should be able to use low temperatures for heating, pre-heating of air for ventilation and production of hot tap water, and there should also be a central control unit in each building allowing separate control according to zone division and temperature-based utility control (according to need);
- super-isolating windows should be evaluated;
- the buildings should have time and utility control of lighting, photosensitive cells on outdoor lighting, and low-energy lighting in office and common areas.

One actual measure to reduce the energy consumption with regard to traditional ventilation systems is utility-based control of ventilation in bigger rooms and offices, as well as regulating the number of cycles of air change in the ventilation system. The main solution to meet the requirements of the EMP was the sea-water heat pump. Apart from this, a relatively low proportion of floor space per employee and utility control for lights and ventilation were included in the design. The project has experienced difficulties keeping up with the energy limits and is only marginally within the limits of the building codes.

## Favourable conditions for realising sustainable architecture

The three case study buildings demonstrate that it is possible to realise sustainable buildings within the dominant aesthetic discourse of architectural design. The architects of the Kvernhuset project as well as those of Telenor Fornebu seem to come from the dominant aesthetic paradigm in Norwegian architecture, with little experience in sustainable building design. The three building projects also seem to have escaped the image traditionally linked with sustainable design, as they are neither typically high-tech nor low-tech. The projects seem to integrate ideas and techniques stemming from both positions, while at the same time having highly modernist features that probably fit well into the dominant, aesthetically focused architectural discourse in Norway. This merging of elements from the traditional high-tech and low-tech approaches may also indicate that this controversy is on the wane.

In particular, the Kvernhuset building is a good example of how it is possible to find a way around the problem of aesthetics. It is evident that the actors in this case have managed to translate sustainability and energy efficiency into something considered commendable by most architects, as the project has received a great deal of attention and publicity in both national and international journals and expositions, as well as being nominated for a prestigious architect-prize. The project includes elements from high-tech as well as low-tech approaches to sustainable building design, using advanced technology in combination with passive measures such as adjustment of the terrain and the conditions on the site. The architects used the Kvernhuset project to illustrate that it is not necessary to write 'ecology' on a building to demonstrate that it is ecological; they avoided the use of 'ecological exclamation marks' and refused to use the technology as the design, trademarks or symbols of ecology. According to the architect, ecology implies that solutions grow together. Thus, the project may definitely be seen as a reference project that can inspire architects to build sustainable architecture, without being trapped in an extreme high-tech or low-tech expression.

The analysis of the final products of these three building projects illustrates that the future is not as gloomy as one might think on the basis of the overall architectural discourse in Norway. Some actors in the building industry take the challenge of building sustainable and energy-efficient buildings seriously when the conditions are right. It is important to note that the instruments we are talking about in relation to these projects operate almost at the lowest levels of the regulatory system: funding by the EcoBuild programme; architect competitions that integrate sustainability, energy and environmental criteria; guidelines from Statsbygg (the prime mover initiating the Pilestredet Park competition and creating the city ecological programme for Pilestredet Park); inspiration from working with Local Agenda 21 issues (important for the municipality of Fredrikstad); and advice and workshops organised in collaboration with NABU. This list shows that there exist quite a few measures that can be used at low levels, but these instruments do not seem to be very coordinated, and it is questionable whether they are initiated from the top.

First and foremost, the realisation of these three projects shows the importance of having devoted and competent people to implement them at all levels of the process – from building owner to architect and from consultant engineer to researcher. It is important to enrol actors (architects and consultant engineers) who take the challenge of realising sustainable buildings seriously and who do not view these challenges as trivial or gimmicky. In order to do this it is necessary to choose good professional co-workers and consultants and not to be too preoccupied with price. To go a step further in realising sustainable design, it seems necessary to include enthusiastic participants who are willing to take a few chances when choosing solutions.

The Kvernhuset project is a particularly good example of this, as it shows how important it is to have actors who are dedicated to the intentions of the project. Furthermore, the different actors in the project perceived this kind of dedication as a positive experience. They claim that it felt good to be a part of a process where everyone pulled in the same direction. This is probably one of the greatest advantages of the Kvernhuset project. It used a series of measures that can be included in such projects to ensure that those participating are committed to the idea of creating environmentally sound architecture. Examples of such measures are workshops (which also contribute to the development of new ideas and the spread of knowledge), seminars and inviting the participation of actors known to be committed to these kind of ideas, for example the HVAC consultant in the Kvernhuset project. The architect competition itself may also be seen as an incentive to promote sustainable buildings. However, it is only when environmental criteria are given real value and are used as a basis for deciding among different concepts and projects, as in the Kvernhuset case, that the competition can be a tool for promoting energy efficiency. Owing to the thoroughness and deep commitment of the actors, the Kvernhuset project appears to be able to realise its goals without the use of an environmental management programme. It is obvious that in order to do this it is vital to have an equally committed building owner.

Having a building owner with a powerful set of visions seems particularly important when projects do not have external incentives or control mechanisms for turning the project into a sustainable one. According to the actors in the Kvernhuset case, a sine qua non for being able to take environmental issues into consideration is to have a creative, determined, curious and inquisitive building owner. In the case of the Kvernhuset project the building owners obviously put a great deal of thought into what they wanted from the project. According to the architects it is also necessary that the building owner makes demands and is willing to go through with the process, as a lukewarm building owner will most likely choose conventional solutions. There also seems to be a positive effect in having a rather open approach to the building project in the beginning, as this does not rule out any solutions. It is also important for producing visions.

However, to realise a building project according to sustainability or environmental concerns it seems necessary to translate the visions into clear and consistent goals and demands. In the Telenor project and the Pilestredet Park project this has been done in terms of EMPs. Having an EMP seems to be crucial for achieving environmental goals, best illustrated by the Pilestredet Park project. This seems to be particularly the case when the building owners are not keen on environmental and energy issues and have been pushed into such considerations by regulations. It is also an advantage when the EMP is at the basis of the sales contract, and particularly when selling public property to private developers. Thus, the EMP of Pilestredet Park may be regarded as a judicial incentive, which probably contributed to making it a lot easier to make decisions on the basis of energy efficiency and sustainability. It also seems to be crucial that the requirements of the EMP are clear and to the point. The demands should be non-negotiable, as in the case of Pilestredet Park, where the building owner tried to negotiate the requirements when purchasing the building. For an EMP to work it is important that it be a premise from the start, even before an architect competition is held. It is also crucial that the EMP is followed properly, as was done in the Pilestredet Park project, and that the procedures for ensuring that the programme is followed apply to everyone in the project, right down to the people doing the actual construction. It also seems to be an advantage for an independent actor to follow the process and check that the procedures are overseen properly, so that the programme's requirements are carried out (as in the Pilestredet Park case).

An EMP makes it easier to realise new solutions, as architects and consultant engineers feel that solutions can be adopted that otherwise would not have been accepted for economic reasons or because there isn't enough time to elucidate them. The EMP in Pilestredet Park facilitated some solutions that are good in terms of energy use and that would have been difficult to implement if the process had been different. One example is the reduction in window areas and bow windows according to the wishes of the contractor. This contractor said that it is almost impossible to persuade architects to do this in a normal project. When it comes to energy specifically, contractors feel that normally they have little power to decide and that the architect often wins. However, when the demands are specific and are also part of the architect's contract, he or she has to take them into consideration. Another solution selected in Pilestredet Park because of the EMP is the use of district heating. The building site was in an area regulated for district heating. Normally exemption from the requirements for district heating may be granted on application, which is quite common, as district heating is more expensive. However, in this project exemption was not an option, because of the ecological requirements for the area.

Having to follow an EMP and to document and prove that its demands have been fulfilled was something new to most actors in the Pilestredet Park project. The EMP did not seem to reduce creativity. On the contrary, when the demands were put into practice they were regarded as stimulating imagination in developing environmentally sound solutions. In sum, all the actors seemed to think that participation in the Pilestredet Park project and the need to follow an EMP was a positive experience.

In the Telenor project the EMP seems to a have exerted only a minor influence on energy decisions. There is no doubt that other solutions could have been chosen that would have lowered the energy consumption of the building significantly more. However, considerations concerning aesthetics, user requirements, functionality and economy were considered more significant. In some cases the environmental demands were perceived as useless. For example, it seemed impossible to find consistent information or experiences that showed the environmental gains or disadvantages of building with different materials.

One of the classic discussions between architects and building owners is about glazing and window areas. This was also one of the main controversies in the Telenor Fornebu project. The feature that Telenor regards as the strongest environmental goal is the average floor usage per employee of approximately 22 square metres, which is considered to be quite low. However, the project manager admits that this was decided after it was determined how large the project should be so that it fitted the goals of the project perfectly and that it was not the EMP or energy concerns that led to this outcome. On the contrary it was driven by the discussion about the cost of the building.

However, those involved in the project made some quite important decisions from an energy point of view, and one of the strongest was to minimise emissions. During the first phase of the project, energy consumption was not discussed:

> At this point we thought of having as much glass and light as possible etc. to fulfil the idea and the main design concept. Design is not primarily energy design. It is associated with the site and the programme. The environmental part was a part of the programme, and the compact situation was the answer to that. When we had decided the main concept, we worked further with the different aspects. In the competition, we worked on different solutions energywise, but the owner did not emphasise those things, as they said they did not want to experiment on such a large scale. The solutions that were proposed were based on things that had already been done in other projects, but we could not demonstrate that they would save money or that it had operational advantages for the owner.
>
> (Interview with architect, 21 May 2003)

Thus, the architect did not find the owner to be particularly interested in alternative energy solutions. According to the consultant engineer, Telenor thinks it has fulfilled its visions regarding environmental friendliness by installing the heat pump.

The planning and organisation of the design process before the actual building of the project seems to be one of the crucial conditions for a successful sustainable and energy-efficient building. The process should be broad and open-minded from the beginning, as it is important to enrol as many actors as possible at this stage in order to create a solid basis for the project. This also benefits the production of new ideas. It is very important to allow some time in the planning phase for developing new ideas and trying to come up with new perspectives, as well as having the time to reflect on what is actually wanted from the building. The sooner that collaboration among architects, consultants and users can start, the smoother the process will go and the better the chances of integrating different technical solutions into the building design. Ideally, the HVAC consultant should take part in the planning process before the architect has drawn the first line. A pitfall seems to be determining the project before demands and concerns regarding sustainability are included, thus blocking many alternatives.

Planning a project like Kvernhuset is much more time consuming than an ordinary project as there are many new aspects to be sorted out and integrated into the building, for example integrated solutions and natural ventilation systems. With such a long and wide-ranging process, it is important to avoid providing solutions before knowing what all the questions might be. The process was thought by the participants in the Kvernhuset project to be the most important factor in making the project the success that they thought it would become. What was reported as fruitful in the process at Kvernhuset was the opportunity to see into one another's professional field and being flexible and generous in searching for solutions. To get optimal solutions one must not be afraid of rejecting a solution and starting over again.

The Telenor project offers a different picture with regard to these aspects. Despite the EMP, energy issues had no impact on the process of choosing a winner of the architect competition, according to the manager of the project. The winning project was the one with the largest area of glazing but was chosen on the basis of other qualities, such as architectonic expression and functionality. According to the project manager this was a fair assessment, as he thinks it absurd to make energy consumption the top priority when building a 150,000 square metre office building that is meant to be the landmark building of a large company. Also, when a project and an architectural team with an architectonic idea has been chosen, it would make no sense to then say that something completely different was wanted. The regulations were set two weeks after the architects for the project were assigned, thus already at this point many alternatives were ruled out.

It is a great advantage to include R&D projects when realising sustainable and energy-efficient buildings. This increases not only general knowledge about different solutions but also a feeling of confidence when choosing solutions. Consequently, R&D projects are essential for allowing one to be more creative and experimental in choosing solutions. External funding of R&D projects also allows more time in the planning process and thereby more time when considering alternative solutions. Projects that have been funded by the EcoBuild programme have stressed this funding as one of the factors with a particularly positive effect, as they are able to promote a greater interdisciplinarity in their working methods and a more integrated design process. This means that the different professions must communicate and exchange experiences.

Being supported in this way encourages better professional working environments where people cooperate, talk together and exchange experiences. This is thought to have a positive effect on the implementation of innovative energy-efficient solutions, because the basis on which choices are made is seen as being more secure. Even low-risk technical solutions like the ones chosen for Kvernhuset are reported to be difficult to integrate in ordinary building projects. Thus research projects like the ones discussed here contribute to making the introduction of such solutions a lot easier, as everyone feels safer.

## Conclusions

This study of the planning and design of the three case buildings not only demonstrates that it is possible to design sustainable buildings, given the right conditions; it also shows the difficulty of planning and designing in accordance with considerations of sustainability. It is not just the fact that architects are generally uninterested that makes designing sustainable buildings a problematic task. The three building projects demonstrate that it is not clear how environmentally friendly buildings may be designed: the options are many, and no standard solutions are available. The lack of standard methods for implementing energy-efficient and sustainable technologies has also been demonstrated in other studies. For example, Guy and Shove (2000) show that the effective implementation of the 'principles' of passive solar design has been an elaborate process of case-by-case interpretation, taking account of the orientation and layout of a building and the materials of which it is made. A recent study of the implementation of water-based floor-heating systems also showed the lack of an available, ready-for-use technology and subsequently the importance of 'social learning' in relation to such new solutions (Kongsli 2001).

Social learning denotes processes in which people who develop, implement or use a project are linked in diverse ways in networks, learn from their experiences and interact (Russell and Williams 2002). There are many different types of social learning, of which Sørensen identifies a few: learning by doing, learning by using and learning by interacting. He characterises social learning as a

> combined act of discovery and analysis, of understanding and meaning, and of tinkering and the development of routines. In order to make an artefact work, it has to be placed, spatially, temporally, and mentally. It has to be fitted into the existing, heterogeneous networks of machines, systems, routines and culture.
>
> (Sørensen 1996)

Thus, a concern for social learning implies a need to reconsider the traditional conceptual split between design and use. The key is cooperation and transmission, and intermediaries will often play a crucial role (Williams et al. 2000). The point of the concept of social learning is to demonstrate that implementation processes are long lasting – that things continue to happen after the artefact has been put into use. In our case, this means that the point is to learn how environmental criteria may be employed and realised in practice.

In the Kvernhuset project, the lack of standards for the adoption of energy-efficient technologies and methods is illustrated by the strong emphasis that all actors put on the large amount of social learning that took place in the project. The architects claim to have learned immensely from working on the assignment, as they had little competence in and experience with sustainable architecture before entering the competition. This lack was due to the limited number of such competitions. However, the architects were not the only ones who felt this way. Engineers and other actors also emphasised the processes in which they learned from experience and interaction. Similar attitudes are found in the other two cases as well. In the Pilestredet Park project the developer particularly stressed the positive effects of social learning.

Taking a wider perspective, these projects demonstrate that it is not only the fact that most architects are situated within a dominant aesthetic discourse that may hinder the realisation of energy-efficient and sustainable buildings. The problem is more comprehensive and complex. Thus, there are important flaws in energy efficiency policies, as it is obvious that policy-makers have not managed to facilitate social learning in the measures that have been applied, nor are the usual policy instruments very helpful in supporting the development of more sustainable technologies and related building practices.

The study of the planning and design of these three buildings shows that in order to realise sustainable buildings someone involved in each project needs to take it as their responsibility and see it as in their interest to ensure that considerations of sustainability are taken seriously and attended to. This analysis suggests at least two ways in which this may happen: either the sustainability concerns may be safeguarded by means of duty (an EMP is one way to impose such a duty) or there must be a particular person or people, preferably the owners of the building, who see it as their responsibility to pursue such concerns. Thus, sustainable design is not likely to be attended to if left alone but has to be policed and controlled through the whole design process.

Political initiatives may also be important for the promotion of sustainable architecture. The fact that Fredrikstad was one of five 'environmental municipalities' in Norway was essential for the process of designing Kvernhuset, as sustainability became internalised as the obligatory way of thinking and making choices in the municipality. Even though projects like Pilestredet Park are grounds for optimism, showing that it is possible to realise energy-efficient and sustainable buildings, there are clear indications that the building sector has been neglected in energy and environment policies. The conclusive messages shown by this study of these three building projects may be differentiated according to the three different types of actors. Traditional measures have been insufficient for promoting sustainable buildings.

Actors in the field of policy-making could promote sustainable architecture by promoting social learning, for example by supporting demonstration projects. Another way to ensure that social learning happens is to insist that all projects include an EMP. However, experience from these three cases indicates that it is not sufficient to have just an abstract set of environmental criteria; to ensure sustainable design it is necessary that the criteria are taken into consideration from the start and that someone is responsible for converting them into practice.

Thus, in relation to building owners and developers the obvious challenge relates to working with criteria for sustainability. In order to promote sustainable architecture it is important that the owner works thoroughly with the elaboration of criteria for sustainability and is able to come up with specific goals. Careful attention to its sustainability criteria is probably one of the reasons why the Kvernhuset project was able to go further along these lines than the other two projects.

In relation to the designers (architects and engineers), social learning seems to be crucial, as it gives these professions an opportunity to gain experience from practice. Here we can see the need to make it easier for the experiences gained in such projects to be communicated to the building industry in general. We also need to develop a more efficient learning economy that links the diverse actors who influence and implement design in buildings. This article could be regarded as a modest contribution to such a challenge.

## Notes

1 *Statusrapport Miljøoppfølging 20.04.01*. Prepared by Gasa A/S and Lund and Slaatto Bolig AS, on behalf of Pilestredet Park Boligbygging ANS, Selmer Bolig, OBOS and Selmer Skanska AS. By Marius Nygaard, Gasa A/S, Pilestredet Park Miljøoppfølging. Kontrollskjema. Oslo. (6 June 2001).
2 *Statusrapport Miljøoppfølging 20.04.01*, MOP 3.2.3, Appendix 3.2. By Per Johan Jensen and Selmer Skanska, Oslo (5 February 2001).

# Part D
# Alternative design

# Green buildings in Denmark

## From radical ecology to consumer-oriented market approaches?

*Kirsten Gram-Hanssen and Jesper Ole Jensen*

Gram-Hanssen and Jensen explore the development of green buildings in Denmark over the last three decades, identifying differences in design philosophies and techniques. They look at four approaches to green buildings: as energy-saving devices, as ecological grassroots alternatives, as subsidised large-scale urban projects, and as consumer products in a market approach. Using detailed case descriptions, the chapter asks to what extent it is possible to define some buildings or some approaches as more 'green' than others. The authors suggest that in order to more fully understand sustainable buildings we must account for the social structuring of both the identification of environmental problems and their resulting embodiment in built form.

## Introduction

Green buildings in Denmark vary widely with regard to all aspects of physical and social solutions as well as ideological rationales. Sometimes this has led to controversies among different actors in respect of the definitions and content of green buildings. We present these different rationales and describe how each in its own way has contributed to a general development of green buildings. We argue that a common definition of green buildings is not necessarily needed and that many different approaches to such buildings might be more useful than one.

Wew use the term 'green buildings' as a unifying and neutral notion of what different actors in different contexts have described as 'sustainable', 'resource-saving', 'ecological', 'self-supplying', 'natural', 'healthy', etc. However, in some of our case descriptions, when describing the rationales of actors we use some of their own words. The chapter looks at four approaches differentiated by different understandings or concepts of green buildings and by different actors:

- Green buildings as energy-saving devices: after the oil crisis in 1973, strong efforts were made to develop building technologies to improve energy performance, as well as regulations for implementing these technologies.
- Ecological alternatives emerging from the grassroots: as a radical critique of modern society, a number of alternative and green rural settlements grew up in the 1980s and 1990s, emphasising community, self-sufficiency, alternative technologies, lifestyle and spirituality.
- Subsidised large-scale urban projects: commitment to the 1987 Brundtland Report created a public drive towards green buildings, aimed at testing, approving and institutionalising alternative technologies, with ample public funding, primarily in impressive building projects under the Urban Renewal Act.

- Green buildings in a market approach: in recent years we have seen a trend towards considering green buildings as individual market-driven consumer products. Here green labels and life cycle analysis (LCA) tools aim to give consumers a central role in the development of such products, based on the market and on ecological modernisation rather than on public subsidies.

The different approaches partly follow a historical path. However, it is important to note that these approaches and their actors coexist at the same time. A key question is how far technological development in green buildings has been a matter of interaction between the physical and the social contexts. As a background to this way of analysing and presenting the subject, the chapter starts with an introduction to social theories of technological development, especially in relation to environmental and urban issues.

Very different aspects of green buildings have been emphasised in different historical periods and by different actors. An actor-oriented approach may ask whether different notions of green buildings are just a matter of different social constructions or if it is possible to define them independently of the actors by measuring their degree of sustainability. In the conclusions we try to answer this question, maintaining on one hand that we need to measure 'greenness' or sustainability but on the other that every way of measuring it is problematic and limited.

## Theoretical approaches to technological development

Different theories help in understanding how technologies develop in relation to the social environment: the theoretical field known as the social construction of technological systems (SCOT theories); the theory of ecological modernisation; and new urban technological studies.

### SCOT theories

SCOT is a research area that is based on the view that technology is socially constructed, in opposition to technological determinism, which sees technology and science each as autonomous and separate from society. This area can be divided into three approaches (Bijker et al. 1987).

First is the social constructivist approach, which claims that technological artefacts are open to sociological analysis, especially with respect to their design and technical content. This approach looks at the social structures behind the growth and assimilation of a technology. It introduces the concepts of 'interpretative flexibility', 'closure' and 'relevant social groups', and Bijker's study of Bakelite is one of the core examples (Bijker 1987).

The second approach treats technology as a 'system' metaphor and stresses the importance of focusing on the links and relations between technology's physical artefacts and institutions and their environments. In his study of the electrical system Hughes argues that technological systems are socio-technical, because besides their technical elements they also comprise organisation, legislation, knowledge and financing, woven together into a 'seamless web' (Hughes 1987). He distinguishes between radical and conservative innovations in relation to the existing systems. The success of the new radical technologies depends on, among other variables, how the innovators tackle the 'reverse salients' – the weak parts of new systems – so that the new technology can compete with existing systems. The aim of the 'system builders' is to shape a system by excluding other systems and components and, if successful, by adding momentum to the system, giving increased stability over time.

The third approach takes the system metaphor a step further, developing 'actor-network' theory, which breaks down the distinction between human and non-human actors (Callon 1987; Latour 1987). According to this perspective, to create new technology is to persuade, seduce and motivate actors to participate in a network around the new technology. One of the studies using this approach looked at electric cars, an area in which the successful engineer has to combine consumers, ministries and the battery electrons, convincing them all of the roles they have to play (Callon 1987). A key controversial element in this approach is the consideration of non-human actors, such as electrons, as belonging to the same network as consumers and engineers.

These SCOT approaches focus on technological development in general, with no specific emphasis on green or urban technology. We supplement the approach with insights from theories that follow the same lines but with a more specifically green or urban viewpoint.

### Ecological modernisation

The notion of ecological modernisation brings together discussions of society, ecology and technology, though it is difficult to say if it is actually a social theory, a political programme or a broader discourse in the public debate. Hajer distinguishes between different approaches – or ideal-typical interpretations – to ecological modernisation and to the reactions against it (Hajer 1998). According to Hajer, a central element in ecological modernisation is the rationalising of ecology so that it can be built into programmes, politics and institutions. Another element is about 'technicalisation' of ecology, whereby some of the big international firms, helped by non-governmental organisations (NGOs), are changing moral and ethical concerns into technology and market issues. In opposition to this trend, one critic of ecological modernisation questioned: 'Why try to resolve the ecological crisis by drawing on precisely those institutional principles that brought about the mess in the first place?'

Ecological modernisation is often associated simply with more effective production methods and win–win situations where companies can earn money on cleaner technologies. According to Spaargaren, however, the central point in ecological modernisation is not that greening of production can bring profit but that a process of monitoring and guarding of all the major substances and energy flows follows modernisation, through the introduction of instruments such as LCAs and environmental performance indicators (Spaargaren 2000). In this approach, the objective of ecological modernisation is to bridge the gap between the technical and social environmental sciences, by bringing real material flows into the over-socialised social sciences and to bring social systems and human behaviour into the under-socialised natural and technical sciences. Furthermore, the task as outlined by Spaargaren is to introduce a more consumer-led perspective into the theories to make an effective tool for analysing domestic consumption of, say, water and energy. The question that Hajer and other more radical social ecologists ask is whether ecology is primarily a question of material flow management or whether it is a cultural task of redefining society. As the case studies demonstrate, questions like this are prominent in the debate and in the technological development of urban ecology.

## Urban technological studies

Ecological modernisation discusses ecology in relation to social and technical questions, but urban and housing issues have not yet become significant in this area. Recent studies have rectified this lack. Guy and Shove have used the SCOT approach, among others, to understand the development of different paradigms for energy efficiency in buildings (Guy and Shove 2000). Graham and Marvin combine SCOT theories with spatial political economy to describe recent developments in urban technologies and state that cities are the greatest 'socio-technical hybrids' of them all (Graham and Marvin 2001). One of the inputs for a spatial or geographical political economy is Castells' theory of how urban structures (as well as everything else) are changed in the new, integrated, globalised society of networks (Castells 1996, 1997, 1998). Castells describes how new information technologies are some of the prime supporters of global networks of everything from criminals to NGOs and big international companies. As some of the old structure of the capitalist society fades away, for example the nation state, new structures built on the power of identity emerge. Before 11 September 2001, Castells had already described the strength of global networks of religious fundamentalists and had also described the influence of the global green movement.

## Four paradigms of green building in the Danish context

Using these theories of technological development in an urban and ecological context, we describe four different paradigms that can be found in the Danish development of green buildings.

### Green buildings as energy-saving devices

The first period of sustainable building in Denmark began in 1956, when the Suez crisis threatened the country's oil supply. Denmark was heavily dependent on imported oil for heating in buildings as well as for all its other energy-consuming activities, so the crisis gave strong support to researchers' ideas for increasing the energy efficiency of buildings. However, the first attempts to gain the attention and support of authorities in regulating energy efficiency in buildings and to begin research studies in energy efficiency failed, as the Suez crisis faded and oil prices fell to their lowest point ever. Thus the development of the first low-energy houses was largely the result of a few visionary and ambitious people. One such was Professor Korsgaard at the Danish Technical University. The professor and his colleagues at the Thermal Insulation Laboratory were ready and able by 1975 to build the zero-energy house, the first solar heated house in Northern Europe (Fig. 10.1). This gained major national and international attention, making the zero-energy house one of the most renowned examples of low-energy houses of its time.

The zero-energy house's aim was to show that it was possible to build a house at a reasonable cost with already existing technology and that it could be heated and provided with hot water simply through the use of solar heat, efficient insulation and recycling of heat from ventilated air. Theoretically the only external energy supply would be electricity for normal domestic consumption and for pumps and ventilation. The 120-square-metre house was supplied with a 42-square-metre solar collector, and hot water

*10.1 The zero-energy house of 1975 garnered major national and international attention.*

for seasonal heat was stored in a 30-cubic-metre insulated water tank, the first of its kind in Denmark. The house was built with insulation (mineral wool) as the prototype constructive element, reducing the cold bridges. Other elements included switches to turn off the convector fan when the windows were opened and a ventilation system with heat exchangers, a feature widely used today in low-energy buildings. A two-year monitoring period showed that the house had very low heat consumption, although not quite zero – one main reason for this was that the heat loss from an underground storage tank was much higher than expected.

An important factor in the attention given to the zero-energy house was that in the 1960s and 1970s Denmark experienced strong economic growth and the construction of more than a million new detached houses – an extremely high number, given the population then of approximately five million. These houses were all built with ample space, and little consideration was given to energy consumption, and therefore half of all imported oil was used to heat buildings, making oil a heavy burden on the national budget. Given this, it is no wonder that the first low-energy buildings were also designed as detached houses.

The zero-energy house was the first of a series of several other types of low-energy building in the following years, the most remarkable of which were the Hjortekjærhusene (six low-energy buildings built in 1978–9) and Skivehusene projects (1977, 1979 and 1984) (see Box 1). These buildings demonstrated potential for energy savings of up to 70 per cent, but with large variations among them. The amount of energy consumed for heat, although considerably lower than in traditional houses, was often higher than calculated. Surveys showed that the main source of this was the heat distribution system and furthermore that the question of heat storage was crucial (Byberg 1984).

This indicated a lack of development of other technical components and the necessity for a parallel development of the local infrastructure. Moreover, at the end of the 1970s it was clear that diffusion into the market of the concept of low-energy building was slow. The whole building market had declined, and low-energy buildings cost more than traditional buildings, largely due to the fact that anything developed from a prototype will be relatively expensive (Byberg 1984). On the other hand, findings from these pioneer low-energy buildings have to a large extent been incorporated into Danish building regulations and consequently have had a major impact on the construction of new buildings (Saxhof et al. 1988).

---

**Box 1: Examples of low-energy buildings**

| | |
|---|---|
| The zero-energy house (Lyngby) | 1975 |
| Hjortekjærhusene I (Lyngby) | 1978 |
| Hjortekjærhusene I (Lyngby) | 1979 |
| Skivehusene I (Skive) | 1977 |
| Skivehusene II (Skive) | 1979 |
| Skivehusene III (Skive) | 1984 |
| Tubberup Vænge I (Herlev) | 1986 |
| Tubberup Vænge II (Herlev) | 1989 |
| Havrevangen (Hillerød) | 1993 |

---

The oil crisis of the 1970s also led to a fundamental restructuring of Danish energy policy. The Ministry for Energy was formed in 1975, and in 1976 the Programme for Energy Research was launched, leading over the next 25 years to massive research and development projects concerning energy efficiency in buildings and renewable energy (Energistyrelsen 2000). These projects were strongly influenced by the people who were behind the first low-energy buildings. The development of low-energy buildings in Denmark can therefore be described not just in terms of technical development, but also in terms of its basis in an 'infrastructure' consisting of political and financial support, institutional security (the Thermal Insulation Laboratory was established in 1959) and access to influential legislators. Energy research in Denmark can be characterised as a 'closed community' (Guy and Shove 2000), with close relationships between researchers, ministries and industry enabling, such influence.

The researchers' efforts are to some degree parallel to Thomas Hughes's notion of 'system builders' (Hughes 1987). A moot point is whether their low-energy buildings are to be seen, in Hughes's terminology, as radical or conservative technology. On one hand, the ideal was to establish a system that is based on low-energy buildings and a renewable energy supply, which would mean a radical break with the existing energy infrastructure. Furthermore, potential 'reverse salients' (such as problems with heat storage) reduced the economic competitiveness of the low-energy buildings. For those making low-energy buildings it was also a problem to get integrated effort from the rest of the actors in the building industry. On the other hand, low-energy building has, in Hughes's terms, to a large extent been institutionalised, as basic concepts have now been incorporated in building regulations, and must accordingly be considered a conservative technology. This viewpoint also reflects a certain flexibility in the existing system (in spite of the momentum, according to Hughes), allowing change and adaptation to new demands, rather than requiring the substitution of a whole new system.

Although the low-energy building approach peaked, in terms of public attention, in the 1970s, the funding, research and influence on building regulations have remained until today, and there has also been a major diffusion of technologies to other types of sustainable buildings. Recently, however, funding for energy research has, for the first time since the energy crises in 1973, been drastically reduced, which implies a radical change for low-energy building and research. But from 1985 'sustainability' widely replaced 'energy saving' as the key term in green buildings. This was due to the Brundtland Report, which made possible a much broader interpretation of the themes and technologies relating to green buildings.

### Grassroots alternatives

A very different approach to green buildings is found in grassroots and citizen-initiated projects (Box 2). The catchwords for the technology of this approach are closed cycles and self-sufficiency, with inspiration coming from similar actors all over the world. Water and waste should be recycled, energy locally produced from renewable resources and, very importantly, the technologies should be organised in neighbourhoods to strengthen and revitalise local social life. The ecological vision is followed by a social vision of a more holistic everyday life – a life that is not split between work, family and home. In this sense the urban ecological movement follows in the footsteps of the collectivist movement of the 1960s and 1970s, and is a reaction against the lifestyle of detached suburban houses. Furthermore, for some at the grassroots there is a spiritual dimension to the relationship between humans and nature; for others there is an ethical concern for future generations. Common to both groups is that human–nature relation-

---

**Box 2: Examples of grassroots or citizen-initiated projects**

*Projects in existing neighbourhoods*
Baggesensgade 5 (Copenhagen)   1983
Hyldespjældet (Albertslund)        c.1988
Vestergror (Copenhagen)            1988
BO-90 (Copenhagen)                 1992
Øko-byen (Copenhagen)              1984

*New-build eco-villages*
Bofællesskabet Sol og vind (Beder) 1980
Dyssekilde (Torup)                 1990
Andelssamfundet (Hjortshøj)        1992
Munksøgård (Roskilde)              2000
Friland (Djursland)                2002

---

ships need to be reconsidered.

Some projects are in existing neighbourhoods, the most famous perhaps being Hyldespjældet. Hyldespjældet is a 1970s social housing district in a suburb of Copenhagen where a downward spiral of negative social effects was turned into a positive spiral by strong grassroots activity in sustainable ecological and social initiatives. Other projects – for example, Vestergror – had the same ambitions but indifferent results and limited influence on the later regeneration of Vesterbro district. The strongest examples of this type of project are found in the new-build eco-villages, because here the goal was to build from scratch with the right technical solutions and social intentions and not just to patch up existing neighbourhoods.

The three best known eco-villages in Denmark – Dyssekilde in Torup (Dyssekilde 2003; Ranum 1994; Reinholdt 1997), Andelssamfundet in Hjortshøj (Andelssamfundet I Hjortshøj 2003; Reinholdt 1997; Bech-Danielsen et al. 1997) and Munksøgård in Roskilde (Munksøgård 2003; Det Økologisk Råd 2002) – have a lot in common.[1] All were built according to a combined social and ecological vision of a more holistic everyday life where members of the local community take care of each other and the environment. They emerged from study groups where future inhabitants met to discuss their vision and how to realise it. The goals were to build self-sufficient eco-villages with some 100 residents, both owners and tenants, that would also have their own production and service facilities. The idea for Dyssekilde was born in 1982, for Andelssamfundet in 1986 and for Munksøgård in 1995, and so the three eco-villages can be considered as examples of historical development with regard to grassroots ideals and the response of wider society to them. In terms of the way these eco-villages formulated their ecological vision, there seems to have been a move from a more spiritual to a more pragmatic view of nature. The Dyssekilde eco-village had its basis in the spiritual thought and cosmology of the Danish spiritual thinker and writer Martinus (Martinus Instituttet 2003). The village's written vision includes formulations of a 'loving attitude' towards the environment as well as a global holistic view. The Andelssamfundet eco-village is more socio-economically oriented. Its relationship to nature is that 'production and consumption' should be 'adjusted to an ecological balance'. The Munksøgård eco-village seems a little less ambiguous in its goals: it wants to build with 'the most possible concern for the environment'.

Reactions from the surrounding community to the eco-villages also differ. Dyssekilde had quite a hard time finding a municipality that was willing to accommodate its eco-village, but Andelssamfundet and Munksøgård were made much more welcome by the municipalities they contacted. At the beginning the authorities were afraid of getting a new Christiania, the 'free city' in Copenhagen well known for its hippies and hashish. However, once Dyssekilde eco-village was seen to be a positive addition to the old village of Torup, for example with its local kindergarten and a village hall, it was much easier for the two other eco-villages to find suitable sites.

The biggest difference between the three eco-villages is in the way the building process developed. In Dyssekilde the original plan was to build the whole village at once. However, when building started they had to give up this idea for economical reasons, and many of the collective solutions, for instance for solar heating, had to be abandoned and made on an individual basis. The first buildings were built by the owners themselves in 1990, eight years after the first meeting. Many experimented with materials, technology and ideas of what a house could look like. The buildings are organised in five groups according to type: some are domes, some are self-built experimental houses and some are eco-standard houses designed by architects (Fig. 10.2). The community has a windmill, 7 hectares of farmland with ecologically grown crops, a

*10.2  View of the eco-village of Dyssekilde, with its very individual alternative houses.*

green treatment plant for sewage, some workplaces and a kindergarten in the village. Hundreds of visitors come every year to the village to see its alternative and very indi-vidual houses. In terms of resource consumption, the village's heat consumption fulfils the requirements for low-energy buildings in the Danish building regulations, and much comes from renewable resources. The average water consumption in the village as a whole is half the national average, and the same holds for waste production (Dansk Byplanlaboratorium 1995).

The study group that led to Andelssamfundet eco-village initially aimed to find a building material that was completely harmless, and they settled on unkilned, rammed clay earth. However, to comply with Danish building regulations the authorities would not allow them to use this material without first building a prototype house to test the strength and durability of the building method. As in Dyssekilde, Andelssamfundet also had problems in financing the buildings. However, in 1992 the first buildings in rammed clay bricks, with paper granulate as an isolating material in the middle of the thick walls and with compost toilets, saw daylight, and these building principles became central to all later buildings in the village. Because the clay building technique was used for all the houses, Andelssamfundet achieved a much more uniform visual expression than Dyssekilde (Fig. 10.3). In the year 2000, Andelssamfundet had around 200 inhabitants in four groups of buildings. It runs an organic garden of 23 hectares, making it more or less self-sufficient. Moreover, it has willow evaporation basing for the grey (non-sewage) wastewater and some places of work, and like Dyssekilde it receives hundreds of visitors every year. With regard to resource consumption, the village's heat consump-tion fulfils the requirements for low-energy buildings in the latest building regulations, and all of it comes from renewable resources. Consumption of water, some of which is rainwater, is on average less than half the national average level. Waste production is less than a third of the national average (Bech-Danielsen et al. 1997).

10.3 *In Andelssamfundet eco-village all buildings are constructed of the same material: unkilned bricks of rammed earth clay.*

In contrast to Dyssekilde and Andelssamfundet, the eco-village of Munksøgård was intended to be built by professionals. Only a year after their first meetings the future inhabitants had contacted a house building company and professional architects and engineers. In principle the village is built as ordinary dwellings, either rented or owner-occupied, with ordinary financing and with tenders put out through the EU tendering system as required by EU law. The residents, however, wanted to be in control of all principal decisions, but having little experience of building processes they have found this to be hard work. Cost restrictions meant that some of their ecological building solutions had to be abandoned. One example is the village's energy supply. An actor-oriented approach to the ecology shows that the technical professionals are focused on energy consumption, whereas the residents are more focused on the social elements and on dealing with their waste products. To the residents heat recovery sounds like ventilation, with its problems of noise and a bad indoor climate, whereas the common house and the toilet solution sounded much more positive and thus they gave it a higher priority. The first ecological audit of the village showed energy consumption for heating to be much higher than originally planned and even higher than required by the 1995 Danish building regulations. The audit showed that electricity consumption is almost at the same level as the national average. Only water consumption seems to be lower than in other modern buildings, owing to the village's urine-separation system (Foldager and Dyck-Madsen 2002).

These three examples show how building technology developed within grassroots projects where the vision is of ecology as local resource management and closed cycles. From the beginning they encountered many obstacles from the wider society concerned about different lifestyles, building regulations and financing, but slowly the initiatives began to be accepted and maybe even appreciated, not least as examples that garnered awards and received media attention.

One way to understand these developments is through the power of identity in 'the network society' (Castells 1997). The ecological grassroots described here are part

of a social movement aimed at transforming human relationships at their most fundamental level. And this movement is not a local phenomenon. It is part of, if not a global,
at least a Western movement that draws on both practical and philosophical knowledge and inspiration from other countries and continents. It may seem a paradox that
the eco-village is, on the one hand, based on a localised and in some sense pre-
modern worldview of self-sufficiency and, on the other, part of a new late-modern
worldwide network (Gram-Hanssen 2000). However, as Castells writes, this local–
global relation is a general tendency in what he describes as the network society. The
power of this movement in general has been strong; very few people today, including
all the actors in the building sector, are not in some sense aware of environmental
problems. The grassroots influence on practical technological development may be
more questionable.

### The large-scale projects: ecology goes urban

A third approach to green buildings can be described as an attempt to make ecology
urban, especially in existing buildings. Up till the middle of the 1990s the most impressive and renowned examples of green building in Denmark had been rural or
suburban, although it had been realised for a long time that what was needed was a
greening of existing buildings, towns and cities. The third approach became apparent
as a part of the urban renewal programmes in the 1990s, which historically have high
subsidies. These programmes were supported by a number of public initiatives and
funds, including the Ministry of Housing's Action Plan for Green Buildings, and
Project Renovation, a programme for the technological development of urban
renewal. Also, it became necessary to include ecological measures in urban renewal.
For low-energy buildings, this effort was largely driven by massive public subsidies
(national and EU), but also, like the grassroots projects, with an enthusiasm among the
actors involved for creating urban sustainability. There was also a strong ambition for
'professionalisation' of urban ecology. It was commonly understood that the efforts
had for a long time been grassroots-driven – now was the time for the greening of the
traditional actors of the building sector. The main actors in this approach were very
mixed: municipal planners, private architects and consultants, residents and green
NGOs. Another challenge was how to transfer the experiences from rural ecology to
an urban context. To point out good solutions from rural ecology might be one
problem, but to find out which would be transferable was another. It is obvious that
many of the green technologies established in rural environs could hardly be transferred unadapted to the cities.

   The prevailing understanding of 'green' was that of urban ecology: a holistic effort
based on local conditions (physical, natural and social) and with active participation by
the residents (Ministry of Environment 1994). This was intentionally meant as a contrast
to the low-energy building efforts with their single focus on energy and limited involvement of residents. In reality, the projects demonstrated a mix between further development of the experiences gained from low-energy buildings and attempts to incorporate
the technologies from the eco-villages into very conspicuous green features (Box 3).
Some projects focused mainly on energy efficiency, e.g. Skotteparken, the Ecohouse
99 and the Yellow House. Other projects primarily focused on one or two themes, for
instance the Fredensgade block in Kolding, with its spectacular pyramid for the green
treatment of sewage, or the Recycled House in Copenhagen, both projects related to

**Box 3: Examples of green buildings of the 1990s**

*Urban renewal projects*
Grøn by (Slagelse)
Dannebrogsgade 19 (Vesterbro, Copenhagen)
Eriksgade (Vesterbro, Copenhagen)
Fredensgade (Kolding)
Hestestaldskarreen (Vesterbro, Copenhagen)
Hedebygade (Vesterbro, Copenhagen)
The Blue House and the Yellow House (Ålborg)
Studsgade (Århus)
The Recycled House (Copenhagen)

*New social housing projects*
Ramshusene (Svaneke)
Skotteparken (Ballerup)
Det Grønne Etagehus (Vejle)
Ecohouse 99 (Århus, Ikast and Kolding)

urban renewal. Finally, a number of projects included a combination of different green features.

The greening of the urban renewal became a learning process. Early projects like the 1992 Dannebrogsgade 18 project in the Vesterbro district in Copenhagen from 1992 and the 1994 Block 7 in the Sydvest district in Copenhagen had just a few features, such as active and passive solar heating and stormwater collection. They served as learning projects for later and more impressive projects such as Eriksgade (1994–5), Hedebygade (1996–8) and Hestestaldskarreen (1996–8), all located in Copenhagen's Vesterbro district, an urban renewal area.

The Hedebygade project served as the Ministry of Housing's flagship project on urban ecology (Fig. 10.4). The green project in Hedebygade was granted 40 million kroner (about €5.3 million) from Project Renovation and comprised a number of different technologies and solutions applied to 12 buildings on the block. These included technology developed from low-energy housing research, such as sun walls (combining heat recovery, passive solar energy, low-emission glazing and air-type solar collectors), ventilation with heat recovery and low-temperature district heating. Other projects can be characterised as attempts to transform technologies primarily learnt from the grass-roots eco-villages for an urban context, such as reed beds for recycling indoor air, rainwater collection, comprehensive waste sorting, strawboxes for cooking (a feature of green kitchens) and efforts to improve the sense of community. Other elements included technologies such as smart metering, photovoltaics (solar cells) and prisms to channel daylight from the roof through the chimneys and into the flats – in other words, a mix of different technical solutions, many demonstrably effective.

The experience in Hedebygade also shows that it is more difficult to obtain the same level of participation from residents than in the grassroots eco-villages, even though active residential participation is the keyword of urban ecology. The Hedebygade process and the participation of the residents were strongly influenced by the urban

*10.4  The Hedebygade project served as the Danish Ministry of Housing's 'flagship project' on urban ecology. On top of the building is a prism to channel daylight into the flats.*

renewal process. In the beginning the consultants had promised the residents that the number of flats would not be reduced through merging. However, the city council over-ruled this and demanded that a number of flats be merged, meaning that some families would have to leave the block after its renovation. This caused many protests from the residents and resulted in distrust towards the renewal process in general, including the projects. As a result, residents were rather reluctant to get involved in the green projects. A residents' questionnaire completed in 2002 revealed a general dissatisfaction with the planning process of the urban renewal project in Hedebygade, which also affected their views of green projects. The general experience from many projects is that it is difficult to obtain enthusiastic support from residents to a more or less predefined concept, no matter how ecological. However, this probably also reflects the fact that many planners and initiators might have unrealistically high expectations of residents' involvement in green building projects.

Hedebygade is in many ways typical of this type of project. The visual elements of green technologies played a large role in many projects, such as visual indicators of the level of consumption in the block, building or flat. The pyramid in the city of Kolding and the 'energy axis' in the Hestestaldskarreen block are other examples. Moreover, the outcome of the projects was often the result of negotiations between a number of different actors with different ambitions – residents, engineers, architects, owners, municipalities, infrastructure suppliers and green NGOs. This was a natural result of the premises of urban ecology but also reflected the fact that a number of projects were completed as a part of an urban renewal scheme, giving the residents and building owners a large influence on the outcomes of the projects, including the amount and type of green solutions. Many projects, however, experienced other difficulties and barriers. One problem related to the need to adjust local technologies and plans to the technical infrastructure, for instance incompatibility between solar collectors and district heating and between local waste sorting and municipal waste treatment (Jensen 2001). One of the main reasons cited related to the actors, who, in contrast to the scientists involved with low-energy buildings and the eco-villages' grassroots actors, had no experience or expertise with urban ecology projects. The positive aspect is that in many cases the projects included processes that created better understanding, reduced 'cultural incompatibilities' (Summerton 1994) and led to the establishment of compromises and new alliances between the actors involved, including infrastructure suppliers, grassroot organisations, consultants and residents.

It is characteristic of the projects of this period that subsequent monitoring and evaluation has been limited. A recent survey of some of the green projects in the Vesterbro district has shown that it is very difficult to get data from the projects (Lading 2000a). This is partly due to the many optional projects among the residents, making a general overview of the final result more complex and data on consumption and emissions difficult to collect. Moreover, there has been little demand for independent evaluation of the projects, a situation that has often been criticised. The argument for features of ecological renewal to be conspicuous has been that this will inspire residents and other people to a more ecologically conscious lifestyle and behaviour, but again this effect has been difficult to document (ibid).

However, the urban renewal and urban ecology project in the Hedebygade block has been evaluated through an eco-audit performed on the block after its renewal. This indicated that heat consumption (per person) is lower than in similar buildings that were renovated traditionally but larger than expected according to the preceding calculations. Electricity consumption is considerably lower, whereas water consumption is at the same level as in traditionally renovated buildings. The eco-audit indicates the efficiency of the technical solutions. However, there are also some obvious problems in this. Other studies have shown that the composition of the residential population, which might change as a result of renovation, strongly influences consumption rates per person (Jensen and Gram-Hanssen 2000; Jensen 2002). This raises the question of whether the eco-audit reflects the green efforts or the residential composition and makes it difficult to estimate precisely the effects of the ecological project as a whole and of the individual technologies.

This lack of monitoring contrasts with the projects of the low-energy period and the expert-driven initiatives, where many projects had a 'built-in' monitoring programme of several years, allowing learning and further development of the projects. Another contrast to the low-energy buildings is in market diffusion. Whereas the low-energy buildings have influenced other buildings through adaptation of the building regulations, and thereby have become less invisible, urban ecology has primarily had its influence through examples but has had little influence on the building regulations. In contrast, almost any town with any self-respect has one or two 'ecological' buildings.

### Green buildings in a market approach

The fourth approach to green buildings is based on market and ecological modernisa-tion rather than on public subsidies, legislation or grassroots activities. It gives consumers and private companies a central role in the development of green buildings and can be seen as part of a 'new public management' policy. This development was started by the former social democratic government but was further radicalised in 2002 when Denmark got a right-wing government. One of its first initiatives was to cut a number of funds and subsidies for green initiatives and research, including the Acceler-ation Fund for Urban Ecology, established in 2001 to promote and develop sustainable solutions, and the Green Fund, which since 1994 has supported green grassroots initiatives. At the same time, subsidies for urban renewal as well as the Energy Research Programme were reduced drastically. Altogether this represents a step away both from subsidised experimental ecology and from the primarily publicly driven approaches as described previously.

Ørestaden, a new development area in Copenhagen, is a prime example of the vision of business, efficiency and sustainability going hand in hand in this approach and of new urban development that relies on network-based cooperation between public and private companies (Fig. 10.5). The director of the Ørestad Development Corporation has said:

> More and more companies wish to take environmental considerations to promote their company and especially to take care of good working conditions for their employees. The Ørestad Development Corporation seeks to inspire and prompt companies to make an extra effort towards the environment to ensure that both their and our visions of Ørestad become real.
>
> (Lading 2000b)

Cost factors were an obstacle to sustainability in the eco-villages, and the urban renewal projects were subsidised. In contrast, the vision in the market approach is that ecology pays either because of reduced costs in the operation phase or because a positive image is created among consumers. The ecological elements at Ørestaden are that stormwater is collected for a recreational element (waterways) and that the buildings should be five years ahead of the latest building regulations with regard to energy efficiency. Also, public trans-portation is presented as a central element in the sustainability strategy (Ørestadsselskabet

*10.5  Ørestad, a new development area in Copenhagen, uses collected stormwater as a recreational element.*

2000). The new Metro in Copenhagen connects Ørestaden with the old city centre, and fast trains run frequently to Copenhagen airport. However, as the Ørestad Development Company is also responsible for selling the building sites, it describes the facilities for private cars in positive language in some of its recent sales material: 'Getting to, from and around Ørestad by car will be easy. As will parking. Ample parking facilities are being established throughout Ørestad to service the individual districts, mainly in the form of public car parks' (Hesselbæk 2001). As we see from this example, ecological sustainability does not always go well with business and sales arguments.

In Spaargaren's approach, ecological modernisation is not only a question of win–win situations and positive images (Spaargaren 2000). Part of the ecological modernisation paradigm is that ecology has to be measured. While some of the grassroots initiatives and some of the urban renewal examples may have been visually impressive, they were not always convincing in terms of reduced impacts on the environment. One reaction to this is that ecology or greenness has to be measured. Thus the ecological modernisation approach of researchers and engineers has been supported by the development of LCA tools to calculate and compare environmental impacts, e.g. the Building Environmental Assessment Tool (BEAT) (Danish Building and Urban Research 2003). Assessment also includes economic calculations of lifetime costs, which should visualise possible long-term savings through extra investments in green solutions. Many of these tools are used in the design of new buildings, including Ørestaden. Several municipalities have also developed their own environmental manuals and design guides that describe minimum environmental standards for new buildings and urban renewal

*10.6 BO-01 in Malmø has luxury flats at luxury prices, and sustainability has a new audience.*

schemes. Efforts have been made to promote benchmarking and labelling of buildings' environmental standards, such as green audits (direct measures of the consumption flows in the building), enabling an environmental comparison of 'average' buildings.

In housing projects as well as office buildings, in the market approach, the green image has been associated with aesthetic solutions in attractive new buildings and urban areas. In these projects sustainable housing has moved towards an association with individual benefits such as health, comfort, security and high-tech aesthetics in luxury flats and with luxury prices. In Malmø[2], in BO-01, the 'Future City' of approximately 500 dwellings, sustainability is a central theme, defined in terms of ecological, social, technical and human issues (Fig. 10.6). The human issues are described thus: 'Architecture, design and technology are fundamentally concerned with human well-being. Access to greenery, closeness to water, freedom from noise, the availability of silence and sunlight are qualities conductive to human sustainability' (Dalman et al. 2001). This understanding of green housing is far from the ethos of the eco-villages. Ecology is no longer seen in contrast to, but as a part of, comfort and well-being, integrated in attractive new flats that require no lifestyle changes or participation from the residents. Sustainable housing has a new form, a new content and thereby a new audience.

## Conclusions

Green building is not a fixed concept. It is under constant change, definition and redefinition. New 'green' themes are adopted as new global and local problems, situations or risks emerge. Where the energy crisis was the overall theme of the 1970s, zero-energy buildings were the answer, and the relevant actors in developing this were engineers and scientists. When the problem was later formulated as a radical critique of our growth-oriented society, the answer coming from the grassroots was self-sufficient eco-villages and experimentation with ideology, technology and social organisation. When the authorities seriously started to act on the urban ecological scene following their commitment to the Brundtland report, it was through subsidising the different actors to promote impressive examples in an urban housing context. In the new millennium the Danish model of a welfare society is under pressure, and market-oriented approaches have been substituted for public subsidies in many areas. For green building the goal is that the building sector itself can handle its environmental problems, and as a part of this approach manuals and measurement methods are being developed. In understanding these developments there is not one social explanation or theory that is able to capture all. The low-energy building period may be understood as technology development, with individuals acting as system builders and driving forces, whereas the ecological alternatives must be seen primarily as part of a social movement. In the two later approaches, the large-scale urban projects and the market approach, the main actors are, respectively, the authorities and the building sector professionals, but with different roles to play: in the first the authorities act as driving forces, while in the second the professionals are given the role of initiators of an ecological modernisation of the building sector.

This development of green building implies rivalry among the different approaches, in terms of funding, public attention and general understanding of the right strategy to be followed. For instance, scientists involved with low-energy buildings tend to see the ecological approach as far too experimental, with too many technical mistakes and without achieving general results. They fear that the politicians will confuse low-energy buildings with 'eco-buildings', resulting in a lack of funding for research into low-energy buildings. On the other hand, for the ecological approach energy reduction is far from enough to enable sustainability, because the basic problem here is our lifestyle as a whole, including the way we live, work, travel, consume, have social relations and so on. Seen from this point of view, the problems with low-energy buildings are the limited public involvement and the narrow understanding of ecological progress. However, in spite of their differences, there is a gradual sharing between the different approaches of strategies and technologies. For instance eco-audits and LCA methods are now quite widely accepted among most of the actors. Moreover, it is also acknowledged among at least a few of the professional actors that the grassroots actors have been effective in spreading a positive interest in green buildings to the public and political spheres. The concept of closure from the sociology of technology describes how different actors in the process of technological development fight to force their definition of problems and solutions, ending up with closure on one of the definitions or principles and then presenting this as *the* solution (Bijker et al. 1987). For green buildings in Denmark we have not yet seen closure on one type of technology, which might indicate that green buildings cannot be viewed as *one* technology. However, the broader acceptance of eco-audits and LCA methods indicates a closure on the evaluation criteria. This raises the question of whether it is possible in this way to evaluate green buildings objectively.

The different concepts of green buildings presented in this chapter represent different 'storylines'. But does accepting a constructivist view also mean that green buildings are just a matter of storytelling? And is it impossible to define objectively any building as more green than another? We do not think so. Just as environmental risks are real but interpreted differently, some buildings and technologies are able to match the environmental challenges regarding, say, resource consumption better than others.

In this sense we find that the tendency to measure ecology is a positive development. At the same time we must also realise that the question of how to measure ecology will always be open to debate. For example, we know that registering consumption of water and energy depends heavily on the measuring unit. Whether consumption is registered per person or per square metre, or if heat loss is measured differently in district heating systems, may heavily influence the conclusions to be drawn (Gram-Hanssen 2002). The lifestyle and the types of residents in a building have a large influence on actual consumption. Also, the relationship of green buildings to local infrastructure is decisive for the actual environmental benefit in the end (Jensen 2002).

We concur with the argument that ecology is concerned with much more than can be measured – this is the cultural question about redefining social structures as Hajer formulated it in his vision for an ecological modernisation (Hajer 1998). Therefore it is important that measurement methods do not have the leading or only role in defining the future development of green buildings. Instead of seeing the different views of green building as a problem, they should be regarded as a strength for development in general. The motivations and incentives for building green are matters of technological development that are embedded in a number of different social dynamics. In line with these arguments we hope that for the future of green building in Denmark all the different actors, with their different approaches, will remain on the scene and fight for their approach.

## Notes

1  Dyssekilde has been known under several different names, including ØLK and Torup Ecological Rural Community. Dyssekilde is the proper name now, taken from the old farm bought together with the building site.
2  Malmø is on the Swedish side of the new Øresunds region that has been promoted along with the new bridge connecting Copenhagen and Malmø. In using Malmø as one of our examples, we are simply following the global tendency to regard cities and regions as more important than national borders.

# 11

# Leaky walls

## Challenges to sustainable practices in post-disaster communities

*Jamie Horwitz*

The study of communities that have suffered major disasters suggests that they present limited opportunities for design innovation. Horwitz tells three competing stories of how Pattonsburg, Missouri, recovered from the great Mississippi valley floods of 1993 and the resistance by Pattonsburg's citizens to incorporating the strategies of sustainable development into the upland site where they eventually relocated. The first story is told by the expert assistance team (which included Horwitz) that was sent to design the new town. It is full of good intentions and introspection but is ultimately a story about restoring a functional ecology, not about restoring a place. In contrast, the second story, told at the local beauty parlour, was about 'relocating memory'. These seemingly irreconcilable accounts of reality led locals to reject *all* of the recommendations made by the design team. Quite by accident – literally – a third story of Pattonsburg was told by the Hollywood film director Ang Lee. Because the deserted old town presented, in his view, an authentic setting for nineteenth-century life, Lee employed it as a set for *Ride with the Devil*, a $35 million action film released in 1999 to critical and popular disappointment. However, 'for the residents of Pattonsburg, Hollywood's construction provided something that the design assistance team could not – it gave them a shared illusion'. With the benefit of hindsight and illusion Horwitz recognised that 'nostalgia may be the greatest barrier to imagining change, or an "alternative future"'. For Horwitz, nostalgia is 'a form of amnesia in reverse'. 'Instead of forgetting the past, one remembers too much.' On the basis of this latent insight she concludes that 'making oneself at home in a strange place requires far more than the abstract concepts of eco-efficiency'. It requires, in her view, the imagination of artists capable of connecting memory and hope. A sustainable landscape ecology, then, must be rooted in the social construction of places.

> You cannot be an architect without being an optimist.
>
> Daniel Libeskind (Boxer 2002)

## Introduction

Social scientists of architecture and technology have argued for many decades that when designers define the characteristics of new products and settings, they necessarily form a hypothesis about the world into which these things will move (Goodman and Goodman 1947; Rivlin and Wolfe 1985). Theoretical implications of post-disaster case studies suggest that these vulnerable communities present widely varying opportunities for the diffusion of design innovations and 'urban reinvention' (Ockman 2002;

Hoffman and Oliver-Smith 2002). This chapter tells competing stories of one small town's reinvention after the Upper Mississippi River Basin floods of 1993 and the assistance of federal and state agencies as well as sustainable design assistance teams. When seen in retrospect, successful design innovation builds up layers of connections as the social and material dimensions grow entangled and conceal their origins and projections, only to appear years later as inevitable or natural (Akrich 1992: 206). Cultural phenomena that appear inevitable 'transform history into nature', wrote Roland Barthes, producing a mythology that depoliticises everyday life (Barthes 1972: 129). Not all design innovations, however, naturalise. Among those that stand out, not yet embedded in the political or material culture of the United States, are the diverse practices of sustainable architecture.

This chapter questions how the unstable and evolving practices and products of sustainable design integrate with, or change, the architecture of everyday life. Three interweaving and competing narratives introduce the problem. The first, a story of experts, is based on my experience working on a national sustainable design assistance team. This team came about through an extraordinary set of circumstances surrounding the relocation of the small town of Pattonsburg, Missouri, to higher ground above the flood plain of the Mississippi and Missouri rivers (BNIM Architects 1995). This story is also based on reports in the media, in professional literature and on the Internet about Pattonsburg and about the team's efforts. It is a cautionary tale about 'consensus models of eco-efficiency' that seek to implement sustainable architecture as a plan of action rather than as an ongoing transformational process (Guy and Farmer 2001: 146). The second story reflects the disjunction between expert and local culture in this project. It is a narrative that grew from voices I heard at the local beauty parlour by the senior women of Pattonsburg, and it follows the evolution of the town after the residents' move out of the flood plain, and after the design assistance team went on to new projects.

The third story is about makeover and transformation. It is a story that cuts across local and expert voices and elides the inherent conflicts that frame the conditional authority each type of voice gives to the other's way of knowing – an elision that authors as different as Sandra Harding (1991) and Wendell Berry (1988) have written about. This particular narrative does not derive from the design team's proposals or from the reconfigured environment of the newly sited town. Rather, the story begins with the unexpected interference of Hollywood's film industry with the everyday reality of the town. Interpreting this conflation of media and memory helps us understand how the people of this region enjoyed their rub with celebrity and embraced the temporary makeover of their nineteenth-century Main Street as a substitute for their own painful history.[1] With its force fields of cultural authority, Hollywood literally reset the stage in Pattonsburg, causing this witness to begin thinking about the largely overlooked role of imagination, illusion, memory and story in the practice of sustainable architectures, and in the recovery of post-disaster communities.

Sites of physical devastation and human loss – whether targets of terrorism such as the World Trade Center in New York City or the result of watershed management as in the small towns devastated by the floods of 1993 – are psychically charged objects. Architects engaged in reconstruction or memorials on such sites operate in a space where people's emotional investments are complex and ambivalent. Case studies by design historians examine post-disaster reconstruction from earthquake and fire to terrorism or world wars through the extraordinary and ordinary circumstances in which new and progressive form does or does not emerge after war or natural disasters, such as the rebuilding of Lisbon into a modern commercial city after the 1755 earthquake (Maxwell 2002). Case studies by anthropologists who examine catastrophes that follow environmental and technological mismanagement, from Bhopal or Chernobyl to the Oakland firestorm of 1991 in the hills of Berkeley, California, show that:

> As is almost universally the case after a calamity, most of the survivors returned to dwell again in the disaster zone. Most rebuilt homes on the same sites as before. Some re-erected near replicas of their former residences.
>
> (Hoffman 2002: 117–18)

Representations and regenerations of the past life of a place provide a window into disaster-conditioned barriers to sustainable redevelopment. The preoccupation of locals with changing the past (rather than the future) suggests a doubling condition, with analogues in art and literature offering a glimpse into Freud's notion of the uncanny as a coupling of the strange and familiar.[2] This chapter extends the notion of the uncanny to the experience of the human and non-human environment, which is understood to be a significant presence in emotional well-being, especially in the aftermath of a disaster (Akrich 1992; Hoffman 2002).

Disasters come into existence in both the material and the social worlds and, perhaps, in

> some hybrid space between them. When we have a way of theorizing that hybridity, fundamental as it is to human life, disaster researchers will have achieved a great deal not only in our own work, but for the social sciences and humanities as well.
>
> (Oliver-Smith 2002: 24)

## A story of experts

There are several official versions of how 'the experts' came to Pattonsburg. All of them tell a story about professional networks connected to the environment through law or design.

The foundation of our work was the legal network drafted by the Hazard Mitigation and Relocation Assistance Act, signed into law by the Clinton and Gore administration in December 1993. In addition to humanitarian consequences the legislation had significant environmental consequences by transferring ownership of individual parcels plagued by perennial flooding to the local community to maintain as open space in perpetuity (Morrish and Swenson 1994; Philippi 1994). The clear intent of the legislation was to let the reassembled property be returned to wetlands, thus restoring the ecological services damaged by development. This process appeared to signal the final act of a long and wasteful cycle of destruction and rebuilding in the flood plains by the Army Corps of Engineers, and anticipated the innovation of more resilient and renewable infrastructures, buildings and site design. It is a perspective that has been attributed to Gilbert F. White's now famous Research Paper 29, *Human Adjustment to Floods*, first published in 1945 when he was a graduate student at the University of Chicago's Department of Geography (White 1997).

Many different groups of professionals, including this author, did recognise that people living in the region were naturally less enthusiastic about the so-called opportunities that arrived along with the floods in the spring of 1993. The torrential rain storms of that season caused breaches in more than one thousand levees in the Upper Mississippi watershed and caused the Mississippi, Missouri and Grand Rivers to charge through towns and farms, ripping houses off foundations and carrying structures and thousands of animals downstream. Tired of fighting the river, and attentive to promises of financial aid, hundreds of communities applied to participate in what became known as the Buyout Program. Although this had been enacted five years earlier, not until the 1993 disaster did the Democratic leadership at the federal level establish a land-use policy so that purchasing property – ensuring relocation rather than repair – could be used strategically to reverse a century of questionable 'flood-control' practices. Experts viewed this dramatic shift in public policy as the beginning of the slow process of re-educating and coordinating agencies and field agents.[3] Many of the small towns severely damaged from the flood were eligible for federal assistance but were unable to keep residents from dispersing after the government purchased their properties, or they were unable to purchase enough land for the entire town to move.

A decade after the flood, four towns had used the federal aid to completely relocate to higher ground: Valmeyer, Illinois; Grafton, Illinois; Rhineland, Missouri; and finally Pattonsburg, Missouri.[4] Pattonsburg was selected in 1994 to become a national demonstration site and received additional technical and design assistance to model the best practices of sustainable redevelopment. The stage was thus set by the legal network for a drama directed by alliances between the public and private sectors of well-intended experts.

The story that explains how design experts came to Pattonsburg is more nuanced. One version is based upon the heroic activity of what Steven Lerner has termed an 'eco-pioneer'. As the worst floods ever recorded were occurring in the Midwest, Nancy Skinner, who was at that time 'an entrepreneur who sold environmentally safe paint' in Chicago, set the project in motion. Lerner claims that

> Skinner had an idea: since the government was poised to spend $6 billion on flood relief in the Midwest, why not use the funds to relocate communities out of the flood zone so that in the future, federal dollars would not be needed to bail them out again? And why not build these communities using the best available environmental and energy-efficient technologies?
>
> (Lerner 1997a: 50)

As the story goes, Skinner called all over Washington and finally found Bill Becker at the US Department of Energy. Becker's efforts had been instrumental in lobbying to see his own home town relocated to higher ground out of the flood zone in 1978 while he was a resident of Soldier's Grove, Wisconsin. When Becker came to Pattonsburg during September of 1994, he showed a film about how Soldier's Grove not only succeeded in moving out of the flood plain but also decided to use government relief funds to rebuild their business district using passive solar, super-insulated, energy-efficient buildings. Soldier's Grove residents used trees strategically to block the wind, and the town passed the first solar ordinance in the country requiring that any newly constructed commercial building derive at least half of its heating from the sun. Becker knew what the practical and frugal residents of small Midwestern towns could do, and he also knew that the project needed someone who could pull together specialists around the nation who knew how to design and build an environmentally friendly and energy-efficient community. Becker contacted Bob Berkebile (BNIM Architects, Kansas City), who had started the first coalition on environmental issues in the American Institute of Architects (the Committee on the Environment or COTE), and asked him to assemble a team of professionals who could 'travel to flood-devastated towns and help residents plan cost-effective, ecologically sustainable communities' (Lerner 1997a: 50).

The team gathered by Berkebile seemed to share an implicit definition of sustainable development and an informal code of how to work with one another and with communities.[5] Some of these assumptions were later recorded as the *Pattonsburg Design Process* by Chris Kelsey, a member of the team who also worked for BNIM Architects at the time. This record is now accessible on the Department of Energy's website (Kelsey 2003). Three public meetings, each held on Saturdays during the fall of 1994 in the auditorium of the local high school, were attended by citizens, the design assistance team and officials from the state of Missouri's Department of Energy and Department of Natural Resources, as well as representatives of the Federal Emergency Management Authority and the federal Department of Energy. Visiting experts lectured, usually with the aid of slides or films, and showed local citizens examples of programmes and sustainable projects around the country. Small discussion groups, led by an expert team member, met and later reported back to the group. After a round-up session attended by all participants at the end of the day, the expert team went out to dinner and then to the basement of a local motel or church where it would work late into the night and all day Sunday discussing, drawing and writing recommendations and plans.

Among the many aspects of the work, four elements continue to be identified. The following appear under the heading 'Success Stories' on the US Department of Energy's website.

# New Pattonsburg

Pattonsburg Design
Assistance Team

Design Charette
October 14 -16, 1994

Community Plan

Sponsored by
American Institute of Architects

Funded jointly by
U.S. Department of Energy and
Federal Emergency Management
Administration

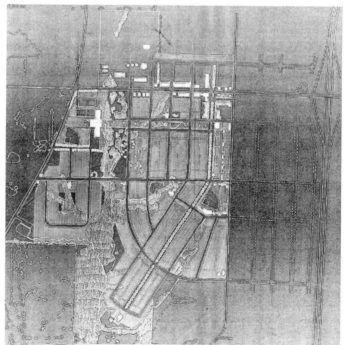

*11.1 The community plan of the Pattonsburg Design Assistance Team, October 1994.*

**Accommodate Pedestrians and Cars**: residents wanted to recreate Main Street in New Pattonsburg and they also wanted plenty of sidewalks. The new plan was designed so that no lot would be more than a five-minute walk from the town center. Cars have easy access, too, as the new town is located immediately adjacent to an interstate interchange and will benefit from the increased traffic.

**Construct Wetlands for Stormwater Management, Wildlife Enhancement and Recreation**: Though a conventional stormwater drainage system has been installed, New Pattonsburg hopes to eventually replace it with constructed wetlands that not only will manage the drainage but also clean the water in a natural park setting.

**Policy Components**: A number of policy documents were drawn up for New Pattonsburg that contain guidance on sustainable community development. They include codes for energy efficiency, solar access, and building orientation, plus guidelines for waste minimization and sustainable economic development.

**Biogas Generation of Electricity**: Pattonsburg's interest in sustainable development has resulted in a regional effort to explore the possibility of generating a portion of the area's electricity using hog manure, a plentiful source of renewable energy. Two large hog farms less than 50 miles from town house up to half a million hogs. Researchers at Northwest Missouri State University in Maryville are studying the feasibility of biogas generation and may incorporate the technology into their planned state of the art swine facility.

(US Department of Energy 2003)

In the virtual environments where these carefully phrased descriptions were published during the tenth anniversary of the floods of 1993 (Kelsey 2003) and in the print media and consultations and conversations in which they are discussed, the sustainable development plan for Pattonsburg offers ideas and encouragement to many people. Yet, there is something more to be learned from the fact that residents ignored virtually all of the recommendations of the visiting experts. In a landscape of oxbows and switchbacks, where hogs are the only inhabitants whose numbers have increased since the Second World War, the residents of Pattonsburg proved resistant to the 'sustainable' plans of the experts. Rather, they instinctively configured a new town that reproduced their social relations but did so without the conscious regard for topographical variations, streams, solar gain, prevailing winds and so on. There was, it now seems clear, no agreement between the professionals and locals about what was being restored.

In retrospect, some of the value conflicts between the team's design proposal and what citizens determined for themselves should have been evident to me when I first visited Pattonsburg. In particular, I believe there was an important impasse with regard to the attitudes that residents shared about reducing the footprint of the town and its impervious surfaces. For example, maintaining a degree of spatial distance in a town of this size ensures a minimum of privacy among people who had moved to town from farms and were not accustomed to seeing their neighbours when they looked out of the window. Cars have a place in rural communities that is hard to quantify or qualify, but I should have noted that no one ever complained about the closest grocery store being eight miles away. Nor did I note that the only local festival that draws people from across the state is devoted to antique cars, or that the truck cabs that could be seen in many backyards are understood by locals not as junk but as a raw material for fixing vehicles – the most common and steady form of employment in this region. The people of Pattonsburg tend to have multiple, seasonally shifting jobs, piecing together a life that represents as a heterogeneous network linked by roads and vehicles. In hindsight it now seems only logical that those who lived in this particular cultural landscape would be opposed to any scheme that limited automobile access or use.

Communities recovering from disaster may or may not be aware of the social and spatial grammars that they share or be able to help outsiders interpret how these tacit rules operate. Such informal social agreements can act as force fields of aesthetic conformity and infighting. In Pattonsburg, while the tacit rules that operate in this community remained largely unstated during our meetings (nobody, it seems, would have corrected us or pointed out how such things work in the town), on two occasions during the public meetings people came alive with interest. Once was when Milenko Matanovic of the Pomegranate Center for Community Innovation in Issaquah, Washington, spoke about the things that hold a community together. He asked people to talk about what they treasured about their town and heard a trove of good stories. Another time was when Pliny Fisk II, co-director of the Center for Maximum Potential Building Systems in Austin, Texas, invited citizens to participate without elaborate words. He held up a sample of ashcrete, an environmentally sustainable alternative to concrete, and talked about building and materials in a manner that people could understand experientially. He then invited people to move around and play with the blocks of a model town. The emotional connection to materials and construction cut through the reserve and discomfort of citizens, where interactions based around drawings and other more abstract representations erected barriers of perception and control. Yet the materials and models employed by Fisk remained abstract enough to be resistant to the undertow of nostalgia.

Such moments of ignition suggest the importance of expressive media in design dialogue and the important connections between the familiar and the strange in generating creative work in art, architecture and literature – from the most popular forms to the most avant-garde. Barbara Eckstein writes: 'A focus on storytelling emphasizes the elusiveness of truth and the complexity of desire. For those who want to plan for a sustainable future, these qualities must be acknowledged and explored' (Eckstein 2003: 14). Attentiveness to or even an awareness of such advice might have proved to be catalytic for Pattonsburg.

## A story of the wall: between the beauty parlour and the historical society

My role on the design assistance team was to help link the design process with the local culture. I began by walking the alleys and streets and then asked if there might be a beauty parlour in town. The 'Do Drop In' parlour was at the other end of Main Street, and with fewer than 400 people still residing in the town, it was alive with older women. As proprietor of the only beauty salon in Pattonsburg, Margaret Lambert was talking about the move to the new site as she curled the white hair of the remaining homeowners on that Friday afternoon in October 1994. Each of these elderly women needed to decide what to do with their property and to consider their options. Should they settle for the government buyout of their houses and move sooner rather than later to senior housing, or watch their homes knocked off their foundations, lifted onto flatbed trucks for the move to higher ground, and run the risk of not being able to sell their house in the future? As she faced them in the mirror, Margaret said that there wouldn't be much to the 'new' town without the old houses and buildings.

Margaret Lambert's inclination towards preservation was evident. Mounted collections of antique hair-fashioning equipment and souvenirs of Pattonsburg's better days hung above the dryers. Running the full width towards the back of the narrow salon was a plastic, accordion-style room divider, separating the salon from and connecting it with the Genealogical and Historical Society next door. As president of the not-for-profit Tree Climbers organisation, she wanted to keep her eye on both places at once. During the many devastating floods, Margaret and her husband Tom Lambert had rescued historical documents, aerial photographs, photo albums, and records of all kinds, including copies of the local newspaper, *The Pattonsburg Call*, dating back to the 1880s. Students from the local school used this collection for research, as it was the only library in town. The 'beauty parlour–historical society' became my unofficial office in Pattonsburg, and period-ically I returned to the new town on several occasions to try to establish a public place for the records and resources of the historical society. Sadly, after Margaret Lambert passed away, the Tree Climbers never unpacked the boxes stored in a trailer on the Lambert farm.

It took four years, but in 1997 Pattonsburg succeeded in moving to safe ground, relo-cating about 40 per cent of its structures alongside Interstate 35. About a dozen houses were carried on flatbed trucks to their newly dug foundations and treeless lots. Dozens of newly manufactured dwellings were delivered and sited (against the recom-mendations of the design assistance team) as far apart as possible without regard for

*11.2 A Pattonsburg house being relocated to the new site.*

*11.3 Pattonsburg on higher ground, with manufactured and relocated houses.*

energy efficiencies or topographic variations, in order to distribute the maximum distance between them – perfectly equidistant, but perfectly inefficient from an ecological perspective. In doing so, the residents reproduced most of the social organisation of the old town but only a few of its spatial and physical relationships.

Rather than transferring any of the material or scale from old Pattonsburg's dignified nineteenth-century Main Street, the retail strip constructed by the locals appears similar to those built at the entry to upscale suburban subdivisions, complete with four lanes and a grassy median. Compared with the design prepared by the planning team, the built version seemed surreal to professionals. With no storm sewer or water retention system, the town is awash in muddy streams of run-off when it rains. The lot planned for the city hall was recently auctioned off to the highest bidder, so that now a funeral parlour sits expectantly at the head of Main Street. Everywhere the eye travels away from Main Street to huge white domes looming in the distance. These domes, purchased from the Monolithic Dome Institute of Italy, Texas, house the newly consolidated elementary and high schools.[6] Providing incredibly high thermal insulation values, which reduce the cost of heating and cooling to the town, the domed school also doubles as a tornado shelter. Although the school offends the aesthetic sensibilities of some architects, it is a tremendous source of pride for the residents. With insurance money from a fire at the old high school (and without any government assistance) the citizens of Pattonsburg succeeded in building a consolidated school complex so that students from the surrounding region would attend kindergarten through to high school in the new town. Although the town still has no grocery store, the combined gas station and convenience store, Total, is visible from town and from the interchange on Interstate 35. It was in this interstate highway landscape that Pattonsburg, a nineteenth-century railroad town from the bottomlands, was reborn as a suburb hundreds of miles away from any urb.

When I bring architecture students and colleagues to the two Pattonsburgs we talk with people at the 'senior center' and then the local high school. The teenagers take the

*11.4a and b Two views of the domed school in the new town of Pattonsburg.*

college students on a tour of both places and tell them how on any given evening you can find old-timers just sitting in parked cars in the empty ghost town, probably near where they used to live. The teenagers know because they're there to park as well, or to race their pick-up trucks and party. I continue to stop by the site of the beauty parlour where I first met Margaret Lambert and her husband Tom and began to understand that for Margaret the problem was not only about relocating the residents of Pattonsburg: it was about relocating memory.

In 2000, several grandchildren and descendants of former residents of Pattonsburg who had moved away from the region before the floods of 1993 decided to form Historic Pattonsburg Inc. This non-profit corporation was

> organized to accept charitable donations and raise funds to be used to relocate and restore (as necessary) buildings and items of historical significance in Pattonsburg, Missouri, Davies County for the purpose of developing and maintaining historical and genealogical museums that will promote and preserve local history.
>
> (www.historic-pattonsburg.org)

The directors of Historic Pattonsburg live in California, Texas and Kansas. Their geographic dispersion did not, however, deter them from moving the old railroad depot to the new town and to raise funds so that eventually the structure might become a museum about the history of Pattonsburg. But, as of yet, one of the only hints that Pattonsburg was a town that had been relocated – other than the strange old houses sitting awkwardly on bare lots – can be found at the Old Memories Café, located on the new commercial strip. Instead of a photograph of the old town or a visual record of the flood, the only images placed above the booths concern a movie made in the old town.

## Hollywood comes to Pattonsburg

When all the households in Pattonsburg had either sold their land to the government and moved their houses to the new site, decided to stay in the abandoned town, or moved away, the city council accepted an offer from United Artists to use their old, newly ghosted town as the set for a Civil War era film. United Artists leased old Pattonsburg for $45,000 as the set for a film about a Missouri family conflict during the Civil War. *Ride with the Devil* is a $35 million film directed by Ang Lee (1999). Lee, who came from Hong Kong to film school in the United States, is well known for immersing himself in the cultural context of each of his films, which include *Eat Drink Man Woman*, *The Ice Storm*, *Crouching Tiger, Hidden Dragon* and *The Hulk* (Lahr 2003). Many residents of the area worked as extras, delighting in riding horses to double for the actors. The inconveniently contemporary properties of the six families who were still living in the old town, complete with their revealing satellite dishes and propane tanks, were camouflaged during filming.

The money United Artists spent on making old Main Street into a film set made everything about it look more attractive. Its pot-holed streets were covered by packed earth, wide slatted-wood sidewalks were laid, the brickwork was painted, and the colourful signs and smaller panes of glass and mouldings returned the graceful proportions and material integrity of the nineteenth-century façades to Main Street. The set for *Ride with the Devil* remade old Pattonsburg by washing it in historical fiction. On the set the relationship between memory and architecture was uncompromisingly porous, never underestimating the load it must carry or the weight of its mass. Ang Lee's eye is so sharp, the details so focused, that the blur of distance, often associated with memory, is forgotten. Especially beautiful was the false work that had to be constructed in order to support the new façades to fill in those unseemly gaps in the historical fabric of the town. These structures, along with the mature trees brought onto the set, were taken down the day filming ended. Nothing was offered to the barren new town, yet some traces of the film-making remained. The set designers had sandblasted off a date that had been chiselled into a stone façade because it was later than the Civil War and then

11.5 *Hollywood makeover of Main Street in the old town of Pattonsburg for the United Artists film* Ride with the Devil.

removed the new number, leaving only scars. The pride Pattonsburg took in being part of Hollywood was, however, stunning. Although *Ride with the Devil* was released in the winter of 1999 to critical and popular disappointment, participation in the process of filming resituated this backwater ruin into the contemporary culture of celluloid illusion, mass media celebrity and the suburbia to which its citizens aspired. For the residents of Pattonsburg, Hollywood's construction provided something that the design assistance team could not – it gave them a shared illusion. Lee's film provided an image of the past, with painful memories removed and yet a great story to tell.

Nostalgia may be the greatest barrier to imagining change, or an 'alternative future'. Nostalgia can be understood as forgetting about change – a form of amnesia in reverse. Instead of forgetting the past, one remembers it too much. This may be what distinguishes nostalgia from the generative preoccupation among many contemporary artists with the former life of places and things. Rachel Whiteread's artwork provides instructive examples of the friction between having a memory and having the physical representation of a memory. Her project known as *The House* conjures up past lives by literally exposing the interior surface of an old house. The sculptor performed this feat by making a wax mould of the house's interior space and casting it in ghostly plaster as a solid rather than void before the supporting structure was torn down. Whiteread's work has been extraordinarily successful in drawing attention to itself, as well as its 'absent host'. But even before this project won the Turner Prize, the English critic Lynne Cooke wrote, 'Whiteread's work shows that when memory and imagination invest in [things] they are able, like Rachel Rosen, to cross over from the realm of the inanimate to that of the living' (Cooke 1992: 146).[7]

In the summer of 1998, Whiteread completed her first sculpture for and about the American landscape – a cast-resin cylinder that replicated one of the ubiquitous water towers perched on building rooftops in New York City's SoHo district. The semi-transparent resin seemed to make visible the forever-invisible interior contents of old wooden cisterns. The resin appears, not like the solid chemical that it is, but like a memory of shimmering water without its tanks. And yet this interior life did not limit interpretation to the past. Rather, I read the sculpture as an invitation to think about the future of water in New York City. By defamiliarising the common yet misunderstood water infrastructure of the city, Whiteread literally makes technology transparent and available to the imagination of citizens. Had the citizens of Pattonsburg been invited to imagine the architecture of their everyday lives in comparable ways, the reconstruction of the town might have proceeded differently. Making oneself at home in a strange place requires far more than the abstract concepts of eco-efficiency.

## Porous boundaries

Disasters and the losses associated with the devastation of property, communities and individuals make them an uneasy and unlikely prelude to radical environmental change, in Pattonsburg, Missouri, or anywhere else. Anthropologists have found that disasters

> undrape canons and law, customs and practices, the novel from the entrenched tradition. In this manner, disasters often reveal the deeper social grammar of a people that lies behind their day to day behavior. Disasters also display and articulate the linkages between local communities and larger structures.
>
> (Hoffman and Oliver-Smith 2002: 10)

*11.6 Rachel Whiteread's translucent watertower in New York City.*

While recovering from disasters, communities may become aware of how these codes operate or the capacity of architects and other experts to work with their explicit and implicit 'social grammar'. In this realm, the citizens of New York are no more transparent than those of Pattonsburg. Since 11 September 2001, New Yorkers of many backgrounds and interests have engaged in planning workshops and forums to voice their opinions about the future of lower Manhattan and the site of the former World Trade Center. Like the citizens of Pattonsburg many New Yorkers wanted to help give shape to a more desirable city. Although the mode of civic engagement varied according to neighbourhood and inclination and the opportunities to participate quickly diminished, public events with invited speakers addressed the deep emotional connections between people and the site of devastation.

One such occasion – a symposium on how architecture could best represent the meaning of ground zero – was sponsored by Columbia University. Although the symposium was quite unlike the design charrettes that took place in Pattonsburg a few years before, the debate that followed it revealed the extraordinary need for an architect to give expression to public imagination and find means to accommodate and translate grief into built form. As reported in the *New York Times*, this symposium on 'Art and Society', held at the New York Historical Society, was to discuss whether or not the ground zero site would become a more suitable memorial if left as a scar rather than rebuilt (Boxer 2002: B1). Leon Wieseltier, a writer and literary critic, advocated an empty space where people could be silent together and mourn. Sherwin Nuland, a philosopher and physician, argued for a garden where people could heal.

Holding up the side for building something to commemorate the loss was the architect Daniel Libeskind. At this date he had just been selected as one of six architectural teams to compete for the contract to design the master plan for the site and its memorial – an honour that his team would eventually succeed in winning. On that evening he showed slides of his projects, each designed in response to a different massive trauma, each designed as a marker for what had been erased but not forgotten. Libeskind argued that the new architecture 'should also move towards a better life, a new topography' (Boxer 2002: B1, B3). He pointed to a slit he had cut in the wall of his Berlin Jewish Museum, which allowed a sliver of light to come through, and said, 'You can never be an architect unless you are an optimist.' As the *New York Times* reported, this exchange then picked up intensity, with Mr Wieseltier responding, 'There is something a little grotesque in the interpretation of ground zero as a lucky break for art.' The critic explained that in the Jewish tradition one mourns and remembers not with buildings and things but with words and rituals.

Libeskind, also a secular Jew, argued for physicality over literary space. Even the Jews, he said, built synagogues and cemeteries. 'I have always been a critic of Heidegger ... Language is not the home. We are not at home in language. We are at home, at home.' Mr Nuland responded, 'I am offended by the thought that there will be a piece of architecture on that spot – because ultimately architecture is about the architect.' When people come to ground zero, he explained, it is not to think about the name Libeskind or Gehry. 'You have a fascist idea of architecture, that comes straight from Ann Rand,' Libeskind said. 'We don't have any more masters of architecture' – to which, Sarah Boxer wrote in the same article in the *New York Times*, 'the audience murmured in protest' (Boxer 2002). The prior murmurs in Pattonsburg were perhaps less audible because they were not amplified in the *New York Times*.

In Pattonsburg, as in New York, citizens erected barriers to a future imagined by others. These barriers were constructed by a shared knowledge of what matters and what exists outside tacit boundaries. One of the barriers to the practice of sustainable architecture may be a distrust of governmental agency and therefore a distrust of the design assistance teams who are sponsored by or participate in federal programmes. Competing stories of narrative power and political influence contribute to the need for strategic networks and cooperative relations across public and private agencies as well as regional and national borders.

Theorising from case studies of disasters, researchers discuss the common longings of victims for a return to order and familiarity. When possible, they argue, people displaced by disaster will rebuild in the same locations and often in the same ways (Hoffman 2002: 117–18). Even communities suffering extensive damage from a disaster that is a result of environmental mismanagement will develop elaborate rituals to recover the same unsustainable environment. The dedication of communities to lost animals and people, as in the Oakland firestorm of 1991, is a common mode of restoring lost familiarity (Hoffman 2002: 132). For example, the hillside property owners of Oakland were highly educated and well informed about the controllable hazards of their environment. Official recommendations for hazard reduction ranged from the removal of eucalyptus trees, because of their highly flammable resin, to building alternative forms of egress and restricting construction on fault lines and hillsides. Residents, however, rebuilt after the fire without fundamental changes in the materials or configuration of the buildings to the landscape or to each other (Platt 1999: 260–70). Like the rural citizens of Pattonsburg these affluent urbanites chose to ignore the advice of local and visiting experts (Platt 1999: 258–60).

Given the massive failure of previous federal flood-control projects, the design assistance team might have predicted that the residents of Pattonsburg would ignore the recommendations of any government-sponsored design team. The history of flood control was, after all, linked to the hubris of controlling the anarchic river and its rogue streams. But that prediction would have required the members of the team to see themselves not only as part of the solution, but also as part of the problem in the long record of flood-control failures.

While narratives about landscape and community can be wilfully separated into distinct histories, these events, like nature and culture, are mutually implicated. It is, in the end, impossible to distinguish the physical fabric of a place from the policies that shape it, the lives of the policy-makers who direct it or the intentions of designers and contractors who visualise and build it. Environmental changes are negotiated individually and collectively, not only through physical construction and technological processes but through narratives that stress the connectivity and porosity between the animate and the inanimate, the human and non-human, the public and private. Sustainable design is not a technological fix. It is a slow and shifting reconstruction that cannot afford to shut out the past as we imagine alternative futures. Memory and hope can be connected, like the permeable wall between the beauty parlour and the Historical Society in old Pattonsburg, where the desire to fashion anew and the desire to engage the past meet in a tentative division and a simultaneous join between oral and written traditions on both sides of this leaky wall.

## Notes

1  The English historian Raphael Samuel develops the theoretical perspective I draw on here, namely that popular memory is altered by the expanding presence of local history in media, museum exhibitions, display houses, etc (Samuel 1994). Moreover, as a result of these mediations, Samuel argues, complex concepts such as 'national identity' become associated with artefacts, buildings and landscapes rather than their elaborated social and political processes.

2  Freud's notion of the uncanny (Freud 1953) can be found in contemporary theory of art and architecture – see, for example, Vidler (1992).

3  Julia Badenhope generously explained this process to me. During the floods of 1993, Badenhope was the extension landscape architect for Iowa and is currently associate professor of landscape architecture at Iowa State University.

4  Curiously, Pattonsburg is not included in many of the journalistic and professional reports about the towns that relocated after the floods of 1993. The most extensive documentation of communities that applied for federal assistance and participated in some way in the Buyout Program is found in the December 1994 publication by William R. Morrish and Carol J. Swenson (1994). Neither this early, extensive report nor an article seven years later that visits the towns that were fully relocated in the Buyout Program identify Pattonsburg as one of the relocated towns.

5  I met Bob Birkebile at a faculty workshop of the Association of the Collegiate Schools of Architecture on sustainable design at the Cranbrook Academy in the summer of 1994. He was a keynote speaker, and when I asked him questions about how the principles he lectured about had affected how he practises architecture he told me about his efforts in the recovery of recently flooded communities. He also explained that in conjunction with several federal agencies he was helping to select one town that would become a demonstration site for a model of 'the best practices of sustainable development', and he asked me to visit several communities in my region and report about the likelihood of their relocation. When I did so, and asked to participate in his future efforts, he invited me to attend the three work weekends in Pattonsburg during the fall of 1994.

6  The Monolithic Dome Institute appears to be both a company and a Christian religious organisation. Periodically institute members visit my college and leave copies of *ROUNDUP*, the institute's journal, which has photographs of the Pattonsburg school.

7  When Rachel Rosen, the leading female 'replicant' in the 1982 film *Blade Runner*, tries to convince Decker, the leading man, that she is human, she shows him photographs of her ostensible family. The photographs evoke an emotional intensity that almost confirms this character's humanness, a virtual proof that she is human and not a manufactured object. The viewer is left convinced that the 'replicant' has at least constructed, if not lived, her archetypal memories.

# 12

# Social research on energy-efficient building technologies

## Towards a sociotechnical integration

*Harald Rohracher*

Rohracher builds on the framework of social studies of technology to explore the experiences of a recent programme of sustainable building in Austria. In particular he identifies the range of socioeconomic influences on the process of design and development. By developing a sociotechnical analysis of 'smart home technologies' and arguments about their contribution to sustainability, he highlights the critical interrelationship between the physical and the cultural. He develops an analysis of how the use and acceptance of sustainable buildings is framed by particular sociotechnical contexts and demonstrates how user needs are negotiated and taken into account in the design and implementation of sustainable technologies. Rohracher points to the importance of viewing the design process as a mutual learning process involving designers, technology producers and users that must underpin any process of successful technology transfer.

## Introduction

New types of green buildings and new building technologies are often taken up at low rates, even if their technical design seems promising. In such a situation, engineers or public authorities often call for sociologists to investigate the attitudes and preferences of potential adopters and to identify social barriers to a wider dissemination of such technologies. However, sociological research has the potential to go beyond investigating attitudes and behaviour and to contribute to a better understanding of the development and use of green building technologies. A number of sociological approaches summarised under the heading 'social studies of technology' provide an integrated view of technological design issues as part of a wider sociocultural context and bring with it not only the chance to contribute to the design and implementation of environmental technologies, but also the possibility of a greater reflexivity in the work of designers or engineers who are confronted with the sociocultural conditions of their own activities. Sociological research into technologies may bring about shifts in perspective, which may also require the rephrasing or reconceptualisation of technical issues. As Guy and Shove point out, 'The simple question, "Who are the real users of current technical research?" threatens to undermine established positions and priorities and open the way for new lines of enquiry' (Guy and Shove 2000: 34).

The shift in perspective of social studies of technology becomes obvious, if we follow Russell and Williams in characterising technology from such a perspective:

- 'Technologies are produced and used in particular social contexts, and the processes of technological change are intrinsically social [ … ];

- technologies function as such in an immediate setting of knowledge, use practices, skills, meanings and values, problems and purposes, and objects which
they act on;
- technologies in many applications are best considered to operate as
sociotechnical systems or configurations;
- technological change is always part of a sociotechnical transformation – technology and social arrangements are co-produced in the same process.'

(Russell and Williams 2002: 48)

From such a perspective environmental buildings cannot be viewed as isolated technical problems. What is needed to promote 'green buildings' is a careful understanding
of relationships and patterns of interaction among those involved in the design, production and use of buildings (Guy and Shove 2000: 29).

In this chapter I ask how sociological approaches, and a sociology of technology in
particular, may contribute to efforts to develop and promote sustainable buildings. The
focus is on an Austrian programme of research, development and dissemination on
sustainable buildings, called 'Building of Tomorrow'. The chapter starts with a review of
socioeconomic projects carried out in this programme and goes on to discuss the case
of energy-efficient 'smart homes' to demonstrate the potential of social studies of technology to gain a deeper understanding of the development of smart homes as part of
sociotechnical change processes and to contribute with such an analysis to the technical design process.

Sociological research within a technology programme like 'Building of Tomorrow'
focuses on a broad range of issues such as post-occupancy analysis of people living in
sustainable buildings; barriers to the introduction to the market of sustainable building
technologies; visions of buildings of tomorrow; analysis of planning processes; experiences of users and their attitudes towards sustainable buildings; and studies of the
development and diffusion of sustainable building technologies. A sociotechnical
perspective will then help us to integrate these sometimes disparate and isolated contributions and embed them in a broader picture of sociotechnical system change.

The example of energy-efficient smart homes, which stand for a specific paradigm of
sustainable buildings,[1] demonstrates how social acceptance and technology design
are part of wider sociotechnical configurations and are simultaneously shaped during
the design and diffusion process. Several levels seem to be influential for this shaping
process: the changing social relations and networks of actors involved when moving
from technology conception to technology adoption; the level of discourses and
guiding visions that orient and restrain the activities of both designers and users; and
the way users appropriate or make sense of technologies. Through these processes,
not only do the interests and strategies of companies and various other actor groups
shape the technological pathways of smart home development, but also broader social
structures such as gender differences[2] or socioeconomic changes such as the restructuring of utility–customer relationships in liberalised electricity markets.[3] The process of
design and adoption of smart homes thus turns out to be dynamic and open-ended and
depends on a number of factors such as pre-existing networks and experiences, the
institutional context of specific user groups and social learning processes between
suppliers, intermediaries and users. Whether smart homes can be a viable pathway of
sustainable building depends not just on getting the technical concept right, but also on

being able to match technical design with other aspects of sociotechnical system change, such as social practices of use or institutional settings.

## The 'Building of Tomorrow' programme

Let us start with the context of our discussion of sociological contributions to the design of sustainable buildings – the Austrian 'Building of Tomorrow' programme. The programme was set up by the Austrian Federal Ministry of Transport, Innovation and Technology (BMVIT) in 1999.[4] One of the design intentions is to take up and build on two dominant developments in Austrian solar and energy-efficient building, developments that are regarded as the most important strands of present research and development (R&D) projects and emerging building practice. One strand of discussion (and a faction of the community of planners and architects) focuses on the issue of energy efficiency and has as its 'technological guidepost' the passive house – a highly energy-efficient building that no longer requires traditional 'active' heating systems (the small amount of heat still required can be provided via the ventilation system). The second focal point, a design type favoured by promoters of renewable energy, is the low energy solar house, which makes extensive use of solar energy and renewable heating systems, thereby not giving the issue of energy efficiency such a central place in design. Both strands have a strong presence in the current debate on the best way to make buildings more sustainable, and they are to some extent represented and promoted by separate constituencies of researchers, architects and other stakeholders. In a way these two design types represent two different logics of ecological design, which in turn are rooted in different conceptions of environmentalism and 'prefigure different technological strategies and alternative visions of sustainable places' (Guy and Farmer 2001: 140).

One of the intentions of the 'Building of Tomorrow' programme is to reconcile these two concepts and enrich the discussion by widening the focus on energy efficiency and renewable energies to include the broader issue of sustainability, including its environmental, economic and social dimensions. The aims of the programme are thus to contribute to the development of buildings that fulfil the following criteria:

- higher energy efficiency throughout the whole life cycle of the building;
- greater use of renewable energy sources, especially solar energy;
- greater use of sustainable raw materials, and efficient use of materials;
- increased consideration of user needs and services;

and to achieve these criteria at costs that are comparable with conventional building methods.

Different types of research, development and demonstration have been funded in past years to better integrate the above criteria into Austrian building practice: generation, preparation and dissemination of knowhow in order to support the technology development process in a way that focuses on the project's aims; concept-led technology and component development; development of innovative building concepts for residential and office buildings; setting up and evaluating demonstration projects; supporting the market diffusion of the 'buildings of tomorrow'.

Although these aims and types of research reveal a strong emphasis on technological R&D and demonstration projects, the programme also developed a strong focus on socioeconomic research. So far about 30 projects have been funded under the category 'socioeconomic'.[5] The programme's management, moreover, adopted the view that the systematic inclusion of this aspect is one of the innovative parts of the programme. Indeed, reviews of research programmes and interviews with research managers in some northern European countries (Denmark, Sweden, Finland and the Netherlands) indicated that research into sustainable buildings rarely emphasises socioeconomic aspects and usually does not go beyond single projects of this kind (Rohracher 2001a). A closer look at socioeconomic building research in the Austrian programme, however, makes clear that the contribution from this side has never been conceptualised in a systematic and consistent way. So far this approach has led to a remarkable number of disparate projects of varying quality.

The socioeconomic projects fall into two main categories, which can also be found in much of the sociological and psychological literature on energy efficiency and energy saving since the early 1980s. The first of these two main approaches is a focus on users' attitudes, behaviour and acceptance of technologies. These perspectives are roughly in line with the tradition of sociopsychological research on energy-efficient behaviour (Yates and Aronson 1983; Costanzo et al. 1986; Kempton and Neiman 1987; Stern 1992). 'Building of Tomorrow' projects focused, for example, on motives for choosing single-family houses (which contribute to excessive land use and increased traffic and energy consumption) as a matter of lifestyle; inhabitants' and experts' expectations and visions about the future of buildings; users' experiences of sustainable buildings and building components; and post-occupancy analyses comparing people living in energy-efficient with those living in traditional buildings or investigating the acceptance of low-energy house components. The second approach focuses on social barriers to the dissemination and use of sustainable building components, and strategies to overcome such barriers. This is one of the 'standard approaches' in the discussion of energy efficiency in the past decades and often promotes the view of neutral technologies that meet unfavourable social circumstances (Howarth and Andersson 1993; Reddy 1991; Sioshansi 1991).[6] Several of the 'Building of Tomorrow' projects dealt with factors supporting the market penetration of sustainable buildings or developed strategies to facilitate, for example, decision-making procedures for the ecological refurbishment of blocks of rented flats through increasing the involvement of tenants.

One of the main shortcomings of such approaches is that they enforce a strict separation between the technical and the social and hardly ever link technology development with sociocultural contexts, institutional frameworks and actor strategies and behaviour. As I will discuss further below, this kind of integration can be provided through approaches that are based on science and technology studies.

### Analysing attitudes, experiences and social barriers

Let us firstly take a closer look at some results produced by a sociological analysis of user attitudes and social barriers to sustainable buildings. This section splits the user perspective into a first analysis of people's expectations and visions when choosing a new house or flat and a second on the experiences of users already living in sustainable buildings.

## Choosing (un)sustainable buildings

Taking a wider view on sustainable buildings, and trying not to focus on the isolated building but taking into account impacts on infrastructures or land use, it makes a big difference whether people live in detached single-family homes spread all over the countryside, thereby contributing to an increase in traffic, energy consumption, land use and other infrastructure requirements, or in blocks of flats and other forms of 'densified housing' (semi-detached houses, terraced houses, grouped single-family houses). It has been an aim of Austrian environmental policy for many years to increase housing density, but little has changed so far. Two sociological studies in the 'Building of Tomorrow' programme set out to investigate the motives behind such choices and the sociocultural and institutional contexts in which they occur (Moser and Stocker 2002; Moser et al. 2002).

As surveys of inhabitants of detached homes and densified housing conglomerations reveal, people don't just want to 'have something of your own' (which they sometimes ranked rather low) or more space inside the dwelling, they also want private outside space, a desire that people see fulfilled mainly by single-family houses (Moser and Stocker 2002). A high-quality location (having low noise, natural surroundings, enough light, a short distance to kindergarten or school) was considered important by all groups and was an important motive in choosing a detached home. The main problem, as the authors point out, is the quality, price and availability of alternative densified housing options. Intelligent planning of such sites, which would still allow prospective owners to adapt the building design to their wishes, would allow adaptation of architectural concepts of prefabricated houses to the requirements of densification, would allow sufficient availability of densified areas with low traffic and safe playgrounds for children and could help stop people moving into the countryside around cities.

It is interesting to further differentiate social groups and their lifestyles with respect to choice of dwelling. Moser and Stocker are especially interested in ways to influence the choice of dwellings and ask questions such as: 'Which lifestyle groups are "indecisive" concerning the type of accommodation they choose [and thus can be influenced]? What are the latent motives that make them prefer certain types of housing? Which images are tied to the conception of a detached house?' (Moser et al. 2002: 6) Indeed, the strength of the need to live in a detached house may vary significantly according to lifestyle. While certain groups regard the possession of their own single-family house as almost obligatory, other lifestyle groups such as 'urban social climbers' or the 'urban establishment' are much more undecided and could probably be influenced by the availability of alternatives and by targeted marketing campaigns. Evidence from qualitative interviews and quantitative surveys shows that the detached house is an archetype, firmly rooted in most people's heads. The authors point out that

> the desire for a detached house can hardly be contested argumentatively, because on a conscious level this desire is determined largely by basic ideas that appeal to people's emotions. A house is associated with family, children, one's own childhood and the realisation of a lifetime dream. Whatever stands in the way of this dream will be re-evaluated intra-psychologically.
>
> (Moser et al. 2002: 7)

Again, the question is how to develop ecologically sound, densified forms of housing that still allow the dream of one's own house or that facilitate the shifting of such meanings and emotions and specifically address groups of people who are less committed to the vision of their own single-family house.

However, as other studies confirm, the shift towards a post-industrial society with greater cultural variety, individualised lifestyles and 'patchwork biographies' may ultimately militate against such highly standardised choices of dwelling. The project 'Built in 2020' (Walch et al. 2001) explores possible developments in living and building for the year 2020 by analysing existing trends and predictions about lifestyles, demographic change and technological developments. Future scenarios are compiled through interviews with building owners, trend experts, planners, architects and building experts. The scenarios and visions centre on different ideal types of building expected to coexist: the 'smart home', incorporating a higher level of new technologies but predominantly used by the upper classes and built in desirable locations; the 'standard home', the future middle-class house, which may be defined primarily by economic efficiency, as a reduction in public subsidies may be expected in coming years; the 'catalogue home', reflecting an increase in prefabrication in the building industry; 'no homes' of people with virtual addresses as a result of new information and communication technologies, constituting a completely new trend in housing; the 'low-level home', which may develop from houses whose occupants do not have the money for maintenance; and finally – the opposite of 'no homes' and 'low-level homes' – the 'homes without limits', the most exclusive way of living in the future. Probably there will also be more variability in the choice of different types of homes during one's lifetime. Walch et al. are led to the conclusion that, firstly, the patchwork of lifestyles may lead to a patchwork of architectures, resulting in greater plurality and individuality in the future, and, secondly, that there will be an ecological optimisation of new buildings. However, it may well be that this optimisation does not lead to increased sustainability when system borders are widened – for example, if transport is included in an analysis, an energy-efficient building in a sparsely populated area may be less sustainable than a conventional one in a city.

## Living in energy-efficient buildings

The sociological research discussed above focuses on the individual choice of type of dwelling against the background of 'archetypal' visions of living and building but also considers the influence of changing social, demographic and economic structures or technological capabilities. Other sociological studies may also contribute to sustainable construction by investigating the experiences of 'users' of green buildings. Better knowledge about the reasons why people choose certain technologies or building features and about their subsequent experiences with components of ecological buildings can contribute to identifying critical problems and increasing the performance of sustainable buildings. Such post-occupancy analysis has more commonly been carried out for large office buildings, to improve the building further on the basis of experiences gained during its initial phase of use (Preiser et al. 1988; Zimmermann and Martin 2001; Cohen et al. 2001) .

Several projects in 'Building of Tomorrow' deal with the experiences of people living in sustainable buildings. Some compared energy-efficient buildings with conventional buildings (Keul 2001), some looked into different types of sustainable housing (blocks of flats, single-family houses, group dwelling projects such as eco-villages) (Ornetzeder and Rohracher 2001), and some focused on specific technologies used in such buildings (Rohracher et al. 2001; Stieldorf et al. 2001; Rohracher and Ornetzeder 2002a).

As shown by a survey of about 400 residents of low-energy buildings, three types of sustainable architecture should be differentiated: group dwelling projects, single-family houses and large-volume residential housing projects (Ornetzeder and Rohracher 2001). The reason for significant differences between these samples is not only that they differ in technical design and performance but also that the social and organisational context differs considerably.

Ecologically optimised single-family houses depend strongly on the initiative and commitment of the home owner (though often in collaboration with a specialised architect). The owner is usually deeply involved in the planning process and in the construction work. Although the prospective users are able to implement many of their individual ideas, these concepts predominantly follow a technical strategy focusing on the use of energy-saving devices, thermal insulation and environmentally friendly building materials. This group of occupants has the highest satisfaction with the building performance, although even in this group factors such as the quality of the building site or the amount of space available in the building are more important than ecological features.

Group dwelling projects (eco-villages) are in most cases private initiatives and often include advanced ecological features and unusual concepts such as low-energy earth houses. Typically, the social process of planning and design in such projects involves several years of discussions – learning and decision processes where usually all members of the group have to deal with ecological, social and technical issues. Compared with single-family houses, there is less space for individuality but more space for a mutual learning process within the group. Although the participatory planning process often leads to strong tensions within the group, residents were in general satisfied with the result. However, the level of satisfaction with their sustainable buildings is significantly below that of owners of single-family houses.

In large-volume residential housing projects, potential users are not usually involved in the planning process. The investors are in many cases interested in realising innovative technological concepts to enhance the public image of the company or to demonstrate that a specific technology works on a large scale. Buildings of this type are often equipped with the latest energy-saving technology, but the use of environmentally friendly materials is rather unusual. The pressure for cost-efficiency may be very high, leading to suboptimal solutions. As it turns out, residents of such buildings are the least satisfied group, not only because of limited living space and the lack of public transport services but because of perceived planning mistakes, insufficient building performance (such as noise or overheating in summer) or lack of support from the housing company. In general, ecological motives appear to be much less important for tenants than for owners of flats or houses.

Focus groups stated unanimously that they saw the chance to participate in the planning process as very important – especially with regard to innovative building concepts. A higher degree of involvement may be seen as an essential precondition for the knowledgeable and appropriate handling of the building and its technical equipment. Consequently, blocks of flats where prospective residents were involved early (sometimes even in the planning process) and where the housing company showed a high level of commitment resulted in a much higher level of satisfaction among residents than buildings where only the technical features were considered important by the planners and developers.

This view is supported by a project that studied the opinions and self-reported behaviour of 114 households in four energy-efficient and four conventional large-volume housing projects in the city of Salzburg (Keul 2001). The interviews did not reveal significant differences between the different groups of tenants in energy-efficient and non-efficient buildings: both groups ranked various features of the flat higher than its ecological performance; both groups had a rather low awareness of their energy bills. However, although both groups appeared to be 'overconfident' about their knowledge of heating and energy saving, residents of low-energy flats were more conscious of energy issues when dealing with the heating system or electric appliances. In general, the issue of sustainability was dominated by waste separation and healthy building materials than energy saving or the use of renewable energies.

The dissemination of sustainable building technology depends not least on the acceptance of specific technological components that are often a constitutive part of green buildings. This is not so much the case for a feature such as a highly insulated building envelope, which is not especially visible to inhabitants and does not make much difference to life in the building, but may be of crucial importance in the case of environmentally optimised mechanical building services or the heating system. Several research projects dealt with the acceptance and experiences of the technical infrastructure of green buildings: mechanical ventilation systems with heat recovery and integrated heating systems (Rohracher et al. 2001), woodchip boilers used for central heating systems (Könighofer 2001) or energy-efficiency applications in smart homes (Rohracher and Ornetzeder 2002a). As it turned out, these technologies often made quite a difference to daily life and sometimes were highly controversial among building experts and residents in buildings. I will come back to the example of smart homes, another controversial subject in the building community. Such controversial building technologies can be the starting point for a sociological analysis that treats social and technological changes in the development of sustainable buildings as mutually constitutive. As with the types of architectural setting of green buildings mentioned above, the functioning and acceptance of sustainable building technologies depends heavily on the social context of their use. While users in single-family houses often identify with the technical features and actively integrate these new technologies into their daily lives, acceptance in blocks of flats (often social housing projects) is generally much lower and depends to a great extent on communication between the building's management and its residents – the way occupants get acquainted with advanced technical features, the reaction to feedback and complaints about such features, and the flexibility of use built into these technologies, which often depends on the vision of the housing company or the planners.

## Barriers to the dissemination of building technologies

Finally, let us turn to a different approach to socioeconomic research often employed in the analysis of sustainable buildings: the analysis of social and institutional barriers to the adoption of sustainable technologies and strategies to overcome these hindrances. Contrasting with the rather individualistic approach taken in analyses of the acceptance of technologies, or in analyses of the motives behind specific choices and the attitudes behind environmentally relevant actions, these studies often deal with the structure of the supply side: the interests and relations of producers, the professional culture of architects or planners, the legal and institutional settings around sustainable buildings, or the effectiveness of certain policies to promote their use. A number of socioeconomic studies in the 'Building of Tomorrow' programme deal with barriers to and success factors for the dissemination of generally innovative green buildings (Biermayr et al. 2001), specific aspects such as the use of renewable building materials (Wimmer et al. 2001) or passive houses (Grabler-Bauer et al. 2001).

Based on expert interviews, case studies and surveys, these studies point to a number of shortcomings, such as the lack of specific knowledge among planners, builders, building contractors and residents about energy-efficient and resource-efficient buildings. Moreover, there are deficiencies at the legal and institutional level, such as the rules for calculating the planning fee (which is based on investment costs and thereby favours expensive systems and simplified, standard planning solutions) and building codes (which make wood constructions more expensive). Problems may also arise from a lack of coordination of support from public authorities, marketing strategies and services offered by architects or planners. Compared with conventional houses, technical elements of sustainable buildings are generally more interdependent, consequently requiring different kinds of collaboration and integration among the various actors involved in setting up the building (see the study on integrated planning procedures by Bruner et al. (2002)). Socioeconomic studies of this kind usually result in policy recommendations for strategies to remove barriers to dissemination – and many of the barriers (building codes, lack of specific knowledge, lack of coordination) are much more amenable to change through policy measures than other barriers, such as lack of knowledge about users' behaviour or attitudes.

Summarising the socioeconomic part of 'Building of Tomorrow', we can say that these studies have become an integral part of an otherwise predominantly technology-oriented development and demonstration programme. The results have been appreciated not only by policy-makers and public authorities, who have received additional inputs for institutional changes and policy interventions to promote sustainable buildings, but also by building experts, planners and manufacturers of components, who have obtained valuable feedback on users' experiences and their acceptance of various design features and products.

## Development and acceptance of smart homes: a sociotechnical view

### The perspective of social studies of technology

Most of the sociological research discussed above is not integrated to any great extent with the design processes of sustainable buildings and concentrates rather on the social perception and impacts of given technologies: the perception of certain types of buildings and technologies; experiences and behavioural changes related to environmental building products; or the identification of social and institutional structures that might support or hinder the widespread use of specific environmental building technologies. This type of sociological research meets the ideas and expectations of engineers and scientists, who often dominate the design and management of technology-oriented R&D programmes. Sustainable buildings, from this point of view, remain a technical concept with its own internal consistency and logic, whereas sociological research is expected to provide knowledge to pave the way to the smooth adoption and broad dissemination of such technologies.[7] However, the impact of sociological research on the design of sustainable buildings may be much higher, if such contributions are

integrated in a broader concept of sociotechnical systems that places the social relations of design, production and use at the centre of analysis. Integrating sociological
analyses with questions of technological design not only improves our understanding of
sustainable buildings but also may provide us with new levers to improve processes of
design and dissemination of sustainable buildings.

Figure 12.1 gives some impression of the main dimensions of sociotechnical
change, which provides the context for understanding the development of sustainable
buildings. Taking sufficient account of the mutual dependence and co-evolution of technology, social structure and strategic action seems to be a better basis for a comprehensive sociological analysis of technology in general, and sustainable buildings in
particular, than focusing exclusively on isolated social aspects such as user attitudes or
institutional barriers to the adoption of certain technologies. As an example of such an
integrated approach, we can analyse the development and acceptance of energy-
efficient 'smart homes' to appreciate the strong interrelatedness of technological
design, actors' interests and expectations, and social structures and socioeconomic
regime changes.

From such a perspective, it is not so much the question of social acceptance of smart
home technologies that is at the centre of interest of social analysis, but rather issues
such as processes of learning between users, designers and other supply-side and
intermediary actors. Analysing actors' experiences and attitudes as an evolving element
of a dynamic sociotechnical system can give us a deeper picture of the processes of
design and use and so seems more promising in improving our understanding and
informing our actions in the implementation or promotion of this technology.

In the following discussion of smart homes the focus is on three levels, all of which
guide the integration of social and technical features of smart homes. The first is the
changing social relations of actors, such as producers, installers, energy advisers or
users, as smart home applications move from technical development to implementation
and dissemination. The discussion tries to cover the social processes of both product
design and product use. The second is the appropriation of smart homes by users who

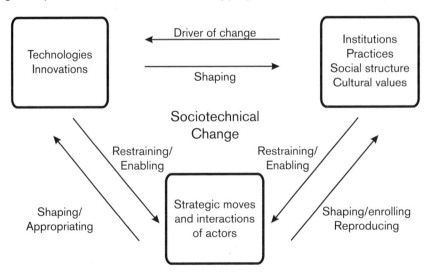

*12.1 Sociotechnical change as the co-evolution of technology, institutions and actor
strategies*

integrate these technologies into daily life, attach meanings to them and develop social practices of use. This level extends from the cultural meaning of artefacts and the life-world of users to the design and redesign of technologies. The third level is the integration of smart homes into social discourses (such as discourses of sustainability) and guiding visions, thus linking users, suppliers and wider social contexts.

### Smart homes as sustainable buildings?

What can we learn from such an approach about the development of (arguably) sustainable smart homes? One of the issues to be dealt with in the 'Building of Tomorrow' programme was the potential of information and communication technology (ICT) for saving energy in so-called smart homes (Rohracher and Ornetzeder 2002a) and the acceptance of such applications by users. Smart homes are certainly a much disputed issue within the community of sustainable building proponents, as technologies in such homes may not save energy and may even be drivers of increased electricity consumption. Apparently there are two pathways such building concepts may take: one in which ICT provides additional opportunities for buildings to be used in a more sustainable way, and another in which ICT adds various applications to ecologically conventional buildings (such as multimedia networks for entertainment and different lighting configurations or electric shutters or blinds on windows to increase comfort and convenience). Which type of smart home will dominate seems uncertain and is rather a question of the social and political contexts of further development than of technological possibilities.

Firstly let us have a short look at the general concept of smart homes. The term 'smart home', as used here, mainly refers to domestic automation. According to Bos and van Leest, 'Home automation is the combining of appliances, information technology and services inside and outside homes and residential buildings into integrated concepts optimally adjusted to the specific needs and behaviour of users' (Bos and van Leest 2001). The concept of smart homes is not a recent one: early prototypes, not to speak of ideas, were constructed in the late 1970s but have never lived up to high expectations about their future rates of adoption. During the past few decades of smart home development the emphasis has shifted from early ideas about 'labour-saving technologies' and then ideas of 'command and control' technologies in home automation to the present services that are based on ICT infrastructure and on integrating the building with external communication networks. Now it may even 'be more useful to think of intelligent systems and intelligent networks rather than buildings' (Clements-Croome 1997: 398).

The commonest applications of automation are in the areas of energy efficiency, comfort and convenience (control of lights and blinds, programmable features) and security and safety (alarm systems, fault detectors). In terms of sustainability, a number of applications could contribute to the energy efficiency of buildings:

- better control and integration of domestic facilities, such as switching off heating and ventilation when windows are open; separate and programmable temperature control for every room and a central switch that enables the user when leaving the house to turn off all unnecessary electric appliances;
- feedback via the Internet on the energy consumption of the building or certain appliances;
- load management and other new services provided by, for example, utilities;

•   intranet solutions in blocks of flats for services such as car sharing.

However, the energy-saving potential of ICT in buildings may be more than outweighed by an increase in electricity consumption triggered by a greater degree of electrification of households and by a further increase in standby losses, as most of the devices connected to the communication infrastructure will be in standby mode. Ultimately, the environmental effects of this type of technology will be determined by how smart home applications are used in practice and the acceptance of specific energy-efficient applications. Nevertheless, it does seem more promising to try to understand and analyse the introduction of smart homes as an ongoing process of sociotechnical change than to concentrate on specific decontextualised sociological results such as the acceptance of such technologies by potential users.

### A sociotechnical analysis of smart homes

The task in sociotechnical approaches is to analyse how smart homes are designed as part of an evolving sociotechnical system that comprises not only new technological opportunities but also, on the one hand, the interests and perspectives of designers, producers and suppliers and, on the other, emerging patterns of use, expectations and experiences of users. Individual actors' expectations and interests are in turn structured by broader socioeconomic developments and are often oriented according to guiding visions or social discourses. This case study analysis used several methods to get an empirically rich picture of these aspects of the smart home as a sociotechnical system.

As a first step interviews were carried out with a number of supply-side actors, not just manufacturers (such as Siemens and Honeywell) but also intermediary actors, such as electricians, housing companies and utilities, which at the same time are often users of smart home technologies. To take account of the issue of energy efficiency in smart homes, the supply-side angle also included the views of energy experts and planners.

The use of ICT for automation of residential buildings is still at an early stage in Austria. Only one housing company has specialised in offering 'multimedia homes', and only a small number of single-family houses have smart home technologies (estimates vary between 500 and 2000). Because of the difficulty of identifying a sufficiently large number of smart home users, no quantitative survey could be carried out. Instead, a limited number of eight households were visited and in-depth interviews carried out with occupants of these smart homes.

However, analysing the situation and viewpoints of actors was only one aspect of the approach. Another step was the active involvement of producers and users in the development of scenarios and requirements for an energy-efficient design of smart homes. Owing to the low number and limited availability of users, a series of three scenario-development workshops was organised with interested supply-side actors (producers, planners, architects and energy experts) and representatives of consumer associations. As a follow-up, several focus groups were set up involving people living in low-energy buildings to discuss the expectations of potential users, images of smart homes and the usefulness of smart home applications developed in the scenario workshops or advertised by producers. The format of the focus groups was chosen to give potential users the opportunity to discuss collectively the problems and advantages of imagined smart home applications, a process that probably would have been much more restricted in individual interviews.[8]

*Reconfiguring actor networks*

A first level of analysis of the development of smart homes is the changing relationships among certain actors involved in the sociotechnical system: the actor network of producers, architects and building companies and their relation to the emerging technology. Smart homes are in an early phase of adoption, with many technologies already in place, though there is still significant leeway in the way they are configured and used. From the perspective of technology suppliers, we can look at the transition from innovation to diffusion as a matter of extending and reconfiguring the actor networks in which these technologies are embedded. Weyer analyses the process of technological development as a succession of three characteristic phases with specific types of actor configurations. Firstly there is the early creation of loose networks and a 'sociotechnical core', then a phase of stabilisation and creation of more stable networks and finally a stage of the breakthrough of a technology (Weyer 1997). The interesting point is that Weyer treats this final phase – traditionally the diffusion of an innovation – as a distinct act of innovation, whereby contexts of use have to be created, the number of actors has to be increased significantly and a coupling of producers and users has to take place, together with a mutual adaptation of technology design and patterns of use. Moving from innovation to diffusion means moving from what is essentially a small and specialised network of actors to a broader network of different and heterogeneous user groups and different groups of professionals. Finding allies and stimulating the interest of users in this broader network means creating contexts of use in interaction with these new actors and adapting the technical system to these new requirements.

It is important to keep in mind, however, that the networks and relations that come into view from the perspective of the production side may differ from the relevant network of social relations that users or consumers find themselves in. As Schwartz Cowan analysed in a historic study on domestic heating in America, moving from consumers through retail and wholesale to production revealed a different picture from that obtained by focusing on production and diffusion. The network of social relations in which consumers are embedded turns out to shape their consumption decisions and defines the range of possibilities of product choice and usage (Schwartz Cowan 1987).

Smart homes and their actor configurations are at the same time embedded in broader sociotechnical regimes and influenced by their dynamics. One such regime change that is especially important for energy-related applications of smart homes is the liberalisation of electricity markets and the ensuing need of utilities to develop add-on services in addition to electricity. Residential gateways connecting smart homes to external communication networks are expected to be a platform for utilities to provide other kinds of services, such as extended load-management features, instant visualisation of energy consumption, or security services. Electricity companies thus turn out to be one of the potential system builders facilitating the integration of technology, services and institutions. As Guy and Marvin convincingly argue, such a development also reconstructs energy consumption practices and the relationship of electricity consumers to producers (Guy and Marvin 1988; Marvin et al. 1999). Smart homes developing in such a context and network of actor relationships (so far there have been only a few field experiments in Austria) may be rather different (and have different potentials for ecological services) from smart homes as 'stand-alone' solutions for the automation of buildings, as is presently the case in the early adoption phase.

What became evident from the interviews with Austrian actors about smart homes is a sociotechnical system in disarray. At the present stage of diffusion of smart homes one of the big problems is that producers, electricians and utilities often follow different pathways (such as utilities treating smart homes as a service platform) and fail to provide cogent scenarios for uses of smart home applications, resulting in difficulties in enrolling new user groups in their actor networks. The problems of introducing smart home technologies point to the requirements and challenge of creating appropriate contexts of use (it is still not clear how and with what aim these technologies will dominate in practice), forging actor networks of heterogeneous groups (there are still various groups – around manufacturers and installers, around building developers and around utilities – with diverging interests and little cooperation) and creating visions that integrate various actors and users. The various interests, the lack of alignment between actors and the isolated, uncoordinated attempts to create applications that are embedded in specific services and concepts of use have not yet been able to create sufficient momentum for the diffusion, modification and acceptance of the technologies.

### Visions of energy-efficient smart homes

Interviews with experts revealed that the different communities connected with smart homes on the one hand and with sustainable buildings on the other differed considerably from one another and had different visions of what tomorrow's buildings should be like. These visions did not usually converge in a 'smart and sustainable home'.

Architects, builders and energy experts with experience of sustainable buildings focused mainly on the building envelope and the 'intelligent' architectural design of the building. Far from hailing low-tech solutions, they saw building services in a supportive role and expected rather a limited use of ICT in sustainable residential buildings. Quite often they stressed the fact that in highly energy-efficient buildings the additional efficiency gains resulting from sophisticated energy-management systems (such as individual room temperature control) were very small and therefore that smart home applications were of limited value for improved sustainability.

Experts on smart homes, in turn, were not interested in the building as a whole, including architectural solutions. A predominant metaphor among smart home supporters when describing the future of smart homes was the automobile, which is in the process of being completely transformed by ICT integration.[9] Social studies of technology point to the importance of metaphors and visions, which serve as collective projections that integrate and orient various forms of actor perceptions and are a way of mediating between different expert and popular cultures. The car seems to be such an orientation point in the discussion about smart homes. It demonstrates the possibility of better control of the environment with ICT and even gives hope that users will uncritically accommodate themselves to new building features. (One of the suppliers asked, 'Which car owner still asks whether he/she really needs electric windows?')

Suppliers still have a strong feeling that convincing users, let alone housing developers, builders and architects, of the added use value of smart homes remains a problem. Their vision of smart homes is not sufficiently matched by the vision of demand-side actors, such as owners or housing companies, as focus groups revealed. Moreover, suppliers have failed to create a coherent network of builders, electricians, housing societies and service providers, which would provide not only technology but also stable institutional structures to set up and use smart homes.

## Appropriating smart homes

If we approach the early diffusion of a technology such as smart homes from the users' perspective, we find that they are far more actively involved in this process than generally expected. Contexts and ways of using a technology are far from clear when an innovation leaves the limited social context of design and production. Designers need to have certain visions of use and certain representations of users in mind when constructing products, and these visions and assumptions to some extent materialise in the physical shape of the product as a script (Akrich 1992). Still, the practices and usages that eventually develop in the course of actually using products and integrating them into daily life, and the values and symbols that are attached to a product by users, cannot be fully anticipated by designers. This process of actively integrating products into daily life, of finding out which way of using products is best suited to a person's own situation, intentions and habits, can be called the appropriation of products. Thus 'one should be careful about accepting the common a priori distinction made between use and design, between user and designer. This distinction implicitly inscribes assumptions that the one is passive (user), the other is active (designer)' (Lie and Sørensen 1996: 8).

Interviews with users of smart homes revealed different groups with specific relations to smart home technologies. Within the group of early adopters is one group of mainly technically interested people with a strong commitment to using these technologies. This group even develops (or tinkers with) additional applications or ways of dealing with them. Undoubtedly there is more potential for electricians or manufacturers to learn from these experienced users than from other groups and to better adapt standard applications of smart homes to practical requirements. For example, one of the users interviewed had developed new ways of reducing heat loss from the hot water system by means of smart control. The second group that may be an important market for smart home technologies was users with a limited number of smart home applications who were mainly interested in a few functions to improve the functionality of certain electrical installations (such as lights, simple security functions, or fewer switches for electric blinds). They had also bought into the idea of a flexible electrical infrastructure in the building that could be adapted to rapidly changing technologies expected in the future, such as a further automation and 'informatisation' of buildings. This group was strongly influenced in its decisions by electricians but, like the first group, was concerned at the idea of being increasingly dependent on this profession. Apart from these two small groups, it appeared to be very difficult to communicate the idea and practical relevance of smart home technologies to potential users.

Focus groups involving people living in sustainable buildings (but without advanced ICT infrastructure) revealed that applications proposed by producers to potential users are still rather abstract. Although there was some basic interest on the part of the focus group participants, the organisational and social contexts of applications such as fault detection and warning have not been developed yet.[10] Creating such contexts will also depend on learning processes and interactions with users and cannot simply be imposed from outside. Attempts to develop integrated packages of applications and new services (such as smart homes for elderly people or the provision of energy-related services by utilities) might be a way to create such contexts of use and practices but have not been very successful so far. The causes for this are manifold, but the lack of collaboration between present actors (for example, between manufacturers and service providers) – and the underestimation of the efforts needed to introduce new technolo-gies alongside new organisational structures, of new actors providing services and of new practices of use developing around these services and technologies – may have played an important part in the lack of success.

### Smart homes and energy efficiency

What does a sociotechnical perspective on smart homes, like the case study just outlined, contribute to design and technology R&D? What has been clearly pointed out is the fact that the contribution of smart home technologies to the sustainability of a building (mainly as a contribution to reduced energy consumption) depends only to a minor extent on the technical availability of corresponding applications. Energy manage-ment (or improved energy information and services) is only one of several other conceiv-able configurations of smart homes – configurations that could even contribute to increased energy consumption.

This analysis of the interrelations of technologies with the interests and strategies of diverse actor groups and with broader socioeconomic trends and contexts shifts the problems of smart and sustainable homes to a different level and sheds light on a number of critical problems that are either not at all or only to some limited extent at the technical level. Given the current interests and visions of crucial actors such as producers or electri-cians, energy-efficient applications have little importance and are not integral to the concepts and visions these actors follow. The only supply-side actors with the interest and substantial resources to implement a concept of smart homes centred on energy issues are utilities providing add-on services to their electricity sales. Even in this case, there are many possible scenarios which involve little energy efficiency and in which utili-ties are seen just as providers of security or entertainment services or only as targeting their add-on services at a premium segment of customers (Guy and Marvin 1998).

Looking at users' practices and perceptions, it is remarkable how much the current development is pushed by technological improvements and how little emphasis has been put on the use value of applications or on the development of appropriate contexts of use. Many of the present applications and services, such as load management or energy feedback, are sometimes rather abstract ideas that do not sufficiently take into account the concrete and daily practice in which they have to be embedded and the improvements they need to provide for current practice and routines.

For a programme such as 'Building of Tomorrow', following the route of smart and sustainable buildings (if seen as promising enough to be followed up at all) should instead mean putting more emphasis on projects that experiment with new applications and that involve users in learning processes about appropriate use practices and contexts of use. Financing the isolated development of energy-efficient applications does not appear as a viable perspective from a sociotechnical point of view.

## Conclusions: sustainable buildings in a sociotechnical context

What this chapter has pointed out is that the introduction of a new technology for sustainable buildings is a complex process of creating new sociotechnical configura-tions and gradually adapting technology design and emerging practices of use. This is far more than a pure focus on technology design, as is the case in most technology-related R&D programmes.

Sociotechnical analysis has the potential to contribute to the design process of sustainable buildings in at least two ways: by enriching the reflexivity and discursive quality of the process; and in a more instrumental sense by providing knowledge relevant to design from sociological studies. On the one hand, such an analysis may contribute to a better understanding of the present situation: the different visions and groups of actors attached to certain development paths of smart homes; the influence of wider socioeconomic contexts such as changes in the electricity or health system, which may provide a viable environment for certain types of smart home applications; the challenge of creating convincing contexts and scenarios of use for smart homes, of closely monitoring emerging practices of using smart home features and of learning from present users. Such an understanding may already have an impact on the way engineers and designers perceive their task and the main problems for the further development of smart homes or sustainable buildings. On the other hand, sociotechnical research may also contribute to the development process of smart homes (or sustainable buildings in general) by mediating between different actor groups and bringing them together, for example in scenario development workshops. Thus the perspective of social studies of technology could facilitate learning processes between producers and users and help to create spaces to experiment with new kinds of uses and to reflect on these experiences. Such ways of directly intervening in the design and policy-making process has been developed further by approaches such as constructive technology assessment (Schot 2001).

To sum up, hopefully this chapter has pointed out that placing sociological analyses related to sustainable buildings in a framework of evolving sociotechnical systems – that is, adopting the approaches of social studies of technology – facilitates the integration of sociological investigations (for example, into user attitudes or into institutional barriers to the adoption of certain technologies) with technological development and design tasks. With such an approach sociological studies may also escape from adopting an engineering-centred problem perspective and may enable a broader perception of the development of sustainable buildings. Such a perspective may help to reframe design problems and may also bring other social groups such as users and their needs and perceptions into the process of developing sustainable buildings.

## Notes

1  An analysis of the rhetoric and practice of sustainable architecture reveals that it is possible to discern several competing logics that exist alongside each other and frame technological decision making (Guy and Farmer 2001).
2  See Anne-Jorunn Berg's paper on the gendering of smart homes (Berg 1992).
3  Guy and Marvin give an interesting analysis of such reconfiguration processes in the electricity sector (Guy and Marvin 1988).
4  More details on the programme can be found at www.hausderzukunft.at. This website also contains summaries of most projects in English and full-text versions of the final reports in German.
5  It should be mentioned, however, that these projects are relatively small, usually not comprising more than one or two person-years of research.
6  Shove (1998) convincingly argues against this picture of 'technical potentials' and 'non-technical obstacles' and demands a new sociotechnical research agenda.
7  See also Guy and Shove (2000) on this issue.
8  As Jaeger points out, focus groups are used in applied social research 'especially to study the dynamics of emotions and arguments triggered by new information, e.g. about a politician or commercial product' (Jaeger et al. 1999: 200). Similarly, the idea of smart homes was new to most of the focus group participants, and a 10 minute video was shown at the beginning to spark off discussion.

9   New cars provide fully technologically controlled environments, where virtually every function – from electric windows to drive-by-wire systems or different climate zones inside the car – is controlled through an ICT infrastructure.

10  There was, for example, a lengthy discussion in one of the focus groups about the possibility and use of applications to detect defects – e.g. of the heating system, washing machine or fridge – and automatically alarming a fault-clearing service or the home owner, who might be on holiday, via mobile phone. Participants found this feature of smart homes quite attractive but immediately turned to the question of what they should do if they got such an alarm while on holiday? Should they allow service people to enter their home in their absence? How would they know what the cause of the fault was? Should they leave a key with their neighbour? These are entirely practical questions, but they point to the importance (and to the failure of present suppliers) of embedding technical features in social practices that are acceptable to users.

# Conclusion

# 13

# Reflection and engagement

## Towards pluralist practices of sustainable architecture

*Simon Guy and Steven A. Moore*

> Imagine ourselves as architects, all armed with a wide range of capacities and powers, embedded in a physical and social world full of manifest constraints and limitations. Imagine also that we are striving to change that world. As crafty architects bent on insurgency we have to think strategically and tactically about what to change and where, about how to change what and with what tools. But we also have somehow to continue to live in this world. That is the fundamental dilemma that faces everyone interested in progressive change.
>
> (Harvey 2000: 233)

In our introduction we characterised the debate about sustainable architecture as exhibiting a tension between the proliferation of ideas associated with 'nature' and a corresponding urge to fix and define a 'best practice' design approach to sustainable architecture. Where public talk about sustainable architecture is expansive there is a corresponding call by building scientists and many architectural professionals to standardise our interpretation of both the environmental problem and our strategies for creating more sustainable futures. The chapters that followed illustrated both the limitations of the standardisation approach and the power of a more dialogical perspective that connects the social and the technical. The examination of heating appliances in Sweden, the controversies associated with constructing 'pedagogical' college buildings in Ohio and California, and the many other cases documented herein – all tell stories of how the citizens of particular places have acted in response to a confusing array of rapidly changing global environmental and social conditions. The actors in these cases have, to varying degrees, hoped to contribute to a body of knowledge that would define the practice of 'sustainable architecture'. Some have developed checklists, others green building codes, a few have experimented with different materials and technologies, while yet others have developed a foundation of shared environmental and social values. Our intent here, however, has not been to favour one approach over another, but to better understand how such lists, codes, practices, buildings and communities are created, contested or legitimated.

Rather than aiming to produce an alternative orthodoxy of sustainable architecture, we set out in this book to document and celebrate the diversity of responses to environmental challenges, and in the process to critique past research on the environmental impact of buildings. Through a variety of theoretical and empirical approaches, we and our contributors have sought to explore the relationship between competing conceptions of environmental issues and the social and technical processes that frame building design. While we hold that more and better building science is surely needed, our approach has been to expand the conventional 'laboratory' to include the study of the cultural contexts within which technological change occurs. In the end, then, our project has been to set an agenda for future interdisciplinary research that would include scientists and sociologists, architects and engineers, philosophers of environmental ethics and of technology as well as citizens themselves.

As we indicated in the introduction, we have divided the contributed chapters into four themes which collectively challenge the conventional view of sustainable architecture as a branch of energy economics (Guy and Shove 2000). So as to challenge our own categories as well as those of conventional building science, we begin this conclusion by revisiting and questioning the validity of the four themes themselves. By challenging our a priori categories through a posteriori analysis we intend to open up other possible interpretations of the research contributed by our co-authors. This brief analysis is followed by a rereading of the individual chapters. The purpose of this re-reading is to highlight the ways in which the contributors both raise questions about the conventional approach of building science and point towards new ways of conceptualising the challenge of sustainable architecture. Finally, this chapter concludes the book by slicing and analysing the data in yet another way: by considering how European and North American authors reflect upon the concept of sustainable architecture and engage their regions differently. In this way the collected chapters become themselves the subject of research as part of the ongoing critical dialogue about sustainable architecture that this book seeks to promote.

## Enframing sustainability

### Revisiting the themes

The four themes that we theorised at the outset – modelling design, responding design, competing design and alternative design – provided a helpful way of interpreting some of the basic arguments made by our co-authors. We do not claim, however, that these four ways of seeing are the only way of ordering their stories. For example, Chapter 8, 'Revaluing Wood', by Ted Cavanagh and Richard Kroeker, which we placed within Part C (Competing design), might have been as easily situated in Part A, 'Modelling design', the discourse concerning standardisation versus plurality. There is, in their analysis of wood technology in eastern Canada, a sub-narrative that is highly critical of standardisation. Similarly, Chapter 6 by Annette Henning, 'Equal Couples in Equal Houses', which we place in Part B, 'Responding design', might have been happily situated in Part D, 'Alternative design'. In this case the sub-narrative is focused upon how designers and manufacturers might significantly alter product design on the basis of anthropological data. Also present in her analysis is another narrative about the influence of gender roles in making technological choices. Our point here is that the themes we have constructed are more porous, more mobile than the table of contents might suggest. The authors might have chosen to be categorised differently or might themselves have constructed various other themes.

Likewise, the contributed chapters have a way of leaking across boundaries, because none of the contributors, let alone the actors in these stories, interpreted the categories of investigation in precisely the same way. As it is with the organisation of this book, so it is with sustainable architecture itself: the categories are fluid. None the less, we hold that such 'thick descriptions' (Geertz 1973) of the cases provide reliable empirical insight into the social and cultural context of technological choices. Although the themes or categories employed are not as precise as a mathematical equation, it is just such interpretive flexibility that helps us to understand how history might be different than it is. Put another way, technological choices are contingent on how professionals, citizens and consumers view their interests at any given time. There are always dominant narratives and sub-narratives, competing discourses that attract and mobilise different affiliates (Nye 2003: 1–20). As John Dryzek suggests, 'Discourses, including environmental ones, help to constitute and re-constitute the world just as surely as do formal institutions or material economic forces' (Dryzek 1997: 201).

Each of the investigations in this book is implicitly concerned with the observation first articulated by Martin Heidegger in *The Question Concerning Technology* (Heidegger 1977: 19–23). Modern technology, argued Heidegger, tends to 'enframe', or limit, our understanding of (architectural) phenomena to narrow categories of quantitative performance, thus 'concealing' or 'challenging' the validity of qualitative meanings. What is important, then, is to consider the multiple possibilities for meaning, the alternative constructions of culture and nature in each case we explore, rather than to limit meaning to narrow calculations concerning efficiency. Each of the four themes or types of design discussed below might be, then, only differing ways of 'enframing' sustainable architecture. By keeping these themes flexible, however, alternative modes of interpretation result.

## Modelling design

A principal concern of three chapters in this collection is the movement in both Europe and North America toward standardising the criteria for assessing the 'goodness' or 'rightness' of green or sustainable architecture. Graham Farmer and Simon Guy (Chapter 2), for example, conclude their study of three office buildings in north east England by rejecting the commonly held assumption that all environmental architecture can be understood as lying somewhere along a linear continuum of light to dark green, technological to organic, or mechanical to passive. Although such a priori categories can be helpful in interpreting competing design strategies, or in classifying internally consistent ideological patterns, they tend to obscure rather than illuminate the complex social dynamics and human intentions involved in building real buildings. Farmer and Guy argue that externally generated and universally applied energy assessment tools such as BREEAM (Building Research Establishment Environmental Assessment Method) tend to 'compress the meaning of green buildings to make them amenable to scientific analysis' and in the process suppress the other motivations and ignore local conditions that frame how people build and live as they do.

In their analysis of two American college buildings, both constructed to teach how building design can influence environmental performance, Kathryn Janda and Alexandra von Meier focus upon 'the presence, absence and use of "data"'. They find that the demand for and assessment of 'hard numbers' seems to 'raise more questions about building performance than they resolve'. At issue here are competing ideas about what constitutes 'performance', quantitative measurement by external experts at one moment in time or qualitative satisfaction voiced by the inhabitants and measured over an extended period.

Steven Moore and Nathan Engstrom, in their study of 26 residential 'green building programmes' in the United States (Chapter 4), argue that such programmes reflect the latent conceptual fusion of two nineteenth-century movements: environmental protection and public health. Once fused as the concept of sustainability the cultural momentum of these sometimes allergic ideas foreshadows the appearance in the twenty-first century of standardised building codes. However, Moore and Engstrom document at least four competing conceptions of how a private green home might constitute a public environmental good. The authors hold that it remains to be seen which set of political interests will prevail in defining the quasi-scientific standards for sustainable architecture.

All six authors who contributed to the first part of the book implicitly agree that the notion of sustainable architecture has been 'co-constructed' within the general process of modernisation and standardisation foreseen by the sociologist Max Weber at the turn of the twentieth century (Weber 1958; Misa et al. 2003: 10). However, Moore and Engstrom go one step further in their concern about the implications of standardisation by asking the simple question, who gets to set the standards and whose interests will they serve? Concern for limiting the meaning of green architecture thus has not only ontological consequences but potent political consequences as well. But where all these authors stand together is in their support for diverse, pluralistic practices. Technological strategies are not, they argue, indicators of quantitative superiority. Rather, technological strategies are indicators of how diverse groups of people choose to live in a particular place.

### Responding design

Two of the chapters in this volume focus explicitly upon the contexts into which design proposals evolve by recognising the tension between deductive and inductive development processes. The first case examined is of sustainable housing in the Netherlands. Although national policy has set ambitious goals for the construction of sustainable housing, real gains have been 'relatively modest'. Although several demonstration projects have been completed, the technologies employed in them have not proliferated outside these 'islands of sustainability'. In their investigation of this paradox (Chapter 5) Timothy Moss, Adriaan Slob and Walter Vermeulen find that the logic employed by planners, although highly rational, is inconsistent with how things really get done in the worlds of design, manufacturing, approval and construction. Not only do Dutch planners tend to overestimate the authority of key actors, but they wrongly understand housing development as being a linear process dependent upon the removal of non-technical 'barriers' discovered in the process of executing a preconceived development plan. The authors argue for an inverse logic where, rather than working from the top down in a deductive linear fashion, planners would work from the bottom up in an inductive, opportunistic and highly political fashion. Seeking out local opportunities, the authors hold, is far more productive than responding to discovered 'barriers'. Moss and his colleagues argue that planners should engage rather than oppose those local 'actor interests' that are required for both short- and long-term technology dissemination. In this story, housing design is a political practice contingent on local contexts, not a narrowly aesthetic or economic practice contingent on rational patterns of design, development and use.

Annette Henning's research in Sweden also supports the notion that the transfer of sustainable technologies from the drawing board, warehouse or showroom to the home is related to the 'experience, habits and ways of thinking' among a certain group of people. At first glance this observation seems perfectly self-evident; people simply will not buy or use what appears unrelated to their lives. It is, however, one thing to observe that ordinary people tend to seek the familiar and quite another to instrumentally render familiar the new technologies required to achieve sustainable conditions. Henning's argument, as a social anthropologist, is that those who wish to alter the consumption habits of large groups of people – government policy-makers, architects, designers, manufacturers and salespeople among them – would be more successful if they learned to relate new technologies to old practices. This logic suggests that designers may not have the power to change people's minds about their relationship to nature, but they may have the power to design buildings and appliances that are more resonant with local ways of living. The fact that these new artefacts are also resource efficient and produced under conditions that are socially equitable may or may not add ontological value in the eyes of the purchaser.

Both of these chapters argue that sensitivity to cultural context is a necessary part of 'good', or should we say 'successful', design. Many architects and critics will, however, take issue with any proposal for what has been called 'contextualism'. The proponents of this strategy, Britain's Prince Charles for example, argue that new buildings should adopt the massing, form and historical style of the surrounding urban context. In contrast, modernists argue that one social function of architecture is to critique norma- tive cultural practices so as to open up new possibilities for meaning and living. Roland Barthes, for example, has argued that representing the new as the old, the unfamiliar as the familiar, is to destroy 'the historical quality of things', it is to lose the 'memory that the artefact was once made' (Barthes 1972: 142). In opposition to contextualists the progenitors of 'critical regionalism' promote the aesthetic strategy of 'defamiliarisation' in lieu of cloaking the new in the garb of the familiar.[1] Following the logic of Marx, Tzonis and Lefaivre (1991: 3–23) mean by 'defamiliarisation' that architecture should evoke meaning and thought rather than emotion and excitement – that architecture should evoke critical consideration of the cultural and ecological origins of construction prac- tices rather than feed local folk what Kenneth Frampton (1995: 1–28) has called 'scenographic fantasies' that encourage them to withdraw into familiar idiocy. Frampton generally makes a distinction between 'Architecture' and mere 'building', and this may be a way of resolving the apparent conflict here – buildings can be familiar, but never Architecture. However, this conceptual distinction would leave the aesthetic intentions of architecture at odds with the environmental intentions that motivated the Swedish government in Henning's case to radically reduce $CO_2$ emissions and fossil fuel consumption.

This tension between environmentalists and architects is an old one and tends to essentialise the intellectual position of both groups in what we argue is a false dichotomy. There are notable exceptions to such simple bifurcation of possibilities. For example, among environmentalists, Barbara Eckstein and James Throgmorton argue that the stories that will best lead to sustainable conditions are those that 'produce the will to change ... disrupt habits of thought, and defamiliarize conventional expectations' (Eckstein and Throgmorton 2003: 5). Among architects, the 26th Pritzker Prize winner (2002), Glen Murcutt, has demonstrated his ability, in projects like the Simpson-Lee House in New South Wales, Australia, to satisfy the demands of local cultural and ecological context without resorting to the type of aesthetic simulation preferred by Prince Charles. In the view of the editors it is necessary to synthesise the apparent but false dichotomy between Architecture and building through an inductive approach to design that begins with sensitivity to local cultural context. The generation of sustainable cultural practices is not dependent upon the simulation of familiar visual contexts in which new technologies will be utilised. Aesthetic simulation is a degraded form of sensitivity to local cultural contexts and can often be antithetical to the desire to have people live differently than they now do.

## Competing design

James Wasley (Chapter 7), Ted Cavanagh and Richard Kroeker (Chapter 8), and Marianne Ryghaug (Chapter 9) have each reconstructed stories in which competing versions of reality play a major role. We could, of course, make such a claim for any of the cases examined in this collection. What makes these three stories the best exemplars of 'competing design' is that all of the authors interpret their research topic as a competition between dominant and emergent technological narratives.

Wasley, for example, examines the differences and similarities between sustainable or 'green' homes and 'safe homes', those designed for the victims of multiple chemical sensitivity (MCS). His analysis concludes that 'green is not necessarily safe and safe is not necessarily green'. Within these broader categories of house types, or design intentions, there are a number of more specific technological, ideological and ethical points of contention between these two worldviews. Where the builders of MCS houses are primarily concerned with their own health, the builders of sustainable houses are primarily concerned with the health of the ecosystem. Where the builders of MCS houses tend to see dense cities as the source of their illness, the builders of sustainable houses tend to see dense cities as the antidote to suburban sprawl. And where the builders of MCS houses tend to use only pure, natural materials, the builders of sustainable houses prefer to preserve such materials in their natural contexts. Each of these oppositions has led to the adoption of different technologies. The principal lesson of Wasley's research is not, however, that these two narratives are opposed and distinct, but that their dialogical relationship is moving them toward a single version of reality in which human health and ecosystem health cannot be separated. This conclusion is very much like that of Moore and Engstrom in Chapter 4.

As we noted in the introduction, Cavanagh and Kroeker's investigation of wood production in Atlantic Canada would find a comfortable home in Part A, which focuses on the opposition between the desire to standardise and the desire to preserve diversity. Within this higher-order topic, however, their research is also structured as the confrontation between a dominant and an emergent technological narrative. The dominant narrative that they reconstruct from historical evidence is characterised as global, corporate, industrial, large and environmentally exploitative. The emergent narrative, which they reconstruct from their own materials research and contemporary historical and sociological evidence, is characterised as local, private, post-industrial, small and sustainable. Such a dichotomous set of characteristics would seem difficult to combine or hybridise. The authors argue that, although there are hopeful signs that sylviculture practices are becoming more 'heterogeneous', any period of technological transition is volatile. In their view the current unstable situation may just as easily result, not in diverse practices, but in a universal and reductive standard or 'orthodoxy of sustainability'. Unlike Wasley, however, Cavanagh and Kroeker see little evidence or advantage in blurring the realities contained within the opposing narratives of industrial and sustainable wood production.

In Ryghaug's study of three Norwegian building projects she finds, like Wasley, that competing dominant and emergent technological narratives show signs of fusion. Based upon the existing architectural culture of Norway this may seem surprising, because the dominant narrative of architectural production is decidedly formal or aesthetic in its values – in general, Norwegian architects display little interest in environmental or energy issues. In the cases studied, however, Ryghaug concludes that architects moved significantly towards the promotion of sustainable technologies when exposed to relevant issues, when given access to energy management programmes (EMPs) and when environmental criteria were included in the initial building programme.

David Nye has argued that all societies construct technological narratives, because such stories help citizens to explain how they came to live in a particular place in a particular way. These 'foundation narratives' must, however, be periodically rewritten as economic and social conditions change. But just as there are foundation narratives, there are also 'counter narratives' that interpret the situation from the perspective of 'groups that had been silenced in or absent from the original formulation' (Nye 2003: 2–19). In the three chapters discussed above there is little doubt that sustainable architecture is such a counter narrative to dominant industrial practices. The authors of these chapters do not, however, see the prospects for counter narratives to be the same. Wasley and Ryghaug see the dialectic discourse between dominant and counter narratives as leading to the reform or synthesis of both. This model we will characterise as 'evolutionary' or developmental and is consistent with the logic of William James, who proposed in 1907 that: 'Truth *happens* to an idea. It *becomes* true, is *made* true by events. Its verity *is* in fact an event, a process: the process namely of its verifying itself' (James 1975: 97). For Wasley, Ryghaug and James, then, the hegemonic narratives that describe reality are always 'in the making' (James 1975), they are what Rorty would term 'achievements' (Rorty 1998). For Cavanagh and Kroeker, however, narratives become dominant in what we will characterise as 'revolutionary' episodes that are consistent with the logic of Thomas Kuhn (1970) and Paul Hawken et al. (1999). In this model, ageing narratives are understood to be suddenly cast aside in a 'paradigm shift' that favours a radically new explanation of reality, but that also subsumes while discrediting the old story. We will not argue that these two explanations of technoscientific change are mutually exclusive, because in the end the evolutionary and revolutionary explanations both rely on the social construction of reality.

## Alternative design

As in the previous three themes our investigation of alternative design includes multiple interpretations, this time by Kirsten Gram-Hanssen and Jesper Ole Jensen (Chapter 10), Jamie Horwitz (Chapter 11) and Harald Rohracher (Chapter 12). The previous theme to be reread, 'competing design', focused on differing interpretations about the nature of reality; this was an ontological discussion. This theme focuses on differing interpretations of the past and future; this is, then, also a historical discussion.

In their investigation of green buildings in Denmark, Gram-Hanssen and Jensen employ an 'actor-oriented approach' by interviewing the participants in various green building projects so as to determine more precisely what they mean by such terms as 'sustainable', 'resource-saving', 'ecological', 'natural', 'healthy' and so on. The authors find that the understanding and use of this vocabulary has changed over time and that four distinct historical periods, or discourses, are discernible from approximately 1973

– the date of the first OPEC oil embargo – to 2003. They explain this rather accelerated change in language as a continuum of response to the rapidly changing risks to which the citizens of Denmark are subject. Changed language does not simply describe the new chemicals, technologies and energy reserves that steadily emerge from scientific discourse and public talk – it inscribes the future with altered aspirations and possibilities. In this sense sustainable architecture is more a form of 'story telling' than a science – it is a way to literally construct an acceptable future.

In her analysis of post-disaster Pattonsburg, Missouri, Jamie Horwitz examines the three alternative futures that are constructed by experts, by the ladies who frequent the town's only beauty parlour and by Hollywood. These are very different stories indeed. In her telling, the experts first envisioned a sustainable future reconstructed on an upland site, far from the destructive flooding of the Missouri River. This vision of the future was enabled by various eco-efficient technologies and environmental best practices. It had, however, nothing to do with Pattonsburg's past, except its history of devastating floods. The second version of the future, told by locals, envisioned a future dominated by the past. It was enabled by the rejection of all the expert recommendations and the reconstruction of familiar life patterns on the new town site. This vision had nothing to do with sustainability, except in recuperating a lost life-world. The third version of the future, told by Hollywood, was a western genre film scripted into the nineteenth century that used the abandoned town as its set. This vision had nothing to do with the future, except that it enabled locals to adopt a fabricated history that foreshadowed a preferable but imaginary new life. In the author's view, all three visions of the future were unsatisfying. What was missing, she argues, was the power of artists to narrate a future that might connect the future with the past, hope to memory.

Within architectural discourse there is increasing global speculation that the future of the housing industry lies in the synthesis of 'smart houses' and 'green building'. Research teams in Finland, Austria and the United States – both at the Massachusetts Institute of Technology and the University of Texas – are engaged in the design and construction of prototypes that assume a symbiotic relation between these two types of technology. In his research on the topic, Harald Rohracher warns that such assumptions may lack any sociological foundation. Based on the empirical analysis of the 'Building of Tomorrow' programme in Austria, Rohracher's argument is that the future of 'smart, sustainable' housing is not inevitable but that it relies on the ability of architects, engineers and product manufacturers to reconceptualise the housing problem in sociotechnological terms. His findings suggest that

> the different communities connected with smart homes on the one hand and with sustainable buildings on the other differed considerably from one another and had different visions of what tomorrow's buildings should be like.

Utility companies, for example, tend to stress smart houses that provide security and entertainment as add-on services to their premium customers. However, these services are energy consuming and tend to appear as a negative to those customers who are primarily interested in energy efficiency. Sociotechnical analysis, Rohracher argues, might better contribute to the design of smart, sustainable housing by imagining alternative social and technical configurations rather than focusing entirely upon technology design. In this sense his proposal has as much to do with the future of the design professions as to the future of housing. In other words, Rohracher questions the ability of architects and engineers to design successful smart, sustainable housing without both redefining the problem and restructuring the design team to include social scientists.

Each of the three chapters in Part D has hypothesised about the process of what Spinosa and colleagues call 'history-making': the innovative activity of individuals that is based on an understanding that a 'commonsense way of acting ought to take care of things and how it fails' (Spinosa et al. 1997: 162–8). On this basis we conclude that the future of sustainable architecture is contingent on at least three variables: the language that we have available to describe it, our ability to link linguistic descriptions to the social practices of the past and present, and the political will to choose technologies consciously, not as material objects but as expressions of a way of life. To evaluate alternative designs of the future thoughtfully and critically, these authors require that architects develop all three skills: new languages, new linkages and the political will to choose technologies democratically. An alternative to this mandate is to work in collaborative design teams with social scientists as equal members in the project of co-constructing small worlds.

Our rereading of the eleven chapters within the context of the four themes has produced yet another layer of interpretation. The questions that surround the modelling of norms and technologies, the cultural contexts into which technological innovations are thrown, the competing realities that vie for our allegiance, and the alternative futures promised by differing worldviews each help us to interpret reality through legitimate if differing lenses. But readers will understandably want to know how all of this theorising adds up to something more than a collage of our moment in history. The contributions to this book highlight the diversity of ways in which we think about sustainable architecture and of design approaches to sustainable architecture. How, then, do we handle such diversity without collapsing into total relativism?

### From universal models to local stories

One way to avoid the assumptions of relativism – the notion that all truth claims are equally valid – is to look to the epistemology of Donna Haraway. She has rejected the seemingly objective 'god's eye view' of worldly phenomena, a view favoured by traditional science, in favour of 'situated knowledges' in which we interact from particular vantage points with a world of interactive subjects (Haraway 1995: 189). In Haraway's view of worldly phenomena,

> only partial perspective promises objective vision. All western cultural narratives about objectivity are allegories of the ideologies governing the relations of what we call mind and body, distance and responsibility.

In this opposition of 'mind and body, distance and responsibility' Haraway reconstructs the modern Cartesian assumption that scientists who objectively study nature at a distance have no immediate responsibility for what they see through their instruments. She continues: 'Feminist objectivity is about limited location and situated knowledge, not about transcendence and splitting of subject and object. It allows us to become answerable for what we learn how to see' (Haraway 1995: 181). In other words, one can acknowledge the existence of competing views of reality that emerge from other perspectives without abdicating one's responsibility to act on what one has learned to see from one's own particular perspective.

Relativism, for Haraway, is only the flip side of modern totalising objectivity, because both positions deny the stakes shared by humans and non-humans. More problematically, she argues, relativism constructs barriers to 'seeing well'. The obstacles constructed by our distance from phenomena, or by their overwhelming scale, arise only when one adopts a 'god's eye view' of reality (Haraway 1995: 182). Seeing a single truth 'out there' and seeing all interpretations of reality as equally true is, in the end, the same Cartesian attitude. Perceiving only one Truth, or alternatively, perceiving everything as truth, absolves the observer from responsibility. Learning 'how to see' from the limitations of a particular place is, then, the only way to appreciate human complicity in and responsibility for constructing and reconstructing the world. This is an epistemology, we argue, that is consistent with the assumptions found in only some versions of sustainable architecture, but one that allows us to appreciate all versions of sustainable architecture. David Schlosberg has argued that Haraway's epistemology ultimately stands on the shoulders of the 'radical empiricism' proposed by the American pragmatist William James at the turn of the twentieth century (Schlosberg 1999: 16). This observation will become significant to the reader in what follows.

If our perspective of events is partial, but we have learned to see historically, it suggests that we can tell stories, or competing narratives of reality. Narratives are a rhetorical tool through which we can re-imagine sustainable architecture in particular times and particular places with focused, if limited, goals. The literatures of urban environmental ethics and of urban studies both look to narratives to understand the emergent meaning of sustainable architecture and urbanism.

From the literature concerning urban environmental ethics, Aver de Shalit (2003: 17) characterises urban narratives as those 'thick' stories that we tell both to visitors and to our fellow citizens that explain how we live in our particular places. The people of Austin, Texas, for example, inevitably refer to the cold, pure water of Barton Springs as the principal icon of the karst limestone geology that underlies the Texas Hill Country. For Austinites these springs, located at the edge of the Balcones geological uplift, explain everything from why people settled in central Texas in the first place, to rainfall patterns, to their choice of building materials, to economic choices, to racial settlement patterns and much more. The slow development of such local thick descriptions serve to both express and engage locals in the construction of regional environmental ethics (Light 2003).

From the literature concerning urban studies, Barbara Eckstein (2003: 13–38) expands upon such logic by arguing that the telling of urban narratives is a principal way to conscript listeners into a dialogue with strangers about how we might live differently than we do. Urban narratives differ from what we described above as 'technological narratives' only in emphasis. Living differently in a place requires different technologies. Thus a successful campaign for a new light-rail transit system requires, for example, a new story about how the technology will change the lives of a majority for the better. Urban and technological narratives both invite citizens to add their own interpretations of reality to the story of their place and in the process become co-authors of a future enabled by its telling, retelling and evolution. It is, then, the construction of such local urban and technological stories that conscripts new supporters and resists universal models of sustainable architecture (Henderson 1999: 215). These stories and the artefacts they inspire constitute what Kenneth Frampton (1995) has referred to as 'tectonic culture' – a way of building in a place that is no less important than the manner in which people speak. Robert Beauregard similarly holds that

A society without such story telling is one in which technocrats rule and bureau-cracy is unaccountable to citizens. Political leaders lose touch with their constitu-ents and citizens are turned into either clients, passive voters, or both.

(Beauregard 2003: 65)

In sum, we the editors argue that the contributions to this collection illustrate how a move away from the legislation of national or international standards for sustainable architecture, and toward the construction of narratives that conscript citizens into ever-evolving local tectonic cultures, provides a more productive basis for debate about sustainable architectures. This argument, however, requires a clearer understanding of how technologies and human practices are co-constructed.

## The co-construction of sustainable architecture

### *The interpretive turn*

It is fair to say that all of the authors who have contributed to this collection have, to one degree or another, been affected by the general turn to postmodern methods of inter-pretation – be they of film, literature, technology or architecture. These methods rely on the understanding of both nature and science as cultural constructs and point toward an interdisciplinary perspective that emphasises the co-construction of nature and culture, of society and technology, of place and the future.

Rohracher and Ornetzeder (2002b: 73–4) hold that the discourse concerning sustainable architecture has contributed to the erosion of the traditional barriers between technological strategies and social strategies, where quantitative, technolog-ical strategies were always given priority. In their view, sustainable architecture requires a techno-social approach, because in the assessment of the performance of buildings, as in Janda and von Meier's chapter, the behaviour of inhabitants cannot be separated from the efficiency of technological apparatus itself. Ralf Brand (2003: 7–27) has, in his doctoral dissertation, built on this logic by arguing for the co-construction of new tech-nologies and the changed social behaviours that are required to achieve a condition of sustainability. In Brand's analysis, one cannot depend on purely technological fixes, because increased efficiency will only enable more consumption unless behaviour is simultaneously altered. Likewise, one cannot depend simply on inducing more pious behaviour in all citizens, because even from a narrow economic perspective there is no incentive to be the first on your block to sacrifice consumption in favour of an abstract goal.

Brand's study of sustainable urbanism, like the chapters in this collection, rely on advances in the history of technology and the relatively new field of science and tech-nology studies (STS). This emergent discipline includes, among others, scholars from sociology, anthropology and the history of technology and has within its porous bound-aries several interpretive traditions. Without attempting to be comprehensive we can distinguish the following five interpretive traditions, all of which have influenced the contributors to this volume: social constructivist theory, systems theory, actor–network theory, critical theory and pragmatism (Moore 2001: 114–22).

Conventional architectural criticism commonly awards the authorship of large, complex projects involving hundreds of workers to a single architect. We understand, for example, the Institute of Contemporary Art in Boston to be a work of Diller +

Scofidio, not the hundreds of other architects, engineers, contractors, labourers and suppliers who contributed thought and time to its construction, nor the curators, collectors and patrons who first imagined the project and have had significant input in its development. The weakness in understanding architecture as an individual work, or creation, is that the emphasis on authorship easily leads to a 'great man' theory of history – an interpretive tradition given up long ago by nearly every discipline, save the popular criticism of art and architecture. Each interpretive tradition reviewed below argues for the social, rather than individual, construction of architecture and technology.

The first tradition in the STS field is social constructivist theory. Bijker and Law (1992), among others, have demonstrated the 'contingent' nature of technological agreements. They argue that, in the contemporary economy, the contingent agreements between producers are designed in the flexible interests of managers and investors. In this view, technoscience is understood simply as one 'belief-system' among many (Barnes 1973: 10). Radical social constructivists refuse to grant science any epistemological privilege over other ways of understanding the world. In this argument, social constructivism is pure epistemological relativism of the kind so disparaged by Haraway. Radical constructivists and Haraway do, however, share some common territory. Positivist science assumes a linear model of research and development of technological artefacts. In contrast, both Haraway and constructivists favour a 'multidirectional model' (Pinch and Bijker 1985: 17–51). This model holds that certain directions in technological development die off and others are economically reinforced as members of the society come to share a set of meanings, or benefits, attached to the artefact in question. The point to be emphasised here is that the moment at which the artefact becomes socially 'stabilised' is commonly confused with the moment of 'invention'. 'Different interpretations of nature are available to scientists and hence ... nature alone does not provide a determinant outcome to scientific debate'. The same logic can be applied to technology and to sustainable architecture. In other words, 'interpretive flexibility' is attached to any artefact – it might be designed in another way. This position has been employed very successfully by Michael Gorman (1998) in the study of solar collector development and recyclable fabrics designed by architect William McDonough. It is also reflected in several of the above chapters, particularly Chapters 2, 11 and 12.

Second in the STS field is the interpretive tradition of systems theory, pioneered by Thomas Hughes. Hughes holds that Thomas Edison, for example, was not the inventor of electricity so much as he acted to integrate economic and political systems with scientific techniques that were already available (Hughes 1985: 39–52). In this view Edison was the quintessential entrepreneur rather than the secretive alchemist. What Edison administered was not the invention of techniques, but rather the creation of social agreements that would institutionalise the production and reproduction of previously isolated technologies. Systems theory understands technological innovation not in terms of objects or in terms of techniques, but in terms of the human agreements required to standardise production and thus assure reproduction. Systems theory provides, as in Chapters 2, 4 and 8, a useful perspective from which to study the various certification programmes that are intent on the standardisation and systemisation of 'green building'.

The third tradition is actor–network theory. Bruno Latour, the most well-known contributor to this position, has recognised that the great men of science, rather than being autonomous hero–inventors, are men propped up in the eyes of society by the material process of knowledge production. For Latour (1987), the facts claimed by 'technoscience', far from being the discoveries of disinterested scientists, are demonstrated to be socially constructed by the material interests of the social networks that produce them. Once scientific facts become encased in the 'black box' of peer review, the web of interested agreements that support the artefact cannot be effectively challenged from the outside. Scientific truth, for Latour, is neither the asocial objective Truth imagined by realists nor the interchangeable social constructions imagined by relativists. Rather, Latour (1995) understands truth to be manifest in the relations that emerge between humans and non-humans – by the relations that 'show up' between 'quasi-objects'. This is not a compromise epistemology that reconciles positivism with relativism, but an ontological position that follows from Heidegger's philosophy of relations. If you want to understand how sustainable technologies are produced and reproduced in the world, reasons Latour, don't study what the practitioners of green architecture say, study what they do! This approach was employed in Chapters 2, 5, 11 and 12.

The fourth tradition of STS is the critical theory of technology, best articulated by Andrew Feenberg. Donna Haraway's position, discussed above, is often characterised as the feminist version of critical theory. It is hardly surprising that Feenberg, as an intellectual descendant of the Frankfurt School, would reject what he refers to as the late Heidegger's 'substantive theory of technology'. It is also not surprising that he would simply ignore the social constructivist theory of technology, because, in Haraway's and Feenberg's view, that literature simply ignores the unequal power relationships constructed by market-driven technological systems. Less predictable, however, is Feenberg's rejection of the determinism implicit in the traditional Marxist position towards technology and what he refers to as 'civilizational change' (Feenberg 2002). In the wake of the Soviet failure, and the entirely instrumental use of technology by Soviet managers, Feenberg reverses the Marxist assumption that it is the state that can most effectively control the 'ontological decision[s]' implicit in technological choice (Feenberg 1991: 3). In the place of direct state control of production from above, Feenberg argues for a 'politics of technological transformation', or a 'parliament of things', in which a radical participatory democracy in the design of technological systems is realised. Feenberg argues that a shift towards participatory democracy in the workplace would both reduce the 'operational autonomy' of managers to dominate production in the name of efficiency and increase the ability of workers to realise their own creative potential. In this argument, Feenberg is most concerned with the selection of technologies as the selection of a way of life. He rejects, however, the 'dilemma of development' in which the social concern for worker satisfaction or environmental preservation is understood as a costly 'trade off' in the purely mathematical rationale of productive efficiency. Rather, Feenberg reasons that such civilisational changes are both efficient and life enhancing (Feenberg 1999: 97). This argument is, perhaps, the most directly related to the idea of sustainable architecture and resonates with the assumptions of Chapters 2, 4 and 8.

Finally, the fifth tradition, or perhaps we should say emergent discourse, of STS is pragmatism. It is not an accident that we consider pragmatism immediately after critical theory, because the distinction between these categories of thought is becoming blurred. Larry Hickman (2001: 170) has argued that Feenberg has renovated the critical theory position of his teacher, Herbert Marcuse, to a degree that it is now closer to that of the pragmatist American philosopher John Dewey than to Jürgen Habermas, the last remaining progenitor of the Frankfurt School. Hickman has gathered and reinterpreted

Dewey's work on technology in a manner that is particularly helpful in our consideration of sustainable architecture. First, he proposes that we should think about technology in the broadest possible sense of the term, as did Dewey, who considered language to be a tool and everyday tools to be culture, '*our* culture' (Hickman 2001: 4, 46, 55). 'For Dewey technology is a rich blend of theory and practice that eventuates in new and improved tools for living and out of which new norms develop' (Hickman 2001: 183). Note that the emphasis in this passage is on the simultaneous co-construction of new tools and new norms for behaviour. Hickman proposes that technology is what we use to 'tune up the way we experience the world' and that the world is increasingly techno-logical (Hickman 2001: 23). How then, he muses, 'do we go about tuning up technol-ogy' so that we might live differently than we do – so that we might live sustainably?

Like Haraway and Feenberg, pragmatists generally reject the Cartesian or 'spectator theory' of knowledge (Hickman 2001: 27). It follows, then, that a principal concern of pragmatists is the role of experts, such as architects and engineers, within society. Following Dewey, Hickman (2001: 5, 139) argues that experts should not create policy, nor should they tell citizens what to think. Rather, their role is 'educative'; it is to help fellow citizens understand how they might act on matters of concern such as environ-mental degradation. Dewey did not believe that cities or environments could be planned per se. He did, however, argue that society should engage in the perpetual process of planning. This is not a paradox but the articulation of a developmental model of techno-logical change that rests on direct empirical experience with our natural and built envir-onments, what James called 'radical empiricism'. If we apply this perspective to the human relation to nature, or to sustainable architecture, it suggests that pragmatists favour a developmental approach to technological change. Pragmatist architects, then, would embrace the process of green building but reject rigid universal standards in favour of ever-evolving local discourses. This position too sounds familiar, rather like Chapters 2, 4, 5, 6, 7, 9, 11 and 12.

Readers who have been keeping track of our scorecard that notes which chapters of this volume are affiliated with which interpretive tradition of STS will have noted that we claim multiple affiliations for most chapters. We must argue, then, that these 'logics', as Guy and Farmer (2001) would identify them, are not mutually exclusive. Each logic, or interpretive tradition, is internally consistent, and the assumptions of some traditions are uneasily combined with others. Yet, all of the authors associated with this collection tend to employ multiple strategies for interpretation, even if their most basic assump-tions are dominated by a distinct disciplinary approach. In Rorty's terms, they collec-tively 'offer an account of inquiry which recognizes sociological, but not epistemological, differences between such disciplinary matrices as theoretical physics and literary criticism' (Rorty 1991: 1). Research about buildings is, then, rather like building itself – a pluralist endeavour. And although we have claimed that there is general agreement among many of our contributors that natures and cultures are multiple and co-constructed, there is no final agreement about how as designers and citizens we should respond.

# The politics of sustainable architecture

## *Cultures of engagement and reflection*

To this point we have identified and critiqued the conventional model of sustainable architecture as energy efficiency, followed some illuminating empirical stories and began to reconstruct an alternative theoretical framework for better understanding of sustainable architecture. However, there remains the task of escaping from the trap of endless speculation and interpretation. Recalling the admonition of Richard Rorty (1999: 91) to stop theorising and get on with the business of solving the real problems of women and men, we must think about engagement with the design process and how we might connect our theoretical flexibility with the materiality of design in particular contexts. We can begin this process by again re-reading the chapters in light of their different emphases on interpretation and engagement, contemplation and action, or reflection and emancipation. This entails a certain re-ordering. One of the many possible ways of slicing the data differently is by employing geography – by grouping the European and North American papers to see whether or not we can identify competing styles or assumptions.

Andrew Jamison, an American environmental academic who has lived and worked in Europe for thirty years, argues that such a geographical re-sorting is justified by 'a huge difference between American writings, with their patriotic enthusiasms and their sticking to the "facts", and European writings, with their cosmopolitan sophistication and speculative theories' (Jamison 2001: 90). Jamison is 'struck by the discursive dissonances, the interpretive imbalances, between the hemispheres'. In light of Jamison's impressions we can re-read our contributions from the perspective of their commitment to critical theory or practical engagement (or both). We have found that Jamison is not the first to categorise Europeans and North Americans in this way.

Critical theorists, Max Horkheimer principal among them, have tended to paint American engagement in the world as dangerously naïve. Horkheimer and his colleagues were not just critical of American political and business interests; they also criticised the cultural attitudes of American politics and business, as exemplified by the writings of American pragmatist philosophers, John Dewey in particular. Horkheimer describes pragmatists as Enlightenment positivists overly impressed with the 'institutions and goals of industrial technology' (cited by Hickman 2001: 72). Dewey, a contemporary of Horkheimer, was characterised as simply too unsophisticated to recognise the degree to which modern technology is complicit with the underlying values of liberal capitalism.

In response to this line of criticism, the philosopher Larry Hickman argues that Horkheimer's critiques are themselves deluded by the myth of elite objectivity and distanced from community-based inquiry held accountable by adequate checks and balances. Dewey himself argued the reverse of Horkheimer: that it is not the fault of technology if it is imagined and controlled by the few for their own benefit; rather, the fault lies with a more general failure to employ technology in solving real problems. For Dewey the problem was not too much democracy or too much technology as Horkheimer proposed, but too little of both. So, where critical theorists reduced American pragmatism to a simple 'philosophy of action', Hickman (2001: 80, 179) retorts that pragmatism is a 'philosophy of production'. He means by this that 'the goal of inquiry is not action, but the construction of new and more refined habits, tools, goals and meanings. In short, new and more refined products'.

Richard Rorty has also responded to the critical theory characterisation of American pragmatism. Rorty begins his response, however, by acknowledging that critical theory and pragmatism share two key assumptions: firstly, that the Enlightenment substituted faith in human reason for faith in supernatural guidance, and secondly, that human reason is still not capable of describing nature as it is (Rorty 1999: xxvi). As important as these shared assumptions may be, any further agreement between Horkheimer and Dewey then seemed unlikely. Where critical theorists find Americans generally naïve, Rorty finds the American optimism to be courageous because they have been the first society to 'renounce hope of justification from on high – from a source which is immovable and eternal' (Rorty 1998: 28). In rejecting both religious myths and the ideological absolutes of orthodox Marxism, Americans have no one to blame but themselves for the various environmental and political risks that confront them.

Rorty's second line of response to the critics of pragmatism is that, in response to the acknowledged horror of the US-sponsored wars waged against Vietnam, Afghanistan and Iraq, critical theorists themselves have become 'spectatorial and retrospective' rather than genuinely political (Rorty 1998: 14, 36). He means by this that the Leftist culture critics of both Europe and America have become disengaged from the day-to-day politics of city hall, the school board meeting or the zoning struggle, let alone international struggles. Rather than engage directly in the project of making life better for those of our fellow citizens who suffer, critical theorists have retreated into academia to observe a troubled world from a distance. From Rorty's partial perspective, which we noted in the introduction (Rorty 1999: 36, 94), the advocates of critical theory have come 'to prefer knowledge to hope' and as a result their 'disengagement from practice produces theoretical hallucinations'.

To illustrate this tension between reflection and engagement we can point to the architectural theorist Paul Shepheard. Shepheard, a European who has taught frequently in American universities, has arguably applied the outlook of a European philosophical postmodern who is sceptical of Enlightenment meta-narratives to the world of green architecture by arguing:

> Sustainability is usually configured as a piece of critical theory against the American way of life. I am suggesting the opposite: that it is a part of the American hegemony's desire for perpetuity, a device for making America last forever.
>
> (Shepheard 2003: 285)

In other passages Shepheard conflates American 'ecologists' and 'special forces guys' as 'twenty-first century Jesuits, who want you to do what they say for your own good' (Shepheard 2003: 193, 227). This characterisation of Americans in the field is followed by a characterisation of their assumptions towards nature: he holds that 'ecologists do not view the world as an emergence but as a defiled paradise, confusing the ideal with the material all over again'. Like Horkheimer before him, Shepheard paints Americans in general as a dangerously naïve presence in the world. Shepheard's fear, shared by other postmoderns, is that the modern desire to create order in the world has inevitably produced unintended consequences – new forms of disorder that are even more malignant than the conditions that motivated our actions in the first place. His hypothesis (Shepheard 2003: 176–8) is that the doctrine of sustainability is only Enlightenment science by another name and constitutes a new meta-narrative of global domination, a 'desire to automate the future' (Shepheard 2003: 194). But in Shepheard we find, not the preservation of difference so valued by other postmoderns, but the same logic of homogenisation and standardisation that we criticised in the conventional building science view of sustainability. For Shepheard, sustainable architecture appears as a single set of powerful ideas – a hegemony – that is internally consistent, and does not extend beyond the deep ecology of Arne Naess. By ignoring the pluralism inherent in practices of sustainable architecture, Shepheard has conveniently essentialised sustainable architecture in order to allow him to make a critical argument about the totalising impulses of science in the service of authoritarianism.

According to Rorty, the pragmatists Whitman and Dewey felt that modern Europeans tried much too hard to produce knowledge and authority as a precursor to action (Rorty 1998: 23). The postmodern turn exemplified by Shepheard appears to have turned dependency on scientific or philosophical authority to fear of any knowledge claims and subsequent paralysis of action. However, there are other European traditions of thought that connect strongly to American pragmatism. Rorty points to Wilhelm von Humboldt's argument that any form of social organisation must pursue 'human development in its richest diversity' (ibid.). For Rorty, these ideas come together in John Dewey's call to treat ideas of right and wrong, 'not as signifying a relation to some antecedently existing thing … but as expressions of satisfaction at having found a solution to a problem' (Rorty 1998: 28). In this way we move from being what Rorty, referencing Dewey, calls 'spectators' to being 'agents' of change, committed to 'protocols of social experiments whose outcomes are unpredictable' (Rorty 1998: 37).

So what are the ideological affiliations of the contributors to this book? Are some critical theorists and others pragmatists? Can we divide along geographical or national lines? Are some positivists and others constructivists? Again following Rorty (1999: 42), we argue that the endless assessment of ideological purity that might help us to distinguish eco-feminists from deep ecologists, eco-socialists from Earth-firsters!, or 'gaias' from Sierra Club members is not productive. As Schlosberg argues, 'plurality is not a phenomenOn to be categorized, but rather needs to be the concept at the centre of the analysis' (Schlosberg 1999: 38). It is to the development of a pragmatic architectural practice of critical pluralism that we finally turn.

## Critical pluralism

### The pragmatics of practice

Employing pragmatic logic similar to the above, David Schlosberg has proposed that

> there is no such thing as environmentalism. Any attempt to define the term in a succinct manner excludes an array of other valid definitions. 'Environmentalism' is simply a convenience – a vague label for an amazingly diverse array of ideas that have grown around the contemplation of the relationship between human beings and their surroundings.
>
> (Schlosberg 1999: 1)

Through this book we argued for diversity in ways of seeing and practising sustainable, green, regenerative or ecological architecture. However, we should note that Schlosberg's proposal for a 'critical pluralism' relies, not simply on liberal tolerance for difference, but on what he calls 'agonistic respect' (Schlosberg 1999: 16). We take this turn of phrase to mean 'the cultivation of care for the positions and responses of others'. Schlosberg (1999: 6–10) has rejected mainstream, or liberal, environmentalism for two principal reasons. Firstly, those liberals who manage mainstream organisations – the 'big ten' in the United States, for example – have increasingly alienated and marginalised many previously vital grassroots groups. These include communities of colour fighting environmental racism issues, eco-feminists, eco-anarchists and so on. Secondly, the organisational structure of liberal environmental organisations has rendered liberal environmentalists indistinguishable from the very corporate and government organisations that they contest. By reducing environmental action to direct-mail solicitations, legislative lobbying and litigation, the practice of environmentalism has been abstracted from local environmental and social contexts. A very similar critique of American mainstream environmentalism has been rigorously constructed by Robert Brulle (2000). Following Schlosberg and Brulle, we argue that the same pattern of professionalisation and abstraction is occurring with regard to sustainable architecture.

To be clear, this is not an argument to return to the 1970s and promote straw-bale construction as a tectonic panacea for the earth. It is, rather, an urgent call to 'acknowledge' and 'recognize', as Schlosberg (1999: 4) would have it, the diversity of practices that might point to alternative sustainable futures. In this way we may begin to chart an agenda for future research that would challenge the orthodox, isolated categories of building design, building science, social science and industrial ecology and 'engage' in critical, interdisciplinary research.

As must be clear by now, we do find new sources of salient theory in the writings of those who are productively blurring the distinction between critical theory and pragmatism – Dewey, Hickman, Feenberg and Rorty in particular. Unfortunately, these authors have written relatively little on the topic of architecture and even less on the topic of sustainable architecture. The absence of research in this area provides a demand for architectural theorists, such as Joan Ockman (2000), to continue investigating any affinity between pragmatism and architectural production. It also creates a demand for symposia that would initiate dialogue between interested practitioners, architectural theorists, philosophers and the public. Pragmatic practice is, then, a second agenda item for further research.

Proposals for critical pluralism are also coming out of the discourse concerning 'civic environmentalism' initiated by William Shutkin (2000) and Andrew Light (Light and Katz 1996; Light 2003). A critical literature is growing on the relationship between democratic participation and the resolution of environmental problems. Called also 'ecological citizenship', such proposals have in common the belief that environmental problems will not be solved without substantial civic participation. This concept has been practised for some years, as in the 30-year-old Philadelphia 'Green City Strategy', as the building of neighbourhood parks and community gardens without a theoretical basis to inform them.[2] The existence of such community-based 'programmes' provides an opportunity to expand them into architecture and urban design. Alternative modes of civic engagement in architectural production are, then, a third agenda item for further research.

Fourthly, we need to open up and explore the language we use to talk about sustainable architecture. As Andrew Jamison has suggested, 'More fluid terms are needed: dialectical, open-ended terms to characterize the ebbs and flows, nuances and subtleties and the ambiguities of environmental politics' (Jamison 2001: 178). There is a need for 'statements that are open rather than doctrinaire' (Schlosberg 1999: 189) and statements that 'conscript' rather than alienate (Henderson 1999: 53, 204). We must encourage a debate in which 'discourse is never-ending, and solidarity is forever creating new networks and mosaics' (Schlosberg 1999: 103).

Finally, there is the very postmodern issue of identity. We opened this concluding chapter with a call from David Harvey to imagine ourselves as 'insurgent architects'. Architects, which for Harvey include all of us involved in designing, developing and inhabiting lived spaces, must 'desire, think, and dream of difference', we must collectively 'imagine how it is to be (and think) in a different situation' (Harvey 2000: 237–8). Echoing the pragmatists we discussed above, Harvey maintains that 'as real architects of the future we cannot engage in endless problematization and never ending conversations' (Harvey 2000: 245), but that we must have available 'some special sources of critique, from which to generate alternative visions as to what might be possible' (Harvey 2000: 237–8). It is our hope that we have contributed some critical resources that might help stimulate that 'never ending debate' about sustainable architectures.

## Notes

1 Tzonis and Lefaivre credit the term 'defamiliarisation' to Victor Schlovsky, a member of the 'Russian Formalists' who coined the term around the time of the Bolshevik Revolution. See also Schlovsky's 'Art as Technique', in L. T. Lemon and M. Reis (eds), *Russian Formalist Critique* (Lincoln, NB: University of Nebraska Press, 1965).
2 See www.pennsylvaniahorticulturalsociety.org/phlgreen/ui_launchinggreencity.htm (accessed 10 March 2004).

# Bibliography

Adam, B., Beck, U. and van Loon, J. (eds) (2000) *The Risk Society and Beyond: Critical Issues for Social Theory*, London: Sage.

[AF&PA] American Forest and Paper Association (2002) *International Wood News* (newsletter), April 2002, Washington, DC: AF&PA (www.afandpa.org/).

Agterbosch, S., Vermeulen, W. and Glasbergen, P. (2004) 'Implementation of Wind Energy in the Netherlands: The Importance of the Social-Institutional Setting', in *Energy Policy* 32: 2049–66. Available at www.sciencedirect.com (accessed 14 January 2004).

[AIA] American Institute of Architects (1990) *An Architect's Guide to Building Codes & Standards*, Washington, DC: AIA.

Akrich, M. (1992) 'The De-scription of Technical Objects', in W. E. Bijker and J. Law (eds), *Shaping Technology/Building Society: Studies in Socio-Cultural Change*, Cambridge, MA: MIT Press.

Allen, L. (2000) 'Seeking Higher Ground', in *Preservation: The Magazine of the National Trust for Historic Preservation*, July/August: 38–43, 93.

Almlund, P., Elle, M., Jessen, A. and Hoffmann, B. (2001) *Økologisk renovering og vedligeholdelse af parcelhuse*, Copenhagen: Ministry of Environment and Energy.

Almqvist, A. (1993). *Han och hon och huset. Drömmen om ett eget liv*, Gävle, Sweden: Statens Institut för Byggforskning (SB:61).

Andelssamfundet i Hjortshøj (2003) *'Co-operative Community, Hjortshøj'*, www.ecovillage.dk/ (accessed 2 June 2003).

Anink, D., Boonstra, C. and Mak, J. (1996) *Handbook of Sustainable Building: An Environmental Preference Method for Selection of Materials for Use in Construction and Refurbishment*, London: James & James.

Appadurai, A. (1990) 'Introduction: Commodities and the Politics of Value', in A. Appadurai (ed.), *The Social Life of Things: Commodities in Cultural Perspective*, Cambridge: Cambridge University Press.

*Architectural Review* (1999) 'Greening Architecture' (special issue), 1224 (February).

Ardener, S. (1997) *Women and Space: Ground Rules and Social Maps*, Oxford and New York: Berg.

Ashford, N. and Miller, C. (1998) *Chemical Exposures: Low Levels and High Stakes*, 2nd ed., New York: John Wiley & Sons.

Austin Energy Green Building Program (2003). www.ci.austin.tx.us/greenbuilder/history1.htm (accessed February 2003).

Banuri, T. and Marglin, F. A. (eds) *Who Will Save the Forests? Knowledge, Power and Environmental Destruction*, London and Atlantic Highlands, NJ: Zed Books.

Barber, B. (1984) *Strong Democracy: Participatory Politics for a New Age*, Berkeley: University of California Press.

Barnes, B. (1973). 'The Comparison of Belief-systems: Anomaly Versus Falsehood', private collection of S. Moore.

Barthes, R. (1972) *Mythologies*, New York: Hill & Wang. (Originally published 1957.)

Beauregard, R. A. (2003). 'Democracy, Storytelling, and the Sustainable City', in B. Eckstein and J. Throgmorton (eds), *Story and Sustainability*, Cambridge, MA: MIT Press.

Beauregard, R. A. (1995) 'If Only the City Could Speak: The Politics of Representation', in H. Liggett and D. C. Perry, *Spatial Practices*, London: Sage; 59–80.

Bech-Danielsen, C., Schjerup Hansen, J. and Jensen, O. M. (1997) *Økologisk byggeri i de nordiske lande* (TemaNord 1997: 575). Copenhagen: Nordisk Ministerråd.

Beck, U. (1992) *Risk Society: Toward a New Modernity*, London: Sage.

Beck, U. (1995) *Ecological Politics in the Age of Risk*, Cambridge: Polity Press.

Benes, P. and Benes, J. (eds) (1984) *Itinerancy in New England and New York*, Boston, MA: Boston University.

Bentham, J. (1838) *The Works of Jeremy Bentham. Introduction: An Introduction to the Principles of Morals and Legislation* (ed. John Bowring), London, 1838–43. Reprinted New York (1962): Russell & Russell.

Benton, J.R. and Short, L. M. (1999) *Environmental Discourse and Practice*, Oxford: Blackwell.

Berg, A.-J. (1992) *The Smart House as a Gendered Socio-technical Construction*, Dragvoll, Norway: Centre for Technology and Society, University of Trondheim.

Bergmann, I., Meir, M., Rekstad, J. and Weiss, W. (2003) 'Architectural Integration of Collector Arrays', in W. Weiss (ed.) *Solar Heating Systems for Houses: A Design Handbook for Solar Combisystems*, Solar Heating and Cooling Executive Committee of the International Agency (IEA), London: James & James.

Berry, W. (1988) *The Work of Local Culture*, a publication of the 1988 Iowa Humanities Lecture delivered 13 November 1988 at the Harlan Community High School, Harlan, IA. Copies available from Iowa Humanities Board, Oakland Campus, Iowa City IA 52242.

Biermayr, P., Baumann, B., Schriefl, E. and Skopetz, H. (2001) *Erfolgsfaktoren zur Markteinführung innovativer Wohnbauten*, Vienna: BMVIT.

Bijker, W. (1987) 'The Social Construction of Bakelite: Towards a Theory of Invention', in W. E. Bijker, T. P. Hughes and T. J. Pinch (eds), *The Social Construction of Technological Systems: New Directions in the Sociology and History of Technology*, Cambridge, MA: MIT Press.

Bijker, W. and Law, J. (1992). 'Do Technologies have Trajectories?', in *Shaping Technology / Building Society*, Cambridge, MA: MIT Press; 1–20.

Bijker, W. E., Hughes, T. P. and Pinch, T. J. (eds) (1987) *The Social Construction of Technological Systems: New Directions in the Sociology and History of Technology*, Cambridge, MA: MIT Press.

Bilger, B. (1993) 'Shaking the Rafters', in *Earthwatch*, July/August: 11.

Birdwell-Pheasant, D. and Lawrence-Zúniga, D. (1999). 'Introduction: Houses and Families in Europe', in D. Birdwell and D. Lawrence-Zúniga (eds) *House Life: Space, Place and Family in Europe*. Oxford and New York: Berg.

Björklund, U. (1983). 'Fritidsdrömmen. Ideal och verklighet i östsvensk skärgårdsbygd', in A. Hjort (ed.) *Svenska livsstilar. Om naturen som resurs och symbol*. Stockholm: Liber Förlag.

Blanton, R. E. (1994) *Houses and Households: A Comparative Study*. New York: Plenum.

Blid, H. (1989) *Education by the People – Study Circles*, Ludvika, Sweden: ABF.

BNIM Architects (1995) *Flood Waters of Opportunity: The Relocation and Redevelopment of Pattonsburg MO* (a technical assistance report of the Pattonsburg Design Assistance Team). The American Institute of Architects, the City of Pattonsburg and the Missouri Department of Natural Resources – Division of Energy, sponsored by the US Department of Energy, Federal Emergency Management Administration, and prepared by BNIM Architects, Kansas City MO.

[BREEAM] Building Research Establishment Environmental Assessment Method (2004) 'BREEAM and EcoHomes', www.bre.co.uk/services/BREEAM_and_EcoHomes.html

Bookchin, M. (1962) *Our Synthetic Environment by Lewis Herber* (rev. ed.), introduction by W. A. Albrecht, New York: Knopf.

Booth, S. (1999) 'Reconstructing Sexual Geography: Gender and Space in Changing Sicilian Settlements', in D. Birdwell-Pheasant and D. Lawrence-Zúniga (eds) *House Life: Space, Place and Family in Europe*, Oxford and New York: Berg.

Borden, I. and Dunster, D. (1995) *Architecture and the Sites of History*, London: Butterworth Architecture.

Bos, J. and van Leest, E. (2001) *[ … Switch ON/OFF … ] Home Automation and Energy*, The Hague: B&A Group Research & Consultancy.

Boxer, S. (2002) 'Debating Ground Zero Architecture and the Value of the Void', in the *New York Times*, 30 September, B1, B3.

Boyd, D. K. (1921) 'Standardization of Building Codes', in *Architecture and Building* October: 77–8.

Branch, M. (1993) 'Smart Buildings', in *Earthwatch*, July/August, 9–11.

Brand, R. (2003) 'Co-Evolution Toward Sustainable Development: Neither Smart Technologies nor Heroic Choices', Austin, TX: doctoral dissertation, University of Texas at Austin.

Brulle, R. (2000) *Agency, Democracy, and Nature: The US Environmental Movement from a Critical Theory Perspective*, Cambridge, MA: MIT Press.

Bruner, S., Geissler, S. and Schöberl, H. (2002) *Vernetzte Planung als Strategie zur Behebung von Lern- und Diffusionsdefiziten bei der Realisierung ökologischer Gebäude*, Vienna: BMVIT.

Bunn, R. and Ruyssevelt, P. (1996) 'Ecological?', in *Business Services Journal*, December.

Burgess D. (1996) 'Forests of the Menominee: A Commitment to Sustainable Forestry', in *Forestry Chronicle* 72/3: 268–75.

Burley, D., Horsefall, G. and Brandon J. (1992) *Structural Considerations of Métis Ethnicity*, Vermillion, SD: University of South Dakota Press.

Butti, K. and Perlin, J. (1980) *A Golden Thread: 2500 Years of Solar Architecture and Technology*, Palo Alto, CA: Cheshire Books.

Byberg, M. R. (1984) *Lavenergihuset - en døgnflue?* in B. Saxhof (ed.), *Aktuel energiforskning: Laboratoriet for Varmeisolering 1959–1984* (Meddelelse nr. 150), Lyngby, Denmark: Danmarks Tekniske Højskole, Laboratoriet for Varmeisolering.

Callon, M. (1987) 'Society in the making', in W. E. Bijker, T. P. Hughes and T. J. Pinch (eds) *The Social Construction of Technological Systems: New Directions in the Sociology and History of Technology*, Cambridge, MA: MIT Press.

Campbell, S. (1996) 'Green Cities, Growing Cities, Just Cities? Urban Planning and the Contradictions of Sustainable Development', in *APA Journal*, 62 (3) (Summer): 296–311, 468.

Canada Senate, Senate Subcommittee on the Boreal Forest (1999) *Competing Realities: The Boreal Forest at Risk*, Report of the Sub-Committee on Boreal Forest of the Standing Senate Committee on Agriculture and Forestry. Available at www.parl.gc.ca/36/1/parlbus/commbus/senate/com-e/bore-e/rep-e/rep09jun99-e.htm (accessed 30 May 2003).

Canadian Society of Forest Engineers, Nova Scotia Members (1944) 'Forestry, Economy and Post-War Reconstruction in Nova Scotia', in Nova Scotia Department of Lands and Forests, *Annual Report*, Nova Scotia: DLF.

Castells, M. (1996, 1997, 1998) *The Information Age: Economy, Society and Culture*, vols I–III, Oxford: Blackwell.

Castle, H. (2001) 'Editorial: Green Architecture', in *Architectural Design* 71 (4) (July): 5.

Carlsson-Kanyama, A. and Lindén, A.-L. (2002) *Hushållens energianvändning. Värderingar, beteenden, livsstilar och teknik - en litteraturöversikt*, Stockholm: Forskningsgruppen för miljöstrategiska studier, Stockholm University (Fms-rapport 176), April 2002.

Carson, R. (1962) *Silent Spring*, Boston: Houghton Mifflin.

Carsten, J. and Hugh-Jones, S. (1996) *About the House. Lévi-Strauss and Beyond*, Cambridge: Cambridge University Press.

Cavanagh, T. (1997) 'Balloon Houses: The Original Aspects of Conventional Wood-Frame Construction Re-examined', in *Journal of Architectural Education* 51: 5–15.

Cavanagh, T. (2002) *Who Designed Your House? A Technological and Cultural History of Conventional Wood Construction, 1790–1880*, Ann Arbor, MI: UMI dissertation (Lehigh University).

Cavanagh, T. (2004). 'No Here There', in *Architectural Design* (March).

[CBC] Canadian Broadcasting Corporation News (2003) 'Softwood Lumber Dispute', www.cbc.ca/news/indepth/background/softwood_lumber.html (accessed 20 February 2003).

Chadwick, E. (1965) *Sanitary Conditions of the Labouring Population of Great Britain*, Edinburgh: Edinburgh University Press (first published 1842).

Clarke, A. (2001) 'The Aesthetics of Social Aspiration', in D. Miller *Home Possessions: Material Culture Behind Closed Doors*, Oxford and New York: Berg.

Clements-Croome, T. D. J. (1997) 'What do we mean by intelligent buildings?', in *Automation in Construction* 6: 395–400.

[CMHC] Canada Mortgage and Housing Corporation (1997) *A Comparison of Canadian and German Building Methods, Codes and Standards for Wood-frame Construction*, Ottawa: CMHC.

[COFI] Canadian Organization of Forest Industries (2001) 'Shanghai/BC to sign agreements to open lumber markets in China', www.cofi.org/whatsnew/releases/2001oct30.htm (accessed 12 July 2002).

Cohen, R., Standeven, M., Bordass, B. and Leaman, A. (2001) 'Assessing Building Performance in Use. 1: The Probe Process', in *Building Research and Information* 29: 85–102.

Cole, R. J. (1998). 'Emerging Trends in Building Environmental Assessment Methods', in *Building Research and Information* 26 (1): 3–16.

Cole, R. J. (1999) 'Building Environmental Assessment Methods: Clarifying Intentions', in *Building Research and Information* 27 (4/5): 230–46.

Commoner, B. (1971) *The Closing Circle: Nature, Man, and Technology*, New York: Knopf.

Cook, S. J. and Golton, B. L. (1994). 'Sustainable Development and Concepts and Practice in the Built Environment – A UK Perspective', in International Council for Research and Innovation in Building and Construction (CIB), *Sustainable Construction* (CIB TG 16).

Cooke, L. (1992) 'The Site of Memory', in *Double-Take: Collective Memory and Current Art* (exhib. cat.), London: South Bank Centre and Parkett.

Cordulack, J. (1975) *The Artisan Confronts the Machine Age: Bureau County Illinois, 1850–1880*, Ann Arbor, MI: UMI, University of Illinois Urbana.

Cowan, R. (1985) 'The Consumption Junction: A Proposal for Research Strategies in the Sociology of Technology', in W. Bijker, T. Hughes and T. Pinch (eds), *The Social Construction of Technological Systems*, Cambridge, MA: MIT Press.

Costanzo, M., Archer, D., Aronson, E. and Pettigrew, T. (1986) 'Energy Conservation Behavior: The Difficult Path From Information to Action', in *American Psychologist* 41: 521–8.

Cubitt, H. (1906) 'A Comparison of English and American Building Laws', *American Architect and Building News* (May): 178–80.

Cutter, B. (1993) *Softwood Lumber Grades* (Agricultural Publication G05053), School of Forestry, Fisheries and Wildlife, University of Missouri-Columbia. Available at http://muextension.missouri.edu/explore/agguides/forestry/g05053.htm (accessed 30 May 2003).

Dahlgren, R. and Driscoll C. (1994) 'The Effects of Whole-Tree Clearcutting on Soil Processes at the Hubbard Brook Experimental Forest, New Hampshire, USA', in *Plant and Soil* 158: 239–62.

Dakman, E., Nordh, I.-B. and Eriksson, S. (2001) *BO01 Framtidsstaden: Mässkatalog*, Malmö: BO01 Framtidsstaden.

Daly, H. (1996) *Beyond Growth: The Economics of Sustainable Development*, Boston: Beacon Press.

Danish Building and Urban Research (2003) *BEAT 2002: Building Environmental Assessment Tool*, Hørsholm, Denmark: By og Byg. Available at www.dbur.dk/english/publishing/software/beat2002/index.htm (2 June 2003).

Dansk Byplanlaboratorium (1995) *21 gode eksempler på byøkologi – i byfornyelse, renovering, nybyggeri, lokalplaner, kommuneplaner og temaplaner*, Copenhagen: Dansk Byplanlaboratorium.

Daun, Å. (1974) *Förortsliv. En etnologisk studie av kulturell förändring*, Stockholm: Bokförlaget Prisma.

Dawson, R. (1944) 'Report on Forest Industries', in *Royal Commission on Provincial Development and Rehabilitation*, vol. III. Halifax, Nova Scotia: Kings Printer.

Denzin, N. and Lincoln, Y. (1994) *The Handbook of Qualitative Research*, Thousand Oaks, CA: Sage.

Det Økologiske Råd (2002) *Munksøgård - Erfaringer og anbefalinger*, Copenhagen: Det Økologiske Råd.

Devall, B. and Sessions, G. (1985) *Deep Ecology*, Salt Lake City: G. M. Smith.

[DOTC] Department of Trade and Commerce (1965) *The Outlook for Canadian Housing in Britain as seen by Members of the Home Builders Mission from Britain*, Ottawa: DOTC.

Douglas, M. and Isherwood, B. (1988) *The World of Goods: Towards an Anthropology of Consumption*, London: Allen Lane.

Drerup, O., Mattock, C., Rousseau, D. and Salares, V. (1990) *Housing for the Environmentally Hypersensitive: Survey and Examples of Clean Air Housing in Canada*, Ottawa: Research Division, Canadian Mortgage and Housing Corporation.

Dryzek, J. (1997). *The Politics of the Earth: Environmental Discourses*, Oxford: Oxford University Press.

Dudley N., Jeanrenaud J.-P. and Sullivan F. (1995) *Bad Harvest? The Timber Trade and the Degradation of the World's Forests*, London: Earthscan.

Duffy, D. and Meier A. (1992) 'Do Appalachian Herbaceous Understories Ever Recover from Clearcutting?', in *Conservation Biology* 6 (2): 196–201.

Dunn, S. (2000) *Micropower: The Next Electrical Era*, Washington, DC: Worldwatch Institute.

Duurzaam Huis (2004) 'The Sustainable House Leidsche Rijn', www.duurzaam-huis.nl/read/english (accessed 14 January 2004).

Dyssekilde (2003) 'Økosamfundet Dyssekilde', www.torup-by.dk/undersider/dyssekilde/okosamfund.htm (accessed 2 June 2003).

Eckstein, B. (2003) 'Making Space: Stories in the Practice of Planning', in B. Eckstein and J. Throgmorton, *Story and Sustainability: Planning, Practice, and Possibility for American Cities*, Cambridge, MA: MIT Press.

Eckstein, B. and Throgmorton, J. (eds) (2003) *Story and Sustainability: Planning, Practice, and Possibility for American Cities*, Cambridge, MA: MIT Press.

Edquist, C. and Edqvist, O. (1980) *Sociala bärare av teknik. Brygga mellan teknisk förändring och samhällsstruktur*, Kristianstad: Zenit Häften.

Edwards, B. (1996) 'The Ethics of Green Practice', in *Architects' Journal* 203 (8): 48–9.

Edwards, B. and Hyett, P. (2001) *Rough Guide to Sustainability*, London: RIBA Publications.

Elle, M. (2001) 'Infrastructure and Local Agenda 21 – the Municipality of Albertslund in the Copenhagen Region', in S. Guy, S. Marvin and T. Moss (eds) *Urban Infrastructure in Transition: Networks, Buildings, Plans*, London: Earthscan.

Elle, M., van Hoorn, T., Moss, T., Slob, A., Vermeulen, W. and van der Waals, J. (2002) 'Rethinking Local Housing and Energy Planning: The Importance of Contextual Dynamics', in *Built Environment* 28 (1): 46–56.

Energimagasinet (2003) 'Ny branschorganisation ska skapa trygg pelletvärme', in *Energimagasinet* (June): 20.

Energimyndigheten (2003a) *Värme i Sverige 2002. En uppföljning av värmemarknaderna*, Eskilstuna, Sweden: Energimyndighetens förlag.

Energimyndigheten (2003b) *Energiläget 2003*, Eskilstuna, Sweden: Energimyndighetens förlag.

Energistyrelsen. (2000) 'Energiforskningsprogrammet: Årsberetning 1999', www.ens.dk/graphics/ENS_Forskningogudvikl/online_publikationer/Energiforskningsprogrammet_aarsberetning_1999.htm (accessed 12 February 2003).

Evans, B. (1997) 'Solar Power Gets Serious', in *Architects' Journal* 205 (24) (19 June): 44–5.

Evelyn, J. (2001) *Sylva: Or a Discourse of Forest Trees*, Brough, Cumbria: Summerfield Books.

Farmer, G. and Guy, S. (2002) 'Interpreting Green Design: Beyond Performance and Ideology', in *Built Environment* 28 (1): 11–21.

Farmer, J. (1996). *Green Shift: Towards Green Sensibility in Architecture*, London: World Wildlife Fund.

Fearon, J. D. (1998) 'Democracy and Deliberation', in J. Elster (ed.), *Deliberate Democracy*, Cambridge: Cambridge University Press; 44–68.

Feenberg, A. (1991) *Critical Theory of Technology*, New York: Oxford University Press.

Feenberg, A. (1995) 'Subversive Rationalization: Technology, Power and Democracy', in A. Feenberg and A. Hannay (eds), *Technology & the Politics of Knowledge*, Bloomington, IN: Indiana University Press; 3–22.

Feenberg, A. (1999) *Questioning Technology*, London and New York: Routledge.

Feenberg, A. (2002) *Transforming Technology: A Critical Theory Revised*, New York: Oxford University Press.

Feenberg, A. (2003) 'Values and the Environment' (lecture delivered at the University of Texas, 26 February 2003). Available at http://wnt.cc.utexas.edu/~csd/documents/dis-papers/values.pdf (accessed 10 March 2003).

Fernow, B. (1912) *Forest Conditions of Nova Scotia*, Ottawa: Commission of Conservation.

Fiedler, F. (2004) 'The State of the Art of Small-Scale Pellet-based Heating Systems and Relevant Regulations in Sweden, Austria and Germany', in *Renewable and Sustainable Energy Reviews* 8 (3): 201–21.

Finnish Forest Certification Committee (1997) *Development of Forest Certification in Finland*, Helsinki: Ministry of Agriculture and Forestry.

Fischer, F and Hajer M. A. (1999). *Living with Nature: Environmental Politics as Cultural Discourse*, Oxford: Oxford University Press.

Fitch, J. M. and Bobenhausen W. (1999) *American Building: The Environmental Forces that Shape It*, New York: Oxford University Press.

Fitzpatrick, F. W. (1908) 'Shoddiness of American Building Construction', in *Architectural Record* (January): 52–4.

Florida Green Building Coalition (2003) http://floridagreenbuilding.org/ (accessed February 2003).

Foldager, I. and Dyck-Madsen, S. (2002) *Munksøgård: En økologisk bebyggelse ved Roskilde: Erfaringsopsamling og anbefalinger*, Copenhagen: Det Økologiske Råd.

Folkestadt, B. H. (ed.) (2000) *From Airport to Sustainable Community: Sustainable Fornebu*, Oslo: Statsbygg.

Foucault, M. (1975) *Discipline and Punish: The Birth of the Prison*, Harmondsworth, Middlesex: Pelican Press.

Fouke, J. (ed.) (2000) *Engineering Tomorrow*, New York: Institute of Electrical and Electronic Engineers.

Frampton, K. (1995) *Studies in Tectonic Culture*, Cambridge, MA: MIT Press.

Frampton, K. and Moore. S. A. (eds) (2001) 'Technology and Place', introduction to theme issue in *Journal of Architectural Education* (Spring): 121–2.

Freud, S. (1953) 'The Uncanny', in J. Strachey (trans. and ed.), *The Standard Edition of the Complete Psychological Works of Sigmund Freud*, vol. XVII. London: Hogarth Press.

Friberg, T. (1990) *Kvinnors vardag. Om kvinnors arbete och liv. Anpassningsstrategier i tid och rum*, Meddelande från Lunds universitets geografiska institutioner, avhandling 109.

Frumkin, H. (2002) 'Urban Sprawl and Public Health', in *Public Health Reports* 17 (May/June): 201–17.

Fryer, W. (1891) 'The New York Building Law', in *Architectural Record* (July-September): 69–82.

Fryk, H. (ed.) (1999) *Energi från skogen*, Uppsala: SLU Kontakt 9.

FSCCanada (November 2002) 'Description of process and results for the Maritime Standard', www.fsccanada.org/maritimes/index.shtml (accessed 30 January 2003).

Gaile, W. B. (1956). 'Essentially Contested Concepts', in *Proceedings of the Aristotelian Society* 56: 167–98.

Gamborg C. and Larsen J. (2003) 'Back to Nature – A Sustainable Future for Forestry?', in *Forest Ecology and Management* 179: 559–71.

Garvey, P. (2001) 'Organized Disorder: Moving Furniture in Norwegian Homes', in D. Miller, *Home Possessions: Material Culture Behind Closed Doors*, Oxford and New York: Berg.

Gaunt, L. (1985) *Bostadsvanor och energi - om vardagsrutinernas inverkan på energiförbrukningen i elvärmda småhus*, Meddelande M85 :14. Gävle, Sweden: Statens institut för byggnadsforskning.

Geertz, C. (1973). *The Interpretation of Cultures: Selected Essays*, New York, Basic Books. Reprinted (1993) London: Fontana Press.

Geertz, C (1993) *Local Knowledge*, London: Fontana Press.

Giedion, S. (1948) *Mechanization Takes Command: A Contribution to Anonymous History*, New York: Oxford University Press.

Gilman, R. (1986) 'Energy Update: An Interview with Amory Lovins', in *In Context* 14: 27. Available at www.context.org/ICLIB/IC14/ALovins.htm (accessed 12 June 2003).

Goodman, P. and Goodman, P. (1947) *Communitas: Means of Livelihood and Ways of Life*, Chicago: University of Chicago Press.

Gordon, H. (2000). 'Sustainable Design goes Mainstream', in D. E. Brown, M. Fox and M. R. Pelletier (eds) *Sustainable Architecture: White Papers*, New York: Earth Pledge Foundation.

Gorman, M. (1998) *Transforming Nature: Ethics, Invention and Discovery*, Boston, MA: Kluwer Academic Press.

Grabler-Bauer, G., Guschlbauer-Hronek, K., Berger, M., Seidl, J. and Krapmeier, H. (2002) *Das Passivhaus in der Praxis. Strategien zur Marktaufbereitung für das Passivhaus im Osten Österreichs*, Vienna: BMVIT.

Graham, S. and Marvin, S. (2001). *Splintering Urbanism: Networked Infrastructures, Technological Mobilities and the Urban Condition*, London: Routledge.

Gram-Hanssen, K. (2000) 'Local Agenda 21 (LA21): Traditional Gemeinschaft or Late Modern Sub-politics?', in *Journal of Environmental Policy and Planning* 2: 225–35.

Gram-Hanssen, K. (2002) 'Technology and Culture as Explanations for Variations in Energy Consumption', in *Proceedings of ACEEE 2002 Summer Study on Energy Efficiency in Buildings*, August 18–23, Asilomar, Pacific Grove, California.

Groves, M., Miller, F. and Donovan R. (1996) 'Chain of Custody', in V. Viana, J. Ervin, R. Donovan, C. Elliot and H. Gholtz, *Certification of Forest Products: Issues and Perspectives*, Washington, DC: Island Press.

Gullestad, M. (1984) *Kitchen-Table Society: A Case Study of the Family Life and Friendships of Young Working-Class Mothers in Urban Norway*, Oslo and Bergen: Universitetsforlaget.

Gullestad, M. (1992) *The Art of Social Relations: Essays on Culture, Social Action and Everyday Life in Modern Norway*, Kristiansand, Norway: Scandinavian University Press.

Gunnemark, K. (1998) *Hembygd i storstad. Om vardagslivets praktik och den lokala identitetens premisser*, Gothenburg, Sweden: Etnologiska föreningen i Västsverige.

Guy, S. (2002) 'Sustainable Buildings: Meanings, Processes, Users', introduction to special issue of *Built Environment* 28 (1): 5–10.

Guy, S. and Farmer, G. (2000) 'Contested Constructions: The Competing Logics of Green Buildings', in W. Fox (ed.) *The Ethics of the Built Environment*, London: Routledge.

Guy, S. and Farmer, G. (2001) 'Re-interpreting Sustainable Architecture: The Place of Technology', in *Journal of Architectural Education* 54 (3): 140–8.

Guy, S. and Marvin, S. (1996) 'Transforming Urban Infrastructure Provision: The Emerging Logic of Demand Side Management', *Policy Studies* 17 (2): 137–47.

Guy, S. and Marvin, S. (1998) 'Electricity in the Marketplace: Reconfiguring the Consumption of Essential Resources', in *Local Environment* 3: 313–31.

Guy, S. and Osborn, S. (2001) 'Contesting Environmental Design: The Hybrid Green Building', in S. Guy, S. Marvin and T. Moss (eds), *Urban Infrastructure in Transition*, London: Earthscan.

Guy, S. and Shove, E. (2000) *A Sociology of Energy, Buildings, and the Environment: Constructing Knowledge, Designing Practice*, London and New York: Routledge.

Guy, S., Graham, S. and Marvin, S. (1997) 'Splintering Networks: Cities and Technical Networks in 1990s Britain', *Urban Studies* 34 (2): 191–216.

Guy, S., Marvin, S. and Moss, T. (eds) (2001): *Urban Infrastructure in Transition: Networks, Buildings, Plans*, London: Earthscan.

Haarman, H. R., van Leeuwen, E. N. and de Haan, M. A. R. (2000) 'Sustainable Building Policy in the Netherlands', in *Milieu (Journal of Environmental Sciences)* 15 (2): 62–70.

Haas, P (1990) *Saving the Mediterranean: Political Economies of International Change*, New York: Columbia University Press.

Hagan, S. (2001) *Taking Shape: A New Contact Between Architecture and Nature*, Oxford: Architectural Press.

Hajer, M. (1995) *The Politics of Environmental Discourse: Ecological Modernization and the Policy Process*, Oxford: Oxford University Press.

Hajer, M. (1998) 'Ecological Modernisation as Cultural Politics', in S. Lash, B. Szerszynski and B. Wynne (eds), *Risk, Environment and Modernity: Towards a New Ecology*, London: Sage.

Hal, J. D. M. van (2000) 'Beyond the Demonstration Project: The Diffusion of Environmental Innovations in Housing', Delft: PhD dissertation, Technical University Delft. Best: Aeneas.

Hal, A. van and Dulski, B. (1999) *Sustainable Housing in Europe*, Delft: Boom-Duijvestein.

Hannigan, J. (1995) *Environmental Sociology: A Social Constructivist Perspective*, London: Routledge.

Hansen, E. (1997) 'Forestry Certification and its Role in Marketing Strategy', in *Forest Products Journal* 47 (3): 16–22.

Haraway, D. (1995) 'Situated Knowledges: The Science Question in Feminism and the Privilege of Partial Perspective', in A. Feenberg and A. Hannay (eds) *Technology and the Politics of Knowledge*, Bloomington, IN: Indiana University Press; 175–94.

Harding, S. G. (1991) *Whose Science? Whose Knowledge? Thinking from Women's Lives*, Ithaca, NY: Cornell University Press.

Harris, L. (1984) *The Fragmented Forest*, Chicago: University of Chicago Press.

Harvey, D. (2000). *Spaces of Hope*, Berkeley, CA: University of California Press.

Haughton, G. (1997) 'Developing Sustainable Urban Development Models', in *Cities* 14 (4): 189–95.

Hawboldt, L. and Bulmer, R. (1958) *The Forest Resources of Nova Scotia*, Halifax, Nova Scotia: Department of Lands and Forests.

Hawken, P., Lovins, A. and Lovins, H. (1999) *Natural Capitalism: Creating the Next Industrial Revolution*, Boston, MA: Little, Brown.

Heaton, K. and R. Donovan (1996) 'Forest Assessment', in V. Viana, J. Ervin, R. Donovan, C. Elliot and H. Gholtz (eds) *Certification of Forest Products: Issues and Perspectives*, Washington, DC: Island Press.

Heidegger, M. (1977) *The Question Concerning Technology and Other Essays*, trans. and with an introduction by W. Lovitt, New York: Harper & Rowe.

Henderson, K. (1999). *On Line and on Paper*, Cambridge, MA: MIT Press.

Henning, A. (2000) *Ambiguous Artefacts: Solar Collectors in Swedish Contexts. On Processes of Cultural Modification*, Stockholm Studies in Social Anthropology 44, Stockholm: Almqvist & Wiksell International.

Henning, A. (2001) *Hem och härd, del I. En litteraturstudie om Sverige och Skandinavien*, Solar Energy Research Centre (SERC), Dalarna University, Sweden. ISRN DU-SERC-72-SE.

Henning, A. (2003a) 'Solvärme och svenska värderingar', in *Hett om kalla fakta*, Vetenskapsrådets temabok 2003.

Henning, A. (2003b) *Tio hushåll om elkonvertering. Hem och härd, del II*, Solar Energy Research Centre (SERC), Dalarna University, Sweden. ISRN DU-SERC-82-SE.

Henning, A. (2004) 'Social Anthropological and Interdisciplinary Research on the Conversion of Electrically Heated Single Family Houses to Heating by Combined Pellet-Solar Systems', in *Biomass and Bioenergy* 27 (6): 547–55.

Hesselbæk, B. (2001). *Ørestad - Expanding Copenhagen City* (2nd ed.), Copenhagen: Ørestadsselskabet.

Hickman, L. (2001). *Philosophical Tools for Technological Culture: Putting Pragmatism to Work*, Bloomington, IN: Indiana University Press.

Hoffman, S. M. (2002) 'The Monster and the Mother: The Symbolism of Disaster', in S. Hoffman and A. Oliver-Smith (eds) *Catastrophe and Culture: The Anthropology of Disaster*, Sante Fe: School of American Research Press.

Hoffman, S. and Oliver-Smith, A. (eds) (2002) *Catastrophe and Culture: The Anthropology of Disaster*, Santa Fe: School of American Research Press.

Horkheimer, M. (1946) *Eclipse of Reason*, 45 no. 29, cited in L. Hickman (2001), *Philosophical Tools for Technological Culture*, Bloomington, IN: Indiana University Press; 72.

Hoorn, T. M. M. van, van der Waals, J. F. M., Vermeulen, W. J. V. and Slob, A. F. L. (2001) *$CO_2$ Reduction in New Housing Estates: A Workshop as Building Block*, Bilthoven: Dutch National Research Programme on Global Air Pollution and Climate Change. Report no. 410 200 096.

Howarth, R. B. and Andersson, B. (1993) 'Market Barriers to Energy Efficiency', in *Energy Economics* 15: 262–72.

Hughes, T. P. (1985). 'Edison and Electric Light', in D. MacKenzie and J. Wajcman (eds), *The Social Shaping of Technology*, Philadelphia: Open University Press; 39–52.

Hughes, T. P. (1987) 'The Evolution of Large Technological Systems', in W. E. Bijker, T. P. Hughes and T. J. Pinch (eds), *The Social Construction of Technological Systems: New Directions in the Sociology and History of Technology*, Cambridge, MA: MIT Press.

Hughes, T. (1989) *American Genesis: A Century of Invention and Technological Enthusiasm, 1870–1970*, New York: Viking Press.

Hugh-Jones, S. (1996) 'Inside-Out and Back-to-Front: The Androgynous House in Northwest Amazonia', in J. Carsten and S. Hugh-Jones (eds), *About the House: Lévi-Strauss and Beyond*, Cambridge: Cambridge University Press.

Hunter, M. (1990) *Wildlife, Forests and Forestry: Principles of Managing Forests for Biological Diversity*, Englewood Cliffs, NJ: Prentice Hall.

Irwin, A. (2001). *Sociology and the Environment*, Cambridge: Polity Press.

[ISO] International Organization for Standardization (1998) *ISO/TR 14061/1998: Information to Assist Forestry Organizations in the Use of Environmental Management System Standards ISO 14001 and ISO 14004*, Geneva: ISO.

[IUCN] International Union for the Conservation of Nature and Natural Resources (1980) *World Conservation Strategy*, Morges, Switzerland: IUCN.

Jaeger, C. C., Schüle, R. and Kasemir, B. (1999) 'Focus Groups in Integrated Assessment: A Micro-cosmos for Reflexive Modernization', in *Innovation* 12: 195–219.

Jaffee, D. (1991) 'Peddlers of Progress and the Transformation of the Rural North', in *Journal of American History* (September): 511–35.

Jakobsen, L. and Karlsson, J. C. (1993) *Arbete och kärlek. En utveckling av livsformsanalys*, Lund: Arkiv förlag.

James, A. V. and Kalisperis, L. (1999) 'Use of House and Space: Public and Private Family Interaction on Chios, Greece', in D. Birdwell-Pheasant and D. Lawrence-Zúniga (eds), *House Life: Space, Place and Family in Europe*, Oxford and New York: Berg.

James, W. (1975). 'Pragmatism, a New Name for Some Old Ways of Thinking: Popular Lectures on Philosophy', in F. H. Burkhardt (ed.), *The Works of William James*, 19 vols, Cambridge, MA: Harvard University Press.

Jamison, A. (2001) *The Making of Green Knowledge: Environmental Politics and Cultural Transformation*, Cambridge and New York: Cambridge University Press.

Jensen, J. O. (2001) 'Green Buildings in an Infrastructure Perspective', in S. Guy, S. Marvin and T. Moss (eds) *Urban Infrastructure in Transition: Networks, Buildings, Plans*, London: Earthscan; 120–35.

Jensen, J. O. (2002) 'Green Buildings as a Part of the Infrastructure: Supporter, Symbol or Stranger', in *Built Environment* 28 (1): 22–32.

Jensen, O. M. and Gram-Hanssen, K. (2000) *Livsstil og energiefterspørgsel* (SBI-meddelelse 133), Hørsholm, Denmark: Statens Byggeforskningsinstitut.

Johnson, R. (1986) *Forests of Nova Scotia: A History*, Halifax, Nova Scotia: Four East Publications.

Junkala, P. (1998) 'Man and Home: The Home, its Physical Premises and Limits from the Perspective of Male Graduates Born in the 1960s', in *Ethnologia Scandinavica* 28: 108–16.

Kanke, S. (2003) 'HVAC Equipments of EMU: The Construction of the Kitasato Hospital Environmental Health Center', in *Proceedings of the 2003 International Symposium on Indoor Air Quality and Health Hazards*, Tokyo: Architectural Institute of Japan and United States National Institute of Environmental Health Sciences, 2: 67–78.

Kelsey. C, (2003) 'Pattonsburg's Design Process', www.sustainable.doe.gov/articles/Pattonsburg_design.shtml (accessed 15 June 2003).

Kempton, W. and Neiman, M. (1987) *Energy Efficiency: Perspectives on Individual Behavior*, Washington, DC and Berkeley: American Council for an Energy-Efficient Economy.

Kennedy, J. F., Smith, M. G. and Wanek, C. (eds) (2002) *The Art of Natural Building*, British Columbia: New Society.

Keul, A. (2001) *Energiesparprojekte und konventioneller Wohnbau – eine Evaluation*, Vienna: BMVIT.

Kroeker, R. (1998) 'Development of Timber Structures Based on a Study of Indigenous Wood Use in North Eastern North America', in J. Natterer and J.-L. Sandoz (eds), *Proceedings of the Fifth World Congress of Timber Engineering*, Montreux, Switzerland: Presses polytechniques et universitaires romandes.

Könighofer, K. (2001) *Anforderungsprofile für Biomassefeuerungen zur Wärmeversorgung von Objekten mit niedrigem Energiebedarf*, Vienna: BMVIT.

Kongsli, G. (2001) *Vann, varme og virkelighet. En studie av sosial læring ved innføring av vannbåren gulvvarme*, master's thesis/STS report 50/2001, Centre for Technology and Society, Norwegian University for Science and Technology.

Kovacs, P. and Weiss, W. (2003) 'Space Requirements', in W. Weiss (ed.), *Solar Heating Systems for Houses: A Design Handbook for Solar Combisystems*, Solar Heating and Cooling Executive Committee of the International Agency (IEA). London: James & James.

Kugelberg, C. (1999) *Perceiving Motherhood and Fatherhood: Swedish Working Parents with Young Children*, Uppsala: Uppsala University.

Kuhn, T. S. (1970). *The Structure of Scientific Revolutions*, 2nd ed., Chicago: University of Chicago Press, 1970.

Kvernhuset Ungdomskole (2000). 'Kværnhuset ungdomskole Bygger skole i pakt med naturen', in Byggmesteren, 10/2000. Kvernhuse Prosjekt. Available at www.sintef.no/units/civil/ark/ar/Norsk/Prosjekter/Kvernhuset (accessed Jan 2003).

Lading, T. (2000a) *Byøkologi i lokalområder - kortlægning: Byøkologiske projekter i København med offentlig støtte, primært i perioden 1994-2000*: Udkast pr. 02.04.2001, Copenhagen.

Lading, T. (2000b). Ørestad. In T. Lading, *De store bygningers økologi*. København: Dansk Center for Byøkologi.

Lahr, J. (2003) 'Becoming the Hulk: How Ang Lee Found his Inner Green Monster', in *The New Yorker*, 30 June.

[Larden Muniak and Youn] Larden Muniak Consulting Inc. and Sang-Man Youn Architect (1998) *Expanding the Korean Market for Residential Wood-frame Construction: Final Report*, Ottawa: CMHC.

Latour, B. (1987) *Science in Action: How to follow Scientists and Engineers through Society*, Cambridge, MA: Harvard University Press.

Latour, B. (1995) *We Have Never Been Modern*, Cambridge, MA: Harvard University Press.

Laurie, B. (1989) *Artisans into Workers: Labor in Nineteenth-Century America*, New York: Hill & Wang.

Lawrence, R. (1987) 'What Makes a House a Home?', in *Environment and Behavior* 19 (2) (March), 154–68.

Lee, A. (1999) *Ride with the Devil*. Hollywood: United Artists.

Lerner, S. (1997a) 'Skipping Town', in *Yes! The Journal of Positive Futures* (Winter 1997/1998). Accessible at http://63.135.115.158/

Lerner, S. (1997b) *Eco-pioneers: Practical Visionaries Solving Today's Environmental Problems*, Cambridge MA: MIT Press.

Lewis, D. (Pir II Arkitektkontor AS) (1999) 'Une école en forêt, Fredrikstad, Norvège', in *L'architecture d'aujoud'hui* 324 (Sep/Oct): 40–5.

Lewis, D. (2000) 'School in Fredrikstad van Pir II en Duncan Lewis', in *De Architect* (Dec): 42–3.

Lewis, D. and Associates + Pir 11 Arkitektkontor AS (1999) 'Kvernhuset Ungdomskole Fredrikstad', in *Mama* 25: 26–31.

Lie, M. and Sørensen, K. H. (1996) 'Making Technology Our Own? Domesticating Technology into Everyday Life', in M. Lie and K. H. Sørensen (eds), *Making Technology Our Own? Domesticating Technology into Everyday Life*, Oslo: Scandinavian University Press.

Light, A. (2003) 'Urban Ecological Citizenship', in *Journal of Social Philosophy* 34 (1) (Spring): 44–63.

Light, A. and Katz E. (eds) (1996) *Environmental Pragmatism*, London and New York: Routledge.

Lindqvist, M., Orrbeck, K. and Westerberg, U. (1980) *Bostaden i norm och verklighet*, Gävle, Sweden: Statens institut för byggnadsforskning M 80: 4.

Londos, E. (1993) *Uppåt väggarna i svenska hem. En etnologisk studie av bildbruk*, Stockholm: Carlssons Bokförlag.

Long, N. and Long, A. (eds) (1994) *Battlefields of Knowledge*, London: Routledge.

Longfellow, H. (1847) *Evangeline, A Tale of Acadie*, Boston: William D. Ticknor & Company.

Loveday, A. (1983) *The Rise and Decline of the American Cut Nail Industry*, Westport, CT: Greenwood Press.

Lövgren, K. and Ramberg, K. (1997) *Vardagsliv och boende i Bro*, Vällingby, Sweden: Mångkulturellt centrum 2.

McCally, M. (2002) 'Environmental Health and Risk', in M. McCally (ed.), *Life Support: The Environment and Human Health*, Cambridge, MA: MIT Press; 1–14.

McDaniel, R. R. Jr, (2001) 'Complexity Science and Health Care Management', in J. Blair, M. Fottler and G. Savage (eds) *Advances in Health Care Management*, vol. 2, New York: Elsevier; 11–36.

McDonough, W. and Braungart, M. (2002) *Cradle to Cradle*, Washington, DC: North Point.

McHarg, I. L. (1969) *Design with Nature* (1st ed.), Garden City, NY: The American Museum of Natural History (by) the Natural History Press.

MacKenzie, D. and Wajcman J. (1985) *The Social Shaping of Technology* (1st ed.), Philadelphia: Open University Press.

Macnaghten, P. and Urry, J (1998). *Contested Natures*, Cambridge: Polity Press.

Manzini, E. (ed.) (1986) *The Material of Invention*, Cambridge, MA: MIT Press.

Marrey, B. (ed.) (1994) *Le Bois: Essences et Sens*, Paris: Arsenal.

Marsh, P. (2000) 'In Praise of Bad Habits', lecture to the Institute for Cultural Research at the King's Fund, London, 17 November (author's collection).

Mårtensson, M. and Pettersson, R. (1998) *Försörjning, vardag och miljö. Miljö, kultur och vardagsliv i hushåll*, Rapport nr 1. Stockholm: Sociologiska Institutionen, Stockholms Universitet.

Mårtensson, M., Pettersson, R. and Wadeskog, A. (1993) *Försörjningssätt, sociala könsförhållanden och lokal ekologisk utveckling. Rapport från en pilotstudie*, Arbetsrapport nr 2. Stockholm: Sociologiska Institutionen, Stockholms Universitet.

Martinus Instituttet (2003) 'Martinus Institute, Frederiksberg', www.martinus.dk (accessed 2 June 2003).

Marvin, S., Chappells, H. and Guy, S. (1999) 'Pathways of Smart Metering Development: Shaping Environmental Innovation', in *Computers, Environment and Urban Systems* 23: 109–26.

Maxwell, K. (2002) 'Lisbon: The Earthquake of 1755 and Urban Recovery under the Marques de Pombal', in J. Ockman (ed.) and Buell Center for the Study of American Architecture, *Out of Ground Zero: Case Studies in Urban Reinvention*, New York: Prestel.

May, E. (1982) *Budworm Battles: The Fight to Stop the Aerial Insecticide Spraying of the Forests of Eastern Canada*, Halifax, Nova Scotia: Four East Publications.

Meier, A. von (2001) *Energy Realities: Rates of Consumption, Energy Reserves, and Future Options*, testimony to the US House of Representatives Subcommittee on Energy, Committee on Science, 3 May 2001. Pub. no. 107–35. Accessible at www.house.gov/science/committeeinfo/docs/pubs.htm

Meiss, P. von (1998) *Elements of Architecture: From Form to Place*, London and New York: Van Nostrand Reinhold.

Melosi, M. (2000) *The Sanitary City: Urban Infrastructure in America from Colonial Times to the Present*, Baltimore: Johns Hopkins University Press.

Miljørigtig Projektering (1998) *Håndbog i miljørigtig projektering – bind 1 og 2*, Hørsholm, Denmark: Byggecentrum.

Miller, C. (1999) 'Are We on the Threshold of a New Theory of Disease? Toxicant-induced Loss of Tolerance and its Relationship to Addiction and Abdiction', in *Toxicology and Industrial Health* 15: 284–94.

Miller, C. and Ashford, N. (2001) 'Multiple Chemical Intolerance and Indoor Air Quality', in J. Spengler, J. Samet and J. McCarthy (eds), *Indoor Air Quality Handbook*, New York: McGraw-Hill.

Miller, D. (1992) *Material Culture and Mass Consumption*, Oxford: Blackwell.

Miller, D. (2001a) 'Behind Closed Doors', in D. Miller *Home Possessions: Material Culture Behind Closed Doors*, Oxford and New York: Berg.

Miller, G. T. (2001b) *Environmental Science: Working with the Earth*, 8th ed. (annotated instructor's version), Pacific Grove, CA: Brooks/Cole.

Milton, K. (1996). *Environmental and Cultural Theory: Exploring the Role of Anthropology in Environmental Discourse*, London: Routledge.

Ministerie van VROM (1995) *Action Plan for Sustainable Building*, The Hague: Ministry of Housing, Spatial Planning and Environment.

Ministry of Environment (1994). *Recommendations on Urban Ecology*, Copenhagen: Ministry of Environment.

Ministry of Foreign Affairs et al. (1996) *The Danish National Report to Habitat II*, Copenhagen: Ministry of Foreign Affairs et al.

Mirbach, M. von (1997) 'No Magic Bullet: What Forest Certification Can't Do, and What it Shouldn't Do', paper presented at Certification Criteria and Indicators: Global Approaches to Sustainable Forest Management International Conference, 23 September 1997, Prince George, British Columbia.

Misa, T., Brey P. and Feenberg A. (eds) (2003) *Modernity and Technology*, Cambridge, MA: MIT Press.

Moffat, A. (1998) *Forest Certification: An Examination of the Compatibility of the Canadian Standards Association and the Forest Stewardship Council Systems in the Maritime Region*. Ann Arbor, MI: master's thesis, UMI.

Moore, S. A. (2001) *Technology and Place: Sustainable Architecture and the Blueprint Farm*, Austin, TX: University of Texas Press.

Moore, S. A. (2004) 'Architecture, Esthetics, and the Public Health', unpublished manuscript.

Morrish, W. and Swenson, C. J. (1994) 'Recovery and Resettlement: A First Look at Post-Flood Recovery Planning Issues in the Upper Mississippi River Valley', Minneapolis: Design Center for American Urban Landscape, University of Minnesota.

Moser, P. and Stocker, E. (2002) *Einfamilienhaus und verdichtete Wohnformen – eine Motivenanalyse*, Vienna: BMVIT.

Moser, W., Reicher, D., Rosegger, R., de Frantz, M. and Havel, M. (2002) *Was ist so schön am Eigenheim? Ein Lebensstilkonzept des Wohnens*, Vienna: BMVIT.

Moss, T. (2003) 'Utilities, Land-use Change and Urban Development: Brownfield Sites as "Cold-spots" of Infrastructure Networks in Berlin', *Environment and Planning A* 35 (3): 511–29.

Munksøgård (2003) 'Det Økologiske Bofællesskab Munksøgård, Roskilde', www.munksoegaard.dk (accessed 2 June 2003).

Nash, G. (1987) 'The Social Evolution of Preindustrial American Cities, 1700–1820', in *Journal of Urban History* 13: 115–46.

National Association of Home Builders (2002) *Summary of Green Building Programs*, Upper Marlboro, MD: NAHB.

Neil, R. (1998) 'A 2x4 Window of Opportunity', in *Logging and Sawmilling Journal*. Available at www.forestnet.com/archives/June_98/manufacturing.html (accessed 18 February 2003).

Nijkamp, P. and Perrels, A. (1994) *Sustainable Cities in Europe*, London: Earthscan.

Nordell, K. (2003). *Kvinnors och mäns energianvändning*, Rapport till Energimyndigheten. Gothenburg, Sweden: Kulturgeografiska institutionen, Handelshögskolan vid Göteborgs universitet.

Nordenmark, M. (1997) 'Arbetslöshet, kön och familjeliv', in G. Ahrne and I. Persson (eds), *Familj, makt och jämställdhet*, Rapport till Utredningen om fördelningen av ekonomisk makt och ekonomiska resurser mellan kvinnor och män, SOU 1997: 138. Stockholm: Arbetsmarknadsdepartementet.

Novem (1999) *Duurzaam bouwen monitoring. Resultaten Plannen van Aanpak 1995–1999*, The Hague: Ministerie van VROM.

Nova Scotia Legislature, *Statutes 1758–1980*, Halifax, Nova Scotia: Nova Scotia Legislature.

Nye, D. (2003) *America as Second Creation: Technology and Narratives of New Beginnings*, Cambridge, MA: MIT Press.

Ockman, J. (ed.) (2000) The Pragmatist Imagination: Thinking about Things in the Making, with a general introduction by J. Rajchman and an afterword by C. Nelson Blake. New York: Princeton Architectural Press.

Ockman, J. (ed.) and Buell Center for the Study of American Architecture (2002) *Out of Ground Zero: Case Studies in Urban Reinvention*, New York: Prestel.

[OHC] Office of the High Commissioner for Canada in London [1967?] *The Maples: A New Concept in Housing*, London: OHC.

Olgyay, V. and A. (1963) *Design with Climate: A Bioclimatic Approach to Architectural Regionalism*, Princeton, NJ: Princeton University Press.

Oliver, C. (1999) 'The Future of the Forest Management Industry: Highly Mechanized Plantations and Reserves or a Knowledge-Intensive Integrated Approach?', in *Forestry Chronicle* 75: 229–45.

Oliver-Smith, A. (2002) 'Theorizing Disasters: Nature, Power, and Culture', in S. Hoffman and A. Oliver-Smith (eds), *Catastrophe and Culture: The Anthropology of Disaster*, Sante Fe: School of American Research Press; 23–49.

Ørestadsselskabet (2000) *Miljøvision for Ørestad*, Copenhagen: Ørestadsselskabet.

Ornetzeder, M. and Rohracher, H. (2001) *Erfahrungen und Einstellungen von NutzerInnen als Basis für die Entwicklung nachhaltiger Wohnkonzepte mit hoher sozialer Akzeptanz*, Vienna: BMVIT.

Orr, D. W. (1993) 'Architecture as Pedagogy', in *Conservation Biology* 7: 226–8.

Orr, D. W. (1997) 'Architecture as Pedagogy II', in *Conservation Biology* 11 (3): 597–600.

Orr, D. W. (2002) *The Nature of Design: Ecology, Culture, and Human Intention*, New York: Oxford University Press.

Orr, D. W. (2003a) 'Can Educational Institutions Learn?: The Creation of the Adam Joseph Lewis Center at Oberlin College', in P. Barlett and G. Chase (eds), *Strategies for Sustainability: Stories from the Ivory Tower*, Boston, MA: MIT Press.

Orr, D. W. (2003b) 'Better Angels of Our Nature', in *Harvard Design Magazine* 18: 41–5.

Orser, C. (1991) 'Historical Archaeology and the Capitalist Transformation of the Illinois Countryside', in E. Schroeder (ed.), *Landscape, Architecture, and Artifacts: Historical Archaeology of Nineteenth Century Illinois*, Springfield, IL: Illinois Historic Preservation Agency.

Overland, C. and Sandberg, T. (2003) *Nulägesanalys – värmekällors andelar av värmemarknaden för småhus*, Stockholm: Svensk fjärrvärme.

Palmqvist, L. (1999) 'Bondebebyggelsen', in T. Hall and K. Dunér (eds), *Svenska hus. Landsbygdens arkitektur – från bondesamhälle till industrialism*, Stockholm: Carlsson Bokförlag.

Paulsen, A. (ed.) *The Telenor Fornebu Project*, Oslo: Telenor. Accessible at www.Telenor.no/fornebu (accessed June 2003).

Pearson, A. (1998) 'Solar so good', in *Building Services* 20 (8) (August): 14–18.

Pearson, D. (1989) *The Natural House Book: Creating a Healthy, Harmonious, and Ecologically-Sound Home Environment*, New York: Simon & Schuster.

Pennsylvania Horticultural Society (2004). 'Launching the Green City Strategy', www.pennsylvaniahorticulturalsociety.org/phlgreen/ui_launchinggreencity.htm (accessed 10 March 2004).

Pepper, D. (1996) *Modern Environmentalism: An Introduction*, London: Routledge.

Persson, T. and Nordlander, S. (2003) 'Conversion of Electrically Heated Houses to Pellets and Solar Heating', *Proceedings of ISES Solar World Congress*, Gothenburg, Sweden, June 2003.

Peters, T. (1996) *Building the Nineteenth Century*, Cambridge, MA: MIT Press.

Petersen, J. E. (2002) 'The Environment and Oberlin: An Update – Judging the Success of the Environmental Studies Center', in *Oberlin Alumni Magazine* 98 (1): 18–23. Accessible at www.oberlin.edu/alummag/oamcurrent/oam_summer2002/feat_enviro.htm (accessed 12 June 2003).

Philippi, N. (1994) 'Revisiting Flood Control: An Examination of Federal Flood Control Policy in Light of the 1993 Flood Event on the Upper Mississippi River', May 1994 off-print from Wetlands Research Inc. Chicago, IL, 60604.

Pinch, T. J. and Bijker, W. E. (1985). 'The Social Construction of Facts and Artifacts: Or How the Sociology of Science and the Science of Sociology Might Benefit Each Other', in W. Bijker, T. Hughes and T. Pinch (eds), *The Social Construction of Technological Systems*, Cambridge, MA: MIT Press; 17–51.

Pir II Arkitektkontor (1998) 'Kvernhuset ungdomskole blir "nyhetens hage"', in *Byggeindustrien* 14: 50.

Platt, R. (1999) *Democracy and Disaster: The Politics of Extreme Natural Events*, Washington, DC: Island Press.

Preiser, W. F. E., Rabinowitz, H. Z. and White, E. T. (1988) *Post-Occupancy Evaluation*, New York: Van Nostrand Reinhold.

Ranum, M. (1994) 'Naturen mellem drøm og virkelighed', Roskilde: unpublished integrated dissertation, Roskilde Universitetscenter.

Raynsford, N. (1999) 'The UK's Approach to Sustainable Development in Construction', in *Building Research and Information* 27 (6): 419–23.

Reddy, A. K. N. (1991) 'Barriers to Improvements in Energy Efficiency', in *Energy Policy* 19: 953–61.

Reese, W. L. (1980) *Dictionary of Philosophy and Religion: Eastern and Western Thought*, New Jersey, Humanities Press.

Reinholdt, L. (1997) *Bosætningseksperimenter: Lærestykker om fire eksperimenterende lokalsamfund på vej mod bæredygtighed*, Aalborg: Svanholm Forlag.

Reis, M. (2000) 'University Buildings that Educate: The Ecology of Design', in *Environmental Design and Construction* (March/April). Accessible at www.edcmag.com/

Riley, J. (1999) *Southern Ontario Woodlands: The Conservation Challenge*, Toronto: Federation of Ontario Naturalists.

Rilling, D. (2001) *Making Houses, Crafting Capitalism: Builders in Philadelphia 1790–1850*, Philadelphia: University of Pennsylvania Press.

Rivlin, L. and Wolfe, M. (1985) *Institutional Settings in Children's Lives*, New York: J. Wiley.

[RIVM] Rijksinstituut voor Volksgezondheid en Milieu (National Institute for Public Health and the Environment) (2000) *Milieubalans 2000*, Bilthoven, Netherlands: RIVM.

Roedekro Kommune (2000) 'Lokalplan Ø 2.1 – For et boligområde ved Øster Løgum, Roedekro kommune', www.iea-shc.org/task23/ (accessed 13 January 2004).

Rohracher, H. (2001a) *Forschungs– und Technologieprogramme zu 'Bauen und Umwelt'. Eine vergleichende Analyse ausgewählter nordeuropäischer Ländern*, Graz: IFF/IFZ.

Rohracher, H. (2001b) 'Managing the Technological Transition to Sustainable Construction of Buildings: A Socio-technical Perspective', in *Technology Analysis and Strategic Management* 13: 137–50.

Rohracher, H. and Ornetzeder, M. (2002a) *Intelligent and Green? Nutzer-zentrierte Szenarien für den Einsatz von I&K-Technologien in Wohngebäuden unter dem Gesichtspunkt ihrer Umwelt– und Sozialverträglichkeit*, Vienna: BMVIT.

Rohracher, H. and Ornetzeder, M. (2002b) 'Green Buildings in Context: Improving Social Learning Processes between Users and Producers', in *Built Environment* 28 (1): 73–84.

Rohracher, H., Kukovetz, B., Ornetzeder, M. et al. (2001) *Akzeptanzverbesserung von Niedrigenergiehaus-Komponenten als wechselseitiger Lernprozess von Herstellern und AnwenderInnen*, Vienna: BMVIT.

Rohwedder, W. J. (1998) 'The Pedagogy of Place: What Do Our Campuses Teach', in *Academic Planning in College and University Environmental Programs*, proceedings of the Symposium on Academic Planning in College and University Environmental Programs, Sanibel, FA.

Rohwedder, W. J. (2003) 'A Pedagogy of Place: The Environmental Technology Center at SSU', in P. Blaze Corcoran and A. E. J. Wals (eds), *Higher Education and the Challenge of Sustainability: Contestation, Critique, Practice, and Promise*, Dordrecht, Netherlands: Kluwer Academic Publishers.

Roodman, D. M. and Lenssen, N. (1995) *A Building Revolution: How Ecology and Health Concerns are Transforming Construction*, Worldwatch Paper 124, Washington, DC: Worldwatch Institute.

Rorty, R. (1991) *Objectivity, Relativism and Truth*, Cambridge: Cambridge University Press.

Rorty, R. (1998) *Achieving Our Country: Leftist Thought in Twentieth-Century America*, Cambridge, MA: Harvard University Press.

Rorty, R. (1999). *Philosophy and Social Hope*, London: Penguin.

Rosengren, A. (1991) *Två barn och eget hus. Om kvinnors och mäns världar i småsamhället*, Malmö: Carlsons Bokförlag och Skaraborgs länsmuseum.

Ross, R. (1994) *The Chicago Gangster Theory of Life: Nature's Debt to Society*, London: Verso.

Rousseau, D. and Wasley, J. (1999) *Healthy By Design: Building and Remodeling Solutions for Creating Healthy Homes*, 2nd ed., Vancouver: Hartley and Marks.

Rubin, R. (1988) *Critical Condition: America's Health in Jeopardy*, Washington, DC: National Committee for Quality Health Care.

Russell, S. and Williams, R. (2002) 'Social Shaping of Technology: Frameworks, Findings and Implications for Policy with Glossary of Social Shaping Concepts', in K. H. Sorensen and R. Williams (eds), *Shaping Technology, Guiding Policy: Concepts, Spaces and Tools*, Cheltenham: Edward Elgar.

Ryghaug, M. (2002) *Towards a Sustainable Aesthetics: Architects Constructing Energy Efficient Buildings*, Trondheim, Norway: PhD thesis, Department of Sociology and Political Science/Institute for Interdisciplinary Studies of Culture, STS report.

Safley, T. and Rosenband, L. (eds) (1993) *The Workplace before the Factory: Artisans and Proletarians, 1500–1800*, Ithaca NY: Cornell University Press.

St Pierre, J. and Vail D. (2201) 'Sustaining the Many Values of Maine's Forests', 'Sustain Maine' op-ed series in *Times Record*, 31 August 2001.

Samuel, R. (1994) *Theaters of Memory*, vol. 1: *Past and Present in Contemporary Culture*, London: Verso.

Sandbach, F. (1980) *Environment, Ideology and Policy*, Oxford: Blackwell.

Sanderson, R. (1969) *Codes and Code Administration*, Chicago: BOCA.

Saxhof, B., Schultz, J. M. and Wittchen, K. (1988) 'From Zero Energy House to the 1st and 2nd Generation Low-Energy Houses at Hjortekjær, Denmark', in Ingemar Höglund (ed), *New Opportunities for Energy Conservation on Buildings – Putting the Results over a Decade of Research into Practice*, Bulletin No. 153, Stockholm: Royal Institute of Technology.

[SCB] Statistiska Centralbyrån (2002) *Energistatistik för småhus 2002*, EN 16 SM 0302. Accessible at www.scb.se

Schatzberg, E. (2002). 'Book Review of Natural Capitalism, Hawken et al.', in *Technology and Culture* 43: 218–331.

Schlosberg, D. (1999) *Environmental Justice and the New Pluralism: The Challenge of Difference for Environmentalism*, Oxford and New York: Oxford University Press.

Schneidereit, P. (2002) 'N.S. Forestry Industry Responds to Ecologist', in *Halifax Herald*, 10 December 2002.

Schot, J. (2001) 'Towards New Forms of Participatory Technology Development', in *Technology Analysis and Strategic Management* 13: 39–52.

Schwartz Cowan, R. (1987) 'The Consumption Junction: A Proposal for Research Strategies in the Sociology of Technology', in W. E. Bijker, T. P. Hughes and T. Pinch (eds), *The Social Construction of Technological Systems*, Cambridge, MA: MIT Press.

Scofield, J. H. (2002a) 'Early Performance of a Green Academic Building', in *Transactions* 108 (2). Atlanta: American Society of Heating, Refrigerating, and Air-Conditioning Engineers.

Scofield, J. H. (2002b) 'The Environment and Oberlin: An Update – One Scientist's Perspective on the Lewis Center', in *Oberlin Alumni Magazine* 98 (1): 19, 22–3. Accessible at www.oberlin.edu/alummag/oamcurrent/oam_summer2002/feat_enviro4.htm (accessed 12 June 2003).

Scofield, J. H. (2002c) 'Ongoing Conversation about the Lewis Center', http://energy.physics.oberlin.edu/Essays/ScofieldResponds.htm (accessed 12 June 2003).

Selman, P. (1996) *Local Sustainability*, London: Paul Chapman.

Shalit, A. de (2003). 'Philosophy Gone Urban', in *Journal of Social Philosophy* 34 (1) (Spring): 6–27.

Shepheard, P. (2003) *Artificial Love: A Story of Machines and Architecture*, Cambridge, MA: MIT Press.

Shove, E. (1998) 'Gaps, Barriers and Conceptual Chasms: Theories of Technology Transfer and Energy in Buildings', in *Energy Policy* 26: 1105–12.

Shove, E. (2003) *Comfort, Cleanliness + Convenience: The Social Organization of Normality*, Oxford and New York: Berg.

Silvester, S. (1996) 'Demonstratieprojecten en energiezuinige woningbouw', Rotterdam: unpublished dissertation, Erasmus University of Rotterdam.

Sioshansi, F. P. (1991) 'The Myths and Facts of Energy Efficiency: Survey of Implementation Issues', in *Energy Policy* 19: 231–43.

Shutkin, W. (2000) *The Land that Could Be: Environmentalism and Democracy in the Twenty-first Century*, Cambridge, MA: MIT Press.

Sierra Club (2000) 'Environmentalists Hail US Government Decision to Ban Pesticide: Call on Canada to Follow Suit', www.sierraclub.ca/national/media/us-pesticide-ban-00-06-08.html (accessed 15 June 2003).

Sierra Club (2001) 'Forest Stewardship Council Finds J. D. Irving, Ltd Pesticide Use Violation of Standards', www.sierraclub.ca/national/media/fsc-cert-concerns-00-01-21.html (accessed 24 August 2004).

Sierra Club (2002) 'NGO Statement on the Softwood Lumber Dispute', www.sierraclub.ca/national/forests/softwood-lumber-statement.html

Silverstone, R., Moreley, D, Dahlbergh, A. and Livingstone, S. (1989) *Families, Technologies and Consumption: The Household and Information and Communication Technologies*, CRICT discussion paper, Uxbridge, Middlesex: Brunel University.

Sjögren, A. (1993) *Här går gränsen. Om integritet och kulturella mönster i Sverige och Medelhavsområdet*, Värnamo, Sweden: Bokförlaget Arena.

Sørensen, K. H. (1996) *Learning Technology, Constructing Culture: Sociotechnical Change as Social Learning*, STS Working paper 18/96. Trondheim: Centre for Technology and Society, University of Trondheim.

[SOU] Statens offentliga utredningar (1995) *Omställning av energisystemet. Underlagsbilagor, del 2*, Statens offentliga utredningar 140 no. 2, Stockholm: SOU.

Spaargaren, G. (2000) 'Ecological Modernization Theory and Domestic Consumption', in *Journal of Environmental Policy and Planning* 2 (4): 323–35.

Spaargaren, G. and Mol, A. J. P. (1992) 'Sociology, Environment and Modernity: Ecological Modernization as a Theory of Social Change', in *Society and Natural Resources* 5.

Spinosa, C., Flores, F. and Dreyfus H. (1997) *Disclosing New Worlds: Entrepreneurship, Democratic Action, and the Cultivation of Solidarity*, Cambridge, MA: MIT Press; 162–8.

Statsbygg (2000). *Byøkologi i praksis*, Prosjektnytt: brochure from Statsbygg 3/1998/ 2000.

Steele, J. (1997) *Architecture Today*, London: Phaidon.

Stern, P. C. (1992) 'What Psychology Knows About Energy Conservation', in *American Psychologist* 47: 1124–232.

Stichting Bouwresearch (1999) *Duurzaam Bouwen, Nationaal Pakket Woningbouw [Sustainable Building: National Package Housing]*, Rotterdam: Stichting Bouwresearch.

Stieldorf, K., Juri, H., Haider, R., König, U. and Unzeitig, U. (2001) *Analyse des NutzerInnenverhaltens in Gebäuden mit Pilot– und Demonstrationscharakter*, Vienna: BMVIT.

Strom, E.-B. (1998) *Telenors utbygging på Fornebu. Miljøoppfølgingsprogram [The Environmental Management Programme]*, environmental consultant, Telenors Fornebuprosjekt, 9 September 1998.

Sudjic, D. (1995). 'Green Utopias', *The Guardian*, 27 October: 24–5.

Sudjic, D. (1996). 'A House in the Country', *The Guardian*, 2 June: 7.

Summerton, J. (ed.) (1994) *Changing Large Technical Systems*, Boulder and San Franscisco: Westview Press.

Swedish FSC Working Group (1997) Front Paper to Proposed FSC Standards for Forest Certification, www.fsc-sverige.org/standard/Referral/referral.htm (accessed 30 May 2003).

Telenor, Fornebu. www.telenor.no/fornebu/english/about.shtml (last accessed June 2003).

Thomas, N. (1991) *Entangled Objects: Exchange, Material Culture, and Colonialism in the Pacific*, Cambridge, MA: Harvard University Press.

Trudgill, S. (1990). *Barriers to a Better Environment*, London: Belhaven Press.

Tyson, B. (1998) 'Transportation and the Supply of Construction Materials: An Aspect of Traditional Building Management', in *Vernacular Architecture* 29: 63–81.

Tzonis, A. and Lefaivre, L. (1991) 'Critical Regionalism', in S. Amourgis (ed.) *Critical Regionalism: The Pomona Proceedings*, Pomona, CA: College of Environmental Design, California State Polytechnic University; 3–23.

US Department of Energy (2003) 'Success Stories: New Pattonsburg, Missouri', www.sustainable.doe.gov/success/dpnewpat.shtml (accessed 15 July 2003).

US House of Representatives (2002) *The Renewable Roadmap to Energy Independence*, field hearing before the US House of Representatives Subcommittee on

Energy, Committee on Science, 21 February 2002, pub. no. 107-5. Accessible at www.house.gov/science/committeeinfo/docs/pubs.htm

Umweltbundesamt (1998) *Nachhaltiges Deutschland. Wege zu einer dauerhaft umweltgerechten Entwicklung*, Berlin: Umweltbundesamt.

[UNIDO] United Nations Industrial Development Organization (1969) *Production Techniques for the Use of Wood in Housing under Conditions Prevailing in Developing Countries*, Vienna and New York: United Nations Publication.

University of Texas School of Nursing and Student Community Center (2003). www.uthouston.edu/sonscc/ (accessed 24 February 2003).

Upton, C. and Bass S. (1996) *The Forest Certification Handbook*, Delray Beach, FA: St Lucie Press.

[USDA] US Department of Agriculture (12 July 2002). www.fas.usda.gov/info/agexporter/bigtime.html (accessed 10 February 2003).

Vail, D. (1990) 'The Internal Conflict: Contract Logging, Chainsaws and Clear-Cuts in Maine Forestry', in T. Banuri and F. Apffel Marglin (eds), *Who Will Save the Forests? Knowledge, Power and Environmental Destruction*, London and Atlantic Highlands, NJ: Zed Books.

Vale, B. and Vale, R. (1996). 'Urban Design: The Challenge of Sustainability', in *Journal of Urban Design* 1 (2): 141–4.

Venolia, C. (1988) *Healing Environments: Your Guide to Indoor Well Being*, updated, Berkeley, CA: Celestial Arts.

Vidler, A. (1992) *The Architectural Uncanny: Essays in the Modern Unhomely*, Cambridge MA: MIT Press.

Waals, J. F. M. van der (2001) '$CO_2$-Reduction in Housing Experiences in Building and Urban Renewal Projects in the Netherlands', Amsterdam: PhD thesis, Utrecht University: Thela Thesis.

Waals, J. F. M. van der and Vermeulen, W. J. V. (2000) 'Sustainable Building: Lessons for Local Policy Processes', in *Milieu (Journal of Environmental Sciences)* 15 (2): 103–10.

Waals, J. F. M. van der and Vermeulen, W. J. V. (2002) 'The $CO_2$-Reduction Workshop: Dutch Experiences with a Participatory Approach', in *Journal of Environmental Planning and Management* 45 (4): 549–69.

Waals, J. F. M. van der, Joosen, S., van Geleuken, B. P., Groenenberg, M. C., Kneepkens, M. and Vermeulen, W. J. V. (1999) *$CO_2$-Reduction in Building Locations: A Survey and Three Case Studies about the Role of Options for $CO_2$ Reduction In Planning Processes*, Utrecht: Utrecht University, Bilthoven, Dutch National Research Programme on Global Air Pollution and Climate Change, Report no. 410 200 036.

Waals, J. F. M. van der, Vermeulen, S. M. J., Vermeulen, W. J. V., Glasbergen. P. and Hooimeijer, P. (2000) *Energiebesparing en stedelijke herstructurering, een beleidswetenschappelijke analyse*, Utrecht: DGVH/Nethur partnership 10.

Waals, J. F. M. van der, Vermeulen, W. J. V. and Glasbergen, P. (2003) '$CO_2$-Reduction in Housing: Experiences in Urban Renewal Projects in the Netherlands', *Environment and Planning C: Government and Policy* 21 (3): 411–27.

Walch, K., Lechner, R. and Tappeiner, G. (2001) *Gebaut 2020 – Zukunftsbilder und Zukunftsgeschichten für das Bauen von morgen*, Vienna: BMVIT.

Wallensteen-Jaeger, R. (1975) *Kök och stök när seklet var ungt*, Stockholm: LTs förlag.

Wasley, J. (1995a) 'Environments for the Chemically Sensitive as Models of Healthy Building Construction: Eight Case Studies from an Architectural Perspective', in

*Proceedings of Healthy Buildings '95: An International Conference on Healthy Buildings in Mild Climates*, Milan, 475–80.

Wasley, J. (1995b) 'Multiple Chemical Sensitivity Syndrome and "Traditional Concepts of Architecture"', in *83rd ACSA Annual Meeting Proceedings*, 537–40.

Wasley, J. (1996a) 'Health and/or Sustainability: MCS and Eco-Design' in *Proceedings of the 1996 Eco-Design Arts Conference*, 10.1–10.6.

Wasley, J. (1996b) 'Environments for the Chemically Sensitive as Models of Healthy Building Construction: Issues of Architectural Space Planning', in *Proceedings – 84th ACSA Annual Meeting and Technology Conference*, 60–5.

Wasley, J. (1997) 'Environments for the Chemically Sensitive as Models of Healthy Building Construction: Issues of Ventilation', in *Architecture: Material and Imagined, Proceedings of the 85th ACSA Annual Meeting and Technology Conference*, 81–6.

Wasley, J. (2000) 'Safe Houses and Green Architecture: Reflections on the Lessons of the Chemically Sensitive', in *Journal of Architectural Education* 53 (4): 207–15.

Waterson, R. (1996) 'Houses and Hierarchies in Island Southeast Asia', in J. Carsten and S. Hugh-Jones (eds) *About the House: Lévi-Strauss and Beyond*, Cambridge: Cambridge University Press.

Weber, M. (1958) *The Protestant Ethic and the Spirit of Capitalism*, trans. by T. Parsons, New York: Scribners.

Weber M. (1958) *Basic Concepts in Sociology*, trans. and with an introd. by H. P. Secher, New York: Philosophical Library.

Weiss, W. (2003) 'Solar Combisystems and the Global Energy Challenge', in W. Weiss (ed.) *Solar Heating Systems for Houses: A Design Handbook for Solar Combisystems*, Solar Heating and Cooling Executive Committee of the International Agency (IEA), London: James & James.

Weyer, J. (1997) 'Konturen einer netzwerktheoretischen Techniksoziologie', in J. Weyer, U. Kirchner, L. Riedl and J. F. K. Schmidt (eds), *Technik, die Gesellschaft schafft*, Berlin: Edition Sigma.

Whan, E. (2000) 'Thirty Years of Intensive Forestry Management in Ontario', draft paper. Accessible at www.wildlandsleague.org (accessed 15 May 2003).

White, G. F. (1997) 'Classics in Human Geography', with a discussion of G. F. White (1945) 'Human Adjustment to Floods', Research Paper 29, Chicago, IL: University of Chicago, Department of Geography, in *Progress in Human Geography* 21 (2): 243–50.

Wilhite, H. (2000) 'The Social Construction of Comfort: A Challenge for Sustainable Consumption Research and Policy', unpublished paper, Oslo: Department of Social Anthropology, Oslo University.

Williams, R., Slack, R. and Stewart, J. (2000) *Social Learning in Multimedia, Report, Research Centre for Social Sciences*, Edinburgh: Technology Studies Unit, University of Edinburgh.

Wilson, A. (2003) 'Lighting Controls: Beyond the Toggle Switch', *Environmental Building News* 12 (6): 1, 9–15.

Wimmer, R., Janisch, L., Hohensinner, H. and Drack, M. (2001) *Erfolgsfaktoren für den Einsatz nachwachsender Rohstoffe im Bauwesen*, Vienna: BMVIT.

Windhorse Farm (2003). www.windhorsefarm.org (accessed 15 May 2003).

Wines, J. (2000). 'The Art of Architecture in the Age of Ecology', in D. E. Brown, M. Fox and M. R. Pelletier (eds), *Sustainable Architecture: White Papers*, New York: Earth Pledge Foundation; 12–18.

Winner, L. (1977) *Autonomous Technology: Technics-out-of-Control as a Theme in Political Thought*, Cambridge, MA: MIT Press.

Winter, M. (1998) 'Solar Synthesis', in *Architecture Today* 89 (June): 24–30.

Yates, S.M. and Aronson, E. (1983) 'A Social Psychological Perspective on Energy Conservation in Residential Buildings', in *American Psychologist* 38: 435–44.

Yearley, S. (1991) *The Green Case: A Sociology of Environmental Issues, Arguments and Politics*, London: Harper Collins.

Zharen, W. von (1996) *ISO14000: Understanding the Environmental Standards*, Rockville, MD: Government Institutes.

Zimmermann, A. and Martin, M. (2001) 'Post-occupancy Evaluation: Benefits and Barriers', in *Building Research and Information* 29: 168–74.

# Index

Page numbers in *italics* indicate illustrations; page numbers in **bold** refer to tables

Adam Joseph Lewis Center (AJLC) (USA)
      32–3, *33*, 34, 36–41, *39*, 44–9
   and teaching 46–8
   temperature control 38, 41
Andelssamfundet, Denmark 172, 173, *174*
architecture, as individual work 231–2
Austin Energy Green Building Program (USA)
      **61**, 62–3, *62*
Austria
   'Building of Tomorrow' programme 203–18
   smart homes 212–14

Barrhaven Community Housing for the
      Environmentally Hypersensitive
      (Canada) 111, *114*, 115, 119–21
Bentham, Jeremy, utilitarianism 54
bio-pellet heating, Sweden 90, 96–100, *97*, *98*
biogas, electricity generation 190
BO-01, Malmø, Sweden 181, *181*
BREEAM, environmental assessment 21,
      22
building codes
   England 53
   and fire prevention 53
   green 51–70, **61**, *62*
   history 53–4
   and public health 51, 53–7
   United States 55–6, **61**, *62*
building regulations, and sustainable building
      77–9
Building Research Establishment
      environmental assessment method 21, 22
'Building of Tomorrow' programme, Austria
      203–18
buildings, use of natural resources 15, 31
Built Green Colorado (USA) **61**, 63–4, *64*

Campbell, Scott, on sustainable development
      59–60, *59*
Canada
   light-wood frame building 136–7

wood production 131, 133–4
   *see also* Nova Scotia
Central Square Offices, Newcastle-upon-
      Tyne (UK) 18–20, *18*, **18–19**, 21–2,
      26, 28
Chadwick, Edwin, and public health 54–5
clay bricks 173
climate, and domestic architecture 91
$CO_2$ reduction 76, 86
Commerzbank, Frankfurt (Germany) 57, *58*
contextualism, in architecture 225
critical theorists, disengagement 236
cultural context, and good design 225

Denmark
   eco-villages 172–5, *173*;
   low-energy buildings 168–71, 182
   sustainable architecture 165–83,
      *174, 177, 180*, 227–8
   zero-energy house 168–9, *169*
   *see also* Scandinavia
Denver, Colorado (USA), green building code
      **61**, 63–4, *64*
disasters
   as opportunities for innovation 185–94,
      197–9;
   people's reaction 186–7, 190–5, 197–9
   reconstruction after 186–7, 198
domestic architecture, Sweden 91–5, *93*,
      181, *181*
domestic heating
   aesthetic considerations *98*, 99–102
   cultural attitudes 89–103
Doxford Solar office, Sunderland (UK) 16–18,
      *17*, **18–19**, 21, 22–3, 26, 28
Drerup, Oliver, 'safe' houses 115–16
Dyssekilde, Denmark 172–3, *173*

eco-villages
   attitudes to 207
   Denmark 172–5, 173

ecological citizenship 238
ecological modernisation, technological
    development 167
Edison, Thomas, as entrepreneur 232
Edwards, Brian, on sustainable architecture
    4–5, 15
electricity, generation from biogas 190
energy consumption, green buildings **19**, 21–2,
    152–3, 168–9, 173–4
energy efficiency
    attitudes to 208; green buildings 4–6,
        21–2, 34, 40–1, 44–5, 49, 168–71
    and information and communication
        technology (ICT) 211–12
    passive houses 203
    smart homes 211–12, 214, 216
    and sustainable architecture 4–6, **19**,
        21–22, 34, 150–154, **151**
energy-efficient buildings, attitudes to 206–8
energy markets
    and local authorities 84
    and sustainable housing 82–3
England
    building codes 53
    public health 54–5
environmental assessments, green buildings
    20–3
environmental hypersensitivity *see* multiple
    chemical sensitivity (MCS)
environmental illness *see* multiple chemical
    sensitivity (MCS)
environmental knowledge, forms of 7–9
environmental management plans (EMPs),
    sustainable architecture 152–4,
    156–8
environmental preservation 56–7
environmental technology
    and green housing 83–4
    and housing market 82
Environmental Technology Center (ETC)
    (USA) 32–8, 32, 40–3
    air infiltration 42–3
    public reactions 40–2
    and teaching 45–7
environmentalism, nature of 237–8
Europe, wood consumption 126

Feenberg, Andrew
    on green architecture 9–10
    on technological development 233
fire prevention, and building codes 53
First Nations people, wood construction 139
Florida (USA), green building code **61**, 64–6,
    65
Forest Stewardship Council (FSC) 126–9,
    132–3
forestry, 'whole-tree' 133
Foucault, Michel, on public health 54–5

Geertz, Clifford, on local knowledge 3
gender, and heating systems 96–7, 99, 102
Germany, light-wood frame building 136–7
good design, and cultural context 225
grassroots projects, green buildings 171–5
green architecture
    and energy efficiency 4–6, 21–2, 34
    ideology 24–6
    nature of 16, 223
    and 'safe' houses 107–22, 226
    *see also* green buildings; sustainable
        architecture
green building codes 51–70
    assessment 63, 64, 66, 223
    logic **61**, 66–8
    standardisation 68–69
    United States 60–9, **61**
Green Building Council (USA) 69, 141
green buildings
    citizen-initiated 171–5
    Denmark 165–83, 227–8
    energy consumption **19**, 21–2, 152–3,
        168–71, 173–4
    environmental assessments 20–3
    market approach 179–81
    renewable energy **19**, 34
    and social context 9–10, 30
    urban 175–9
    variety 3
    waste production 173
    water consumption 173–4
    *see also* green architecture; sustainable
        architecture
Green City Strategy, Philadelphia (USA)
    238
ground zero, redevelopment 198
Groundwork Trust Eco-Centre, South
    Tyneside (UK) 16, *17*, **18–19**, 21,22,
    26, 28
Gulf War syndrome 108–9; *see also* multiple
    chemical sensitivity (MCS)

Hajer, Marteen, on environmental knowledge 8
hallway, functions 92, *93*
Hammurabi, King of Mesopotamia, building
    codes 53
Haraway, Donna, nature of knowledge
    229–30
Hedebygade, Copenhagen 176–9, *177*
Heidegger, Martin, technology and
    architecture 223
house building, wood 134, 135–9, *138*,
    *140*
housing market, and environmental
    technology 82
hybrid buildings 27–9
Hyett, Paul, on sustainable architecture 4–5,
    15

Information Centre for Sustainable Living, Netherlands 78
information and communication technology (ICT)
  and energy saving 211–12
  practical aspects 218
  smart homes 211–12, 214

James, William, on truth 227
Japan, wood standards 131

kitchen, functions 92–4, 103
Kvernhuset, Norway 146–8, **147**, 150–2, **151**, 155–6, 158–60

language, of sustainable architecture 229, 238–9
Latour, Bruno, on scientific truth 232–3
Leadership in Energy and Environmental Design 69, 141
Lee, Ang, Ride with the Devil 195–6, *196*
LEED programme, green building code 69, 141
Libeskind, Daniel, on ground zero 198
light-wood frame buildings 136–7
living room, functions 94–5
local authorities
  and energy markets 84
  and sustainable development 75
low-energy buildings
  Austria 203
  Denmark 168–71, 182

Maine (USA), forestry practices 133
MCS houses *see* 'safe' houses
Midwest (USA), house building 138–9
Milton, Kay, on environment 2–3
modernisation, and standardisation 52
multiple chemical sensitivity (MCS) 107–9
Munksøgård, Denmark 172, 174, *174*

nature preservation *see* environmental preservation
Nelms house ('safe' dwelling) (Canada) 116–18, *116*, *117*, 120–1
Netherlands
  building regulations 77–8
  CO reduction 76, 86
  Information Centre for Sustainable Living 78
  sustainable development 75–6, 224
New Mexico Earthship 57, *59*
New York (USA), ground zero 198
North America
  light-wood frame building 136–7
  wood consumption 126

Norway
  sustainable architecture 145–61, **147**, *148*, **151**, 227
  see also Scandinavia
Nova Scotia
  history 124–125
  wood production 124–6, *125*, 130, 132–3
  *see also* Canada

Oberlin College, Ohio (USA) *see* Adam Joseph Lewis Center
Oetzal house ('safe' dwelling) (USA) 111, 112–13, *113*, 118–19
Ørestaden, Copenhagen (Denmark) 179–80, *180*

passive houses 203
Pattonsburg, Missouri (USA)
  employment opportunities 190–191
  as film set 195–6, *196*, 228
  relocation 185–96, *189*, *192*, *193*
  schools 193, *194*
  sustainable development 188–90, 228
people
  attitudes to sustainable architecture 231
  choice of home 205–6
  and energy-efficient buildings 206–8
  reactions to disasters 186–7, 190–5, 197–9
*photovoltaic panels 17, **19**, 21, 85*
Pilestredet Park, Oslo (Norway) **147**, 148–9, *148*, **151**, 152–3, 156–7
Pitman house ('safe' dwelling) (USA) *110*, 111–112, *111*, 118
plywood 135
politics, of sustainable architecture 235–7
pragmatism, and technological development 233–6
public health
  and building codes 51, 53–7
  England 54–5
  and environmental preservation 56–7
  United States 55–6
public transport, and sustainability 179–80

rammed clay bricks 173
renewable energy, green buildings **19**, 34
Rorty, Richard
  on pragmatism 236
  on sustainable architecture 2, 3, 4

'safe' houses
  choice of materials 109–11, 113, 115, 119, 120
  design 109–18, *110*, *111*, *114*, *116*, *117*
  and green architecture 107–22, 226
  site selection 118–19
  ventilation 111, 112, 116–18

Scandinavia
  gender roles 95–6, 99, 102
  *see also* Denmark; Norway; Sweden
Schlosberg, David, on environmentalism
    237–8
science and technology studies (STS) 231–4
SCOT theories, technological development
    166–7
Shepheard, Paul, on sustainability 236–7
smart homes
  energy efficiency 211–12, 214, 216
  information and communication
      technology (ICT) 211–12, 214
  social acceptance 202–18
  sociotechnical aspects 209–14
  and sustainable building 209–18,
      228–9
  users' attitudes 215–16
social acceptability, sustainable building
    203–9
social constructivism, and technological
    development 232
solar heating, Sweden 100–2, *100*
Soldier's Grove, Wisconsin (USA),
    sustainable rebuilding 188
Sonoma State University, California (USA)
    *see* Environmental Technology
    Center
standardisation: green building codes 68–9
    and modernisation 52
subsidies, for sustainable building 78–9,
    80
Sudjic, Deyan, on sustainable architecture
    5–6, 15
sustainability, and public transport
    179–80
sustainable architecture
  concepts of 57–60, *59*, 223–4
  costs 35–37;
  Denmark 165–83, *174*, *177*, *180*,
      227–8
  and energy efficiency 4–6, **19**, 21–2, 34,
      150–4, **151**
  environmental management plans (EMPs)
      152–4, 156–8
  and human behaviour 231
  ideology 24–6
  language of 229, 238–9
  Norway 145–61, **147**, **151**, 227
  politics of 235–7
  Sweden 181, *181*
  and technology 231
  and urban narratives 230
  *see also* green architecture; green
      buildings; sustainable buildings
sustainable buildings
  and building regulations 77–9
  design routes 81

information transfer 79, 80
  politics of 73–88
  and smart homes 209–18, 228–9
  social acceptability 203–9
  sociotechnological studies 201–18
  subsidies 78–9, 80
  technology lag 79
  urban environments 73–87, 175–9,
      *177*
  wood 124, 134, 135–9, *140*, 141
  *see also* green architecture; green
      buildings; sustainable architecture
      sustainable housing
sustainable development, and local
    authorities 75
sustainable housing
  and energy markets 82–3
  and environmental technology 83–4
  residents' opinions 177–8
  *see also* sustainable buildings
Sweden
  climate and domestic architecture 91
  domestic architecture 91–5, 93, 181, *181*

  domestic heating 89–103, *97*, *98*, *100*,
      224–5
  green housing 181, *181*
  *see also* Scandinavia
systems theory, and technological innovation
    232

technological development
  and pragmatism 233–4
  and social constructivism 232
  theories of 166–8
technological innovation, and systems theory
    232
technology
  dissemination 75, 79, 83, 208–9
  and sustainable architecture 231
technology lag, sustainable building 79
Telenor Fornebu, Oslo (Norway) **147**, 149–50,
    **151**, 153–4, 157–8
truth, nature of 227, 229–30, 232–3

United States
  building codes 55–6, 60–9, **61**, **62**,
    *64*
  environmental preservation 56–7
  Green Building Council 69
  public health 55–6
  *see also under individual projects*
urban environments, sustainable building
    73–87, 175–9, 177
urban narratives, and sustainable architecture
    230
urban technological studies, technological
    development 168

utilitarianism, and public health 54
Utrecht (Netherlands), Information Centre
    for Sustainable Living *78*

ventilation, 'safe' houses 111, 112,
    116–18

Waring, George, and public health 55
waste production, green buildings 173
water consumption, green buildings
    173–4
Weber, Max, on standardisation 52

Whiteread, Rachel:
    *The House* 196
    translucent watertower 197, *197*
wood
    over-exploitation 123–4
    production 132–3, 134–9, 226
    standards 125, 129–30, *130*
    sustainable building 124, 134, 135–9,
        *138*, *140*, 141
    sustainable use 126–9, 132–3, 226

zero-energy house, Denmark 168–9, *169*

eBooks – at www.eBookstore.tandf.co.uk

# A library at your fingertips!

eBooks are electronic versions of printed books. You can store them on your PC/laptop or browse them online.

They have advantages for anyone needing rapid access to a wide variety of published, copyright information.

eBooks can help your research by enabling you to bookmark chapters, annotate text and use instant searches to find specific words or phrases. Several eBook files would fit on even a small laptop or PDA.

**NEW:** Save money by eSubscribing: cheap, online access to any eBook for as long as you need it.

## Annual subscription packages

We now offer special low-cost bulk subscriptions to packages of eBooks in certain subject areas. These are available to libraries or to individuals.

For more information please contact webmaster.ebooks@tandf.co.uk

We're continually developing the eBook concept, so keep up to date by visiting the website.

# www.eBookstore.tandf.co.uk